CROSSCURRENTS *Modern Critiques*

CROSSCURRENTS *Modern Critiques*

Harry T. Moore, *General Editor*

Frederick R. Karl

C. P. Snow

THE POLITICS OF CONSCIENCE

WITH A PREFACE BY
Harry T. Moore

Carbondale

SOUTHERN ILLINOIS UNIVERSITY PRESS

FIRST PUBLISHED, APRIL 1963
SECOND PRINTING, SEPTEMBER 1966

For *Judith*

AT THE TIME this preface is being written, the present book is the only one devoted to a full consideration of the novels of C. P. Snow. Frederick R. Karl has made a thorough and illuminating analysis of all of Snow's fiction, from his detective story of 1932 (Death Under Sail) to the latest volumes in the Strangers and Brothers series. And for that series Mr. Karl has compiled an interesting table of events, paralleled by one which lists the principal facts of C. P. Snow's own life.

Charles Percy Snow, who is now formally Sir Charles Snow, was born in 1905 in Leicester, in many ways the counterpart of those Midland or Northern cities which have subsequently produced the writers known as the Angry Young Men (in another book in this Crosscurrents series, William Van O'Connor gives good reasons for preferably using the other name they are known by which supplies the title for his volume: The New University Wits). Though Snow came from poverty, like many of them, his work has little in common with theirs, largely because he is a figure of the Establishment. Similarly, he has little in common with two prominent earlier writers who, like him, were poor boys who obtained their education by winning scholarships: D. H. Lawrence and H. G. Wells. Wells was, like Snow, a man with scientific interests, but both his social-comedy and his science-fiction novels are generally different from the works of C. P. Snow, though the latter's second book, New Lives For Old (1933), is somewhat in the vein of Wells's fantasies.

As a professional scientist, Snow was a Fellow of Corpus Christi College, Cambridge University, in the 1930s. In the big war which followed, he supervised the scientific personnel in the Ministry of Labour. His novel Strangers and Brothers, which was to give its name to the series he is still writing, came out in 1940. It now appears that it will run to eleven volumes. Among the eight which have appeared so far, The Masters (1951), the story of an election in a Cambridge college, has attracted the most attention.

Mr. Karl's subtitle, The Politics of Conscience, indicates the lines along which he attempts—very successfully, I think—to determine the quality of Snow's current series of novels. As Mr. Karl points out in expanding his ideas, Snow demonstrates what it is like to be a "good" man in the twentieth century, continually fighting the temptations of ambition in a materialistic and competitive world. Mr. Karl traces the working out of this concept through the various novels. His statement to the effect that Snow is becoming a major writer will be challenged by some readers; certainly it is in contradiction of F. R. Leavis's attack on Snow in 1961. Leavis, in his farewell lecture at one of the Cambridge colleges, allowed the author of The Masters no talent whatsoever. Mr. Karl, characterizing this attack as "intemperate," deals with it very sensibly and gives it no more space than it deserves; but he finds some grains of truth in parts of Leavis's lecture.

C. P. Snow has, since Leavis's onslaught, been subjected to a far more formidable one: vigorous and trenchant, its reasonableness is reinforced because the attacker doesn't forget his manners. The Earl of Birkenhead, in The Professor and the Prime Minister (1961), says Snow is entirely wrong in his own attack upon E. C. Lindemann (Lord Cherwell), who was Churchill's scientific adviser during the war. In Snow's Godkin Lectures at Harvard University in 1960, he spoke slightingly of Lindemann's attitudes toward radar and strategic bombing. Lord Birkenhead's reply might serve as a model for those who wish to disagree with C. P. Snow.

Discussing Snow's attacks upon the innovators in literature, Mr. Karl shrewdly points out that "if literature were to follow the course suggested by Snow, it would become an arm of social criticism; the 'untruths' that literature should tell us would soon be transformed into social commentary"; it would become merely "newsworthy instead of creative." Yet, within the limitations Mr. Karl discerns in Snow's esthetic thinking, and sometimes in the working out of Snow's novels, he finds much that he can praise.

And certainly C. P. Snow, however stodgily conventional he may seem at times, is a writer who has given us some important reading experiences. The provincial origins and early life of the protagonist of the Strangers and Brothers series, Lewis Eliot, are effectively rendered. Similarly, Eliot's adventures at Cambridge, in a London law office, and among wartime scientists are presented with an authenticity and narrative interest that make them seem, just now, very good—though whether Mr. Karl's application of the term "major" is as yet quite safe remains to be seen. Mr. Karl mentions C. P. Snow in relation both to Thackeray and Galsworthy, but only the future can tell whether Snow will survive, like Thackeray, or sink into virtual oblivion, like Galsworthy. Whatever Snow's ultimate fate, I doubt that he will disappear like Galsworthy; his talent is certainly greater than Galsworthy's, so badly overrated in his own time.

In any event, Mr. Karl has written a stimulating discussion of Snow. It is revelatory and critically perceptive, and it is definitely worth the attention of those who read modern fiction seriously.

HARRY T. MOORE

University of Colorado
December 6, 1962

ACKNOWLEDGMENTS

THE AUTHOR WISHES to thank the following publishers: Farrar, Straus & Cudahy, for permission to use material from the chapter on Snow, "The Politics of Conscience: The Novels of C. P. Snow," which appeared in his *Contemporary English Novel* (1962). Macmillan & Co., Ltd. and Charles Scribner's Sons, for permission to quote from *Strangers and Brothers* and *The Search*.

CONTENTS

C. P. Snow

THE POLITICS OF CONSCIENCE

1 THE POLITICS OF
CONSCIENCE

WITH THE PUBLICATION of *The Conscience of the Rich* in 1958 and *The Affair* in 1960, C. P. Snow is clearly emerging as a major literary figure. Both novels are part of *Strangers and Brothers,* the continuing series on which the scientist and civil administrator turned novelist has been working since 1940. Through his narrator, Lewis Eliot—who functions somewhat similarly to Marcel in Proust's great novel—Snow has set out to examine the moral conscience of England in the years following World War One. No iconoclast or protestant, Snow is primarily concerned with the inner workings of traditional institutions and the ways that these elements of society are perpetuated; thus, his interest in lawyers, scientists, academicians, and administrators: all the groups who have assumed power in the twentieth century and make the decisions necessary for civilized life.

Snow's characters, as we meet them in *Strangers and Brothers,* are usually involved in a test or conflict when personal ambition and social conscience are at stake. Anxious to catch the conscience of an individual when subjected to everyday temptations, as well as to the large temptations that make or break careers, Snow is understanding about those who are unable to resist quick rewards, and unsentimental about those who retain their principles despite the promise of personal gain. In short, Snow is that phenomenon among twentieth-century novelists: a serious moralist concerned with integrity, duty, principles, and ideals.

The fiction that Snow writes is akin, in technique and manner, to the average Victorian novel of Thackeray, George Eliot, or John Galsworthy, although it is less complicated in narrative structure and character development than the work of the former two and more closely reasoned than that of the latter. Snow eschews the impressionism and symbolism of Joyce, Virginia Woolf, Lawrence, and Conrad, and in so doing returns the novel to a direct representation of moral, social, and political issues. His novelistic world is not distorted or exaggerated; his art rests less on artistic re-creation than on faithful reproduction, careful arrangement, and common-sensical development of character and situation. His society is one in which people live, not intensely as in novels, but solidly immersed in careers and ambitions.

Specifically, Snow asks, what is man like in the twentieth century? how does a good man live in a world of temptations? how can ambition be reconciled with conscience? what is daily life like in an age in which all things are uncertain except one's own feelings? If, by some not impossible chance, the world were suddenly to be destroyed and only Snow's novels recovered by a future generation, the historian of that day would have a fairly good idea of what a responsible twentieth-century man was like merely by following the author through the vast labyrinths of a bureaucratic society where the individual, without visible guidance, must himself find his way or be lost. In his intense realism of conception and execution, Snow believes that man must constantly come to terms with himself in every act, and that the conscious individual is responsible only to himself for whatever course he does take. In brief, he has the faith of a moral agnostic.

Consequently, in what is one of the best volumes in the series, *The Conscience of the Rich* (1958), Charles March—a long-time friend of Lewis Eliot's—with full awareness of what he is doing cuts himself off from his family circle by choice of profession and wife. The consequences of his act, he knows, will be his disinheritance from family, fortune, and religion. Yet his choice is not heroic, certainly not comparable to Stephen Dedalus' to fly from Ireland. March decides, rather simply, that he is unfit for law and more suitable for medicine, at the same time standing behind his wife when he finds that she is a communist out to ruin the name and reputation of his rich uncle, Sir Philip. He is no idealist, no Don Quixote tilting at windmills; instead, he recognizes that life forces choices—often almost invisible to the outsider—which in themselves mock pretentiousness. The fact that a person can recognize the choices involved is, to Snow, an indication of his maturity; often the decision itself is secondary to the realization that it must be made. Accordingly, the burden of decision is the sole heroism that man is ever called upon to bear. By choosing his wife and his career as general practitioner, March chooses the way of manhood, although had he opted for his father, family, name, and religion instead, Snow suggests, he would by no means have been hypocritical or reprehensible.

The entire series of *Strangers and Brothers* is concerned with the conflicts that moral issues impose on basically decent people. Lewis Eliot, Snow's narrator, is himself of moderate abilities, more renowned for his solidity and good judgment than for his talents, which are not exceptional. Eliot is clearly a man of our times: ambitious, but aware of conscience; anxious to gain comfort and power, but cognizant that advancement means moral struggle and compromise with ideals; desirous of recognition, but afraid to lose dignity in achieving it.

From his beginnings as a poor schoolboy with dreams of a better future, Eliot has been aware of what happens to the individual when he loses his sense of judgment; to avoid chaos, he learns, one must be moderate and flexible. Even though personal interest will count for a great deal with Eliot—Snow emphasizes his ambition in *Time of Hope* (1950) when he takes a long chance on winning a law scholarship—his decisions are rarely indecently personal. He recognizes that in a world in which personal interest *is* necessary the only test of a "good" person is how far he responds to the demands of decency and responsibility, how committed he is to values that go beyond personal ego and will.

Throughout all the volumes of *Strangers and Brothers*, whether they are concerned with Eliot's public life as lawyer, academician, and civil administrator or his private life with the schizoid Sheila Knight, conscience becomes the guiding force, at times almost an obsession. This word, evoking as it does a sense of provincial Victorian morality and smug religiosity, is used here as the sole basis for a secular society. Snow, however, drops the moralistic and didactic connotations of the word, and, as a twentieth-century novelist, equates it with responsibility, the area within which each individual who has the power of choice must make decisions. Thus, George Passant, Eliot's friend —whose superabundant id runs like a counter theme to Eliot's calm judgment—is an incomplete man despite the nobility of his ideals; for he, in the long run, lacks the protective coloration of conscience, and he is punished by losing an administrative post for which he is perhaps over-equipped.

Passant, unlike Eliot, becomes for Snow a man whose insufficient sense of responsibility mocks his ideals, one who fritters away in inconsequential acts a truly remarkable talent. The world is divided, Snow suggests, between the Passants and the Eliots; the one voracious in his intellectual appetites, but weak in judgment; the latter less capable, less talented, but able to muster control when needed. In the modern world, it is evidently the semi-talented who lead.

In *Homecoming* (*Homecomings* in England, 1956), Eliot recognizes that the George Passants are too brilliant and undependable to find easy niches, while the good second-rate man can rise almost to the top. Similarly, in *The New Men* (1954), Luke, the brilliant scientist, is almost too bright for those he has to lead, and it is Eliot's brother, Martin, who could supersede him, relatively mediocre as Martin is. A man like Hector Rose, who as a top administrator manipulates people, is sure, with his moral certainties and conforming imagination, that he knows who shall rule the world. He turns down the Passants so that his own position will not be threatened, for the genius, if permitted, can make rules of his own; for genius Rose offers judgment, for original thinking the comfort of safe conformity. In the growing bureaucracy, the administrator, as Max Weber has firmly persuaded us, makes the important decisions and wields the significant power. Moreover, Eliot recognizes that Rose *is* probably right—he does favor the percentages; but what a human waste results from enforced conformity!

One of the real issues in our century, Snow indicates, is how to utilize the talents of a man for the benefit of the country and for his own benefit. *Homecoming, The New Men, The Masters* (1951), as well as parts of the other novels, show Eliot as he at various times must pass upon the worth of men. The only way to work with people, he recognizes, is to assume their faultiness—and then work with them. In *The Masters*, he supports Jago for master *because* Jago is human enough to recognize his fallibility, and his opponent is not. If, like the nineteenth-century liberal, we suppose the perfectibility of the world and of people, then we are basing hopes upon an unattainable ideal which by its very deceptive nature is dangerous to hold. If one presupposes frailty and imperfection, then one knows where to compromise. Thus, Lewis Eliot works with what is available, and what he succeeds in obtaining is always less than what is desirable, but always more than what he would have gained by bull-like methods.

This way of life is not inevitably a *moral* compromise, but the compromise between what one wants and what one can hope to obtain in an imperfect world. To recognize that one must keep his moral person intact, and yet realistically see that others might not also be aware of or able to act upon this knowledge, is to be mature in Snow's world. In a society in which the traditional hero and villain no longer have meaning, the man of moral stature who can work with the material at hand is the real hero. Society, Snow indicates, depends upon the kind represented by Eliot: dedicated to some extent, but responsible and flexible enough to change when he sees that in flexibility lies the road to social and political survival.

Evidently, with this kind of hero and this kind of subject matter, Snow is not going to be brilliant, eccentric, or even strikingly original. His hero seems middle-aged from youth on, and the novelist himself argues that life works its way out in compromises. From either hero or novelist, little of sensational value can possibly result. There will be few severe dramatic turns in the narrative, few visions or conversions in the main characters, little violence of action or emotion; the ripples on the surface of life will be small indeed. Eliot rarely sparkles, is hardly romantic, seems more imposed upon than imposing. He is, in several ways, a staunch Victorian, only one with a more realistic sense of social fact and greater moral flexibility than most. He derives, in part, from Mr. Knightly of Jane Austen's *Emma*; he is, as well, a more sophisticated Dobbin (*Vanity Fair*); and among twentieth-century characters, he recalls Conrad's Marlow, although Eliot is more intelligent and less restricted by a rigid world of honor, integrity, and loyalty. He is not above expedience, as we shall see; and at times he displays sadistic tendencies. He can be cruel as well as patient, self-protective as well as understanding.

No matter how one chooses to look at Eliot, he is not a romantic character. His shabby beginnings—like Snow's own—imposed a sense of reality, and his calling as a lawyer keeps him close to facts, not to flights of imagination. He is, as his acquaintances often tell him, solid, even prosaic, and very safe; people confide in him, ask his opinion, honor his judgment. Yet he has charm of a sort: as an intelligent man in a world of unintentional nonsense, he is almost an anomaly, as Snow himself is as a novelist. Both the creator and created are plain men. As Lionel Trilling has written (*The Griffin*, IV, no. 2— Feb. 1955—8), he could imagine Snow's having asked himself what qualifications he had to be a novelist, only to answer depreciatingly: "No strange or violent or beautifully intense vision of life. No new notions of the moral life—on the contrary, a set of rather old-fashioned notions chiefly about loyalty and generosity. The best he could muster under the moral head was a belief that it was quite hard to live up to even these simple notions. 'It is not much to make novels with,' Mr. Snow thought."

Snow's prose, as well, is marked by plainness, an innocuous prose that rarely does more than indicate essentials. His style is, as it were, virtually an absence of style when we use the word to signify something distinctive. There is, also, a curious lack of development in his power of expression from first novel through last, as though Snow refused to tamper with something that he considered adequate. The following passages come, respectively, from his first novel, *Strangers and Brothers*, and his last novel, *The Affair* (page references to the Macmillan—London—edition).

> George, of all men, however, could not be seen in half-truths. It was more tolerable to hear him dismissed with enmity and contempt. He could not be generalized into a sample of the self-deluded radicalism of his day. He was George, who contained more living nature than the rest of us; whom to see as he was meant an effort from which I, his oldest friend, had flinched only the day before. For in the dock, as he answered that question of Porson's [the prosecuting attorney], I flinched from the man who was larger than life, and yet capable of any self-deception; who was the most unselfseeking and generous of men, and yet sacrificed everything for his own pleasures; who possessed formidable powers and yet was so far from reality that they were never used; whose aims were noble, and yet whose appetite for degradation was as great as his appetite for life; who, in the depth of his heart, was ill-at-ease, lonely, a diffident stranger in the hostile world of men. [p. 308]

> In the study next door, my brother [Martin Eliot] was interviewing a pupil, and Francis Getliffe and I were alone. He was a couple of years older than I was, and we had known each other since we were young men. I could remember him thin-skinned, conquering his diffidence by acts of will. He still looked quixotic and fine-

featured; his sunburned flesh was dark over his collar
and white tie. But success had pouched his cheeks a
little and taken away the strain. In the past few years
the success which he had wanted honorably but fiercely
as he started his career and which had not come quickly,
had suddenly piled upon him. He was in the Royal
Society and all over the world his reputation was as high
as he had once longed for it to be. In addition, he had
been one of the most effective scientists in the war. It
was for that work, not his pure research, that he had
been given the C.B.E. whose cross he wore on his shirt-
front. For a combination of the two he had, two years
before, been knighted. [p. 11]

In the early passage, Snow is describing a man who seeks
failure as some men seek success; while in the latter, he is
concerned with a man who turns every enterprise into
fame and reputation. The prose to describe each is virtually the same, and yet both passages almost call out for
parody in their honesty of intention, sincerity of statement, and naive feeling that such words can actually catch
the nature of people. Even the vocabulary is similar in
these two passages written twenty years apart: particularly,
the word *diffident*, which enters into almost every Snow
description of character and must appear at least a hundred times in the series, sometimes several dozen times in
one novel. What the two passages indicate is Snow's fixity
of purpose, his refusal to let any external influences creep
in to upset his balance or question his methods, a refusal,
ultimately, to change or grow. In terms of writing style
alone, he has probably developed least among any of the
serious contemporary novelists; there is no indication that
he has ever doubted his initial attempt, so modest are his
intentions, so limited his creative aims.

Similarly, Lewis Eliot's talents are modest, his ambitions
within reason, and his successes out of proportion to his
intentions. He does his work quietly, without fuss. His
virtues are those of calm and rather colorless efficiency,
and he is obviously insufficient to carry the weight of
eight fairly long novels. Therefore, around him, Snow

has created several recurring characters, of whom only George Passant has so far been mentioned. Another is Charles March, Eliot's rich friend who begins in law and ends in medicine; a third is Roy Calvert, the center of *The Light and the Dark* (1947), whose brilliant scholarship is vitiated by his headlong plunges into depression amidst periodic hysteria. As these are Snow's weightiest characters, so the most interesting of the novels are *The Masters*, his best known, and *The Conscience of the Rich*, his penultimate; also of consequence is the aforementioned *The Light and the Dark*, which covers the same time period as *The Masters*, while emphasizing different aspects of Calvert's and Eliot's relationship to the Cambridge College where they are Fellows. The three novels, with Calvert and Eliot within the first two, and Charles March the center of the third, form a trilogy concerned with the use of power, whether it be the tangible power of politics in a political world, or the power politics of Cambridge Fellows, or the power struggle of individuals to realize their own potential. In his stress upon various aspects of power, Snow, almost alone among his contemporaries, is concerned with the thrust of the individual will as it seeks its justification.

ii

In attempting to write a fictional history of the years following the first World War, Snow to gain texture and weight has used the now common devices of overlapping situations and characters. The trial of George Passant in *Strangers and Brothers* foreshadows the trial of Donald Howard in *The Affair*; the election of Roy Calvert to a Fellowship in *The Light and the Dark* adumbrates the election of a Master in *The Masters*; Charles March leaves law for medicine as Lewis Eliot himself leaves law for a College Fellowship and then for government administration. Working along with overlapping situations are recurring characters who turn up either in the flesh or in memory. Snow's use of recurring characters and scenes helps prevent stringiness, a defect common to long series of novels. In the earlier days of the novel, the "stringy" narrative was the form of the picaresque novel, a method appropriate to a time when there was little attempt at psychological depth and when the surface behavior of the character *was* the character. With the advent of the psychological novel, as developed by George Eliot and Thomas Hardy and consolidated by Conrad and Joyce, the picaresque had to disappear, for it permitted only a relatively unsophisticated view of human nature.

The chief ways to modify the picaresque have come through experiments in the doubling of characters and scenes and particularly in the use of time. Conrad and Ford were pioneers here, both agreeing that chronological time sequences have little to do with the way that life operates and the way people think. Their aim was to upset clock time through a rearrangement of material that would approximate the haphazardness of life.

After Conrad, Virginia Woolf, and Joyce, the straightforward narrative employed even by a relatively conservative practitioner like Snow was passé. In the present generation of English writers, Snow himself, Lawrence Durrell, Anthony Powell, among others, have all worked with time in order to find a working method. In France, the influence of Proust remains supreme, coming down to the present in the variations of Beckett, Michel Butor, Alain Robbe-Grillet, and Nathalie Sarraute, all of whom upset clock time and impose psychological time upon the structure of the novel. In a novelist like Butor, time assumes a significant place either for reasons of suspense and narrative plotting, or for psychological import.

In a writer like Powell, time, as the title of the series (*The Music of Time*) indicates, is to be arranged musically, with the past entering and re-entering like a musical motif, arranged and rearranged, modulated, and harmonized. For him, things in the past continue to well up; events come back as though eternally recurrent, "like those episodes of early experience seen, on re-examination at a later period, to have been crowded together with such unbelievable closeness in the course of a few years; yet equally giving the illusion of being so infinitely extended during the months when actually taking place." Time here becomes a Fury which pursues its characters and makes them feel guilty for not having changed internally as they are altered externally. In their need to avoid boredom, in which they often knowingly demean themselves, the one thing they cannot escape is time.

Snow himself occasionally works with Proust's so-called "privileged moments" in which a substance, flavor, meeting will recall almost an entire previous existence, and in this way he is actually closer to Powell's use of time than, say, to Durrell's. Durrell's purpose in the *Quartet* is to gain simultaneity by having the unchanging substance of the narrative screened through the eyes of different characters and thus modulated accordingly. While an earlier novelist like Conrad was concerned with making the reader *see*, Durrell goes further and asks what he actually sees and whether he can even be sure that he has seen. The substance becomes ever-moving and ever-changing. In Snow's hands, there is some attempt at simultaneity, for many of the events in the sequence overlap, but Snow is very sure of what everyone sees. Also, the sequence is controlled by Eliot in a way denied to Darley in Durrell's *Quartet*. As an experimenter of a sort, Durrell raises quasiphilosophical questions of subject-object relationships. As a conservative, Snow raises no such questions: he *knows* what a subject and an object are. The only area in which phenomena can be uncertain is that internal area where decisions are determined by the unconscious; but these decisions—what leads Lewis Eliot to marry Sheila Knight, for example—are in the very areas Snow avoids.

Snow's sequence, despite the several instances of overlapping sequences, was conceived as a chronologically straight narrative, with the looping of time simply a way of bringing in new material, not a means of seeing the same material from different aspects. Despite his grounding in modern physics, which assumes relativity, Snow works with fixed points. Although he remarks that Lewis

Eliot is actually different from the way he seems to others, nevertheless he has Eliot operate with a hard core of reason, except in certain personal matters, which makes him predictable. It is precisely the fixed nature of his material and his chief character which causes Snow to seem curiously old-fashioned despite the contemporaneity of his material: scientists, bureaucracy, atomic fission, power struggles. Snow comes up against the old novelistic question: who suggests reality more effectively, the novelist like Snow who presents what is, or the novelist (say) like Kafka who indicates a view of bureaucracy that seems more visionary than realistic? One returns, inevitably, to Aristotle's distinction between History and Poetry. Snow, according to the terms of his involvement, is concerned with History, although, to his vast credit, he can create dimensions that move outside History.

The distinction is a crucial one, for in his essays as well as his fiction, Snow has become a spokesman for the literary right, the conservatives who wish to write as though the novels of Conrad, Lawrence, Joyce, Kafka, Mann, Proust, Gide, and Faulkner had never occurred. We grant that the severe pressure of external events has resulted in a partial reaction against the art novel, which had its roots in Symbolism, and Snow seems to be the logical leader of this quasi-defined movement, if it is even that. As a former scientist, civil administrator, and director of an electric company, as a pragmatist in philosophy and a benevolent and enlightened man in social questions, Snow disdains those who refuse to see the novel as solidly based in realistic fact. Unlike Wallace Stevens, who came to poetry with something of the same background, Snow does not see fiction as imaginative, but curiously views science as an imaginative art and makes literature into a category of social science.

Thus, we note Snow's distortion of the significance of stream of consciousness, his attacks on experimentation, his suspicion of involved symbolism, his assumption that the "anti" writer is somehow subversive of human qualities and irresponsible toward the hopeful thing that is life. Snow and those who agree with him (novelists as well as critics) argue that the whole movement attributed to Symbolism narrowed the novel, which can be re-charged only by writers who face the "real" world, by which they mean man's daily hopes and fears. Yet Snow's ideas, tending as they do toward the naturalistic, would, if realized, restrict the novel by reducing human motivation to its tangible elements and human actions to a chartable course. It is odd to find a scientist whose logic is Aristotelian becoming a Platonist in his distrust of the false poets who tell us "untruths." Snow's literary reactionaryism would raise barriers to imaginative fiction; for English life, taken straight without the "embroidery" Snow rejects, does not provide the depths and heights of behavior suitable for strictly realistic fiction. Snow unfortunately confuses the potentialities of the English novel with those of (say) the Russian.

All this is not by way of making Snow the whipping boy for much that is far outside his personal control. His work is merely symptomatic, not the cause. At his best, he transcends his own doctrines, and at his worst, he remains intelligent and reasonable, qualities that many of the writers he opposes could well learn from him. Also, he provides a valuable corrective to the novelist who isolates a small area of reality without regard for the whole, a practice that has increased as novelists have retreated from the larger confusions. Nevertheless, even as we recognize and pay tribute to Snow's achievement, we must cite the dangers for the novel implicit in his view. The novel thrives on realism, but the realism is not that of the big events, the political struggles, or the social conditions as reflected in history.

In his anxiety to close the gap between science and the humanities, Snow simplifies the nature of the humanities. Very often, the humanities create doubt, while science seeks certainties. Very often, the gap—not the result of ignorance but the consequence of the complex things in question—must indeed remain a gap, for the scientific point of view cannot be contained within literature. Inevitably, one returns to the imaginative writers, often the very ones Snow castigates for unreality.

It is all very well to praise Tolstoy and Dostoyevsky for

their social realism, but when one tries to apply their ideas to life, as ideas, one finds that they do not fit Snow's plans at all. As ideas, the Russian writers' views are almost the opposite of what Snow embraces: Tolstoy advocated a rejection of administration, bureaucracy, industrialization, success, ambition, and everything else that Snow says modern man must embrace discreetly; Dostoyevsky had apocalyptic visions in which man found salvation through faith in Jesus Christ, while most of Snow's intelligent characters are nonbelievers or dogmatic atheists. In Snow's world, religion is a medieval superstition toward which indifference is the best policy. Tolstoy's and Dostoyevsky's "social realism" would hardly satisfy Snow's own views, nor would (say) Balzac's; obviously, social realism in itself—apart from the literary and imaginative trappings—does not fit Snow's formula.

By using Eliot as a central narrator, Snow himself sacrifices a great deal of the novel's potential multiplicity to gain what he calls social realism. In practice, everything must be viewed through Eliot's eyes, and there is a consequent loss of motivation and density in the other characters. What Eliot fails to see, we must assume is not present. Further, decisions which are made within another's consciousness cannot be dramatized. This drawback is particularly acute in a character like George Passant, who comes to us solely as Eliot sees him. How Passant feels, how he reacts to disappointment after disappointment, how he reconciles his talent with his achievements, all these we see with Eliot's eyes, not Passant's. When Henry James used a central narrator— for example, Strether, in *The Ambassadors*—he gained a sense of discovery: as the reader reacts, Strether reacts. Rather than simply a filter or sifter, Strether becomes the reader's eye, and his experiences become the reader's. With Snow's Eliot, we gain little sense of discovery; we merely come to see things as someone like Eliot reacts to them. The loss is obvious; no matter how perceptive, wise, or discreet Eliot might be, he becomes predictable. Perhaps it is Snow's failure to have Eliot's private weaknesses appreciably affect his public life that narrows the range of the sequence to the reasonability of Eliot himself.

Connected with the narrowing influence of Eliot is Snow's prose, which, as we saw above, may be effective perhaps to catch a world of administration but is incapable of probing into the more diffuse world of irrationality. Even when trying to come to terms with a schizoid like Sheila Knight or a manic depressive like Roy Calvert, Snow does not use prose appropriate to their states. He uses, rather, the factual, occasionally compassionate tone of administrative prose that is more suitable to outline a procedure than to limn a psychopathic personality. At the very beginning of the series, in *Strangers and Brothers*, Snow reveals the detailed precision, the almost scientific calculation of his style: "The firelight shone on the new, polished silver. I [Eliot] held out my hand, took the case, looked at the initials J. C. [Jack Cotery] in elaborate Gothic letters, felt the solid weight. Though Jack and I were five years older than the boy [Roy Calvert] who had given it, it had cost three times as much as we had ever earned in a week." (pp. 11–12)

The emphasis upon enumeration and the keyed-down flatness are generally indicative of Snow's prose style, although several passages are superior to that quoted. The inescapable point, however, is that Snow, like Wells, for example, has forsaken "romantic" prose for "scientific" prose, just as he forsook so-called modern techniques for the more straightforward narrative of the post-Victorian novel. And yet, curiously, he like most of his contemporaries is concerned with catching the tones of the age and delineating its struggles and tensions. Notwithstanding, he divorces the style of that delineation from the thing itself.

Snow's remarks in a recent article on modern fiction ("Science, Politics, and the Novelist: Or the Fish and the Net") in *The Kenyon Review* (Winter 1961) are illuminating. For there he praises a scholar, George Steiner, for having written a book about Tolstoy and Dostoyevsky without knowing Russian. And the scholar practices textual criticism, Snow remarks with admiration. Of what use, we ask, is textual analysis if it is an analysis of the translator's prose, precise and effective as the latter may be? Is not Snow begging the issue entirely in his attempt to simplify cultural differences, of which language is a major manifestation? Is he not claiming that the content is identical in both the original and the translation, and that language itself therefore makes relatively little difference?

In minimizing linguistic differences, Snow as well tends to minimize both cultural and human differences. While it is admirable and enlightening to talk about the elements that make men similar, it is misleading to assume even for the sake of argument that the similarities are greater than the differences. Snow at his best recognizes that men are more nearly strangers than brothers, that they are strangers not only to others but also to themselves. When his fiction manifests these uncertainties in human relationships, then Snow demonstrates the complexity, not the simplicity, of the world. Then he shows that textual analysis is meaningless unless it is an analysis of what the writer wrote, not of what the translator translated.

As in his attitude toward textual analysis, so in his view of human problems Snow is uneasy if no resolution is foreseeable. Too often, Snow believes what Crawford claims in *The Affair*, that sensible men make sensible decisions. While this remark does come from Crawford, who is relatively uncomplicated and now old and tired, nevertheless it does to a large extent reflect Snow's own views. The several court scenes, the election of a Master, the procedures over the nominations for College Fellows —all these are the concerns of a novelist who does assume that sensible men do make sensible decisions, and that discussion and judgment, not revolutionary tactics, can prevail. They are the beliefs of a man who assumes that logic and nonviolence are still attainable; ultimately, they become the basis of Snow's qualified view of progress, the characteristic meliorism of the scientist. They are the

assumptions of a man who believes that justice will inevitably prevail in a democratic society. In this area, we
have Snow's limitations as a novelist: he thinks more like a
scientist than a humanist in that he wishes to translate
hypotheses into conclusions.

The alternative does not have to be Beckett's brand of
nothingness, although the tones of Beckett's work often
seem more suitable for a description of contemporary life
than Snow's logical pursuit of justice, or even injustice.
Even when the latter prevails, there are reasons for it: if
George Passant is refused a permanent civil-administra-
tion post, there is injustice involved, true, but it is per-
petrated within a system which Eliot nevertheless accepts
as the best man can create. When Hector Rose decides
that George, although brilliant, is unstable, Snow can see
Rose's argument, while strongly disagreeing with it. Eliot
does not castigate the system so much as feel it goes wrong
in this situation. Underlying Eliot's response to Rose's
decision is his feeling that the Roses will not make too
many mistakes of this sort.

Once again, this is not to claim that Snow totally
ignores irrational forces, like certain self-destructive tendencies submerged in man. There are several passages in
Strangers and Brothers, as well as in *The Masters* and *The
Conscience of the Rich*, in which irrationality prevails:
in Eliot's courtship of Sheila, in his brother Martin's
choice of Irene, in Eliot's early decision to try to be an
attorney against overwhelming odds, in Charles March's
choice of medicine over law, in Roy Calvert's intemperate
attack upon his patron. Here, there are forces working
which dictate choices that lie beyond reason, although
some of the decisions ultimately prove correct. Within
men, Eliot believes, there are forces operating which are
inexplicable, self-destructive, and powerful enough to
overturn well-balanced minds. Snow writes: "I [Eliot]
believed that some parts of our endowment are too heavy
to shift. The essence of our nature lay within us, untouchable by our own bonds or any other's, by any chance
of things or persons, from the cradle to the grave. But

what it drove us to in action, the actual events of our lives
—those were affected by a million things, by sheer chance,
by the interaction of others, by the choice of our own
will." (*The Light and the Dark*, pp. 366–67)

One feels, however, that these unreconciled inner conflicts simply act as halters on ambition; they do not affect
what the person finally chooses to do: he moves ahead,
even while hobbled. Only he moves more slowly than he
had planned. Characters like Sheila and Roy are of course
outside any help, but they are not representative. In fact,
they fail precisely because Snow does not make them
representative: they have conflicts which remain insoluble,
although the nature of the conflict is rarely adequately
developed. Both have childhoods that seem regular
enough, although both develop psychopathic tendencies,
Sheila's need to withdraw from successful, ambitious people, and Roy's obsession to find a master. The only character in the sequence besides Eliot (in part) who is
fleshed out both internally and externally is George Passant. Here is a man truly trapped by what he is, a man
who finds escape impossible and who rationalizes what he
is and what he has done: in brief, a human being. While
George twists and turns alternately to accept and reject
himself, Eliot comes to terms with everything and moves
on, virtually undeterred by his inner failings.

In comparing Snow with Graham Greene, an exact
contemporary also interested in conscience and morality,
we see how Greene moves *within* the character, while
Snow merely pays his allegiance to the inner man before
getting down to what really interests him: the outer,
public creature who must make decisions. There is a
dichotomy in Snow that does not exist in Greene. The
latter is interested primarily in souls—how they are saved
or damned, or, in many cases, how they are tortured. The
outer man is secondary; the public roles of his characters
are never very satisfactory precisely because their souls are
not satisfactory. Snow, however, wants to show man functioning in the larger world, not man praying or playing,
but man working and making, *homo faber*; and yet he also

wants to see why that particular man acts that way—what his motivation is, what his causal psychology is, what he really is. These ambitions should bring Snow back to the inner man in a much more profound way than he is willing to go, and precisely here he fails us in a way that Greene does not.

One way Greene satisfies us comes through his use of jagged imagery to describe human behavior, the nervous note in his prose that seems an amalgamation of Hemingway and Conrad. In *The Power and the Glory*, Greene writes of the whisky priest that he "drank the brandy down like damnation." Catching the point in a fleeting image, Greene is able to merge language with content. With equal ambition although different stress, Snow is discursive, losing tautness and incisiveness because for him language is not imagistic. In his use of language, Snow loses the quality of being, the metaphysics of behavior that Greene is capable of catching. This failure limits his explanation of human behavior, and partially vitiates his assumption that people are neither good nor bad but merely expedient and self-seeking. The failure of adequate language makes his work seem more logical and rational than his plan calls for, for in one image of despair, were he capable of projecting it, he could catch not only sadness but a tragic sense of life.

iii

Snow began his writing career concerned not with sadness but with detective mysteries. *Death Under Sail* (1932) is standard mystery fare, showing Snow's ability to deduce information and to present data logically and coherently, qualities that would stand him in good stead in the trial and election scenes of the *Strangers and Brothers* sequence. In the following year, Snow published a Wellsian tale of science fiction, *New Lives for Old*, concerned with the discovery of a hormone which eventually causes the moral breakdown of the West. Then, in 1934, he published his only serious novel outside the series, *The Search*, which curiously foreshadows many of his later themes. This novel is an apprenticeship-like study in which the protagonist instead of growing up to be an artist becomes a scientist, as it were, a *Naturwissenschafter-roman*. For Snow in the early 1930's, the new culture hero was already the scientist, the man who would lead where once the artist led. Arthur Miles is the scientist as hero: his revelations are not artistic or religious but those experienced in the laboratory or in searching the skies. Instead of composing great music or writing great poetry and novels, Miles measures electric signals in a darkened room or charts figures and plots curves. The papers he writes are not for court consumption or even the little magazines but for the attention of the Royal Society; instead of images, he creates figures.

This is by way of saying that Snow's scientific interests have always prevailed over his literary ones, and although he sincerely wishes to bring understanding to the two cultures, his view is still that of the scientist who somehow wishes the humanities could be less ambiguous and more "scientific." Even as early as *The Search*, Snow's discussion of human affairs is limited because it so clearly lacks passion, is already scientifically oriented. For the man interested in public power, human emotions, although a necessary intrusion, must be contained. Except for Lawrence and possibly Joyce, this is the tradition of the English novel from *Robinson Crusoe* on: that the successful man is successful because he can control and limit his feelings. Thus, later, Lewis Eliot is angry with Sheila Knight because she has upset his career, angry because his uncontrollable love for her destroyed his chances. For Snow, the "feeling" side of life is interesting, even compelling, but relatively unimportant; rather, what a man has done in his career (measured against what other men of similar age have done) fascinates him. Like Crusoe, he is interested in his stockpile for the future.

In several other ways as well, *The Search* presages the later series. Miles' shift from scientist to writer suggests Snow's concern with the two cultures, prefiguring Eliot's own shift from law practice to academic law and Charles

March's change from law to medicine. Further, the squabble over the Institute in the early novel indicates Snow's concern with how things get done, with how dedicated men can fight among themselves and then finally reach a compromised solution, the forerunning of the elections and trials of the later novels. Also, there are several passages concerned with the temptation to cheat on scientific experiments, the partial substance of which became *The Affair* twenty-six years later.

Principally, the early novel demonstrates Snow's flexible view of people and the decisions they will make, his realization that we must base our liberalism on human beings who are cruel and cowardly. He suggests that faith in people is still possible even though they are frail, and that liberalism in the past failed precisely because it believed in the perfectibility of human beings. The somewhat jaded Snow even in his twenties saw that administrative decisions involved expedience and compromise, that Arthur Miles would be willing to sacrifice his friend Sheriff in order to gain the Assistant Directorship of the Institute, as later Martin Eliot would sacrific Sawbridge. He perceived that such things must be accepted—that our notion of morality must gain new dimensions—if society is to continue; or else we must retreat into orthodoxy and let the worst prevail while we wait for the best to reform themselves.

iv

With Snow's work, certain tendencies in the English novel from Jane Austen to the present have come full circle. Although lacking Jane Austen's irony as a comic freeing force and as a means of returning her characters to a social norm, Snow uses man's social conscience as a way of avoiding chaos. Moreover, in his concern with man's moral nature, in his use of a straightforward narrative technique, and in his understanding and forgiveness of temporary deviations from "correct" behavior, he is indeed close to the mature Jane Austen of *Emma* and *Persuasion,* as well as to several other of the major nineteenth-century novelists. In still another way, Snow has returned to the moderation and proportion of the Greek dramatists, finding in their attitudes the wisdom necessary to preserve a balanced society in which personal interest is both present and necessary. Snow recognizes that personal ambition, if unfettered, can destroy decent life, and that with civilized people the only test of a "good" man is how far he responds to the demands of decency. The power of conscience becomes, under these conditions, a social necessity.

2 STRANGERS AND BROTHERS
and TIME OF HOPE

ALTHOUGH *The Search* after its publication in 1934 attracted considerable attention, Snow felt that it was, for him, a false start. As he writes in a Note to the second edition of the novel: "It was a false start because of the things it did well as well as the things it did badly. I wanted to say something about people first and foremost, and then people-in-society, in quite a different way, and at quite a different level, from anything in this book. So I had to put it on one side, and find my way to a form which would give me a chance of saying what I wanted to say." The sequence called *Strangers and Brothers*, named after the title of the first volume (published in 1940, covering 1925–33), fulfilled this desire of saying "something about . . . people-in-society." The title itself is apt, denoting as it does Snow's concern with making brothers of strangers, with reducing the isolation that each person suffers because of his inability to connect with his fellow human beings.

It is possible to see Snow's entire career as a way of bringing people closer together, not of course through the vulgar way of the evangelist or the popular humanitarian, but through demonstrating man's common aims. In his now well-known pronouncements on bringing together the scientific and humanistic communities, Snow is simply pursuing the same theme: that the similarities among men are sufficiently great to warrant their rapprochement. In the world of knowledge, this attitude would mean the creation of a new type of men, the "New Men" Snow called them in his novel of that name. In politics, this attitude would mean mutual understanding, a reduction of nationalism, and the spirit of compromise. In the social world, this attitude would mean that each individual should gain understanding of more than himself, that he should pursue more than selfish ends, although naked selfishness is also to be expected.

In a way, Snow comes to the reader as a wise uncle who has seen the world and returned to report that while it is possibly as bad as we have always thought, it is also the only one we can expect to know. The message is hardly reassuring—it is not expected to be—but it does cut through a great many complications. It tends to take the ground from under those who bewail the nature of the world, for Snow agrees that we should not overestimate it. It tends to comfort those who seek a secular faith, for Snow tells them that a secular morality is indeed possible if each man questions his own ambitions, goals, and judgments. It tends to pacify those who claim that progress is virtually illusory, for Snow himself accepts a very limited view of man and progress, holding that while man is often capable of decent behavior, on occasion we should expect him to be expedient and self-seeking.

What Snow holds out for "people-in-society" is a distinctly restricted view of happiness, one less tortured than Greene's and Beckett's but also less optimistic than Henry Green's. In fact, happiness is not Snow's primary concern. As we have seen above, he is more concerned with how man functions than with how man reacts to what he does. Snow wants to see things done, regardless of the toll, regardless of the loss in human happiness. Society is always greater than the individual, and the cause or goal is always greater than the person who seeks it, although Snow nevertheless believes quite strongly that the individual has his rights. Had John Stuart Mill written novels, they might have sounded like Snow's: fiercely individualistic, yet concerned with social patterns, with the ways in which the individual compromises society and society compromises the individual.

Obviously, with these concerns, *The Search* was not the right start for Snow, involved as that novel is with the details of scientific discovery, with a young man's revelations as his eye catches new configurations in the microscope. Only the end of *The Search* foreshadows Snow's growing involvement with the larger community of men, for there Arthur Miles turns from pure science to history; he becomes a writer, much as C. P. Snow shortly afterward also did. Snow catches his protagonist's conversion at the end of the novel when Miles recognizes that his friend, Sheriff, has falsified scientific evidence in order to insure his advancement. Were Miles to remain in science, it would be his duty to report the deception and ruin his friend, for personal considerations count little when science is involved. But Snow is already questioning what science means against the background of a world filled with would-be brothers who are strangers. Scientific fraud remains a dreadful thing, but except for those dedicated to pure research, it is relatively insignificant; what is more important, now, is history, the record of mankind's folly as Miles sees it.

Snow himself turned to a branch of history when he started *Strangers and Brothers* in the late 1930's, a time when social and political issues were ready to explode. In the twenty odd years that Snow has been working on the sequence, from *Strangers and Brothers* in 1940 to *The Affair* in 1960, the world has indeed exploded; and his "New Men" are politically and socially conscious scientists, dedicated men who have been created by the new world and who, in turn, will help create the still newer world. It is these men who should bear the responsibility of decision, Snow suggests; they should become increasingly important in government, in public affairs, in the decisions that affect men's lives. Snow's sequence, then, is a "history" of our times, from Eliot's modest beginnings to the creation of men who can either destroy or improve society.

At least at its inception, the series was to be broader than Powell's *Music of Time*, which is more concerned with breakup than with even qualified progress; grander than Durrell's *Quartet*, which stresses personal happiness —what is love? how does one gain and lose it?—more than it does social and political man; more expansive than Doris Lessing's *Children of Violence* series, which has failed to move out into a large enough view of the world; more extensive than most major series in our century except Proust's *Remembrance*, which is a book that Snow could never write. The broad and ambitious gesture is evident in Snow's plan as it took root after *The Search* had proved inadequate for what he wished to say. It was nothing less than an examination of modern man. Later, we shall see how the novels themselves fall short of Snow's ambitious intentions, in which the plan was in excess of the fulfillment.

For such an ambitious undertaking, *Strangers and Brothers* was a modest beginning. Curiously, the novel gains much of its interest from the character of George Passant rather than from Lewis Eliot, who is Snow's surrogate. In fact, as the series grows, it is George Passant who acts as counterpoint to Lewis Eliot, with George's failure a contrast to Eliot's growing administrative success. George Passant as a young man has energy, an analytical mind second to none, and ideals—all the qualities that should insure success without loss of conscience. Early in the novel, he idealistically defends the rights of Jack Cotery in the latter's fight to continue at school while enjoying remission of fees. Without regard for self, George fights the case and wins, although at the expense of his own reputation with the authorities.

From the outset, we have a typical Snow situation in miniature: a good deed committed which will compromise the doer's future. Under these conditions, should a discreet man attempt to do good deeds? How far should one measure his own chances against the good he wishes to do? To what extent is a person committed to his own future at the expense of another's chances? At what point does a private good cross or compromise a public good? These are the questions that Eliot asks himself, and his answers are typically compromised, for while he is also idealistic and anxious not to injure others, his actions are discreet, neither heroic nor treacherous. Rather than confronting "evil," Eliot minimizes it: he compromises it, while being sure to secure a foothold from which he cannot be dislodged.

George Passant never provides these defenses, and therefore he answers with action, immediate and, for him, indiscreet. It is a minor triumph of Snow that as he gains the reader's sympathy for George's idealism, he also gains the reader's horror at George's headlong plunge toward destruction, at his waste of talent and energy. As a political liberal, Snow admits that good deeds are excellent; however, as a conservative in personal matters, he suggests that one has the obligation to protect oneself. One must play situations by ear and make decisions accordingly. Pure idealism is self-destructive, just as selfishness and greed are reprehensible. There is of course no punishment except that meted out by one's peers for indiscretion. In the response that George makes to Jack Cotery's situation, Snow provides an epitome of the entire series.

Mixed in with George's idealism is a great deal of presumption. He assumes that he has made a greater hit with the committee than the situation warrants, and when the decision goes partially his way he is sure that he tipped the balance. The fact of the matter is that the committee reached a compromise in order to cut the ground out from under him. He received something of what he wanted only to keep him from getting more. The committee has reacted as most committees react, but George's presumption deceives him. It is just this self-deception that cripples his career, and it is precisely this lack of self-deception that secures Eliot his qualified success.

George Passant gains immediate interest because he achieves stature as much by his failings as by his idealism. At every turn, he compromises himself. Like Kafka's K., he is beaten back by forces seemingly outside his control, often at the moment he thinks he has gained what he desires; like Tantalus and Sisyphus, he has a taint on his past that makes the water recede as he starts to drink or makes the boulder roll down when he reaches the peak of achievement. There is in George the substance of heroic failure, and like Tantalus and Sisyphus, he always returns to the job of doing the impossible.

While we admire George's recuperative powers, Snow comments that he retains part of his energy from his ability to fool himself. George remarks that: "I believe in progress, I believe that human happiness ought to be attained and that we are attaining it. . . . The world I want will come and you know it." Olive, Jack Cotery's pursuer, comments that George gives far more than he receives, that he fritters away his real opportunities: "If he hadn't come across such a crowd [the group that George attempts to "educate"], he'd have done something big." Olive seems to have struck George's flaw: that he *must* dilute his talents in order to avoid facing them, that he *must* compromise his vast energies through some weakness he is unable to control. According to this reasoning, George is predetermined to fail despite his great gifts, which in several ways surpass Eliot's.

At his trial for fraud, George—who is partially guilty— makes an eloquent plea for freedom, for joy, for personal happiness: "If there's to be any freedom in men's lives, they have got to work out their behavior for themselves." And earlier, "But I believe that while people are young they have a chance to become themselves only if they're preserved from all the conspiracy that crushes them down." George has organized his group in order to give them freedom from social strictures, to show them that they can be themselves. Yet other, less noble motives are involved in George's actions. He also uses his position of power to solicit girls to the farm where the so-called freeing process occurs. Later, he agrees to make money from the farm, in connection with his other enterprises. Thus, at the moment George pleads for his beliefs, his actions have partially compromised his ideals.

Here is Snow at his best, for at the trial itself, he mixes what he and the reader favor with unfavorable arguments and actions. The trial is vaguely reminiscent of the trial of Meursault in Camus' *The Stranger* in that both Meursault and George are being tried for what they are rather than for what they have done. Meursault's crime, among others, was his failure to weep at his mother's funeral; while George's crime is his sensuality, his libertarianism, his subversion of the young. Behind both is the trial of Socrates, who too was accused of being a bad influence on society. What Snow raises here is the entire question of justice, just as later, in *The Affair*, he is concerned with the nature of justice when the defender is personally unpleasant, even repellent.

Yet nothing is fully clear. For behind George's legitimate appeal for freedom is the self-seeking, the partially guilty young man who uses the group for his own purposes. George's idealism is blunted, his intelligence compromised, his ambitions besmirched. At the trial, Herbert Getliffe defends George successfully by belittling the very things that his client most believes in. Getliffe pleads passionately that George was naive and innocent, that he honestly meant to do good but that he had no notion of what people were really like.

> He wanted to build a better world on the basis of this freedom of his: but it's fatal to build better worlds until you know what human beings are like and what you're like yourself. If you don't, you're liable to build, not a better world, but a worse one; in fact you're liable to build a world for one purpose, and one only, that is just to suit your own private weakness. I'm certain that is exactly what all progressively minded people, if you'll let me call them that, are always likely to do unless they watch themselves. They usually happen to be much too arrogant to watch themselves. . . . He's been too arrogant to doubt his idea of freedom: or to find out what human beings are really like. He's never realized— though he's a clever man—that freedom without faith is fatal for sinful human beings. Freedom without faith means nothing but self-indulgence. Freedom without faith has been fatal for Mr. Passant himself. Sometimes it seems to me that it will be fatal to most of his kind in

this country and the world. Their idea of progress isn't just sterile: it carries the seed of its own decay. [p. 300]

What is involved in Getliffe's plea for George is an indictment of the so-called false liberal, the man who plunges in to save the world without understanding its nature. What is also involved, however, is the unsavoriness and hypocrisy of these words when they come from someone like Getliffe, who represents the complacent Establishment, the man who would like to be a judge, the man who, as we later see, is himself mixed up in somewhat shady dealings in stocks. What is also involved is that George can escape punishment simply because this kind of self-righteous argument appeals to the court. Getliffe adds that the court must beware of being prejudiced against such a headlong, foolish man like Passant, even when its prejudices are absolutely right. In order to dilute the charge of fraud, Getliffe undercuts the only substantial thing that George stands for. Getliffe's speech is an adequate but depressing symbol of Snow's view of the way the world works.

Snow provides a further twist in that Eliot sees still another George, the one who explains his actions positively while he lies awake nights afraid of his little world, remorseful over his frustrated aspirations, aware of fear and guilt. "He was less honest than those who saw in his aspirations only the devices of a carnally obsessed and self-indulgent man. He was corrupt within himself. So at the time when the scandal first hung over him, he was afraid, and already dissatisfied, tired of the 'little world.' But this answer which he made to Porson [the prosecutor] was the manner in which he explained it to himself." (p. 286) Eliot sees George's noble words as an attempt to reason away his misgivings. And yet Eliot partially misreads George, for beneath the fear, the rationalizations, the sensuality, and the self-deception is a person who goes after the right heads, who is indulgent with the needy and energetic in the pursuit of freedom, a man who throws down the gauntlet to the complacent and the stodgy.

Eliot perhaps sees George in a limited way—without losing his admiration for the man—because he is readying himself to become part of the very Establishment which condemns the Georges. When, later (in *Homecoming*), George is turned down by Hector Rose for a permanent position in the Civil Administration, Eliot dissents from the majority opinion, but indeed continues as part of the Establishment that has rejected George. Eliot dissents within the limitations of safety. He has made his mark as a man of judgment for the very reason that his judgments are limited, are not radical, even when radicalism may be called for. He is obviously going to misjudge George who judges radically even when the situation calls for limitations. The two are diametric opposites, with just enough sympathy to keep the friendship going. The difficulty is that while we know how Eliot views George, we never really see how George views Eliot, whether he fully recognizes that beneath the exterior of the man he has helped, there lurks the nastiness and ambition that will necessitate expedience and compromise.

Strangely, George recognizes these qualities in other people, and possibly because he does recognize them, he is able to work with them. Early in *Strangers and Brothers*, Mr. Passant tells his son that people live within the absolutes of good and evil, and George immediately draws a zigzag to indicate how he thinks people live. That is, people live in constant movement between good deeds and bad actions. They may be going in one direction when they relax, perhaps spurt in another direction, until the downstrokes may be longer in some cases than in others, or the reverse. With this view of people, George is prepared for the truth: that human nature is capable of great good and great evil, and he must work with that notion if he hopes to do anything.

In the course of all this idealistic talk and compromised action, George is created, a figure of energy and optimism who will hover over the series as a contrast to Eliot. As George's fortunes fall, Eliot's proportionately rise, although he too is held back by uncontrollable forces within him. The possible alternative to both is provided by

Martineau, the partner in George's firm of solicitors who leaves his business and takes to the road seeking sainthood. Martineau's motivation is not clearly established beyond the explanation that he had some kind of revelation which made secular life impossible for him. Snow is clearly uneasy with this type of person—the recluse who seeks salvation through rejection of the world—and does not include another character of this sort. Obviously, this alternative is not for Eliot or Passant. The latter's sensuality would hardly be satisfied by rejection, and Eliot's ambition is part of his fiber. He must seek what the world offers, find out how much he can gain, and then settle down with what his capabilities permit him.

At this early point in the series—with the intervention of the war the next volume, *The Light and the Dark*, was not to appear for seven years—Snow could have developed his work in several ways. From the first volume, however, it becomes clear that he has at least partially rejected the possibility of the panoramic novel. Almost immediately he settled down into the kind of everyday gossipy detail that precludes the grand design. Just as Snow's plain prose is the opposite of the grand style, so his plain ground-plan is the opposite of the grand design. It is clear that he will work scene by scene, so that the completion of the plan occurs through details. There will be little sense of sweep such as we feel in Durrell's Alexandria *Quartet*, even though Snow's material as he later develops it is concerned with the frontiers of science and the great, behind-the-scenes decisions made by administrators.

There seems, then, almost initially a fundamental opposition between the material Snow is developing and the style or tone of his method of development. As he moves out from the small worlds of *Strangers and Brothers* and *Time of Hope* into the larger worlds of *The Light and the Dark, The Masters, The New Men,* and *The Conscience of the Rich,* he retains the same style and method for material that is considerably more ambitious. *Time of Hope* (published in 1949, covering 1914–33) is concerned with a small boy's world, his growing pains and his partial transcendence of his early poverty; evidently, this kind of world is quite different—in kind as well as degree—from the world of atomic science, the decisions that can affect the future of England and the world, the development of the Barford project, the choice of civil administrators, and all the other aspects of complex political life. Nevertheless, Snow's approach to both is fundamentally the same: to present what is occurring through small scenes in which personal and public matters are intermixed. What works for one, however, is partially unsuccessful for the other. There is a deadening of the excitement that the later material calls for. The somewhat wooden prose is not up to the poetry of man's effort to chart the unknown.

Snow's placid style and unadventurous technique are relatively unimportant in the novels whose action occurs from 1914 to the mid-1930's, but as soon as the tempo of public life quickens, then the technique is inadequate to the intention. It is here that Snow's literary conservatism cuts into material that he takes very seriously. Certain aspects of life are amenable to his style; as we have seen in *Strangers and Brothers,* he can effectively build up character and situation with the tools at his command. But the coming of the war and the development of the atomic bomb, not to mention the administration of these new forces, all call for a more daring method. Snow might still have honored his attacks on experimental techniques and yet have arrived at some approximation in style of the material he wished to present. As it is, there are several aspects of the material left over, so to speak, simply because the technique cannot come to terms with it; the result is a loss of what Snow really wishes to catch. For here, he is obviously more interested in public issues than earlier, and yet his method still sweeps up the details of private squabbles and personal reactions.

This avoidance of a grander style, then, hurts the series as a whole, although it works well in those novels in which just this kind of honest prose and method are called for. There is also another factor involved: Snow as a novelist shows little or no development. His material changes; he does not. There is none of the growth into stylistic discovery that one hopes for from one novel to the next, none of the experimentation on a large or small scale that shows the author is trying to confront his material with all he has. Snow seems to have been fixed from the beginning; the Snow of 1940 is the Snow of twenty years later with *The Affair*. Although he has become somewhat more adroit in his handling of character and situation, essentially he has not changed. For a long series, the style becomes deadening; what works for a novel or two seems wooden over the long haul. The prose unfortunately lacks the modulations and nuances which would vary the pace and flow.

Durrell recognized this very point in his tetralogy, for his prose—while perhaps too flamboyant in parts—jumps and scintillates, becoming alive with images and metaphors. Admittedly, Durrell had exotic material to begin with, but Snow in his later novels certainly had exciting material with the war and the bomb. However, even with less exciting material, an author can create tension. Snow's realism has come back to haunt him.

The unadventurous technique might have been qualified somewhat had Snow attempted irony, so that he could have enlarged the single authorial point of view. Snow uses Eliot much the way Conrad used Marlow, and yet Conrad gained some distance on Marlow even while using him as spokesman for a sane and conservative point of view. This distance Conrad gained through the use of irony, for irony specifically provides another voice for the material. If we momentarily look at the novel tradition that Snow is close to, that brought to near perfection by Jane Austen, we can see that she rarely takes her heroines straight but, rather, treats them ironically. That is, we see her heroines as they think they are, as others see them, and also as the author sees them. The heroine, accordingly, is rarely fixed; there are shadows and silhouettes and ambiguities. Through irony, Jane Austen can distinguish between character and personality, between substance and superstructure. In the creation, we find a heroine capable of many tones and colors, one who is rarely constant—all this within a rather severely limited social frame of reference.

Snow of course has the freedom of word and movement that no female—or even male—novelist could possess in the early nineteenth century. And yet he gains far fewer nuances from his protagonist than Jane Austen or Dickens obtained from characters much more limited in mobility and behavior. From the chronological beginning of the series, from *Time of Hope* (1914–33), Snow presented Lewis Eliot "straight," that is, as he is. Even when other characters see him, they agree about the basic Eliot: moderate, judicious, honorable. Only the women in Eliot's life view him differently, as a man less pleasant than his exterior presents. Nevertheless, in the Author's Note to *The Conscience of the Rich*, Snow speaks of the inner design of the series as a "resonance between what Lewis Eliot sees and what he feels." Snow means specifically that Eliot first observes certain emotional experiences as they occur in others, and then in a different context finds himself going through the same or similar experiences. Thus, Eliot notices the love of power and the renunciation of power in others, only to go through these experiences himself, first as a lawyer, then as a College Fellow, and finally as an administrator.

As design, this is valid enough. In performance, however, these incidents become somewhat flat when they are the sole way of opening up what a person is. After eight volumes in the series, Eliot has not taken on flesh. In his lack of real desire and in his ability to sublimate sex as conditions necessitate, he seems close to Robinson Crusoe; yet Snow makes him need sex and seek sex. There is here, as elsewhere, a failure of imagination. We ask whether this cold man would even bother with sex at all, or else we ask whether this man once he is involved with sex actually feels anything. Socially, also, Eliot seems to feel little. Although he is capable of putting up with every kind of nonsense and seeing some value in every kind of fool, we are expected to accept him as discriminating and intelligent. The only other possibility is that Eliot goes along with everyone to further his own career, but then how would Snow explain him as a man of integrity?

The confusion in his creation is not the planned confusion of the design, for example the confusion one finds in a novel by Virginia Woolf or E. M. Forster, in which confusion is itself thematic. If anything, Snow's intention is the opposite. How often he has attacked the kind of novel in which confusion becomes a justification for the book! Snow desires precision, and it is here, paradoxically, that he hurts his own cause. Eliot acts too often like a machine, without the blurred purpose that seems human. Early in his life, as he fumbled for a career, Eliot arranged his public life with machine-like precision, and this precision remained even after his disastrous marriage. As one character remarks to him, he can compartmentalize his wounds and continue to function in the public world. Yet this very ability to arrange his feelings, to sort them out and see which he will react to, makes Eliot desiccated as a character, if one is compelled to take him straight.

Here, as we have seen, ironic treatment by the author would create another dimension or another voice. Then the singleness of Eliot's intentions might have been given the complexity of life. Clearly, irony provides more than even another dimension of character: it indicates to the reader one way in which he can take the character, not necessarily *the* way, but an alternative to the behavior of the character and the way other people view him. It complicates, it provides wit, it gives depth. Taken straight, Eliot makes Snow's various points about contemporary life, but he takes on few of the resonances that would make him exciting. When the reader has finished with the eight volumes, he almost immediately forgets Eliot and thinks solely about the choices and decisions involved in the books.

And yet this is not at all the point Snow wishes to make about people. If, like Beckett, he did believe that people do drift away into nothingness, then he could partially justify the insubstantiality of his characters. But Snow, on the contrary, believes very strongly in people; he likes people, and he likes to see good in people even when they do their best to hide it. His is a peopled world: he is fascinated by the possibilities of their behavior, by the potential of their actions, by their techniques of defense and offense, by their sheer ability to resist what would drag them down into misery and suicide. Snow is a positive man, a yea-sayer, a believer in humanity despite its admitted shortcomings. Unlike Beckett, he thinks certain things count, and he thinks that human decency can and does prevail in certain controlled situations. Within this frame of reference, then, it is necessary for Snow to create real people, for it is the reality of people that concerns him. He is principally concerned with the fact that people can survive despite their evident shortcomings, that George Passant can remain buoyant after succeeding defeats, that Eliot can remain ambitious despite the drain his wife makes upon him, that a college or country can survive the squabbles that go into policy making. Snow is concerned with survival *despite—despite* all the things that tend to frustrate the human spirit. Within these terms, people must really be people, and here in what should be his very area of strength, the author, at least partially, fails us.

Having rejected irony, Snow might have viewed Eliot's career in a different light and brought him home a success, or, alternately, a failure. That is, *with* irony it might have been quite possible to chart the middle course that Snow did and still create an individualized human being, as Tolstoy did with Ivan Ilych. Without irony, it might have been easier to do Eliot "straight" as a success or failure and that way caught the human note. Evidently, Snow wanted the middle ground, irony or not. A success would mean heroizing his protagonist, giving him qualities that Snow feels are lacking in a democratic age. Eliot develops despite limitations that are as severe as his talents: the two elements circumscribe each other, with the resultant character a keyed-down man who is frustrated in his search for success, but who has too many qualities to fail completely.

Further, Snow avoids other absolutes, whether religious or social. Life is the result of compromise, and the good man is the one who compromises what must be compromised to insure continuity while forsaking as little principle as possible. But, from Snow's point of view, principle must be forsaken in a situation that would otherwise create stalemate. To recognize the degree to which one must compromise is to demonstrate maturity. With the rejection of absolutes, with the rejection of irony, Snow is left with a middle-of-the-road character who must somehow come through, curiously a man of integrity who will compromise himself, a judicious man who will display expedience. What often remains is stodge and woodenness set out as the best that we can expect from man.

This view of Eliot would be perfectly acceptable if Snow himself intended it. Perhaps, it may be argued, that for Snow to see his Eliot as a joke on mankind—as the best our age can produce—is for him to assume idealistically that man is capable of more, when realistically he knows that he is not. Perhaps, this argument may go further, Snow has reached the point of wisdom whereby he recognizes that we must peg our hopes low, and by expecting relatively little actually gain more than we hoped. With this assumption, even the stodgy Eliot really is preferable to those around him; and were we forced to choose between Eliot and any of the characters surrounding him, we would unhesitatingly select Eliot. The point, Snow suggests, is not that a man compromises his ideals—such a view would be sophomoric in the light of what the real world is—but that a man must know when he is compromising and must recognize when to stop. The mere fact of it we must, as mature people, accept. As I remarked above, this assumption could be perfectly valid; but only if Snow were working ironically; for, then, stodge would characterize the man of the future.

There is, instead, only some very gentle irony, what in

fact borders on nostalgia. The title of the first volume—
Strangers and Brothers—indicates the mildly ironic assumption that people who should be brothers are really
strangers, and that while it is advantageous to close the
gap, it is doubtful if they ever will approach each other.
There is also mild irony in the title *Time of Hope*: the
irony implicit in our childhood view of immortality. This
is a time of hope, Snow suggests, because one does not
recognize the barriers, the virtual impossibility of imposing
one's will upon the world. This is an irony of personal
sentiment, however, rather than one based on a view of
the world. Ultimately, what happens is that Snow, for all
his sophistication, for all his flexibility and refusal to be
shocked by any behavior, simplifies the world. A world of
the middle-way related without irony is inevitably a
simplification of the real world; a world in which reason
rules is inevitably a softening of the real world, as Conrad,
Lawrence, and Joyce so well recognized. Too often Snow
feels that the decisions men make in their public functions
indicate a great deal about them, when actually their decisions are an exterior response to survival at the most
superficial level. What actually goes into that particular
decision is what counts, and here Snow treads softly.

There is a kind of healthiness implicit in *Time of Hope*
which accepts that the will, even when partially frustrated by uncontrollable forces, will triumph once a man
recognizes his limitations. Thus in this volume which
carries Lewis Eliot back to 1914, when he was nearly nine,
Snow tries to set the background for his protagonist's
checkered career. However, there is really very little in
Eliot's background to give a key to the kind of person he
will be. In fact, the few incidents that Snow does provide
would seem to point to a different kind of person. Eliot is
early "wounded" when before his entire class his poverty-
stricken position is brought home to him by his teacher.
Eliot's mother has scraped along so that her son can give a
large sum to a war subscription fund being collected in
his class. She finally saves ten shillings, an amount considerably more than the average donation. With great

pride, Eliot brings the sum to the front of the room. The teacher accepts the money with surprise and then launches into a speech to the effect that the donation would be better used toward paying off his father's debts. This advice comes at the exact moment that Eliot has expected praise for his large contribution. What was to have been a hard-earned triumph becomes humiliation, and intensifies his disadvantageous position vis-a-vis society.

This situation is perhaps the nadir of Eliot's fortune as a child and would appear to indicate a person who will go on to make his mark, driven furiously by a will impelled to seek success. It entails the kind of rejection Thomas Sutpen suffers in Faulkner's *Absalom, Absalom!*, a rejection that results in his obsessed need to prove himself. The next great humiliation occurs when Eliot is pursuing Sheila Knight, the withdrawn, psychoneurotic girl whose morbid attractions are more than he can withstand. After ostensibly making a date with Eliot, Sheila shows up at a Christmas party with another man. The humiliation Eliot feels harks back to the incident over the war contribution, both incidents indicating to him that there is cruelty, real cruelty, operating in the world. Eliot says: "I saw in her and in myself a depth which was black with hate, and from which, even in misery, I shrank back appalled." (p. 192) Thus ends Eliot's innocence.

These two incidents, the outstanding personal ones in Eliot's first twenty years, do little to adumbrate the character who turns out to be a judicious, social Fellow and administrator. One other point should also be considered: Eliot's rejection of his mother's affection, a rejection that he draws upon to explain himself and yet one which seems low-keyed indeed while his mother is alive. Eliot actually shows little emotional reaction to his mother, and when Snow informs us that he has rejected her affection and possessive love, it comes virtually as a surprise. Yet this rejection is supposedly a crucial one, for Snow bases many of Eliot's future emotional attitudes upon it. Towards the end of *Time of Hope*, Snow writes about Eliot:

Somehow I was so made that I had to reject my mother's love and all its successors. Some secret caution born of a kind of vanity made me bar my heart to any who forced their way within. I could only lose caution and vanity, bar and heart, the whole of everything I was, in the torment of loving someone else. Sheila, who invaded me not at all and made me crave for a spark of feeling, was so wrapped up in herself that only the violence and suffering of such a love as mine brought the slightest glow. [p. 414]

Here, supposedly, is the key to Eliot's masochism and sadism, most evident in his relation to women and quickly noticed by the shrewd Sheila. And yet this depth of uncertainty, this penchant for cruelty, this need to suffer in order to gain an orgasm (in one place, Eliot speaks of almost performing rape on Sheila during their sexual intercourse) never really comes through as planned. Snow must himself have recognized this inadequacy, for when pushed to explain, he retreats to the mystery of the self and thus begs off. After Eliot's humiliation and shock at the Christmas party, Snow writes: "I felt a sense of appalling danger for her [Sheila], and, yes, for me: of a life so splintered and remote that I might never reach it; of cruelty and suffering that I could not soften. Yet I had never felt so transcendentally free."

What this and other passages amount to is the valid enough belief that forces operate below the surface of behavior which are inexplicable and uncontrollable. Yet Snow proceeds throughout the series as though everything else is eventually explicable, and his style is that of a man who believes phenomena can be explained. Eliot is able, in Snow's workmanlike prose, to examine his own feelings, to sift out the reasons for them, and then to justify his behavior. To catch the morbid forces sweeping through Sheila Knight and Lewis Eliot, Snow would have needed a much different approach, one whose tone conveys the irregular and the irrational, even the self-destructive.

Yet, ironies within ironies, some of the most potentially interesting sequences in the series pertain to Eliot's self-destructiveness: how he forces himself to be hobbled by circumstances. We would like more along these lines, more preparation for what Snow plans to do with Eliot. Percy Lubbock in his *Craft of Fiction* talks about the need for preparing a change of attitude or a new tone in the novel. What preparation does is to relieve the novelist of unnecessary and often tedious detail to carry through his point. Lubbock remarks that Balzac emphasizes Eugénie Grandet's boredom by preparing the reader for her long dream of Charles—so that the actual dream does not need much explanation. On a lesser scale, this method would be valid for Snow's presentation of Lewis Eliot. Eliot has reached a certain point at which ambition and will are to be frustrated by emotional quantities he cannot control. Yet the reader has not been prepared for what may be Eliot's most significant characteristic: his self-destructiveness.

The fault here lies in the development of *Time of Hope*, which, along with *Homecoming*, is primarily devoted to Lewis Eliot, bringing him from childhood through his professional life as a lawyer, just prior to his acceptance of a college Fellowship. The fault, perhaps, is that Eliot's childhood is not enough that of a child; it is too much an adult's view of childhood. There is too little childish reality, too much adult interpretation of what a child is like. Snow is unable to move within Eliot and unable to make him into a child, although the circumstances and people (his father, for example) surrounding him are authentic, even touching. This kind of evocation, which several of Snow's American contemporaries have caught perceptively, is beyond his power, concerned as he chiefly is with adult preoccupations. Of course, once Eliot has grown and enters the world, Snow's abilities come to the fore, and in maturity and intelligence he outstrips many of those same American writers.

Nevertheless, in pursuing the reality of a man's public decisions, Snow slights many of the forces that make a man what he is. There is little sense of life as itself, life apart from one's social contacts. Even with Sheila Knight, there is little attempt to explain her psychopathic need to help others, to gather around her the helpless and the hopeless. True, Snow presents her parents, her shrewd but hypochondriacal father, her stupid but domineering mother; but even here there is no indication how they turned their daughter into the psychotic creature she is, a withdrawn sado-masochistic woman unable to follow the dictates of her sense, self-destructive in every move she makes, hating herself and everyone around her except those who need her. Again, we are faced with a lack of preparation; Snow simply unfolds what has occurred after the fact. The nature of the fact—how people get that way —falls outside of his purview, and when he does tentatively deal with it, he fails to convince. Snow's talent is manifest chiefly when people have reached the point at which they are involved in public life.

The key word is *involved*. One reason, perhaps, why Snow is weak on childhood influences is that childhood contains few involvements: decisions are relatively simple, resting as they do mostly on physical needs. The child, after all, can control little of his own destiny—that is part of the agony of childhood—and Snow is principally interested in people who try to will their destinies. Thus, childhood, for this adult novelist, offers little of the complexity or the involvement that an adult situation offers. Snow tells us Eliot is like *that* because of his rejection of his mother, and because of the "wound" he received with his contribution to the war subscription list. A further "wound" has come at the hands of Sheila Knight at the Christmas party. Yet these three major incidents, plus a few minor ones, do not explain Eliot, should not even pretend to explain him.

With these necessary preliminaries out of the way, we can see *Time of Hope* as a typical apprenticeship novel, not unlike *The Search*: that is, the protagonist expects success, but life partially frustrates him, and he must settle for less. In its fashion, this novel chronicles the childhood of the "hero," his aspirations and ambitions, his growing circle of friends, his first successes (here academic), his first love (for Sheila Knight), his mental development and emotional maturation, his various ordeals, and his subsequent awareness of his role in life. Then Snow rewrites the traditional script and brings it into line with contemporary developments. Instead of having the hero go forth to conquer, now that his chief obstacle has been removed (his law examinations), Snow hobbles him with two destructive tendencies, one physical and one psychological.

The physical ailment is Eliot's illness diagnosed (wrongly) as pernicious anemia. Once sick, Eliot becomes aware of his mortality and finds his will tested with even greater severity than when he was studying for his examinations. He finds he cannot reveal he is sick or else he will lose his chance. As a junior in Getliffe's office, Eliot can hold his position only because he is there; let him relent or show weakness and someone else will swiftly replace him. Such is the nature of the competitive world. Every man is expendable if he cannot keep the pace, and Eliot must carry on despite his physical need to capitulate. With his examinations behind him, the illness becomes his second ordeal. Eliot comes to know the dread of a man who sees the thrust of his life passing outside his own control, who senses that he is no longer the sole master of his destiny: "I had the sense, which all human beings dread, . . . of my life being outside my will. However much we may say and know that we are governed by forces outside our control, and that the semblance of volition is only an illusion to us all, yet that illusion, when it is challenged, is one of the things we fight for most bitterly. If it is threatened, we feel a horror unlike anything else in life." (p. 323)

So strongly does Eliot feel about this possible loss of control that he contemplates suicide. He sees self-destruction not as an abnegation of will but as an imposition of it. With suicide, "one's life is, in the last resort, answerable to will." This blunting of the thrust of the individual will is of course part of Snow's acceptance of man's limitations. Even in a man-centered universe which has dispensed with God's services, man must not become epical or heroic. He must accept that the mere force of circumstances—what the Greeks explained as the phenomenon resulting from *hubris*—can frustrate his calculated pursuit of material success. He must settle for less, even though in his youth he had sought riches as his right. "What else is there?" both Eliot and Snow ask, and the answer is that there is little else. Every man is entitled to his pursuit of his dreams, although, Snow adds, he has also to accept the consequences of his ambition.

The consequences for Eliot are embodied in the form of a chemical action that decimates his red blood corpuscles; the will of man proves futile when it struggles against the will of pernicious anemia. Whereas once the Greek hero, full of self-importance and anxious to challenge the gods, was brought low by those very gods he hoped to emulate, now anemia brings down a man who had hoped to go all the way. His ambitions stymied by a few less red blood corpuscles than necessary, his body weakened by loss of muscular control, his psyche afflicted by disturbances of the nervous system, Eliot becomes a battleground: his youthful desires mocked by the failings of his body. He is split into two, and at twenty-five suffers the agony of perhaps dying without knowing whether he would have prevailed, a Keats struck down while under attack.

Eliot's physical failing brings sadness, perhaps even a tragic sense of life. Certainly, it deepens his perceptions and makes him more aware of human frailty. Also, it forces him to take another calculated risk. Sick as he is, he must return from Mentone, where he is recuperating, to pick up his practice, or else lose everything and see another replace him. He must drag himself around London and calculate his strength in his every move. Suddenly alerted to the absurd claims of his body, Eliot finds his dream world spinning away into nothingness. He no longer dreams; now he wishes merely to survive. In one stroke, Eliot is brought down to earth, caught as he is by the inexplicable absurdity of the universe. Even though his career continues, this period is a turning point in his development as a human being.

The second destructive tendency in Eliot is a psychological one that almost destroys his career while it also makes a shambles of his private life. In this novel, Eliot's attachment to Sheila is carried up to and through their marriage, and then examined in greater detail in *Homecoming*. Sheila's relationship with Eliot further indicates Snow's point that "we are governed by forces outside our control," that free will is partially an illusion in a world where certain inexplicables mock reason. Certainly, Eliot is sufficiently forewarned about the connection, not only by his friends, but also by Sheila herself. "Lewis, if I married you I should like to be a good wife. But I couldn't help it—I should injure you. I might injure you appallingly." (p. 243) When they discuss their future, or even their present, there is little meeting of minds. When he says that he wants "to find some of the truth about human beings," she retorts that she "believe[s] in joy," although she claims she is unable to love anyone. Eliot answers that he must love a woman who will not force herself within his affections. She is reckless with her emotions, squandering them over people who will never reciprocate, while Eliot is closed about his feelings, giving them only to Sheila, who, too, will never reciprocate them.

Despite her plea that she pursues joy, Sheila is death-oriented, while Eliot, despite his infatuation with Sheila, is fiercely life-oriented. At one point, Snow catches imagistically her death-oriented frigidity as she stares into the Thames from Westminster Bridge. "Too cold to jump," she remarks to Eliot while they gaze into the ice-slivered black water. Frigid herself, she ironically finds the river too cold. At the same time, Eliot is burning with life, "defeated and hungry with longing." He has gone walking with her despite his injured heel, a further instance of his masochism, especially since his attempt to reach her sexually earlier in the evening had failed. He had virtually tried to rape her only to have her pull away and scream that she could not go any further. The freezing night air, the frigid Sheila looking into the river and contemplating suicide, the limping, frustrated, dissatisfied Eliot all come together to make this little scene a mockery of man's foolish belief that he controls his destiny. To recognize his foolishness is part of Eliot's education.

At the end of the novel when Eliot hovers indecisively over whether or not to let Sheila go, he must choose between prison and freedom. He must also choose the kind of professional future he wishes, for with Sheila as a burden, his career is crippled. Then once again his career crosses with George Passant's. In the summer and fall of 1932, Eliot hears of George's trouble with the farm and subscription list, the substance of the second half of *Strangers and Brothers*. At the same time that George's future is jeopardized, the now married Eliot lies beside Sheila and faces, as he well recognizes, the corrosion of his own future. So, too, George, with the case coming up and his chances of winning slim, faces a corroded future, the hopes of both destroyed by forces they have themselves set into operation. Eliot blames Sheila for the shortcomings of his career, forgetting that he somehow sought to evade success in the very decision to marry her. That George blames no one is admirable, but he continues to face the future as though his fraud had never occurred. His optimism is untarnished, although circumstances seem to mark him as a small-town solicitor for the rest of his life.

Both, then, are contained, and both, after the trial, must rebuild their futures. Having been passed over as the defensive lawyer in favor of Getliffe, Eliot must face anew what he is and what he can do. The forward thrust of his career that began ten years before with George's help has slowed; and Eliot's predicament is as severe now as then. For in addition to seeking his own way, he has the burden of Sheila. In a moment of Proustian recall, Eliot sums up what the first twenty-eight years have meant: "Anyway, for a second, I remembered how I had challenged the future then [ten years before]. I had longed for a better world, for fame, for love. I had longed for a better world:

and this was the summer of 1933. I had longed for fame; and I was a second-rate lawyer. I had longed for love: and I was bound for life to a woman who never had love for me and who had exhausted mine." (p. 414) And yet Eliot retains some hope. As he indicates, he has perceived certain truths, and he finds that he must live with them. One of them is the nature of his career: he will never go all the way. The other is the nature of his private life: he will remain anxiety-ridden until he or Sheila dies. With the facts upon the table, Eliot knows the worst; he has seen himself and his fate.

For Snow at this point, it becomes a matter of revising Eliot's earlier dreams. As a pragmatist, Snow keeps his ear close to the ground, and what he hears is something very unstriking: that man survives because of his adaptability. Unlike a creature from a Beckett novel, a Snow-man does not give up the struggle and await annihilation. These are not novels of apathy or indifference; there are still choices to be made, minor victories to be won, and personal deficiencies to be overcome. For a secular writer like Snow, there is no alternative. In a Graham Greene novel, Eliot at this point would be transformed into someone like Scobie (*The Heart of the Matter*), tied to the wrong woman, his career a shambles, his energy wasted, his tendencies suicidal. There is, however, little sense of that complete rejection of life in Eliot's bleakness. His attitude is more a compound of disappointment, frustration, and dissatisfaction—all feelings that, one by one, he can resolve. His despair is not cosmic; the hound of heaven is not chasing him, and he must live up to only his own view of the future.

As Snow leaves Eliot in these two volumes, the two concerned with his apprenticeship, and moves on to his public life, we already see in operation Snow's secular philosophy. The key is Eliot's ability to compartmentalize his problems and deal with them as they arise: not to struggle with them en masse and become dragged down by their weight. Implicit here is the qualified optimism of the liberal who recognizes all the shortcomings of his position.

When, later, Snow argues about the need for men to question their own infallibility, he sees this step as the first toward stability. Eliot has this quality in abundance. His experiences as a lawyer and then with Sheila have pointed up his deficiencies. And as he no longer expects perfection from himself, so he does not expect it from others. He expects weakness, he looks for imperfections; when he finds them, he is not surprised, and is able to turn them into necessary action. It is not unusual that Snow later transforms Eliot into a successful administrator. For in Snow's world of choice and selection, the administrators will inherit the earth. While lacking meekness, they can, however, control their emotions, and in the contemporary world that is sufficient for success.

WITH *The Light and the Dark* (published in 1947, covering 1934–43), Snow moved Eliot into his official life. Now established as an academic lawyer at a Cambridge College, Eliot is 29, having forsaken his law practice except for two days of consultation in London, where his wife still lives. With his problems having been partially solved by his separation from Sheila, Eliot is himself not of primary importance here. Instead, Snow picks up Roy Calvert, the young man we first met in *Strangers and Brothers* who indiscreetly gave Jack Cotery an expensive gift. Roy there is simply a rich, impetuous youth who indulges his whims, one of which is his temporary attachment to Jack. Roy's name threads through that book and then recurs in *Time of Hope*, where Sheila admires his ability to throw himself heedlessly into his feelings; it is also Roy who calls Eliot to bring him home to work out George Passant's case.

After the interruption of the war years, when Snow was himself active in administration, it was fitting that he should turn to a young man—Roy is five years younger than Eliot—who grew to maturity during the preparations for the war and then fought in the conflict itself. In addition, Roy is something special, for intellectually he is about the best his country can produce: a brilliant scholar, a witty conversationalist, a personable, generous young man. But he is lamed by a recurring manic-depression, his inner disease comparable in some ways to Eliot's less obvious and more easily-controlled self-destructiveness, and to George Passant's excessive sensuality.

In a way, Roy's mental illness is an adequate symbol of the 1930's: his periods of depression comparable to its, his moments of elation also its. In Roy, Snow has caught a figure who is sacrificed to his age; he is, in his way, its conscience. Of course, Snow does not intend only allegory, for he makes Roy's disturbance an inner conflict as well as a symbol of outer malaise. Snow admirably avoids a straight sociological interpretation in which his young man is victimized by a corrupt age. Corrupt it surely is, but Roy is also possessed by demons for which the age is not responsible, for which, in effect, no one is responsible. Roy's crippling moods are part of every human being's inheritance that keeps him from functioning at his best, and that forces him to come to terms with what he is. This quality—present as it is in nearly all of Snow's major characters—prevents heroes, precludes freedom from doubt, and bars complacency. By suggesting that torture is as much within as without, it forces self-knowledge.

Roy, then, must try to reconcile the inner with the outer man. The outer is dazzling: good-looking, brilliant, rich, accomplished. The inner is a shambles: insecure, uncontrollable, rude, nihilistic. Split between his two selves, Roy finds himself in a world that truly alternates between light and dark. The title ostensibly refers to the beliefs of the Syrian group known as the Manichees, into whose history Roy is encouraged to do research. According to Manicheean belief, man is a battleground between the forces of light and those of dark. In this struggle, man's spirit is equivalent to the light, his flesh to the dark. Thus, the struggle is between flesh and spirit, with the desired outcome that the spirit overcome the flesh, and make worship of the flesh a matter of guilt. Applied to Roy's situation, the light, or the spirit, indicates his drift toward life; the dark—his flesh, the periods of depression—suggests his drift toward death. Thus, Roy is created as embodying the twin antinomies implicit in man's existence, the twin forces whose struggle against each other keeps him aware of self. The guilt feelings about the body which Freud saw as necessary to progress at the very same time he saw them as destructive of the individual, the Manichees interpreted similarly: man can never rest easy about himself.

It is fitting that Roy's major scholarship should be concerned with beliefs which come so close to defining what he is. The lights and darks of Roy's existence are always there, as much as they are in Hamlet. Roy is perhaps a kind of modern-day Hamlet, one for the twentieth century as much as Shakespeare's was for the seventeenth, both torn between their quest for decency and an inner torment that twists them into making unnatural responses. Hamlet, of course, has some objective reasons for his torment, while Roy's are more internalized, part of his self-destructive mechanism; but that distinction is surely the distinction between not only the two characters but the two ages—what was manifest in one is internalized in the other. The forces operating are, nevertheless, similar. Like Hamlet, Roy is a young man of considerable intellectual gifts which fail to assist him in the very area where he most needs help. Roy seeks absolutes to fill a void within him, like Hamlet's "Yea, from the table of my memory / I'll wipe away all trivial fond records." Yet Roy is an honest man. As he seeks to fill the void within —what Hamlet filled with oaths of revenge—he does not permit himself to be deceived by false beliefs. As he seeks, he finds nothing. There is no external equivalent for what he lacks. Had there been a murderous uncle to do away with, Roy would have killed; had there been a victimized father to avenge, Roy would have sought revenge. His, however, is not an "antic disposition" to be put on or off; it is something outside of volition, like Hamlet's moments of hysterical elation. He drifts toward death in his desire to surmount the depression, to test his will as it confronts the thing he fears most.

Both Hamlet and Roy in a somewhat restricted way are existential heroes; both toy with death as the way out, and both resist death when it finally comes. Both play out the game even though they know they are doomed to certain fates, and both find inexplicables in their existence: Hamlet's ghosts, Roy's moods. In their relationship with women, also, they are strangely similar. Two-thirds through *The Light and the Dark*, Roy comments about Joan Royce, the Master's daughter who loves him: " 'I've got to look pretty reasonable when Joan comes. It's important, Lewis. She mustn't think I'm ill.' He added, with a smile: 'She mustn't think I'm—mad.' " (p. 277) The difference in this respect between Roy and Hamlet is that while the latter feigns madness to disguise himself, the former must feign sanity also to disguise himself. Again, each age makes a differing claim upon them.

Inevitably, Roy's actions lead him increasingly closer to death, just as the chain of events around Hamlet lead him toward his death. Roy's situation is somewhat worse, for he has no control over his drift, while Hamlet does himself make many of the decisions which determine his future; but, of course, we are not attempting to find congruity between the two characters. Instead, what is interesting is to see that Snow, whether consciously or not, has worked with an analogue that deepens the reader's understanding of Roy and gives him the kind of substance that Eliot himself rarely enjoys.

This is not to claim that Snow is equally successful with every aspect of Roy. On the contrary, Roy's depressions are rarely fully cogent, for Snow—as in his description of Sheila Knight's withdrawal from reality—rarely uses sufficiently imaginative languages or images to convey the unusual and the irrational. Also, the Roy Calvert we saw briefly in *Strangers and Brothers* gave little indication of the Roy we meet here. In the earlier volume, he was simply impetuous and indiscreet, not manic or depressive, or even "odd" in any significant way. His gift to Jack Cotery manifested a schoolboy's crush on an attractive charming man some years older; it was not a direct homosexual action on Roy's part. The very opposite is true, for Roy's sensuality is totally woman-directed. All we can see in the indiscreet gift is a boy dissatisfied with his home and seeking a "style," which he misidentifies in Jack. Similarly, the Roy we see in *Time of Hope*, published after *The Light and the Dark*, but covering the preceding twenty years (from 1914 to 1934) again gives little indication of the tormented young man of twenty-four we meet here. When a novelist presents a character in one place who is considerably changed in the next, he is obligated to suggest the changes, if not to explain them. This Snow failed to do with Lewis Eliot, even though he devotes a good part of one volume to his childhood, and he fails to do it with Roy Calvert.

This failure does not destroy the characterization, but it does thin it out and make it less than fully credible. There are great difficulties involved in creating a character who is partially mad, for the question immediately arises: in what way is he mad when madness is so relative that a perfectly sane man may have *his* moments of madness? Not only must the differentiae be made clear, but the elements of madness must themselves be clearly defined. Somehow, madness must appear to be mad, not simply the unusual actions of a person basically sane. Here, too, Snow partially fails us, although he goes as far with Roy Calvert as his style and method will permit. The very qualities, then, that would distinguish Roy from the others remain partially undefined.

Nevertheless, in Roy Calvert Snow has his sole "contemporary" protagonist; that is, one who lives close to the edge of death or nonexistence, one who remains substantially outside the restrictions of reason and fully savors the absurdity of his plight. As a consequence of his illness, Roy has the kind of awareness that comes only from the very sick who have been forced to face themselves on sharply varying planes of existence. Roy experiences life more intensely than the others because his mind might at any time descend into the nihilism of his depression. The depression, like the artist's "wound," perhaps gives impetus to Roy's brilliance, perhaps makes him aware of how little time he may have before his desperation returns.

Living as he does on a different plane of existence from the other College Fellows, Roy falls in with Eliot. The latter differs from him in almost every possible way, and yet beneath the skin they share certain attitudes. Principally, they connect in their relationship to forces which will destroy them. Roy even suggests that Eliot took him on, as he took on Sheila, because of a hidden streak of madness in him. Roy's drift toward death is of course stronger than Eliot's toward destruction. In both his elated and depressed periods, Roy finds himself moving closer and closer to nullity. Only in complete negation of life can his real wishes be fulfilled; and yet he fears death. When his wish to die is about to be fulfilled, he discovers the kind of stability that makes life worthwhile, or at least preferable to death. Roy is much the more intense of the two, the better mind, the wittier personality, the stronger in his negation. Eliot almost always has the ability to compartmentalize his deficiencies—he has rational control over them—while Roy, like the truly wounded, must founder when possessed.

In his varying moods, from melancholy to manic, Roy reveals a range of emotions never experienced by Eliot, who moves in a social world too small to contain Roy. While the young scholar lives through other people, and is often given support through interchange with them, he rarely finds them sufficient, at times merely using them as props for his ego. The novel, accordingly, is itself less a plotted narrative than a series of episodes in which Calvert can reveal himself; and what he reveals is perhaps of greater interest than that afforded by any other Snow character, with the possible exceptions of Charles March and George Passant. The narrative of the novel returns to the manner of the picaresque, but the hero is less on the brink of adventure than on the verge of destruction.

The dramatic conflict of the novel centers, for the most part, around Roy's election as a Fellow to a Cambridge College, the precursor in its way of the election of a Master in *The Masters*. Roy is undeniably brilliant, but his personal life leaves something to be desired, and his petty enemies, less talented than he, are more afraid of his philandering than desirous of gaining his abilities in their College. His work in reconstructing an obscure language,

Soghdian, that had hitherto been undecipherable, secures his place as a scholar of repute. But Roy is obviously not fulfilled by his scholarship; he is unable to come to terms with himself, and often his absorption in philology is simply an escape for his energies. When unoccupied with his work, he falls back on his feelings and finds them wanting. Accordingly, he needs to believe in something since he cannot believe in himself. He wistfully admires the Master, Royce, for his innocent religious faith despite all his knowledge which should have undermined it. Roy searches for absolutes, particularly for the authority of God, willing to accept any kind of dogma and practice if only he could believe in a supreme authority. But he is unable to summon the final faith which would make God real to him, and once again he is thrown back upon himself, where he recognizes his insufficiency. At one point, he makes a pitiful admission to Eliot: "Listen, Lewis. I could believe in all the rest. I could believe in the catholic church. I could believe in miracles. I could believe in the inquisition. I could believe in eternal damnation. If only I could believe in God." (p. 82)

In his mixture of depression and elation, Roy, again like Hamlet, assumes the mantle of a tragicomic clown, striking at hypocrisy and crassness wherever he sees it, while also mocking his own anxieties and carelessly injuring himself. In one way, a source of honesty, in another, an immature imp, Roy causes terror to those who recognize his moods. He attacks, indiscreetly, the pretentiousness of Sir Oulston Lyall, a Near East expert, and by so doing almost brings down upon himself the entire scholarly world. Yet while what he does is admirable, the way he does it is not sporting—he attacks Sir Lyall with insufficient evidence, and he does it before a gathering of their peers, after the old scholar has generously supported Roy's application for a Fellowship. Thus Roy comes close to the reactions of several of Snow's major characters, including Eliot himself, George Passant, and Charles March: he is torn between honesty and gratitude, between what involves personal integrity and what is considered sporting, between the claims of his own nature and the demands of a social conscience.

In another way, Roy's inability to have faith in God is obviously his inability to have faith in himself, for in lieu of God he throws himself into the German revolution of the 1930's in order to identify with power and authority. In the Germans under Hitler, Roy finds the kind of power that appeals to his weaker side and completes him, although he entirely rejects anti-Semitism and even helps a Jewish couple (the Puchweins) to escape persecution. The sheer dramatic force of the movement entices him, and he loses his ability to distinguish between power for good ends and power in itself. In one way, Roy here is close to the disgruntled German intellectuals who supported the Nazi movement because it satisfied them emotionally, even economically, at the same time suspending their intellect to do so. In addition, of course, Roy is trying to exorcise demons which have pursued him in every aspect of his life.

Eliot disagrees violently with him and argues the facts of German expansionism. He also warns about the very nature of power, how it must be relegated with care and would best be kept out of men's hands. "No one is fit to be trusted with power," he tells Schäder, the Nazi official, as Roy listens. Eliot goes on: "I should not like to see your party in charge of Europe, Dr. Schäder. I should not like to see any group of men in charge—not me or my friends or anyone else. Any man who has lived at all knows the follies and wickedness he's capable of. If he does not know it, he is not fit to govern others. And if he does know it, he knows also that neither he nor any man ought to be allowed to decide a single human fate." (p. 253)

Eliot of course argues human imperfectibility and the consequent need to work out institutions that will protect people against themselves. In contra-distinction, Roy searches for perfection—his search for God, or for God in himself—and deceives himself about the nature of the world. The two positions are clear: Eliot's realism about the frailty of human beings and Roy's idealism or romanticism that humanity is capable of everything. This point recurs in different form in *The Masters* and becomes the reason for Eliot's support for Master of the imperfect Jago over the "perfect" Crawford.

This distinction, which Eliot draws with acerbity, is crucial for the series and for Snow himself. It is obviously a completely democratic point of view, and it assumes that institutions work well when they avoid extremes, even at the expense of genius. Such institutions may not produce an Einstein, but neither will they nourish a Hitler. This view provides Eliot's partial condemnation of George Passant, and it explains why Snow often has the second-rate man assume necessary power while withholding it from one clearly superior. The second-rate man, by the very fact that he recognizes his limitations, will be more careful in his use of power than the man who thinks he can go all the way. The second-rate man has feelings of humility, for he sees what he lacks to be absolutely first-rate; and this humility acts as a hobble upon his ambitions. It cuts down his pretensions, and eventually, in policy, it works to the advantage of the institutions he perpetuates. Humility or self-recognition rather than the wilful use of power will keep society stable and operating.

This point becomes doubly significant when we recognize that Snow is writing about one of the most tumultuous periods in man's history, when the Nazi movement seemed supreme precisely because men like Roy, innocently or not, worshipped its worship of power. As against the vacillating old fogies who determined England's foreign and domestic policies in the 1930's, there was the dynamism of a regime which could get things done. Even though the Cambridge College where Eliot and Calvert are Fellows is at the fore of the novel, the background—the forces that eventually claim Roy—is always intruding and not to be lain to rest. What is frightening is the attraction that the Nazi movement can have for the dissatisfied, even when the worshipper is as intelligent as Roy.

And yet, Eliot understands to some extent what Roy is going through, how all his academic attainments are insufficient to fill the void. Eliot himself had felt just such a void and in marrying the schizoid Sheila Knight had tried to effect a relationship with a woman whom he strongly suspected could not be reached at all. In fact, Sheila is as empty in her way as Roy in his, except that she lacks the mental equipment to keep herself busy: her depression alone defines her.

Roy's desire to seek death as the sole solution to his periods of depression leads to his enlistment in the air force, where he feels sure he will die. Yet once he starts his series of raids over Germany, he becomes afraid. Now married, with a child, he wants to play with death as an abstraction, as a possible escape from the dark periods which he dreads, but death as a tangible quantity he comes to reject. Fearing death and also fearing one side of life, Roy becomes a haunted individual living in a kind of no man's land where there is no satisfaction. He does die, but his problem remains after him: there are unforeseen forces which man is rarely able to conquer or even sustain, and these, irrespective of his talents, will destroy or weaken his will so that he becomes ineffective, a plaything of circumstances. Even while working out the intricacies of Soghdian, Roy finds only intermittent escape from his problems, and nothing that approaches a solution. Also, his marriage and family provide only temporary relief, and when their values do take hold it is too late: he has set into inexorable motion the forces that will destroy him.

It is difficult to see how Snow could have argued otherwise against the background of the 1930's. Most of the old certainties were already gone or rapidly disappearing: the modern mood was being fixed. It was becoming apparent that decent men were almost helpless, that a humanistic education and profession were inadequate; that, ultimately, at least for Snow, only the scientist might be able to restrain the tide of destruction.

What makes Roy's death certain is the fact that wartime

freezes his choices; it precludes free will. And precisely as Roy is frozen within his choice, so the individual, Snow suggests, is frozen within his character: Eliot, Sheila Knight, George Passant, and the numerous minor characters like the College Fellows and Royce, the Master. The darkness within Roy is the darkness of death, the very substance of wartime. There is implied here a tragic situation, with a tragic character: that Roy recognizes what he is and what can save him at the very moment the times claim him, and he becomes a victim to what the old men of the 30's have set into motion. His fragmentation of personality is the division forced by an age in which wholeness has become impossible.

This novel is Snow's sole attempt to write tragedy; and Roy Calvert is his sole serious attempt at a tragic hero. He certainly has the potential: he is of sufficient stature, he has a flaw which he is unable to control, he has self-awareness and knowledge; and yet, curiously, Roy is not really a tragic character. Perhaps Snow failed to convey the tragic sense of life because he inadequately charted any sense of decline in Roy; even though he seems doomed, Roy chooses part of what will destroy him. Further, there is not sufficient cosmic maladjustment, a quality that Snow's method and temperament can hardly convey. There is tragedy intended, but Snow is so little the tragic writer that Roy does not transcend the story as the tragic hero must. When he goes out to his death by air, he is pitiful rather than tragic; the tones of the novel suggest hope and guarded optimism, even though Roy is the victim. Moreover, Roy is victimized by circumstances; he does not sufficiently defy them. Snow, evidently, is caught in the same dilemma as his contemporaries: a belief in democratic institutions reduces the range of the protagonist, and without heroes it is difficult to have tragedy, unless it is social tragedy. The hero has become the victim. Only Graham Greene has attempted to transcend these restrictions, but his success is often dependent upon the reader's acceptance of his religious dogma.

Snow provides a possible alternative for Roy's hopelessness in the religious beliefs of his clerical friend, Ralph Udal. Udal, however, accepts his religious faith as easily as if it were a feature or a limb, something he was born to and would have for life. He wears it facilely and lightly; his is not the faith of a Greene or Mauriac character, who must struggle through the dark night of the soul to establish his belief. While Roy struggles through *his* dark night to find some anchor for his self-doubt, Udal can so order his life that he keeps one day a week for spiritual exercise. Roy had originally admired Udal for the latter's freedom from self, from the very chains that shackle Roy to his affliction. Now Roy sees Udal as absorbed in self as everyone else; he sees, further, that Udal's religion is simply an excuse for self. It is not a great passion, but something he can turn on and off as he sees fit. Religion, under these conditions, is the same as business, philology, the sexual act: it does not sustain a man. Roy, subsequently, turns away from Udal, once more frustrated in his search for a way that will make sense. The Udal he had admired now turns out to be no better than the usual run of College Fellows dedicated to their own egos.

A great passion might have sustained Roy, but what great passion is possible in the 1930's in England? What is there to believe in? Turning outward after the disappointment of looking inward, Roy finds the same nullity. Wherever he turns, the nada of existence strikes him. Even in Rosalind, the girl who persistently tracks him, he finds little more than sexual satisfaction. In Joan, the Master's daughter, he also fails to find comfort from his furies, despite her tenderness and intelligence. Women, then, solve nothing. Roy continues his quest for salvation from self while in the background the dying Master, Royce, is ever there as a reminder of the larger world, a dying Master whose death is going to split men as divisively as Roy himself is split.

Although Eliot's affairs poke through sporadically— Sheila dies in 1939, the year the war breaks out—this novel belongs almost solely to Roy Calvert. And even though Roy partially fails as a tragic hero, and the novel as a tragedy, there is sufficient compelling material to make this one of the three best in the series (the others being *The Masters* and *The Conscience of the Rich*). Surely, Snow tried more here than he did elsewhere. In *The Masters*, he cut his range to chart the ins and outs of an administrative struggle when men must use the power they hold. While he somewhat weakened the intensity of their decisions by his use of analytical reason to chart their motivations, nevertheless he did work out a complex of cross-purposes which convey the feel of a power struggle with all its pettiness and backbiting. Likewise, in *The Conscience of the Rich*, he dramatized material where his insight into the nature of moral decisions stood him in good stead; and he made full use of this talent in presenting Charles March and his wife, Ann Simon.

In *The Light and the Dark*, however, he was trying something almost radically different, particularly after the orthodoxy of *Strangers and Brothers* seven years before. Primarily, he has skirted the world where normal decisions and acts count and moved into the dark area where devils reside. This is a novel of torment—as far as Snow can go— rather than resolution: the torture of Roy Calvert's own existence, the pain of Eliot's married life, the gradual decline of Royce, the beginning of the war that will claim Roy, the frustration of Joan Royce as she unsuccessfully tries to lead Roy into the light, the tragic death of the Boscastle's son, Humphrey, the suspicion of fraud in the scholarship of Sir Oulstone Lyall, the confidence of the Nazis as their revolution proves increasingly successful, the decadent world of Willy Romantowski and his friends. Implied in so much death and suffering is the breakup of an entire way of life, and it is only Snow's lack of intensity that prevents this novel from gaining tragic stature.

There is even the further twist that Eliot must assume part of the guilt for Roy's death, for Eliot had once told him, when Roy was suicidal, that the most dangerous thing to do was to fly. Half whimsically and half meaningfully, Roy reminds Eliot of this advice. Now afraid and desirous of resigning, Roy does not intentionally wish to blackmail Eliot emotionally, but what is on his mind slips out. Perhaps he tells him because he knows that Eliot, having lived with Sheila Knight for several years, can understand the nature of torture. All this is a burden, but it is one that Eliot can bear, for he knows to what a limited extent he is really guilty. He believes that Roy would have destroyed himself in some way, with or without the war:

> He [Roy] had once said, just before the only flaw in our intimacy, that I believed in predestination. It was not true in full, though it was true as he meant it. I believed that neither he nor any of us could alter the essence of our nature, with which we had been born. I believed that he would not have been able to escape for good from the melancholy, the depth of despondency, the uncontrollable flashes and the brilliant calm, the light and the dark of his nature. That was his endowment. Despite his courage, the efforts of his will, his passionate vitality, he could not get rid of that burden. He was born to struggle, to pursue false hopes, to know despair—to know what, for one of his nature, was an intolerable despair. For, with the darkness on his mind, he could not avoid seeing himself as he was, with all hope and pretence gone. [p. 366]

Ironically, Eliot's view of Roy's torment applies to himself as well; the burden of blackness that he carries within originally led him into Sheila's arms. He, too, was born to suffer despair, although his basic sanity makes his situation far less desperate than Roy's.

This, then, is Snow's "black novel," the fruit of the war years. Curiously, it is sandwiched between two novels which are among the most hopeful in the series. Snow's pessimism was temporary, and even in *The Light and the Dark*, there is a sense of the world brought to peace. The residue of the war years did not remain. After *Time of Hope*, Snow moved back into the miniature world of a Cambridge College, leaving behind the problems of the larger world. Even with Eliot's acceptance of man's inherent limitations, the individual can still work out part of his destiny; and it is man's ability to do this that gives Snow his limited optimism. Certainly, the Fellows of *The Masters* believe that their decision is significant; the weight they place upon their judgment demonstrates their assumption that life does count, and that meaningful decisions remain to be made.

The Light and the Dark may ring less true as an artistic creation than the more restricted *Masters*, but in its way it remains true to its times. As Snow's most ambitious undertaking, in terms of its largeness of movement, it contains the blackness denied to the more stable world of *The Masters*. In its very doubts, it conveys the dangerous tones of life in the 1930's, while the later novel, although taking place in the fateful year of 1937, retreats into itself, withdraws into a world of stodge, to use Roy's own word. *The Light and the Dark*, however, provides a counter to stodge in the figure of Roy Calvert. It is unfortunate that Eliot and Snow accept stodge as the norm once Calvert is out of the way. Calvert's best moments came when he pierced people where they were most afraid; in those moments, Snow touched upon a tragicomic theme partially missing in the rest of the series.

IN TERMS OF the series, *The Masters* (published in 1951) is probably the most self-contained novel, taking place as it does within a limited period of time (during 1937) in a limited place (a Cambridge College) with a limited number of characters (the College Fellows). As such, it recalls the Aristotelian unities. It is, in its way, tragedy reworked for the modern world. Its power struggle, Snow suggests slyly, is the modern replacement for tragedy; and it works its way out in terms not of defiance but of expedience, shifting alliances, compromise, and equivocation. Gone are the grand passions, the long decline, the innate violence, the cosmic maladjustment, and in their place are the administrative qualities of moderation, deceit, and manipulation.

Of course, Snow never suggests that this modern version of life is tragic. His is the more urbane point that manipulation and moderation are the best we can hope for, and that a society based on these values, while not startling, also avoids the excesses of abnormal behavior. Above all, it is a stable society; the grand gesture is no longer necessary or even fitting in such a relatively closed society. Snow takes it for granted that society has closed sufficiently so that erratic behavior is contained before it can get too far. Implicit in his attitude is a society that wishes to perpetuate itself, and that holds to certain traditions regardless of the dissensions that may temporarily seem to split it. The setting itself indicates the point: as the novel opens, there is the peace and quiet of an institution that has persisted despite wars, conquests, changes of reign, revolution itself. It has prevailed, and its quiet, soft sounds that Lewis Eliot hears now were heard by the seminarians who settled there 650 years before. "The snow had only just stopped, and in the court below my rooms all sounds were dulled. There were few sounds to hear, for it was early in January, and the college was empty and quiet; I could just make out the footsteps of the porter, as he passed beneath the window on his last round of the night. Now and again his keys clinked, and the clink reached me after the pad of his footsteps had been lost in the snow." (p. 3)

Into the quiet of the court and the comfort of a blazing fire on a cold night comes the first movement of the long and desperate struggle that is to follow. And yet the struggle is less violent than it might have been when we take into account the undercurrents running through the relationships among these Fellows. Their ability to pacify their true feelings and channel them into acceptable modes of behavior indicates that civilization has turned animals into men, a point that Snow is quick to establish. He is anxious to demonstrate what reasonable creatures men are and how fine their decisions may be even when their own interests are at stake. The novel, then, is a series of modulated noises and silences: the foreground of the struggle for power counterpointed to the great traditions of Cambridge as they bear upon the present situation. Within this "fugue" of sound and quiet comes the election of a Master, the rites of which derive from the "election" of a prince to the throne.

The forces set loose in *The Light and the Dark*, particularly the election of Roy Calvert to a Fellowship, are intensified in *The Masters*, which is Snow's fullest treatment of the power struggle within men. Although the focal point is ostensibly the election of a new Master to replace the present one who is dying of cancer, the College is, in fact, a miniature society, and the problem becomes one of how to use the power that is attached to this society. Power, in short, will be the key to the novel. What is power? How do honest men use it and misuse it? how does it change honest and well-meaning men? how are decency and integrity compromised by power? how does power bring out the best and worst in men? Finally, Snow asks, how can power be used to gain progress when power itself, in a college world, is more individual than communal?

The issues that Snow raises are of enduring concern and surely explain the continuing popularity of the novel. The lawyer, the businessman, the medical man, the union worker, as well as the academic—all of these groups can see in the miniature world of *The Masters* an analogy to their own. Further, the various types that Snow sets forth are recognizable in any institution that contains hierarchies, with its varying degrees of patronage to be exploited and honors to be conveyed. There is also something comforting in the fact that the decision, when reached, is not an outrageous one; Snow demonstrates that even when Eliot's candidate loses, there is no tragedy, for the winning man is quite able. Implicit in Snow's treatment is the reassurance his readers must gain: that institutions and traditions prevent men from going wild, and that men's choices even when vehemence is involved are judicious. This attitude is an opiate for the middle class, for Snow falsifies reality to make his point. He tends to blur the more important point that this College, which is to educate the young, is less concerned with that role than with the dispensation of its honors. That is, of course, the way of many a college faculty, but Snow might not have taken it straight. It is, after all, a pity that men should be so picayune even when we fully recognize that they do act this way.

Four years prior to the action of *The Masters*, Lewis Eliot, now much matured from the young, ambitious pusher we met in *Time of Hope*, has left off attempting to establish a law practice and has entered academic law, on the basis of which he becomes a Fellow at a Cambridge College. He retains his outside interests as a part-time consultant to a London firm, but his failing energies make it difficult for him to pursue a full law career. Having already recognized that he would not be first-rate, he has the additional burden of his schizoid wife, whose presence makes social relationships impossible. Also, he is not equipped emotionally and mentally for the long pull, and rather than try it, Eliot takes refuge in academic life, where he finds, to his sorrow, that the tensions and conflicts are not dissimilar to those he wished to avoid in public life.

Eliot is the focus of rationality, the one man who can be relied upon for objective judgments, the man who provides the sole basis of reason upon which the election, however emotional it appears, is to be structured. In the minds of the other Fellows, however, there is evidently the desire for power, whether it be that of giving or receiving: Brown, the conciliator, wants the kind of power that makes other men dependent on him, the power he gains from putting them into jobs that he has designed to suit their talents; Chrystal wants recognition, the deanship, for example, and to be known as a man of power, although he would be satisfied without all the power himself. He desires, as Snow says, to see and feel his own strength. Jago, the candidate of Eliot's faction, wants to be first in order to enjoy the trappings, the titles, the ornaments of power. He is excited by the prospect of the big house the Master obtains, by the entrance of his name in the College register, by the prestige attached to the office, by being addressed as Master. Further, as an ambitious man, he believes there are things only he can do for the College; he therefore ties his own ambitions to its progress and development. In his messianic role, he becomes, as it were, a faulty and weak man with a mission, believing that he is different and anxious to have this difference noted. With power, he would blossom, he believes, although in actuality he might descend into meanness and contempt for others with less prestige. He is not a humble man, but is prodigal with his extravagance.

The limit of power here is the limit of decency. These men are little more than politicians, Snow points out, in the way they conduct themselves and in their quest for power. Involved in secret alliances, after-hour cabals, conspiratorial voting sessions, intrigues toward candidates—all the rituals more suitable for the election of a king than a Master—they work barely within the limitations of decency. They try to be scrupulous and just, especially when near the young, although they know better than anyone else how private ambition compromises public honesty. Their ruthlessness is something they find difficult to equate with their academic idealism, for more often than not they let personal interest dictate where reason should rule. Snow compares their tensions to that induced by war hysteria. They commit "crimes" under martial pressure that they would not commit in peacetime; yet their behavior is not reprehensible, Snow tells us, for in a secular world what else is there but personal ambition and its satisfaction?

Paralleling the drive for official power by the Fellows is the attitude of Sir Horace, a wealthy benefactor of the College, who relishes the power of giving or withholding money as he sees fit. He recognizes that his is power to use, and he is careful to squeeze the full worth from his position. Like Chrystal, he cherishes power just for the feel of it. Strikingly, all the Fellows accept that Sir Horace is an important man simply because his money can do much for them; they understandably worship his power as much as they do their own. They are hard-headed enough to recognize that they are dependent upon Sir Horace, and that his world in a sense makes theirs possible.

In the meeting between the Fellows and Sir Horace, one finds all the crosscurrents of life in the larger world. The sense of *noblesse oblige* which each assumes—a kind of polite blackmail—is a recognition that they are interdependent in their ultimate welfare. The Fellows can guarantee that Sir Horace's cousin will pass his examinations, as well as give him the intellectual respectability which his money can buy. Through them, he can enter into history. He, on the other hand, makes it possible for them to put up new buildings, to expand their facilities, but, most of all, to feel contact with the outside world. His money will give them a sense of power that transcends the confines of the College. In the meeting of the academic and business worlds, we have a union, Snow suggests, between two of the major forces in contemporary society: each admires the other, although each is suspicious of the ideals of one and the practicality of the other. Nevertheless, their differences, in the end, are fewer than their similarities; both, in varying ways, want the same things: power, recognition, the ability to give. Both have the need to expand.

As the time for the election approaches, the will to power demeans all concerned, except Eliot, whose choice never wavers and whose course is one of decency and reason. To gain public power, Snow indicates, one must lose dignity, for in acquiring power there is the loss of the better part of man, particularly the loss of balance. Jago, for example, becomes increasingly hysterical as he fluctuates between success and failure, as he sees the Mastership first slipping from him and then returning within his grasp. The maneuvers behind his back seem like an undermining of his position, and he resents intrigue even from his own side. He wants to think that the Mastership will become his as a result only of his own achievements, and that he alone has the power to assume the title. By dividing the power with others, he feels himself divided, as if he loses part of the honor by having to grant that others have helped him.

Precisely because Jago is insecure and frail, so aware of his fallibility, Eliot favors him over Crawford, the successful scientist who remains to the end sure of himself and his powers. Eliot reasons that *because* Jago is unsure, he will recognize frailty in others, and once the Mastership is his, he will take into account human fallibilities. Power has less chance of destroying him because he will continue to perceive human limitations. Crawford, however, will not question himself or others, and, lacking Jago's flexibility, may use power with the unquestioned assurance that he is doing right.

Perhaps more than any of the other Fellows, Eliot is aware of the flaws of basically decent men and how easily they confuse personal ambition with social conscience. As one who endeavors to be objective—he admits to a dislike for Jago at the beginning of the novel—he tries to probe the area where compromise will yield the most; we remember that he is a trained lawyer. In Crawford, he fears the use of pure power by a man who has never had any doubts about his superiority and perfection; in Jago, he finds a man beset by personal fears and doubts, actually the lesser man on the record. Yet Jago, by virtue of his very doubts, will examine his conscience with more exactitude before taking a course of action. Crawford, the man without a dent in his self-confidence, may be the potential dictator as well as possibly the better Master. Probing the two men—and Eliot has nothing substantial against Crawford, who honorably remains above the politicking— Eliot chooses the lesser man as providing the smaller degree of danger to the academic community.

Crawford finally wins the Mastership when Chrystal, who wants to be known as a man of power, shifts his vote from Jago to his opponent. Amidst all the strands of compromise, Chrystal decides that he has been on Crawford's side for months. Chrystal is, in fact, moved by vacillations he does not even understand, and while having aligned himself with one party, he begins to feel things he does not recognize until he makes his final decision to support Crawford. Men who seem to know their own minds best, Snow suggests, often are beset by doubts and fears below the surface which dictate their final decisions. The drive for power in Chrystal makes him, finally, identify with strength; he needs to be triumphant, regardless of how he compromises himself.

The Master having been chosen, the College seemingly returns to normal, the Fellows putting aside their differences to work together under the new Master. Yet the struggle is not soothed over that easily, for each man has had to look at himself in a new and hitherto undiscovered way. They have all been touched on their most sensitive points, and only Eliot remains unchanged by circumstances, for he knew exactly what he was doing, his actions being free of personal interest. Only he retained his reason throughout, and this because he was unaffected by the emotional crosscurrents. Chrystal, for example, learns something he never knew before; Brown recognizes that even his mature awareness of conciliation cannot take everything into account; Jago must face all his fears and insecurities. Nothing is exactly the same, although the surface will continue smooth. Consciences have been touched, weak spots revealed, wounds uncovered. Yet the Fellows will once again show allegiance to the College, all the time coming to terms with themselves; until a new Master must be chosen.

ii

An outline of the narrative, however, does not convey the substance of the novel. It is curious that most critics in hailing the book simply accepted the "truth" of what Snow says without questioning any of the values implied. Also, they have failed to question Snow's evaluation of the characters, the reason, for example, why Jago is held up for praise by Eliot's faction. In fact, most readers have accepted Jago's superiority over Crawford without quibble, and have not sufficiently judged Eliot's qualified support of the man.

As we have seen, Eliot supports Jago precisely because he is a weaker man than Crawford, less sure of his capabilities and therefore perhaps more prone to question his decisions. In making his selection, Eliot has nothing tangible against Crawford, except, as he ruefully admits, Crawford once called him a barrister manqué. In this respect, he owes something to Jago, for the latter supported him when he entered academic law; Jago, in fact, feels that Eliot is his protégé. Nevertheless, on most social and political issues, it is Crawford with whom Eliot sides. Crawford is a typical liberal scientist whose political beliefs are generally progressive, antitotalitarian, and individualistic. Crawford mouths these views as though he had never questioned them, as though they came with his body. Jago, on the other hand, is conservative, even reactionary: pro-Franco (the Spanish Civil War was the watershed for political opinion), anticommunist (at a time when liberals made common cause with the communists), pro-Chamberlain and anti-Churchill (when for the liberals Hitler was clearly the enemy to reckon with).

Thus it is obviously against his political views for Eliot to support Jago. It is the man himself he admires; the rest is appurtenance. The point is whether Snow makes Eliot's support of Jago appear logical. That is, in the course of events, with a choice to be made between two candidates of such differing views and qualifications, can the decision Eliot makes be justified? Although Senior Tutor, Jago has had an undistinguished career, while Crawford is an eminent scientist, a member of the Royal Society, a man interested in scholarship and achievement. His research in biology is impeccable, and his place in science secure. By the time of *The Affair* sixteen years later, he will have won a Nobel Prize. The choice, then, is between a proud humanist who is politically blind and an egalitarian scientist who often seems more humanistic than his opponent. Snow obviously wishes to indicate more than the choice itself; obviously, he is suggesting here a good deal of what he believes about the world, and therefore the crucial importance of Eliot's feelings.

Implicit in the novel is Snow's assumption that the world is divided into two cultures, but, unlike his views in the later essay discussing that problem, here he opts for the humanist. He distrusts Crawford, not because of his science, but because science has not forced him into the human depths where he has suffered. Jago, however, has suffered. He lives with a shrewish wife, and he has loyally protected her. She has been his burden, ever since their marriage when he was a young don and she his pupil. As a man with a burden, with a wound (in some ways like Eliot's), he has become sensitive to everything that might seem to slight her; and consequently, Snow suggests, he has become generally sensitive to human pain. In his sensitivity he is something of an artist, although unlike the artist he does not transform pain into creativity. Nevertheless, he has the flexibility and awareness of the creative person, while Crawford, we are told, has the complacency of the man who "knows" the truth. It is necessary, then, for Eliot to support the one who displays human frailty because he seems to have imagination and the kind of flair that may be good for the College. Contrariwise, it is necessary to oppose the man who has, in Eliot's eyes, attained a kind of perfection.

All this is what Snow would have us believe. Yet while his case against certain aspects of Crawford is viable, his case *for* Jago is weak. There is a great deal of ego in Jago which Eliot assumes will be dispersed. There is also a great deal of vanity which, again, Eliot assumes will be channeled into College activities. There is, further, a great deal of immodesty, which Eliot believes gives Jago size. The potential of Jago is perhaps promising, but the man as presented offers little, and Eliot's championing of him seems to imply the backing of a friend who has been his patron and the opposition to a man who has seen through him. In theory, what Snow wants to prove seems valid, but in presentation the sensitive, high-strung Jago is perhaps the last one who should be entrusted with the power of the Master. That Snow here opts for the humanist over the scientist is significant, but this particular humanist seems ill-chosen.

Of course, if the reader is willing to see the events from Snow's own point of view, then he recognizes the nature of the compromise. Eliot claims not that Jago is the best man for the job but under the circumstances the better man. And that since a choice must be made, Jago should be selected as the lesser of two evils. What is more important than Eliot's choice of Jago over Crawford is what Snow signifies by making such a choice necessary. In brief, as Snow sees it, we *must* choose between the Jagos and the Crawfords, the inadequate humanists and the unimaginative scientists, when these alternatives present themselves: this *is* the democratic process. Perhaps it is, but it becomes disturbing when Snow's tone indicates that such an alternative is a healthy thing, and that regardless of the outcome—Crawford does win—an institution is assured of decent leadership.

Irony is missed in *The Masters* perhaps as much as in the other novels. Without irony, Snow's "maturity" smacks too much of complacency. When we meet the College community again, in *The Affair*, we see that Crawford, with Brown's help, has done quite well for the College, that it has thrived under his leadership as it was expected to under Jago's. Snow suggests that traditions are sufficient to carry the institution along and force a man to the right decisions even if he may be the wrong man for the job. Despite Snow's openness about society, his modernity, his tolerance of people and their beliefs, he falls back on time-tested traditions and sentimentalizes the College. If English College administration is anything like that in American Universities, then Snow has caught the entire process of an election less brilliantly than he has been credited with doing. The mistakes are often irreversible, and the wounds run much deeper than he is willing to grant.

Snow's forte, obviously, is political intrigue in itself: the behind-the-scenes, smoke-filled room in which caucuses occur, the gesture that indicates compliance, the build-up toward a change of vote, the nuances of canvassing for votes. He is less successful, however, in the very areas where the novel begins and political reporting ends: that is, where inner needs are involved. He makes his characters behave with too much consistency. Jago is consistently anxiety-ridden and presumptuous; Crawford is continuously complacent and stodgy in his commonsensical approach to all issues. Brown lives only by virtue of his manipulations; Francis Getliffe is the idealist, the outraged scientist for whom fair play comes first; Winslow is the soured old man whose accomplishments have failed to satisfy his expectations.

Perhaps it was inevitable that in his anxiety to get on with the behind-the-scenes politicking, Snow could not probe beneath the men involved. What he gives us is a kind of tentative guide to the behavior of the Fellows: we know them by a few lines or by a paragraph, and then once they are established, Snow gets on with the election. Because Snow considers results more than he does what goes into the process, he slights the examination of character in depth. Without such analysis, Chrystal's shift from Jago to Crawford seems motivated more by the needs of the plot than by the inner fluctuations of the man himself. Snow evidently wanted to indicate that something in Chrystal—for example, his need to identify with power—was driving him away from his first choice toward the opposition. However, when it comes time to analyze precisely what it is, Snow retreats into that same area of fuzzy irrationality which appears in several of the volumes. He writes: "I saw men as tough and dominating as Chrystal, entangled in compromise and in time hypnotised by their own technique: believing that they were being sensible and realistic, taking their steps for coherent practical reasons, while in fact they were moved by vacillations they did not begin to understand." (p. 338) Yet, as I have mentioned above, these are the areas that Snow might have probed, instead of withdrawing into the "mystery" of human behavior.

True, there are mysteries of behavior which remain impenetrable, but they must be conveyed not through the statement that they exist but through the quality or tone in which the character is presented. For a man like Chrystal, mysteries seem alien. If in every other aspect of his life except this one there are no mysteries, why, suddenly, here? The mystery of Chrystal cannot be indicated by calling him mysterious; it is the novelist's job to suggest irrationality in action or image. Otherwise, Chrystal's action to support Crawford simply takes Snow out of an impasse by allowing the resolution of the narrative.

As soon, however, as we abstract the situation of *The Masters* from the characters involved in it, the novel gains in significance. If we project the situation beyond the Cambridge setting and see it as symbolic of all democratic institutions, then the novel becomes exciting as political drama. Snow's talents as a master strategist of compromise here stand him in good stead, for in college as well as political life it is compromise and retreat from principle which become the only possible course of action. Eliot, like Snow, has learned his lessons, and he gains the admiration of others for being a judicious man because he knows when to compromise. As we look over the series, we see that Eliot has failed to compromise in very few areas, perhaps only in his defense of George Passant. Elsewhere, he has chosen the course that is less than or different from what he has expected; and yet he has found it relatively easy to live with the compromise. He is a born politician, a born master of deceit. To Eliot's credit, his compromises almost never hurt anyone directly. They are usually compromises over principles, not over people.

Still, Eliot can play a nasty game when necessary. As election fever mounts, he suspects that Nightingale, the dissatisfied scientist, is drifting toward the other side. Nightingale, however, wants the tutorship, should Jago move up to the Master's position, and he thinks that Eliot himself will be a challenge for the position. Eliot assures him that he will not, and that the way may be clear for Nightingale. But as Francis Getliffe points out, Nightingale stands no chance to be tutor whether Eliot wants the position or not. Eliot, Getliffe suggests, is simply giving false hopes to Nightingale to gain his vote.

Such maneuvering is of course in the nature of political life, whether in a college or outside. Yet Eliot never comes to see it as somewhat obnoxious within an institution that should be concerned with education. The novel is curiously lacking this entire dimension, which never really concerns Snow. That is, that such maneuvering, while it is to be expected wherever men have power to dispense, is to be deplored when it pre-empts the educational function of the College. Eliot as educator never appears, and the others are rarely seen with students, or else they are seen as they dismiss a student to get on with their politicking. Clearly, this may be the way men act, but the novelist loses his edge by treating such pompous fools seriously. What is disturbing is Snow's evident admiration for Brown's subtle strategy, for Jago's ambitions to be Master, for Francis Getliffe's drive to be a famous scientist, for Chrystal's desire to be known as a man of power.

What is further disturbing is that Snow accepts people and their frailties as they are, instead of the figures of mockery they should be. These are vain, puffed-up, self-righteous men—our colleagues in whatever enterprises we enter—and it is impossible for them to retain their dignity as they grasp for what they want. In his anxiety to show how institutions work despite man's weaknesses, Snow loses distance on his characters and accepts their faults as facts instead of as sources for ridicule. People in their official functions are usually objects for mockery or satire, as Stendhal and Flaubert realized; taken straight, they are not, as Snow supposes, realistic, but unreal figures supported by their creator simply for the sake of their functions in the novel.

This disclaimer is not to indicate that Snow must satirize his College Fellows to gain perspective on them. What it does indicate is that he must see them as they really are. They are much more insufferable than he is willing to grant. While Snow demonstrates that Brown is capable of the grand gesture (in protecting Roy Calvert), he loses sight of his pettiness. Brown's use of fine wines to make his arguments go down more easily becomes somewhat ridiculous, particularly as he solemnly dedicates a bottle to his latest endeavor. There is pomposity in the man as well as short-sightedness in his views. It is strange that Eliot should swallow Brown almost whole when the latter's social and political views are anathema. Such views do qualify one's admiration of a colleague, especially when they cut as deeply as Brown's pro-Franco convictions. If the political issue is as meaningful as Snow indicates, then it would indeed be difficult to remain happy within the ambience of someone like Brown, reactionary, upholder of the status quo, complacent politically and socially. Why should Eliot trust his judgments in College administration when they are obviously so limited elsewhere?

Yet Snow makes little use of these potential cross-currents. Once he explains how the political land lies, he moves on, as though the political issues can be minimized or forgotten. Only old Pilbrow reacts to Jago's conservatism and throws his support to the more liberal Crawford. Once again, *The Masters* works out as a piece of intrigue and not on the personal level where the subtleties of human relationships count. Admittedly, for the novel to have been fully successful, Snow must have set himself a difficult task. For the election must somehow be integrated with the personal relationships of the Fellows. Actually, the ground plan for such a novel would have to be much more ambitious, requiring further preparation and background than Snow provides.

This speculation is based of course on the novel that Snow did not write. What he did write is a well worked-out treatise on Machiavellian machinations performed by those who should be the best that the country can produce, a book nevertheless full of assurances that institutions and traditions are being safely cared for. *The Masters* essentially is full of confidence about the continuity of those things we should consider important. In the figure of Gay, the old, almost senile scholar, Snow presents a focus for continuity. Gay himself was a Fellow long before many of the present Fellows were even born; his field of study was the sagas, and like his beloved saga men he continues to go on, his vigor and enthusiasm unabated. Gay is a great scholar, perhaps the greatest the College ever produced, and yet he is basically an unperceptive, even a stupid man. He gains his energy from his enthusiasms, and is not enervated by anxieties about other things. For him, life is clear and purposeful, something to be tasted and enjoyed to its fullest. He is above petty politicking, just as he is above reason. Like Conrad's Singleton, he endures: he represents the ability of society to perpetuate itself. And Snow's admiration of the man is there even when Gay acts ridiculously and bores his audience.

In Gay, Snow has pulled off a minor triumph. If Gay were the sole representative of continuity, then Snow would have made his point. For Gay comes to us with just the right amount of humor so that we can suffer his company. But that very humor is lacking in the others, who are also to suggest the continuity of society and its institutions. Had they been treated with the kind of light satire in which Gay is presented, then Snow would have had the right touch for a college atmosphere. Gay's excuse for being slightly ridiculous is his growing senility; for the others, some such excuse might not have been necessary.

One other curious point is involved in the novel. When Pilbrow, the old political liberal who trots around Europe, indicates that he cannot support the reactionary Jago, the outcome of the election is left to Chrystal's vote. Chrystal, as we have seen, is a turncoat; after first throwing his support to Jago, he gradually moves away, until his is the crucial vote giving Crawford a 7–6 majority. As the voting in the chapel proceeds, we learn for the first time that Chrystal's Christian names are Charles Percy, Snow's own. How curious that Snow should use his own names for the turncoat! How much of this was conscious? And what was it supposed to indicate? Could it possibly have been chance? Does this use of names indicate that Snow sympathizes with Chrystal? And in the light of Snow's later attempts to reconcile the humanities with the sciences, how significant is Chrystal's shift from the humanist to the scientist? There are really no possible answers. We can only speculate that Snow, if he intended anything at all, desired to show in Chrystal's choice the mysteries and inexplicables involved in human decisions, and used his own name simply to indicate everyone's involvement.

5   THE NEW MEN

LIKE MOST Snow titles, the title of this volume (published 1954, covering 1939–46) is significant, perhaps more than the rest. For here Snow is trying to define a new race of men, as it were, in whom our faith must rest and upon whose judgments our future may depend. The new men are the best we have, Snow suggests, in the absence of gods, and gods are no longer conceivable even if they were desirable. The title indicates Snow's preoccupation with a secular society, his view that men must meet the challenge of the world *they* have created and that no alternative—no hope for divine guidance or miracles—exists or can exist. We must trust that the new men are really new and that they are adequate for the tremendous burden they must bear.

Who, then, are these new men? Are they the humanists whom Arthur Miles favored at the end of *The Search,* when, like Snow, he moved from science to the humanities? Or are they the scientists whom Snow increasingly came to trust, for example, the upright and idealistic Francis Getliffe of *The Light and the Dark* and *The Masters?* For Snow, in 1954 and before, the new men are those who explore new worlds and come back to tell us about their findings. These explorers cannot possibly be the novelists and poets, for Snow's literary attitudes assume that art should reflect reality, not experiment with it. The *avant-garde* in art and literature he found pretentious, misleading, downright disruptive of human life. Therefore, his growing distrust of the literary man as a possible guide for the future. As he later wrote in *The Kenyon Review*, literature was heading up a blind alley in its emphasis upon decadence and lost hope; literature should affirm, should reflect men's hopes and desires, as the fiction of Tolstoy did. Snow makes these points without righteousness and from the feeling that the modern movement has lost sight of the real drives in man in its stress upon perversities and dislocation.

With this assumption, obviously the literary man—at least until he reforms and changes direction—cannot be a suitable guide for the most difficult time in man's history. What is needed is someone more solid, even more serious, more concerned with immediate problems and willing to face a reality of survival. Like Plato, Snow fears the poets: a new society demands a new race of men, scientists who tell the truth and follow their ideals, men who get something done.

There are further connotations to the title, in that these "new men" are, morally as well as professionally, a new breed of men. In a moral sense, they are men who have been resurrected from the malaise; they are men of courage, perception, conscience: a new race of men who can rise above the immediate demands of their society. They indicate the democracy of science—anyone with the talent can be a new man—but they are at the same time a new aristocracy of the mind and spirit. In their ability to discover and make, they rival the gods, and in their ability to destroy, they rival the devil. Snow puts his hope in their former function, and therefore his use of the title.

For Snow, the scientist is a man of conscience. He is also a rebel who will pursue truth—whatever it is and wherever it leads. The scientist is not the engineer, the hardware man who works with what exists, but the man who explores new worlds by using what the engineer has prepared for him. The engineer makes the tools possible, but the scientist puts them to imaginative use. The new poetry of life must be interpreted by the new men, whose imaginative powers are analogous to those of the great poets of the past. It is vastly to Snow's credit that he does not overidealize these men but sees them as human beings. He recognizes their ability to compromise, their expedience, their occasional nastiness. Nevertheless, as he conceives them, they provide a necessary counter to the military and political men—the real dangers in our day. If opposition were left to the literary man, Snow suggests, solutions would go begging, and problems would, unfortunately, be resolved by politicians and soldiers. The only force that can act as a conscience or brake upon the latter would be the scientists themselves, for the politician and soldier depend for their success on what the scientist can discover. Such is the nature of politics in the world of the atom.

In this world, scientists can act as a counterforce to foolishness. They can, Snow hopes, save us from destruction even while they create the weapons that are destructive. The humanists have fallen into disrepute, so far as the real forces which run the world are concerned, and the scientist has picked up where the humanist left off. Accordingly, the scientist must not only create, he must fight for what he thinks right. An atomic bomb may be a necessity in wartime—even there, many scientists believe it should never have been used—but its control thereafter must be left to sane minds. Here, Snow voices his confidence in the scientist.

What Snow neglects to mention is that the scientist, as well as everyone else, is subject to the forces of his society, and for every scientist who acts as a moral force there will be one who sees science the same way as the politician and the soldier. Such has been the case in the United States, where most scientists have gone along with official policy, which they have little or no hand in forming. One need only cite the Oppenheimer case in 1954, the same year that Snow published *The New Men*. Despite the scientist's general liberalism, despite his historical skepticism, despite his rebellion against many social norms, he is subject to pressures which are outside his control; and these pressures, whether direct or not, force his hand. Also, there is a large school of thought which believes that the scientist must pursue his own kind of truth regardless of what the politicians do. As this reasoning goes, the scientist should keep his nose out of politics, which is no concern of his. At this point, the scientist is little better than the humanist who has retreated from any direct influence upon the body politic. Both pursue their own kinds of truth and leave the management of the world to those who are practical.

One must cite these limitations to Snow's point of view, or else his stress upon the saving nature of science may seem more fruitful than it has proved. His view would be infinitely more valuable if he could establish that science, historically, has ever acted as a moral force against the insanity of the politicians and soldiers. Or if he cannot demonstrate this point historically, then he would have to show why the special conditions of our time have brought around such a change of position. All he has now indicated is that such a change is necessary, a point of view with which not many would quarrel if Snow allowed the humanist more of a position. The humanist and the scientist working together may provide an adequate moral force against the professional managers. The scientist alone, it would seem, is inadequate. After all, many scientists, whether directly or not, have their salaries subsidized by the federal government; most humanists do not.

Once we have noted the purpose of the novel, we can see that the form Snow has set himself is full of problems. For here, more than in most of his other novels, he must work two parallel lines: the public lives of his chief characters as they strive to create an atomic bomb, and the private lives of these men irrespective of the bomb. The two lines must somehow meet to make the characters believable. Yet if we momentarily separate this novel from the entire series, its thinness in private matters is apparent. Without the other novels to rest upon, *The New Men* becomes merely a laboratory demonstration of the role of the British scientist in the formation of the bomb.

There are too many loose ends in the minor characters and too many inexplicables in the major ones. The excitement that the novel generates does not derive from people and their fortunes but from the presentation of an intricate problem in layman's terms: the inside story, so to speak, of the great mystery of the atom, analogous to what the discovery of the heavens must have meant to a discerning man in the seventeenth century and what Darwin's *Origin of Species* must have signified in the nineteenth. But these elements of popular science—like the sections on crystallography in *The Search*—are not sufficient to keep the novel together.

Among the minor characters, the Puchweins, for example—the couple that Roy Calvert had brought over from Germany in *The Light and the Dark*—seem to be significant, but Snow fails to carry them through any significant action. Dissatisfied with her husband, Hanna Puchwein seems to like Martin Eliot, Lewis's brother, and then she chooses Rudd, an engineer who seems completely unsuitable for her. (Later, in *The Affair*, she turns up married to Clark, the most unlikely of choices, for he is a rigid reactionary and she a communist.) Why the private byplay if it is not to add up to anything? If Snow is suggesting some character failing in Hanna in her choice of Rudd, analogous, say, to Lewis's disastrous choice of Sheila and Martin's of Irene, then there would be some point to the development of this character relationship. There is, however, no further point. Hanna begins as a very interesting woman, capable of a great deal, but her role declines. Even so, Snow pursues her deep into the novel, into Chapter XXXV, which is fifty pages from the end. For what purpose? Even after she has been insufficiently developed, Snow writes about her: "It came to her with consternation, almost with shame, that, now her will had come up in earnest against Martin's, she, who in the past had thought him pliable, did not stand a chance. She was outraged by his behavior, and yet in her anger and surprise she wished that when they first met she had seen him with these fresh eyes." (p. 249)

Exactly as this minor character fails to gain the substance Snow evidently intends, so do the relationships among the major characters fail to become meaningful. Snow is anxious to establish the point that both Eliot brothers suffer from some mysterious destructive force which makes them masochistic in their relationships with women. Earlier, we had seen Lewis Eliot's abortive marriage to Sheila, the further details of which Snow is to pick up in *Homecoming,* the next volume after *The New Men.* Here, with Sheila now recently dead, the emphasis is upon Martin Eliot's courtship of and marriage to Irene.

Snow has only briefly mentioned Martin before, in *Time of Hope.* Of course, the difference of eight years (Snow wrongly figures nine *) between them would mean that Lewis was already pursuing a career away from home when Martin was still a schoolboy. But Martin seems to have inherited the same rage for self-destruction in his connections with women that we have seen in Eliot. Curiously, in other respects, the two brothers are wilful, self-reliant, ambitious, and, to an extent, masters of their fates. Yet both choose wives who are wrong for them in the large sense of frustrating their careers. Both select women to whom they are sexually attracted rather than temperamentally suited. At least Sheila seemed intelligent and perceptive, while Irene has only a kind of tumescent femininity or dark sexuality. In some way that Snow fails to explain, she seduces the sober Martin, even though he is aware of her past and, most important, aware of what she means to his career. Of course, as a scientist he is able to leave her behind more readily than Lewis as a lawyer could do with Sheila. Nevertheless, Martin deliberately destroys any domestic equanimity by marrying her; his career, as it turns out, does not suffer.

Snow wishes to show that the relationship is debilitating although Martin's will ultimately proves stronger than

---

* At the beginning of *The New Men*, the time is late February, 1939. Lewis was born in 1905, and internal evidence indicates sometime in late summer or early fall; Snow himself was born in October, 1905. In February, 1939, then, Lewis would be 33, while Martin is mentioned as being 25; the difference is eight years, not nine. Lewis could not be counted as nine years older until the late summer or early fall of 1939. There are several discrepancies of this type in the series.

hers. Snow points the analogy with Lewis's marriage when Lewis says: "It was partly that our loves are entirely serious only to ourselves; years of my own life had been corroded by a passion more wretched than Martin's, and yet, as a spectator of his, I felt as my friends used to feel about mine." The reader receives the impression that this analogy is being made simply *for its own sake,* and that there is no overall significance in terms of the pattern of the novel. If part of the meaning of the novel centers on Martin's will to power and his ultimate rejection of that power for one reason or another, then what importance does his attachment to Irene have? Does it in any appreciable way influence his decisions? The answer must be no.

Then, we are left with one other possibility: that the attachment to Irene is a significant aspect of Martin's will, that in taming her he demonstrates (to himself? to her? to the world?) he can do so, and she becomes, here, a pawn in his development of self-control. This interpretation is valid enough in terms of the marriage of Martin with Irene, but how does it bear upon Martin's public career? What possible integration is there between his mastery of this woman and his mastery of his career? It is here that Snow fails to merge the two aspects of the novel, the interesting public details, the less compelling private ones. The two worlds seem only vaguely connected by Martin's decision to gamble in both; in all other respects, they remain apart.

These are serious faults to the novel, although once the reader accepts that they exist and are irremediable, he can still go on to meet Snow at his strength: in his ability to catch people on their way up, in his control of a complex problem distant from the average layman, in his recognition of the mixed motives which make up a man's decisions, in his ability to probe a bureaucratic world in which one man's decisions may affect thousands. These individual sections of the novel are often effectively done, although in the long run they do not coalesce to produce a finely wrought novel.

For example, from the layman's point of view, the Barford project contains the excitement and suspense involved in any original creation whose outcome remains in doubt. The urgency of the project, its hit-or-miss atmosphere, and the dangers involved in its development—all these Snow catches gracefully and compellingly. Perhaps he is so successful here because people are themselves of relatively little importance, while technical knowledge is significant. Throughout the series, Snow is better in catching the nature of things—institutions, traditions, organizations, procedures, physical quantities—than he is in delineating people. It is the project that holds the reader's attention rather than the people involved in it. Even Luke loses the reader's interest when he goes off to play the piano (badly) while waiting for the atomic pile to be finished. Snow finds little inner life to fill in, and thus Luke has to be moved rather ludicrously to the background in order to give him something to do. This is a failure of people, not events. The events remain meaningful.

Less meaningful, however, is the section devoted to Sawbridge, the suspected communist spy, later convicted and sent to prison for treason. This entire episode appears to be little more than a demonstration of Martin Eliot's will to power. By trapping Sawbridge, Martin establishes himself as the logical head of Barford, the man who can be trusted because his past is clear. Although Luke is clearly the better scientist, it is against Luke, rather than for Martin, that the vote goes.

It becomes obvious, then, that Snow has little interest in the quality of Sawbridge, but sees this episode as simply a way of moving Martin toward the top, which he can later reject. Yet Sawbridge is potentially a more interesting and fulfilling character than Snow is perhaps able to develop. Since almost a third of the novel is concerned with the Sawbridge affair, from Chapter 32 when Martin decides he can make personal capital from prosecuting the traitor, much more should be made of the man. Lewis's own position seems strange here, as though Snow had reached a point in the narrative in which he needed a certain turn to continue the novel along a predetermined course but had been unable to justify this turn in terms of the characters. Snow writes of Lewis Eliot:

> I disliked what he [Martin] planned to do about Sawbridge; but I could not have explained why I minded so much.
>
> I had no doubt what he intended from that night at Stratford, when he put forward his case in front of Luke. He had foreseen the danger about Sawbridge: he had also foreseen how to turn it to his own use. It was clear to him, as in his place it might have been clear to me, that he could gain much from joining in the hunt. [p. 227]

Here, Lewis's uncertainty in the face of his brother's act seems to be Snow's: how does one act when one's brother is clearly going to ride to glory not on his own merits but on the miseries of others? For Lewis Eliot, the point should have been clear; why should he say that he could not explain why he minded so much? The reasons are obvious. Martin hopes to hurdle Luke by trapping Sawbridge, a means toward power that is immoral even if he does trap a spy along the way, perhaps doubly immoral for a "new man."

This uncertainty carries over to the portrait of Sawbridge himself. He is curiously passive and stony, as though an automaton. Surely Snow, who professes to understand and feel affectionate toward "outsiders," does not believe that spies, even when dedicated communists, are stony and impenetrable. And even if they are, for the purposes of the novel they must be developed and warmed into credible characters. Sawbridge, however, does not react at all; he does not even show any real dislike for Martin. With the stakes so high and the results so important, the two sit across from each other as though involved in a friendly chess game. The fault is traceable to Sawbridge's lack of an inner life, the same fault that lames most of the characters. Therefore, when under Martin's attack—an attack, incidentally, that is to destroy his career and place him in prison—Sawbridge can only stare and look sulky. What is called for is a sense of torment, anguish, or even some intellectual response. After all, Sawbridge is a gifted scientist, and therefore a man of some imagination. Would this man of imagination retreat so completely? and even if he did, is this attitude sufficient for a situation that calls for considerable tension? Similarly, Howard, in *The Affair*, six years later, is stony and sulky, completely unresponsive and unyielding in a political situation that calls for some kind of reaction.

On other grounds, Sawbridge's acquiescence destroys dramatic conflict. Martin's progress toward the top of Barford is unimpeded, even unconsciously helped, by the man whose enemy he should have become. Or is there in Sawbridge some force tipping him toward destruction, some inner gyroscope directing him not toward success but toward failure? Again, if this is so, then Sawbridge is a considerably more complicated individual than the one Snow presents. There is, in fact, the suspicion throughout this episode that Snow makes Sawbridge a "stony" communist in order to avoid the exploration of a complicated psyche. Certainly, to invade Sawbridge's mind would entail a psychological exploration on a major scale, and Snow might have found himself forced to explore a Raskolnikov rather than a safely-contained Englishman. Yet it is precisely a Raskolnikov who is called for: the mere fact of someone spying is of considerably less interest than an analysis of why that particular person would spy in those circumstances, especially when the spy is an Englishman spying on Englishmen, not on a foreign power.

Curiously, Snow winds around that very point, as though his avoidance of Sawbridge's mental state were forcing him to vacillate in order to disguise what is obviously missing. Mounteney, a scientist identified with left-wing causes and quite tolerant of communists and fellow travellers, is horrified, nevertheless, that Sawbridge would spy on his fellow scientists and forgo their trust. For Mounteney, the fact alone that Sawbridge is traitorous is sufficient, even though Sawbridge has shared many of

Mounteney's own political beliefs. Mounteney feels that one should play the game; in effect, that political beliefs should not be translated into action when one's own country is involved, and that one honors a trust—a human relationship—before one honors one's political convictions. Now this attitude on its face is a tremendous simplification of the entire problem. Yet Snow more or less allows Mounteney's views to prevail, and that is virtually all we see of Sawbridge, the man who somehow failed what was expected of him.

This view of a complex matter—whether the perpetrator is a simple man or not does not matter—is obviously insufficient. Martin's action, under these conditions, becomes too easy. Once he decides to trap Sawbridge, he must simply apply pressure, and eventually Sawbridge gives in. This sequence of events simplifies the novel by allowing only Martin's motivations to count and by permitting his will to prevail. The thickness and density that would result from an opposing and countering will are forsaken.

The insights that are lost in the major characters are often found on a smaller scale in some of the minor ones, perhaps because they present less of a problem. Such a character is Bevill, who, now in his seventies, is still determined to hold on to his government position and will not give up without a struggle. Here is a man who thrives on controversy and who must remain close to the sources of power. Even though aged and hopelessly out of the real struggle, he will accept whatever he can if it means retaining some power himself.

Such also is Hector Rose, who turns up in a more important role in *Homecoming*, two years later, when he rejects George Passant for a permanent civil administration position. Rose is the perfect administrator, in that he unquestioningly accepts that the present-day world is to be controlled by the bureaucrat. Decisions that count are those made by administrators: the age of the great man is over, the age of the bureau head has begun. In his view, the world has fallen into patterns which men can identify and use to their advantage. That is, the world is an organized one and its events can be controlled. This is the administrator's assumption; and too often it is the one that Eliot himself assumes, despite his occasional disagreements with Rose. There is involved here more than merely an administrative attitude; there is implicit a whole philosophy, one in which the philosopher feels that he has found the key. Only on one occasion is Rose slightly flustered, when he admits, momentarily, that events "get too big for men." Eliot comments that it was one of his rare moments of self-doubt. But it almost immediately passes, and Rose returns to his safe world where he can move his counters and thus determine the future.

The difficulty here is that Rose is a fit subject for satire, not for straight treatment. How can one possibly take him straight, even Snow, for whom "satire is cheek"? Snow writes about him: "Rose was always one jump ahead of official opinion; that was why they called him a man of judgment. His judgment was never too far-sighted for solid men, it led them by a little but not too much, it never differed in kind from theirs." Rose in his office, Bevill in his pseudo-bohemian club—both of these are ridiculous men doing ridiculous things while thinking that the world depends on their decisions. Their ambitions are often selfish, their abilities not great except in a very narrow area, their range not broad; they are simply a breed of men, neither happy nor sad, who have been made possible by the proliferation of administrative power. That they should call the turns as often as they do should elicit horror, not satisfaction that frail beings can carry on so well.

Snow catches these men effectively; what is missing, however, is a suitable tone in which to characterize them. A tone of mockery or irony would be more suitable to their presumption than Snow's flat presentation. On the other hand, with a character like Luke, Snow is more successful despite the lack of any strongly directive tone, simply because Luke has brains and ambitions enough to carry himself. Also, his work engages him fully, and it is admirable work—that of exploring the nature of the universe. Luke is an inventor, a discoverer, a creator: what he does gives him the right to certain pretensions, and therefore his general modesty makes him admirable. When a sense of power, then, begins to corrode his values, we feel that something actual is occurring, that a conflict has been created, and that a real human being has been engaged in a significant way.

As the directorship of Barford begins to seem his, Luke becomes somewhat expedient or safe. He agrees that Puchwein, who has been associated with several left-wing causes and organizations, cannot be retained as the chief chemist at Barford. This Luke grants although he knows that Puchwein is not a spy; he fears, however, that if the leakages at Barford do become public, it would compromise him and the entire project were Puchwein to be present on the job. Luke's sudden cautiousness is complemented at this time by Martin's desire to trap Sawbridge, and thus sew up his own career. Consequently, the two men vie with each other and play the game of expedience, even treachery, for both seek the power of the directorship. Because of the hope for private gain, both commit acts or make decisions alien to their normally balanced judgment. They cannot resist what all men seek: the feel of power.

It is this point that Snow obviously wishes to establish, a point that becomes basic to the entire series. The question now becomes: when does a man cease to compromise himself and injure others? Or, further, when does he see himself clearly enough so that he applies the brakes and allows his sense of decency to prevail? Snow of course believes that every responsible man has this sense of decency and will call it into play before he does too much damage. But this is an administrator's view of human nature, one based on checks and balances, on calculations; it fails to take into account man's compromises which he does not admit even to himself. For Snow, one admits everything to himself, and therein lies part of his simplification of human behavior.

While Luke's expedience rings true in terms of what the young scientist has been, Martin's is not always dramatically cogent. Before Martin's decision to go after Sawbridge, he seemed anything but expedient. In fact, in his anger over the immoral use of the atomic bomb, he drafted a letter whose publication would have ended his public career. He intended to publish it, being barely dissuaded by Lewis's arguments. Of course, Lewis was successful because Martin was not completely sure of his own motives, but nevertheless the thought that went into the letter was hardly that of an expedient man, even if he could be persuaded not to print it. Then, shortly afterward, Martin acquires what seems to be a sudden will to power, the sharp change in attitude apparently unmotivated from one event to the other.

As a consequence, although the novel focuses on Martin, there appear to be gaps in his development. At first, Lewis directly faces his brother with the expedience of rising on Sawbridge's back. Under Lewis's questioning, Martin admits that what Sawbridge has done is less than what outsiders believe, that, as a result, he could be left alone without appreciable national harm. Then, he further admits that he does not mind climbing even at Luke's expense, whom he never liked. These are the decisions and actions of a man suddenly turned nasty and evil; Martin's self-seeking stamps him as a person reprehensible to his own brother, although Lewis comes to feel that to understand all is to forgive all. Then, in a further turnabout, Martin rejects the directorship precisely when it is within his grasp: a still newer man pokes through and displays still another identity which we have not been prepared for. Here we have a Martin who simply wanted to know that he could be head of Barford, that he was the chosen one; the actual power and responsibility are secondary. Like Chrystal in *The Masters*, he wants to be known as a man of power, while the power itself is of minor importance. As an excuse for his new switch, he argues that as director he will be part of the machine and will not be able to think for himself. He remarks further that he wants to do some "real science" in the next ten years, or else he will be finished (by 42).

> He [Martin] told me [Lewis] in so many words that he had not lost faith that science—though maybe not in his lifetime—would turn out for good. From some, after his history, it would have sounded a piece of facile scientists' optimism. From him it had a different note. For to Martin it was jet-clear that, despite its emollients and its joys, individual life was tragic: a man was ineluctably alone, and it was a short way to the grave. But, believing that with stoical acceptance, Martin saw no reason why social life should also be tragic: social life lay within one's power, as human loneliness and death did not, and it was the most contemptible of the false-profound to confuse the two. [p. 301]

Martin's response makes him something of a hero: for the greater glory of science, he will return to research, and he will seek a social life unimpeded by the restrictions that Barford would have placed upon him. Yet part of the motivation behind Martin's rejection of the post is his fear of power, and his sudden loss of will when faced with a position that requires first-rate abilities while he has only second-rate. In brief, his motives are quite mixed, but unfortunately Snow leads him only one way.

Snow's explanation becomes doubly curious when we remember that Martin had attacked Lewis for having allowed himself to be carried along until he had wasted his promise and spent himself on personal relations, a charge, incidentally, that does contain some truth. Yet we now see Martin defending his new action by talking about the freeing nature of social relationships. Further, when Lewis is attacked by Martin for letting himself be carried along, he answers that Martin is too self-centered to understand the give and take of human relationships; that he would sacrifice any of them for his own gain. And yet it was Lewis who had dissuaded Martin from sending the letter protesting the use of the atomic boom for fear that it would ruin the latter's career. These shifts and changes could have been of great interest had they been normally motivated, but they occur as needed, not as developed within the logic of the character. Martin comes around to Lewis's position nearly at the moment Lewis comes around to Martin's, although in neither case is there any indication why each has shifted his ground.

These inexplicable moves, taken together with the failure of several of the minor characters, weaken the fiber of the novel and inevitably create more problems than they solve. Snow seems to have seen the scientific part clearly, while remaining fuzzy elsewhere. Accordingly, whenever he leaves the bomb project and falls back on his characters, the novel drifts out of control.

These new men—even if they are all we can count upon—do not seem much better than the old ones. Has Snow proven, or even established, his point that the scientist should be lauded as the new man of our age? In drawing his distinction between scientists and engineers, Snow carefully shows that scientists are protestants while engineers are accepters who buckle down to their jobs and look no further. It is not unusual, therefore, that heretics, traitors, and spies should come from the scientific class. The political truth of our era is such, Snow suggests, that the brilliant and the imaginative ones whom we must rely upon may also, from a layman's point of view, be politically unsound; and that we must accept that the man who is scientifically adventurous may also be politically adventurous, or at least inquisitive enough to forsake nationalism for internationalism. Unlike the politician, the scientist refuses to play sides, and the fact that the scientist may stand on principle causes major misunderstandings between him and the politician.

Snow further argues in defense of his new breed of men that for the scientist science must be done in the open and must be kept supranational. If science is to develop adequately, it must be through the cooperation of all, not through the efforts of the isolated few. Therefore, scientists cannot accept the alienation of another country if it means the isolation of science so that it can be employed for political purposes. In addition, most scientists—demo-

cratic as they are—are amenable to social change, which
they see as an adjunct of physical change. Obviously, for
them, man's social life cannot stand still, in terms of
necessities and state welfare, when science is exploring
and constructing a new world.

Here, then, is the crux of Snow's defense of his new
men. They are men with consciences who see in atomic
fission the final product of civilization, the greatest triumph of science, not a force for destruction. Also, involved
as they are with human welfare, they are unwilling to see
hundreds of thousands killed for any end, political or
otherwise. In theory, their views are moral, sensitive,
aware of human needs. In practice, however, Snow's
scientists fail to live up to their views: as they jockey for
position, they become little better than the academicians
of *The Masters*, the lawyers of *Time of Hope*, the businessmen of *Strangers and Brothers*, and the politicians
and administrators who run through the other novels.
Perhaps the theory is a blueprint for a race of men yet to
be created, but it is certainly not applicable to the characters Snow presents.

In this novel, Snow was caught among a great many
possibilities, and in attempting to resolve all—the discovery of the bomb, the contribution of the modern
scientist, the personal lives of several characters, the dilemmas posed by important moral decisions—he slighted
each in turn. A novel of 300 pages is far too short for such
ambitions, unless the author can compress much more
severely than Snow does. There are loose ends everywhere,
and even Snow's point about the new men does not
strike the reader as it should. We accept the fact that new
men are necessary, and even that scientists might be that
happy breed, but Snow's demonstration does not convince us that they fulfill the role. Their intentions are
often more "moral" than we have come to expect of public
men, but in practice they act like politicians when a decision presses.

Of course, Snow was trying to avoid ennobling them,
or heroizing them. His purpose was to show them as

ordinary men in all respects except the one affecting their science. Thus, he has Martin marry a woman who can hurt him; he makes the otherwise noble Luke weaken when faced by a large reward; he has Lewis counsel caution even when protest is called for. Their personal responses are those of plain men, Snow suggests, as he recoils from any suggestion that they are heroes. Nevertheless, they are expected to be a new kind of aristocracy, one based on mind and achievement. How to demonstrate this point without distorting its component parts obviously proved too much for the format Snow provides. By its end, the novel has retained interest only in details: in the Barford project and in certain interchanges between the characters, as long as we do not seek consistency in their, or Snow's, attitude.

6 HOMECOMING

IN *Homecoming* (published in 1956, covering 1938–49) Snow considerably restricted his scope after the ambitious undertaking of *The New Men*. The novel returns to a point of time before *The New Men* and carries up to a period shortly before *The Affair* was to begin. As a novel, it is close to *Time of Hope*, for both books are primarily concerned with Lewis Eliot, while the others are focused less on him than on what he sees. Here, Snow centers on Eliot's two marriages and even brings George Passant back for a long episode. The war and its aftermath remain in the background, as though Snow after a brush with public life in *The New Men* and *The Masters* were anxious to return to the individual and his discomforts.

The plurality of the English edition's title (*Homecomings*) indicates three separate returns: Lewis Eliot's fear of returning home as a child, when he felt he never knew what to expect, "this dread of what might be waiting for me"; his fear of returning home to Sheila in Chelsea after his long weekends in Cambridge as a law Fellow, once again full of the apprehension that he had felt in childhood; and, finally, his happy return home with Margaret, his second wife, after their child has recovered, and he has regained, as it were, his manhood. The ending is a happy one: childhood and adult fear has been transformed into contentment and satisfaction. *Homecoming*, then, is to be for Eliot a journey through an inferno in which he is scorched, but eventually a place from which he ascends into heavenly bliss. It is both a love story and a tale of recovery.

It is also a novel in which certain things are settled. Eliot finally obtains the kind of relationship with a woman which can sustain him, although his path to the marriage is characteristically difficult. Also, his career is finally determined, as something less than he had envisaged when he was in the full strength of his ambitions, but also as something more than he had hoped for when he was stricken by anemia. The novel is a middle-aged one in which while some battles are still to be fought, nevertheless resolutions and reconciliations are in sight. There stretches ahead a future of what may pass for happiness and joy and behind a past that clearly indicates misery and frustration.

Yet despite the "comforts" of this novel, Snow touches upon a major theme, one which gives the book contemporaneity. In connection with Lewis Eliot's relationship to himself and to others, Snow asks what precisely a man has to give. And to whom? And behind this question is a further one: what exactly is a man? We are back to the modern man's quest for identity, the familiar quest of the twentieth-century author in search of who he is and what the world is. The search for identity perhaps seems like an unusual pursuit for Snow, whose methods are relatively old-fashioned, and whose view of the world would seem to indicate that *he* knew who everyone is and that such questions are the vapid stuff of arty writers trying to be profound over what appears to be obvious.

The quest for identity has been perhaps the major theme of the most important novelists of this century trying to determine what is stable amidst a world of dislocation. The so-called art novel in England—Conrad, Ford, Joyce, Lawrence, Woolf, Forster, among others—was concerned in many respects with this metaphysical quest. In fact, what often distinguished the art novel from the more popular form was the fact that the "arty" writer questioned the very thing the popular novelist took for granted: that is, who we are, how we got this way, and how we know what we are.

In general, Snow has revolted against what he considers to be the futile questioning of things we can never know. In his attempt to bring the novel back to his kind of reality, he has pursued real people in real situations. His characters are not like Durrell's Alexandrians obsessively trying to find out what they are, but reasonable people involved in making decisions about their careers and their futures; people concerned with finding how they can imprint themselves upon the world. Here, it is less a question of pursuing identity than one of modulating or transforming what are solidly based characters. And yet behind this solid purpose is Snow's concern with the nature of Lewis Eliot, with the distinction between what he actually is like and the face he presents to his friends. As he put the matter later in the Author's Note to *The Conscience of the Rich*: "It [the inner design of the entire series] consists of a resonance between what Lewis Eliot sees and what he feels." Thus, while Snow elsewhere recognizes the social themes in the series, here he stresses that there is an inner dynamic which may have passed unnoticed.

This inner dynamic, which he remarks as essential to an understanding of his purpose, is no less than Eliot's quest for identity. What Snow suggests is that a man may seek his identity in business, law, academia, and amidst well-placed friends as well as amidst marginal creatures and experiences. What he further suggests is that although a man has seemingly made his peace with the world there is no reason to believe that he is satisfied with what he is, or even with the way others see him. There is still an inner dynamic of which he may be unaware, and it is this very dynamic which often provides the design or pattern of his character.

In Lewis Eliot's situation, the question of identity revolves around Eliot's ability, or lack of it, to give himself to others. Specifically, which Eliot is involved in a relationship? Or, put another way, where is Eliot in a relationship? Does what he holds back count as much as what he gives? And why does he have the difficulties with women that he evidently encounters? What kind of man is this, who mixes so well with other people but who curiously lacks something in a close relationship? Does Eliot know as much about himself as he thinks, or are there forces operating which predetermine his acts at the very moment he thinks he is making his own decisions?

With these questions, Snow comes as close to the psychological novel as his method allows. But even here, there is little urgency in his pursuit of the "truth" of Eliot. Furthermore, Snow feels certain things can be resolved; happiness may be a relative factor, but there is a time when a man can say, "I am happy." There is also a time when a man can say, "I have suffered, but I have discovered my true identity." Snow assumes that there is, as it were, an identity waiting if somehow one hits the right combination. This interpretation is perhaps a simplification of his aims, but it does approximate his basic optimism. Perhaps too much direct exposure to people has resulted in the kind of optimism Snow demonstrates; for people in operation—doing their work, carrying on in their daily activities, discussing their hopes and aims—are deceptively substantial. They can be seen as they are only if one sees them in perspective, as both more and less than what they think they are.

Here, Snow slights the problem, for in his busy life, he has evidently seen people from near, and he tends to judge them on the basis of their daily behavior rather than as wholes. He is, consequently, more hopeful of people's fortunes than a psychological examination would warrant. When Eliot does find something satisfactory, there is the assumption that he need no longer seek. Precisely here, Snow draws a sharp distinction between his views and those of the major novelists in the first third of the century who found in the individual's endless pursuit of his identity a vast symbol of the world's dislocation. Snow reduces the symbolic import by making the pursuit simply a man's quest for his real self, with the assumption that he can find it.

This limitation is implicit in the nineteenth-century novelists from whom Snow has received his chief influences, occurring principally in their portrayal of their major characters. With his belief that the human will could overcome great problems, the nineteenth-century novelist, despite his other impressive achievements, was often unable to create fully credible protagonists; more often than not, his success lay in his minor characters and in his arrangement of character and plot. A massive architectonic could disguise the weakness of the main figures so that the limitations of characterization seemed less apparent and less important. In Snow, however, the architectonic is reduced to a single plot, there is relatively little wit, and the minor characters are frequently flawed. What is left is only the reality of the situation, which in itself is insufficient to carry novels whose leading characters are limited to a nineteenth-century view of psychology.

Nevertheless, this novel does effectively create dramatic situations and catch Eliot in moments of real tension. In contrast to *The New Men*, which was most successful in its "public" sections, *Homecoming* succeeds best in its examination of Eliot's personal problems. In this novel, Eliot is revealed, and he becomes almost an interesting character, although Snow still tends to make his qualities too recognizable, too explicable.

Early in the novel, Snow writes about Eliot: "At the springs of my nature I had some kind of pride or vanity which not only made me careless of myself but also prevented me going into the deepest relation on equal terms. I could devote myself; that was all right; so long as I was not in turn understood, looked after, made to take the shames as well as the blessedness of an equal heart." (p. 48) If we take Eliot's explanation at its face, we can see why he has difficulties with women, even while his drifting social life is successful. In flight, he can charm, drift away to the next experience, and still remain uncommitted. Curiously, in Sheila Knight, he finds a tortured counterpart, a girl who cannot be strongly committed to anyone who desires equality. She seeks out the helpless and the needy, for hers is a nature to give, not to receive.

As soon as someone tries to offer her help or advice or even a kind word, she pathologically retreats where she is untouchable: thus, her periods of obsessed withdrawal which create a purgatorial atmosphere in the home.

Yet, Eliot is curiously akin to her. What often passes for selflessness is simply his inability to reject giving help, perhaps for fear that someone might offer it to him. In turn, he has taken on Roy Calvert, Sheila herself, Norman (the fiancé of an employee of his), Lady Boscastle's son, and lent himself to half a dozen other relationships in which he was "needed." Eliot admits that he helps others because there he is not really involved and cannot be reached or hurt. A good part of the present novel is devoted to forcing Eliot into self-commitment, making him recognize that as long as he holds back he cannot enjoy any kind of happiness. He must come to perceive that commitment is necessary, *not* for social gain, but for personal stability.

Sheila, of course, can never recognize this fact, for she is beyond human help, as her suicide later indicates. What she lives upon is unknown to anyone else, perhaps hidden from herself as well. Eliot, however, is "normal" in the sense that he can realize his problem and partially correct it, although his withdrawal into self is almost as fierce as hers. Obviously, the two cannot possibly make a go of the marriage, for each has the same problem: Eliot wishes to help Sheila, not to receive her help, while she thrives on those who need her. Eliot is first attracted to her because she relies upon him, and on this basis he hopes to build a relationship. On the other hand, Sheila has rejected Eliot because he seems self-sufficient, while she battens on someone like Robinson, the disreputable publisher who seeks her money. The marriage is quite impossible, on Eliot's part an act of masochism, on her part an act of sadism. Gradually, their inner desires overlap, and she becomes masochistic as Eliot becomes sadistic. It is at this point in their relationship that Sheila recognizes the futility of it and commits suicide.

Through it all, however, Eliot is buoyed up by a combined masochistic-sadistic pleasure. "It was a marriage in which I was strained as far as I could bear it, constantly apprehensive, often dismally unhappy; and yet it left me with a reserve and strength of spirit, it was a kind of home." (p. 49) This is a view of marriage that is possibly common even when one member is not psychopathic, but when one is, then Eliot's statement gets Snow into psychological areas that are treacherous. Implied in Eliot's statement is his feeling that he gains pleasure only where there is pain, and that Sheila's suicide is perhaps as much a result of her own fears as of Eliot's dependence upon their "sick" relationship. His reliance on her need of him continuously reminds her of what she is, keeps her attentive to her problems, even keeps her ill. Eliot never lets her escape, for he is there, hoping, consciously or not, that she will lean upon him.

In the circumstantial interplay of human relationships, Eliot must therefore bear part of the guilt for her suicide. For throughout their marriage, he resents her intrusion upon his career. Mixed in with his protective love and pity is his antagonism toward her for ruining his chances at the bar. Yet Eliot forced the marriage, a point that is not at all lost upon him and one that intensifies his unconscious sadism. When Sheila commits suicide, for instance, he perceives his petty feelings of her ingratitude. "Suddenly I was angry with her. I was angry, as I looked down at her [dead body]. I had loved her all my adult life; I had spent the years of my manhood upon her; with all the possessive love that I had once felt for her, I was seared because she had not left a goodbye." (p. 81)

While Snow is anxious to indicate Eliot's pettiness, and even seems to excuse it with the shrug that that is the way people are, a good deal more than simple pettiness is revealed. There is here a monstrous egoism that needs further revelation. Why does Snow wait until this late volume, the sixth, to indicate the real nature of Eliot? Why did we expect something different from him, even when in *Time of Hope* he pursued Sheila out of some psychological need of his own?

What has happened in this saga is that Snow has saved revelations about Eliot, or else stumbled upon them himself at this late date. The result is a different Eliot in this novel from the man in the others, even though this volume overlaps with two preceding ones in the series and purports to be a logical extension of the other three. Snow must have recognized the problem of this change in Elliot when he wrote the Author's Note to *The Conscience of the Rich*, for he suddenly felt explanation was necessary. Obviously, the Eliot in *Homecoming* should not be a different creature merely because he has come to the foreground; he should be consistent with the earlier Eliot who hovers over the other characters.

The "new" Eliot is revealed in the remarks of Margaret Davidson, who later marries him: "You want to be private, you don't want to give and take like an ordinary man. . . . You issue bulletins about yourself, you don't want anyone else to find you out. . . . With those who don't want much of you, you're unselfish, I grant you that. . . . With anyone who wants you altogether, you're cruel. . . . With most people you're good . . . but in the end you'll break the heart of anyone who loves you." (p. 163) Where has this Eliot been before? Why has this aspect of him gone unrevealed, or only been hinted at? After five volumes, we now realize that we have known very little of Snow's main character, and that here we have a major revelation. The only previous hints of this aspect of Eliot's behavior came when he rejected his mother's overbearing love, his retreat from her commensurate with her demands upon him. What other revelations should we expect? Is this now the real Eliot?

What occurs as we look more closely at Eliot is that he becomes less and less the figure who could support this saga were we to know everything about him. There is clearly some hypocrisy in Snow's presentation; that is, Eliot must be of some stature to command the center of eight volumes (so far), and yet Eliot diminishes not only as *we* see him but intrinsically. Even more than in his private life, Eliot diminishes in his public life. The episodes with George Passant are particularly revealing, for they demonstrate the impossibility of Eliot's position as Snow presents and seems to accept it.

During the war, Eliot, as an administrator, has obtained for George Passant a position of some trust and power, all under the bureau run by Hector Rose. George is very effective, as everyone admits. As we saw in the earlier volumes, he is a man of large talents, as well as of tremendous energy and confidence. From the reader's point of view, he is perhaps the best realized character in the entire series, and one with whom we sympathize despite his large failings. With the end of the war, the bureau must decide who is to remain as a permanent member of the service and who is to be dropped. George is now 47 years old, only three years younger than Rose, a top administrator.

There is a hearing at which George presents his case for staying with the service. He answers brilliantly, his responses indicating not only a command of detail but also a view of the whole structure of administration. Although Rose agrees that George is a superior person, one thing bothers him: if Passant is admittedly so good, why is he, at 47, starting at the bottom; why has it taken him so long to have found himself? what failings are there in the man that might once again cripple his talents? Rose comments at length:

> And at the same time we take on a definite hazard, not of course a serious one or one likely to materialize in fact, but the kind of hazard that you can't escape if you commit yourself to a man of, I don't want to do him an injustice but perhaps I can reasonably say, powerful, peculiar and perhaps faintly unstable personality. . . . There's a finite chance that we should be making trouble for ourselves. . . . I think I should conceivably have come down in Passant's favor if we were able to consider him for something more senior. He's the sort of man, in fact, who might have been far less trouble as a cabinet minister than he'd be in the slightly more pedestrian ranks of the administrative service. [p. 316]

At Rose's decision, Eliot loses his temper, warning that it is dangerous for any society to make only safe appointments. Rose looks calm and icy, and informs Eliot that the decision was made justly and would stand. Snow then remarks, through Eliot:

> The men I sat with in their offices, with their moral certainties, their comfortable, conforming indignation which never made them put a foot out of step—they were the men who managed the world, they were the people who in any society came out on top. They had the virtues denied the rest of us: I had to give them my respect. But that morning I was on the other side. [p. 318]

Having given them his respect, Eliot has provided himself with a good reason for remaining with the service. His burst of indignation over, he can once again settle down to his job. It never occurs to him that Rose and his colleagues are shallow fools, that as administrators they are not the best that society has to offer, that their complacency has created just the kind of world that Eliot in other circumstances deplores, and that their arguments for safety are simply ways for them to protect themselves and their positions. Snow's tone indicates, on the contrary, that this is the way the world is, and while we may deplore certain actions, we must applaud that the world survives despite injustices. The complacency of the author and his narrator herein becomes stultifying. At this point, satire is necessary, or at least irony; or else Eliot melts into virtually nothing. He has risked his neck for his friend, but he falls back into harness easily enough. As we meet Eliot two or three years later in *The Affair*, he is a high administrator, now in the Atomic Energy Establishment at Barford. The trouble with George Passant is only a ripple in his past: Eliot still believes in what he does and basically in how it is done.

The English attitude toward one's job is often different from the American, if the novelists are themselves to be believed. An American author trying to build some sympathy for Eliot would have him disdain and ridicule Hector Rose, a fit subject for lampooning, not for a little speech lauding his virtues. Next, the American would make Eliot face a great moral decision instead of taking George Passant's dismissal in his stride after consoling himself with a temporary burst of anger at the short-sightedness of administrators. Finally, the American would probably have Eliot drift away to something else. He would go on the road to seek his fortune and prove himself by rejecting the Hector Roses and everything they stand for.

What Eliot's situation calls for is a middle ground between the two points of view. Snow misjudges the serious reader if he thinks Eliot can still remain sympathetic after he resettles into harness. Once again, satire or mockery of some kind is called for. For an Eliot to take a Rose straight is for the two to be equated; they both share the same worlds, and they both have similar ambitions. Yet while the novel calls for Eliot to remain a sympathetic character, under these conditions he appears complacent and expedient. Snow is so immersed in the workings of his little bureaucratic world that he fails to see the humor implicit in a pompous ass like Rose. When Rose speaks, he pontificates as a god would, and his words are taken as gospel. Eliot questions Rose's decisions, as the decisions of gods are often questioned, but he returns to the fold a believer. His shrug reveals that this is the way people are. More thought would have indicated that such people are fit subjects for ridicule.

The loss here of edge and tone hurts both Eliot and the point Snow wishes to make about the present world. If Snow intends to show how this world works, both at its best and at its worst, then he needs some point of view besides Eliot's. He needs his own as well. Too often, Snow and Eliot become one, so that Eliot is not a created character, but simply an extension of the author. Only if Snow had provided some distance on Eliot and had seen *him* as he, Eliot, sees others, only then would Eliot have been caught in a world of real people making important decisions. Snow considerably simplifies people and their decisions by reducing Eliot to one dimension, by seeing Rose in merely one way. There is clearly not enough operating to give the sense of life, people, and events.

Once we recognize the partial failings of Snow's point

of view, then we can go back and see Rose's idea for what it is. Despite the complacency of the man—after we accept that, for good or ill, he exists and that he does make decisions—we recognize the truth of his estimation of George. Here, Snow makes a fine point: that in a complex society such as ours, people are on trial not only for the moment but for the entire content of their lives. They may be admirable, but if they have failed somewhere in the past, this failure will frustrate them at every turn. George is of course perfectly suited for the position under consideration; we see his fitness when he is juxtaposed to Gilbert Cooke, who is retained by Rose although far inferior. But George's past lames him. He has not done enough for a man of 47, and despite his potential he becomes suspect. There is, here, a fearful law operating: that one must start young and sprint all the way in order to reach the top, or else give up the race altogether.

In this world, one cannot afford to make many mistakes. If he does err, he can only do so after he has been accepted; before that, he must appear impregnable. This is a world of nerves, anxieties, jagged tones. And yet can we really claim that George is too honest with his own feelings to survive in such a world? It is to Snow's credit that we cannot put the question that way. For while George may be true to himself, he is not quite honest. His optimism—what Eliot calls his failure to take on any protective coloration—often becomes confused with naïveté. George wishes to operate in the big world, and yet he assumes innocence when experience is called for. He becomes a somewhat foolish man, in that he wants the rewards of the bureaucratic world without becoming aware of the rules. He misses tragedy because he remains unaware of what the game actually is. Were he to understand the rules and then fail to gain his objective, he would perhaps attain tragic standing.

Instead, George appears as a kind of fool, really a clown. He has grown older without growing wiser. He has the mentality of the small town lawyer, and while his knowledge was useful to Eliot when they were both in the provinces, in the city he fails to grow. Here he is relatively helpless, for he has been conditioned by his many years as a solicitor. Rose, then, is right. George has too much resilience, too much bounce, too little sense of personal doom. Change these qualities, and George would be a Lewis Eliot, in several ways more admirable, in others less.

It is George's very ability to go all out, however, that attracts Eliot; the later sees that, like a child, George must be protected. It is also this quality of George that Eliot must himself acquire: he must become committed to feelings, actions, temptations. He must cease to be a spectator. "George was a human brother. He fought with his brother men, he never wanted to be above the battle. He did not understand the temptation, so insidious, often so satisfying to men like me, of playing God: of giving so much and no more: of being considerate, sometimes kind, but making the considerations into a curtain with which to shut off the secret self I could not bear to give away." (p. 228) Here is the beginning of Eliot's retrenchment, his attempt to recoup the values of his life and to rebuild himself into a person who can give.

Yet Eliot rarely follows up this realization, practicing it only in his private life while his public life continues as before. He is an administrator, and his talent is not to create but to rearrange people. Although in *The Affair* we hear that Eliot has written some important books, this aspect of his career Snow slights in favor of his public work. Eliot as a writer never appears; Eliot as manipulator appears constantly. As a manipulator, he continues to be committed to the notion that there is such a thing as moral expedience.

In *Homecoming*, his moral expedience comes out as he attempts to explain the persecution of Sawbridge as a spy (see *The New Men*). Eliot's problem is to justify Sawbridge's trial to Mr. Davidson, Margaret's liberal father. The relevant moral issues concern whether Sawbridge is actually guilty of spying or whether he is being sacrificed for the sake of security. In brief, is the individual being fully protected against the workings of the state, even when the operation of the state demands certain security measures? Here Mr. Davidson questions the boundaries of state jurisdiction. Eliot answers that since a government has a right to protect itself, certain information must be kept secret as long as that government attempts to be effective, and that it depends on what the government does with the information as to whether or not it is a good government. The best one can hope for is that the government does not use its information idly, but that it has to keep information secret Eliot fully believes, even if such a procedure will disquiet those who are the conscience of the government, like Davidson himself. One must simply hope that the information is in the hands of decent men who will not use it to falsify the record or to advance their own positions. Eliot remarks of the whole business: "People of my sort have only two choices in this situation, one is to keep outside and let others do the dirty work, the other is to stay inside and try to keep off the worst horrors and know all the time that we shan't come out with clean hands. Neither way is very good for one, and if I had a son I should advise him to do what you [Davidson] did, and choose a luckier time and place to be born." (p. 250)

With these comments, Eliot hopes to allay Davidson's fears about the nature of the state, and successfully does so. Yet just earlier, Eliot had thought: "I had not enjoyed defending the establishment: but I was also irked by the arrogance of men of decent feeling like Davidson, who had had the means to cultivate their decent feelings without the social interest or realism to imagine where they led." (pp. 249–50)

These thoughts as well as the language expressing them are precisely those of an administrator who by and large accepts the administrative way of looking at things. Eliot alleges that he has not enjoyed defending the establishment—this disclaimer supposedly makes him liberal and broad-minded, somewhat hip—but nevertheless he does go ahead to do so. Also, in defending his position to Davidson, he forgets to mention that Sawbridge's prosecution was an attempt on Martin Eliot's part to vault into the directorship of Barford. Sawbridge may have been a spy, but he was also a scientist whose future was expediently sacrificed to Eliot's brother. How, then, can Eliot remark that we must hope that decent men will administer justice? Nearly all men are decent when there is little at stake, but when there is a great deal—their futures, their ambitions, their status—then their decisions are always mixed, as Davidson shrewdly suspects. For Eliot to argue otherwise is for him to accept the point of view that he ostensibly disclaims. And his alternatives of staying outside while others do the dirty work or remaining inside to hold off the worst are not really the whole of the story. One need not do either. There is the third way in which, like Davidson, one acts as a conscience and pursues a course of action which leaves one free of the establishment and administration. Eliot wants his disclaimer and yet wants to enjoy his glory too. The so-called change that has taken place in him has certainly not affected his public affairs. He is here a hypocritical man only a degree better than his coevals, a man who on the surface seems different from Hector Rose but who in reality is quite close to his administrative chief.

Only in his private life does Eliot learn to give of himself, and that change requires a crisis. In his early relationship to Margaret Davidson, Eliot finds himself in another tortured affair, so much so that Margaret marries Geoffrey Hollis, only to divorce him to marry Eliot. In his pursuit of Margaret after her marriage (she also has a child), Eliot moves from behind his self-protective wall to see if he has something to give. Once he and Margaret are married, they have a child, Charles, but Margaret finds she cannot conceive again without great danger to her life. The child falls ill, deceptively so at first, so that the doctor, Charles March, incorrectly diagnoses the ailment. When the child's condition worsens, they call in Geoffrey Hollis, who makes the correct diagnosis and brings the child safely through.

Involved are a number of conditions which force Eliot's hand: first, that Margaret cannot conceive again; second, that the death of the child would mean that only Maurice, the child of Margaret and Geoffrey, would remain; third, that the child himself has given Eliot an opportunity to move out of himself; fourth, that from Margaret's point of view, the child was her visible hold on Eliot, without which the marriage might well crumble; and fifth, that the illness of the child curiously brings Geoffrey closer to them, for they disliked him because they had hurt him. With a kind of balance restored, shame on both sides is swept away.

Further, Eliot recognizes a point of view which hitherto he had dismissed as irresponsible. Earlier, he and Geoffrey had argued about the nature of responsibility, with Eliot holding for a broad view in which a man tries to influence as best he can the great events of the world. To this, Geoffrey answers that we should concentrate only on the things we can control, commenting that he has even stopped reading the daily paper. Eliot thinks such withdrawal is ostrich-like in its denial of the world's problems, believing as he does that one must have a social conscience. "Partly, Geoffrey seemed to me complacent, speaking from high above the battle; and, like many people who led useful and good lives, even like many who had a purity of nature, he seemed insulated by his self-regard." (p. 263) However, after Geoffrey saves Charles from meningitis, Eliot sees that he is definitely on the side of the species, that by saving children he is in his fashion saving mankind.

In these ways, *Homecoming* resolves Eliot's personal problems. The forward movement of the series seems to have ended, for all that remains is a dip back into the past or a foray into the future to visit some allied problem. Eliot as a person has little more to say: he can only be a sounding board for the ideas of others. The dread of his past homecomings, first as a child and then after his marriage to Sheila Knight, has vanished. Now he can return home to a normal wife and a stable family. He has attained personal happiness. While this resolution bodes well for Eliot, it bodes ill for his role as a character in the series, for we have little more to learn about him. With happiness gained, Eliot is now fixed.

ALTHOUGH *The Conscience of the Rich* (published in
1958) covers a period full of great importance for Lewis
Eliot, this novel does not essentially concern him. The
years from 1927, when he took and passed his bar finals,
to 1936, when the novel ends, contain his entrance into
law practice, his marriage to Sheila Knight, the trial of
George Passant for fraud, his own election to a law
Fellowship at Cambridge, his friendship with Roy Calvert.
In these years, Eliot makes many of his most significant
personal decisions, and he also suffers a nearly fatal illness,
one that almost wrecks his career before it gains momentum. Nevertheless, the focus of the novel shifts to the
March family, principally to Charles March and his father,
Leonard.

As the novel begins, Eliot has finished his law examinations and passed well enough to win a scholarship and be
articled to Herbert Getliffe, a London lawyer and half-
brother of the Francis Getliffe whom we have already met.
Eliot's acquaintance, Charles March, has also passed high,
but not high enough for a scholarship, which he does
not need or want. More talented than Eliot, he is, by
virtue of his background, less motivated by financial in-
security and personal drive. His family, the well-known
Marches, is part of the rich and settled upper class Anglo-
Jewish world that is comfortably and complacently sitting
out the trouble between England and Germany prior to
the second World War. The Marches are not very religious Jews in their practice, but certain conventions have

become important for them. Huge Friday night dinners, with fifty or sixty guests, form the basis of family solidarity; at these gatherings, which the older generation insists upon, the family is consolidated through forced attendance, although the younger people already look upon the dinners as unamusing anachronisms. There, a review of news and gossip prevents any eccentricity from escaping the ears of all, and the family unit becomes a way of exerting social pressure upon the potential deviator. As a miniature world, the family prevents Charles March and his sister Katherine from forgetting their Jewishness by returning them to it, at least once a week.

Here, in Charles March, is Snow's "new man," not at all the scientist who will defend our future. The "new man" as typified by March, and to a limited extent by Eliot, must break with meaningless traditions and strike out on his own, despite those he hurts. His break from family and inherited fortune are signs of his freedom, although his rejection need not be complete or brutal. Whatever he rejects he retains an affection for, but he also knows that peace of mind depends on his right to make his own decisions. He is reasonably ambitious, but he recognizes the moral limitations of ambition without being a prig or even an idealist. He is a supreme realist, for his imagination soars no further than the things of this world. This "new man" is supposedly the best that civilization can produce. He will avoid the extremes, at the same time escaping mediocrity. A Charles March is an aware, liberated individual, perhaps not the best of doctors (as we saw in *Homecoming*) but an able and responsible human being. A world of Charles Marches, even of Lewis Eliots, Snow suggests, would be a sane if unoriginal world, one that for him would be preferable to the one that presently exists.

The importance of this volume to the series is obvious. It is perhaps the best of the novels because it catches both broadly and succinctly the social and political dilemmas of the day. Further, Snow brings back a word— "conscience"—that has become virtually taboo in contemporary fiction. Because of its connotations of religiosity, moralizing, and didacticism, the word has been avoided; even the whole notion that it signalizes has been generally skirted. Snow uses the word and makes it dramatically cogent. Conscience becomes the guiding force for people who recognize that only conscience can hold back chaos. Snow recognizes that in a world in which personal interest does count a great deal, the only thing that can contain chaos is balanced judgment, his synonym for conscience. In a way, Snow has returned, unheroically, to the moderation and proportion of the Greek dramatists, finding in their attitudes the wisdom necessary to preserve a balanced society. And even though his characters are not always responsible for their actions, nevertheless Snow knows that the only test of a "good" person is how far he responds to the demands of decency, how well he retains his balance in a world ready to upset him. In this sense, March and Eliot are culture heroes, for they point the way to the kind of society Snow wishes to see develop. *They* are "new men."

The reader's difficulty with Lewis Eliot, as he develops, comes when he fails to live up to his advance notices. We feel troubled precisely when Snow accepts Eliot's temporizing as inevitable, while at the same time talking about conscience and duty in moral terms. The presentation of Charles March, however, is less ambiguous, for March remains a moral being, both in his conception of his own life and in terms of his duties to others. Rejecting his father's world, he does not reject his father, to whom such an action might prove fatal. Rejecting much of what his wife believes politically, he nevertheless stands by her and forces her to make her own decisions. He allows principles to guide his behavior, although he can on occasion be difficult and stubborn. He is not always admirable as a human being, but he is principled and just when the matter counts.

The leading influence in the immediate March family is Leonard, Charles's father, whose conventional tastes and aims have fixed him in a pre-industrial dream world, unable as he is to come to terms with changing times. His children, of course, are very much of this century, and the conflict between them and the elder March is, in one way, the conflict of one century's institutions with the ideas of another, in a second way, the conflict of Jewish conventions with the non-Jewish attitudes of the nearly assimilated children. The problem, then, becomes one of compromise: how far will the children compromise to keep Leonard satisfied? how far will he move to placate them?

It is here, in this small area of mobility, that Charles March must act. It is true that he must partially compromise, or else be excessively cruel; at the same time, he must satisfy himself, or else he is simply being expedient: placating Leonard so as not to lose his inheritance. Charles's range of movement is narrow, as Snow intends it to be; for his point is that people must usually make choices that are relatively limited.

On Leonard's part, there is always the nagging fear that he has failed to realize what talents he might have had, and that his life, full of crotchets and old-fashioned opinions, is basically meaningless; therefore, the worth he places on tradition, on external forms, on the self-righteous opinions of the family group, on his Jewishness to set him and the family off from the rest of society. His religion is certainly not that which involves the God of Moses or the Covenant of the Ark; it becomes, almost solely, a means of social snobbery. Like Cain, the Marches are marked, and consequently they have good reason, they feel, for retreating into isolation, while maintaining their good living, fine houses, and other signs of material distinction. In many ways, their Jewishness becomes merely an excuse for exclusiveness, a cover for personal deficiencies.

Leonard would have made a suitable companion for Dickens's Pickwick, that pre-industrial gentleman who relied so heavily upon conventional institutions. The choices Pickwick must face are few, but when he needs to make a decision he can fall back upon traditional answers. It is this world into which Leonard fits, frightened as he is of the world of his children, in which choices are made separate from convention and tradition. He is an anachronism, albeit a powerful one.

Nagged by the fear that his own life has been a failure, Leonard lives through his children, turning in hope particularly to his son, Charles. All his rejected dreams center on Charles, and his attachment becomes obsessed with his desire to prove himself and to maintain the family honor. The need for outward success becomes obvious. But Charles, while fond of his father and careful of his feelings, is anxious to break out of the family mold and acts counter to his father's wishes. As a lawyer, he is within a world acceptable to Leonard, but as a doctor earning his own way, he is reprehensible, even slightly ridiculous. Charles's desire to be a doctor—to feel useful by being responsible—indicates to Leonard the breakup of the family unit, for no March with any regard for the family would turn to medicine, especially to general practitioning.

Accordingly, the tensions appear in several ways: in personal terms, Charles's sense of personal responsibility versus his father's sense of family honor; in religious terms, the son's conflict with Leonard's Jewishness, plus the Jewishness of the Marches versus a non-Jewish world; in social terms, family and tradition versus the impending disintegration of the family unit, as well as the ghetto attitude of Leonard versus the cosmopolitanism of Charles and his sister; in political terms, the radicals (the younger people) versus the conservatives (Leonard and his brother, Sir Philip), and within the former group, the communists (Charles's wife, Ann Simon) in conflict with the noncommunist left (Charles, Lewis Eliot, Francis Getliffe); and all this against the background of everygrowing political conflict between England and Germany in the 1930's.

The novel derives its richness of texture from the cohesion Snow gains between the public and private lives of his characters. Here, unlike the characters in *The New Men* or even *The Masters*, people have lives that unfold naturally. Even Leonard, whose crotchets make him an annoying human being, is fully developed: he makes perfect sense as a person as well as a symbol of old-fashioned conservatism. He fits the plot, and he fits as a person. In this novel, virtually for the first time Snow was able to bring together his underlying "resonances," what he considers to be the real pattern of the entire series. These resonances act as motifs: the various struggles for power, as well as its renunciation; the numerous obsessions, possessive and otherwise, that the characters have; the several levels of feeling in Eliot himself.

All of these resonances are viable in *The Conscience of the Rich*, as if this volume, although covering the relatively early years of Eliot's career, were itself a summation of the series. Certainly here, more than elsewhere, Snow successfully presents his point that man must immerse himself in life, as Charles March does, and suffer sorrow, pain, even personal tragedy; that man must make the grand gesture of immersion in reality, even while he recognizes that his will might not triumph, that certain uncontrollable forces might bring him down.

By denying the formal side of his Judaism—and becoming a doctor is an outward symbol of this negation— Charles feels that he has found one of the ways he can counteract his family and gain independence for himself. His religion, tied as it is to tradition and continuity, binds him to a course of action with which he has no personal identification. He feels he will be fixed, unalive, and inactive as long as he remains part of Leonard's world. To be a doctor, however, is to depart from the general line the family has taken in the past, and it is only natural that Charles should equate his change of profession with his disdain for the forms of Judaism his father retains. By overthrowing his career as a lawyer, in which he could be very successful if he wished, he partially nullifies the traces of the past, in particular the traces of his father's very strong control over him.

His marriage to Ann Simon, similarly, isolates him politically from his traditionally conservative family. While he does not share her political views, he stands behind her by refusing to make her head off a communist report that will ruin Sir Philip, Leonard's older brother and the bell-wether of the family. This decision becomes his moral battleground, paralleling in its way his choice of profession. His moral struggle here is merely a continuation of his struggle against the past; the conscience of the rich is working on him to make him individually responsible. To remain a March in the sense that Leonard desires is to remain safe and protected at every turn of fortune, isolated from life by family wealth, position, and name. Charles recognizes that to be safe is to deny life, and his conscience will not allow him to avoid dangers, the first of which is to throw off the family burden, although he is more than willing to retain the love implicit in his father's relationship to him. The crisis over Ann, who must herself, uninfluenced by Charles, decide what to do about the information that will destroy Sir Philip's reputation, becomes the crisis of Charles's own life: here he can achieve manhood through asserting his self or else remain all his life under Leonard's control.

Within this struggle of the individual to realize his own potential, Snow is interested in catching essentially unheroic characters at their moments of decision and watching how they react as whole people. Each act, he recognizes, is moral only when it grows from the whole person; an immoral act, he suggests, will not come from one fully conscious, for the conflict itself confers nobility. Thus, Snow is concerned with mature and knowledgeable people who are aware of duty and discipline, who realize that much of life is a necessary compromise between what one wants and what one can hope to obtain in an imperfect world. The individual, in these terms, is clearly not a traditional hero; on the contrary, the humble everyday acts of living are the sole terms of one's heroism, which is within the reach of *any* moral character. With the hero in Victorian and modern fiction having declined from his traditional position, Snow shows that the, sole kind of hero left is the person who assumes responsibility and makes personal choices, in themselves part of his struggle to gain self-identity.

Charles March and Lewis Eliot are Snow's alternatives to the typical existential hero. Since Snow's society is based on continuing values, people must work, they must pursue ambitions, they must marry and settle down. In such a situation, or in such a civilization, the existential hero would find little place, for he lives on the fringes of the society which for Snow is everything. The existential hero—Dostoyevsky's Ivan Karamazov, Camus' Meursault, Conrad's Kurtz, Gide's Lafcadio, Hesse's Haller, Kafka's K.—values few of the things cherished by a bourgeois society. While he may not be in direct reaction against it, he nevertheless is relatively untouched by it. He lives on a plane where the things of this world are relatively insignificant; attitude is all.

The existential hero cannot of course fall back on any given values except those he accepts himself, and here he overlaps with a typical Snow character. Nevertheless, the differences remain great. Snow's people are solidly within the society that remains closed to the existential hero; in fact, Snow's characters are not even aware of the latter's existence. When Snow tries to present a peripheral figure, he turns to Robinson, a disreputable publisher (in *Homecoming*). For him, Robinson is a typical outsider, and yet Robinson has the aims and desires of everyone else: he simply cannot achieve what he wants. For the existential hero, such is clearly not the case. What everyone else wants leaves him impassive, if he is even aware of the wishes of others. The chances are that he lives within his own bounds, sees things solely from his own point of view, and fails to communicate with anyone else. For with whom can he communicate if he believes the world is nonsensical? Here, however, is not so much a rejection of traditions and institutions as a view of the world which stresses only the worth (or lack of worth) of the individual. Everything else passes.

Further, the existential writer is concerned with inexplicables, while Snow is mainly concerned with the things that do have explanation. The existentialist tries to suggest the nature of the irrational; Snow attempts to show that even the irrational can be partially controlled, although he does admit that there are forces in operation untouchable by the human will. In addition, the quality of nothingness which the existentialist explores is alien to Snow, for his chief characters, while they may feel the emptiness of their existence, nevertheless proceed as though life has meaning, a meaning which they seek and *expect* to find. Both Eliot and Charles March face decisions which contradict any notion of a meaningless universe; in their decisions, they hope to find stability, perhaps even happiness.

The notion of nothingness, which proceeds from the fact that man is a stranger in an inexplicable universe, leads to quite a different kind of despair from what Eliot suffers. Eliot's despair, we are led to believe, is only temporary; there is always the possibility of recovery once he sees his way clear. His feelings of emptiness or nothingness are transitory, for they are not intrinsically part of the universe. Instead, they reside within the individual, and the individual can find the substance of resurrection in his own efforts. Thus, we have Snow's faith, limited though it may be.

The existential writer, moreover, is death-oriented. A good deal of his philosophical outlook is concerned with demonstrating that a man to be truly alive must be aware of death, and ultimately must be able to face it without fear or trembling. In brief, life gains value in direct proportion to the individual's ability to transcend the fact of his death. While Eliot does face death, when early in his career he suffers from something diagnosed as pernicious anemia, he nevertheless does not transcend death so much as transcend his illness through an act of will and determination. Eliot does not accept the irrationality of the universe which can arbitrarily condemn him, although he does examine this possibility; what he does instead is to try to find ways to overcome what appears irrational to him. He applies reason to an inexplicable situation, hoping to overcome it. And he is successful, even though he comes out of the encounter a chastened man now more aware of his limitations.

In Snow's view, then, there is a strong belief in the continuity of both society and the individual. He has no real idea of emptiness or nothingness. Once Charles March decides to forgo law for medicine, he can proceed despite the tremendous obstacles in his way. The obstacles are of the kind that can be dealt with, notwithstanding the difficulties. The will can conquer. In the existential writer, there is little of this belief. For him, the will is baffled at every turn, until the individual virtually gives up; like Kafka's K. or Beckett's various M-characters, he must look to heaven not with hope but with despair, for heaven promises him only something worse than he suffers on earth. He finds he must accept whatever exists; the struggle is over, the battle done.

Snow's view of modern man is close to the way most people like to see themselves; that is, as buffeted by forces they do not understand, but forces nevertheless which they believe they can overcome. We live as though continuity were not only possible, but already present; we assume that despite impending world catastrophe, we will go on: work, marry, have families, settle down into a life-time occupation, pursue hobbies and try to create a milieu of happiness, even joy. Most people live with the assumption that such a world is within their reach. Certainly capitalistic democracy, despite its transformation in the last thirty years, is still based on this notion. Capitalism promises each man his own property, with the assumption that it is his to keep, while democracy promises him equality of opportunity, with the assumption that, given the opportunity, the individual will seek what he wants. This gospel is also not far from what the communists promise, making due allowance for differing views about property. Thus, it would seem as though the reality that Snow reflects is reality as viewed by the majority of people in the western world.

Snow's view that the will, in spite of setbacks, will ultimately give man what he wants if he is willing to persist, is comforting, especially against a background of fiction by Kafka, Beckett, Camus, Sartre, and Conrad. Snow's seems the real world of hope and desire, ambition and set-backs, will and counter-will. Life here is controllable, subject to a man's sense of his own destiny. Even Snow's view of what constitutes wisdom is comforting: it is curiously close to the Greek assumption that with age a man is expected to grow wise. This view assumes that there is wisdom and that there is a self worth cultivating. Implicit here is a belief that things do have a sense of purpose. Snow is among the yea-sayers.

The Conscience of the Rich becomes the working out of this very point: how does a man arrange his own destiny? Here is a clear alternative to the despairing novels of the last thirty years, one that fits a progressive society interested in the welfare of the individual. And this is the notion of reality that most of us live by. On the other hand, the writers who mock this view and who become prophets of doom are generally our major ones, the ones whom we teach in the colleges and the ones whom we pass down from one generation to another for interpretation and analysis. Whose reality is closer to the truth, or are values so relative that each view is equally correct? The distinction that we make must be at Snow's expense. In general, his characters live the way the rest of us do when we are only concerned with what we immediately say and do. As long as we restrict our range of thought and movement, we remain safely within the world that Snow catches. But our lives if restricted to only this world will be somewhat limited. What Snow almost completely ignores is the vast swamp of unconscious and subconscious desires and motivations which often do not work themselves out directly in action or word. Snow's psychology is that of the behaviorists, although somewhat more sophisticated. The mere fact that he tells his story from Lewis Eliot's point of view indicates that the conflicts of the other characters are meaningful only as they are seen by an outsider. Their conflicts in themselves are of little moment; their behavior, on the contrary, is what essentially counts.

The major contemporary writers—the existentialists as

well as the nonexistentialists—have been concerned with that swamp underneath, making those veiled desires and intentions the real stuff of the character. The latter's social behavior is secondary, for that is formed by others. The "real" character is what he has made of himself, what he thinks, how he sees others; the rest does not matter. The existentialist, whether successful or not, sees man as a weak creature capable of a curious grandeur when faced by annihilation. Snow sets his sights considerably lower; man's grandeur is revealed when he makes a good business decision or selects a capable administrative assistant. There is no swamp, no unconscious, no cosmos. Once Charles March decides to stick by Ann Simon as she faces the logical outcome of her political views, he has made a decision that is meaningful and that seals their fate, for good or ill. It is as if his loyalty to her is a final thing. There should, however, be an outgrowth or development from this: their coming-together here might portend a later split; or his loyalty might take something from him and result in his having less respect for her, or she for him; or their very attachment might prove suspect, perhaps based on false assumptions. Snow suggests that there is a final solution, that once Ann recovers from her illness their marriage will be stronger than ever.

The other side of reality—the boredom a person feels in the presence even of someone he loves, the meaninglessness of an attachment that one desires, the hopelessness of the will in facing the really big issues that Eliot himself says a man should consider, the fact that life is always less than what one expects it to be, the emptiness of human relationships and the estrangement a person feels from forces that seem to be directing him—all these sides of reality Snow either bypasses or ignores altogether.

What Snow does with his empirical outlook is as much as can be done with this equipment. To go further would be to delve into the realm which he denies is of primary importance. When he talks of the humanist as opposed to the scientist, or the humanistic view as opposed to the scientific view, he gravitates toward the scientist because the latter is positive, is aware of human progress. Snow is somewhat suspicious of the humanist not only because the latter is ignorant of the scientist's world but because he tends to deny that the world is this way at all. Snow's suspicions go as deeply as Plato's in their common distrust of the poet who tells untruths, who may be decadent, perhaps homosexual, drug addicted, or alcoholic. In political life, Snow is very tolerant of those who deviate, but in literature he deplores the humanists who are concerned with sickness, while he praises the scientists, who are concerned with health. This aspect of Snow's attitude has been little noticed: that he deplores the division of knowledge into two worlds because one of those worlds seems to be contradicting man's potential progress, seems to be leading man back to his worst self. Here, Snow's literary reactionaryism stultifies his common sense, for even though we obviously live with fears and anxieties, Snow wants his humanists to see life whole, and to see it as essentially progressive. Since they often do not see it this way at all, Snow favors the scientist, who looks into the future confident that there is a future and that knowledge is worth pursuing.

This view, then, is the alternative that Snow provides to the existentialists. Like Charles March in *The Conscience of the Rich* and Lewis Eliot earlier, we must arrange our lives and calculate our chances. If we fail to calculate, or to take on a "protective coloration"—what George Passant fails to do—then we fail life. Life rarely fails us. The world is there to conquer if only we find the right formula and the correct code of behavior. Rather than deploring this view of the world, Snow accepts it realistically and is willing to work with it.

Snow's portrait of Leonard March, like the one he draws of Charles, is effective because the old man is caught among several worlds, all of them solid and substantial. Whatever Leonard identifies with has texture and shape, whether it is the banking world of his youth or the professional world of his son and friends. Leonard has had to learn how to come to terms with his gifts and his limitations. He is fixed within a way of live and identified clearly with his generation of conservative businessmen. Leonard was once so secure that as a young man of 32 he decided to retire when he realized his firm was not advancing; and since it refused to take in outside blood, the firm closed while still prosperous. Having with certainty committed this act of renunciation, Leonard is now nagged by the fear that he may have failed to realize his talents. With a life empty of meaningful activity, he stresses tradition as well as personal crotchets and opinions. Leonard, accordingly, is boxed in by solid shapes, and his fixedness allows Snow to catch him as he would a sitting duck.

With Leonard, there are none of the moral hesitations that go on in Eliot or Charles as they move around in worlds beyond them. Leonard does not move, nor does he make decisions that are outside his world of family honor and tradition. He makes his calculations within a small circle of possibility; for he must balance family reputation against the feelings of his children, and he must compromise between the two. His choice is relatively simple even as he sees his kind of world evaporating. When Katherine decides to marry a non-Jew, he perceives that the breakup of the family is imminent, but he knows also that he must hold his daughter's love. His choice is obviously bounded on both sides, and he has little room for maneuver.

In just this restricted area, Snow shows his talent for catching the conscience of an individual. Leonard is a successful character precisely because his old world reactionaryism takes on charm and because he cannot be taken seriously despite his dignity and solidity. Leonard, as is his way, accepts without question his position in upper-middle class society and in his provincial sophistication assumes that what has been good enough for him is also good enough for his son. Snow writes:

> Yet it was true that Mr. March could not credit that a balanced man should want to go to extravagant lengths to feel that his life was useful. He could not begin to understand the sense of social guilt, the sick conscience,

which were real in Charles. To Mr. March, who by
temperament accepted life as it was, who was solid in
the rich man's life of a former day, such a reason
[Charles's desire to be useful] seemed just perverse. He
could not believe that his son's temperament was at this
point radically different from his own. [p. 116]

Inevitably, Leonard is caught between real choices which
can make his life happy or unhappy. The decisions here
are not metaphysical, nor are they necessarily complex.
Leonard March simply has to choose a course of action
that will perpetuate the family tradition: the thing itself
counts. That he can act upon.

Of course, involved in Leonard's choice of action is a
complex of social, economic, and political institutions.
The split in thinking between father and son is indicative
not only of the split between the two generations, but also
of rich and poor, have and have-not, conservative and
liberal: the spectrum of 1930 politics as the Labor Party
and the Conservatives struggled for power. Charles, unlike
his father, cannot accept his riches without question and
is willing to accept poverty (relative poverty, since he
does marry a rich girl) for his ideals. And if impoverish-
ment itself is not actually his fate, he at least recognizes
that he must struggle for what he has, that he cannot retire
at 32 and be useless. He suffers feelings of guilt over his
wealth; men should be responsible, he feels, and the rich
man more than most since he has power to wield. This
acceptance of human responsibility leads to a political
split between Charles and his father, although they would
not break were it not for the other related factors.

The split between generations is further pointed up in
the type of people who receive invitations to Bryanston
Square, the March home. Formerly, only titled and
moneyed young men were invited, and the servants recognized their worth. Now come men like Eliot and
Francis Getliffe (here, Katherine March's fiancé), poor,
pushy young men without connections or wardrobe. The
change in visitor is indicative of the change from Tory to
Labor: the rich young conservative has been transformed

into the forceful left-wing democrat. No longer can the same values be held, and no longer is class inflexible, even though the Marches feel they are holding the line. With birth and economic position relatively minor factors, personal attainment confers status. None of this of course is startling, but it does work well as background for the personal struggle in which Leonard represents the last vestiges of privilege and Charles stands, despite his money, for all those forceful young men.

The novel is of one piece. It comes as a realized chunk of life, principally because Snow has caught a world that has shape and form and substance. The sole part of the book that partially fails is that concerned with the communist plot to blacken the reputation of the Establishment; but few novelists can make a conspiracy seem real and catch it without affectation or distortion. Here Snow falters, simply because the forces in operation are beyond measurement and calculation. The motives of the people —Ann Simon, Seymour (who operates the *Note*, a mud-slinging newsletter), even Charles March—are full of ambiguities that Snow's technique cannot even suggest. All he can do is chart the characters' courses of action and record their talk as they jockey for position.

If, however, the reader accepts this part of the novel as history rather than as literature, he can then see its virtues. Lacking belief in the noncommunist left, people like Ann and Seymour gravitate toward the communists as the sole group capable of action. They both recognize that the communists consider them or anyone else expedient, but they are nevertheless dedicated to some ideal, apart from personal interest or class. Ann is willing to pursue this ideal even though it will mean injuring her in-laws, so alien to personal interest does she see herself. Only her illness makes impossible her choice of what to do about the *Note*, and the decision itself passes on to Charles. Ann, however, is never clearly realized, so close is she to a stereotype: the rich girl who turns on her own class and identifies with the social views of the left. She rarely emerges from this stereotyped characterization, although she is physically attractive and evidently bright. But here Snow is involved in a characterization that needs further depth and more probing than he is willing or able to make. The portrait, and the entire communist conspiracy, suffers.

When Snow returns to the difficult decisions people must make within a social framework, then he is on safe and sure ground. Ann's illness sets up a situation which he can exploit to good advantage. From Leonard's point of view, she is the alien outsider, a traitor to her class, although she too is Jewish and rich. The latter fact perhaps makes it even worse, for in Leonard's view the Jews of the upper class should present a solid front. She, however, forces the issue: bewitcher of his son, daughter of a doctor, believer in the doctrinaire left, a nonbeliever in religion, a scoffer at everything Leonard holds dear. She upsets continuity, she mocks traditions, she is a force for chaos. Leonard wishes her conveniently dead. Hers is a temperament that compels change, that reacts joyously to change, and there is no chance that Leonard can understand, no less accept her. She threatens his entire security. Her part in the communist plot to smear Sir Philip is clearly symbolic of her social role: to discredit the Marches or their equivalent and to climb to power on their backs. With his short-sighted view of the situation, Leonard is sure that his son will return to the family fold once she dies. He becomes desperate to frustrate the forces of anarchy, as desperate as he is to hold on to his son.

Just as Ann's illness is crucial for Leonard, so it is for Charles. For him, Ann is symbolic of his break with everything Leonard stands for. Her death would leave him bare and exposed; for some reason, it would reflect upon him, mark him as a failure. Clearly, he needs her strength as a buffer against the Marches, even while he retains respect and affection for his father. Consequently, when Ann is too ill to take any further part in the conspiracy, Charles is left with the burden of decision: should he use certain information he has to squash the *Note* and thus protect his uncle?

Charles's answer is that he must protect Ann's wishes, that the decision is really hers and he will do nothing to circumvent it. In effect, he argues his own point of view: that the individual must not be coerced into doing what he does not wish to do. Each of them is old enough to make his own choice according to his own conscience. He argues, rightly, that he is not hurting Leonard's peace of mind any more than Katherine does when she marries out of her religion. The situations parallel each other. Katherine is caught between the demands of the family and the demands of her own happiness, and she chooses the latter despite the fact that it will hurt her father. When, later, Charles is faced with the same dilemma—of marrying Ann against the wishes of the family—Ann's leftist political views are as much a disadvantage to the Marches as Francis Getliffe's being a non-Jew. Charles has sided completely with Katherine in her choice of Francis, and expects her help when he must make his decision to let Ann malign Sir Philip. Katherine refuses, claiming that the decisions are different, that it was easy for him but impossible for her. Charles, then, is left alone.

The final section of the novel is aptly called "Alone." The three main characters—Eliot hardly counts in the moral action of this novel—are alone in different ways. Ann, her recovery in doubt, is of course alone in her illness, her contact with the world broken by comas. Charles himself is alone in his decision whether to take action without Ann's agreement. Leonard, however, is perhaps the loneliest of all, for he sees his family slipping away. With his oldest daughter married to a writer and therefore lost, with his second daughter married to a Gentile, and with his son turned general practitioner and married to a communist trouble-maker, Leonard, like the age he represents, is cut off, ready for senility.

Snow in this novel has modestly attempted to bring fiction back to a concern with commonplace human nature without making the novel either journalistic, naturalistic, or prophetic. Accordingly, his characters, also modest in aim and conception, are of mixed qualities, neither totally attractive nor completely forbidding. Charles is spiteful, scornful, yet loyal, and dependable; Eliot himself, merely a sounding board in this novel, makes an art of compromise when compromise is viable and principle is not; Leonard March is idiosyncratic, yet upright, and his eccentricities never make him a caricature—he is of a time and place, and he *fits*. If he has cut himself off from the present, it is because he recognizes that the present is corrosive, and he refuses to let reality interfere with what his inner ear tells him is true. He has been unable to grow with age, and wisdom is clearly not his. Blinded by his own failure, rather than by ignorance, he will not see what he chooses not to see, and he loses his son because of his short-sightedness. Although he retains dignity, he must, as Charles realizes, be superseded.

Essentially, *The Conscience of the Rich* is a novel about individuals; however, it is also a history of England in the 1930's when the Charles Marches could still make their own decisions. Charles's discomfort with his Judaism, for example, is the difficulty of a whole generation trying to strike through to its conscience. In changing times, the old alignments, he finds, no longer make the same sense. Charles's decision to come to terms with himself, then, is the decision the entire age must make. Snow's real talent lies in his ability to demonstrate cogently that the response must come from within, that it must be a moral response, and that it must retain a note of social responsibility while fulfilling the individual. As Lewis Eliot in the earlier volumes had turned inward and in his own moral conscience found a *modus vivendi* that would serve him uniquely, so too Charles March must make peace with his conscience, regardless of the demands that others will make upon him. Only then, can he, unlike his father, realize himself.

AFTER THE COMPLEXITIES of *The Conscience of the Rich*, *The Affair* (published in 1960) which returns to a later Cambridge (1953–54) of *The Masters*, seems anticlimactic, although it is exciting as a suspense story complete with mysterious intrigues and a courtroom scene. Snow's novel superficially recalls James Gould Cozzens' somewhat pompous *By Love Possessed*, which mixed basically unsympathetic characters with legal highjinks to stir up interest that is really less than meets the eye. Cozzens' purpose, however, was to show how morally shaky the people are who hold positions of trust, while Snow's is to demonstrate that justice—at least in England—eventually triumphs despite the moral shakiness of the individuals who make the decisions. Snow is here concerned with clearing the name of one of the College Fellows of scientific fraud. Many of the important characters from *The Masters* are still alive, and they display their talents in much the same way they did in the earlier novel. In fact, the passage of time—the process of how men grow old— is a curious by-product of the novel.

This novel, more than any other of Snow's in the series, takes the form of a mystery-suspense work, with the actual outcome of the College trial held until the virtual end. Snow makes Howard—the Fellow accused of committing a fraud in order to gain academic prestige—into an intense, unlikable young man, a sneering, dominating, complacent Marxist who jeers at the very institutions and people trying to help him. By making the object of injustice himself unpalatable, Snow isolates the act itself and weighs the scales heavily against those who want justice. He stresses that human feelings are not at stake—clearly all feelings run against Howard—but simply the institution of equity for all. Even Eliot, who so often has been willing to accept abstract principles rather than the man, is taken aback by Howard and is wary of helping him, although he is finally drawn into the case.

Snow emphasizes that Skeffington, a rigid conservative who is the very opposite of Howard, despises the latter and everything he stands for, but he must see justice done, no matter whom he hurts. Perhaps one of the weaknesses of the novel lies here: that people like Skeffington are not concerned with human relationships but with the abstraction that justice is at the core of the English people, and it must be done. One of the finer qualities of *The Masters* was Snow's ability to embody the abstractions of different ideals and ideas in the form of recognizable people who fought out their petty ambitions in a daily give and take. No matter who they were, they reacted to each other as human beings, and Snow saw their flaws in terms not of abstract principles but of real people caught between what they wanted and what they saw they could have. The same kind of give and take was dramatized in *The Conscience of the Rich*, wherein Snow did not forsake principles, morality, justice, and those other abstractions which form the spine of *Strangers and Brothers*, but managed to flesh them out. In *The Affair*, the flesh has melted away, and often only the bony abstraction remains. This novel, consequently, seems akin to the earlier novels when Snow's hand was less sure and on occasion more committed to abstract ideas than to people themselves. The rich texture and density that result from mixed motives and ambiguous actions found in *The Conscience of the Rich* have been diluted. The result is often a linear narrative that makes its point but tells us little about life.

Chiefly, most of the characters have little meaning except as carry-overs from *The Masters* or as participants in a drama in which they themselves have no personal interest. Skeffington, for instance, the man who pursues the case with single-minded energy, is a relic of British justice, a man who inexplicably fights for what he knows to be correct even though he despises the object of his struggle. Eliot himself is drawn in against his will; Francis Getliffe does not wish to be bothered; Arthur Brown is afraid of the upset, and so on through the other characters. They all react to the abstraction of justice, not to men themselves. In Snow's previous novels, the reaction, at best, was to both, and the conflicts there were between the man and the principle at stake. Here the man is so personally disagreeable that there is no question of like or dislike; no one could possible feel favorable toward him, and consequently there is little conflict. The characters find they must support justice despite themselves, and while justice is always admirable, it cannot be isolated as Snow separates it without the novel becoming an exercise in English equity.

As readable and suspenseful as it is, *The Affair* (which takes its title from the Dreyfus case), accordingly, has the odor of just such an exercise. Perhaps Crawford's complacent comment at the end of the novel indicates what is wrong with it: "I think I remember saying that in my experience sensible men usually reach sensible conclusions." It was precisely this point that remained in doubt in the more recent novels: that sensible men were perhaps not quite so sensible when their personal needs were involved, and that their decisions were not so just as they might have been had they not been expedient men. In those novels, Snow was able to question the very basis on which men judged each other and to show that motives went more deeply than any disinterested belief in justice, equity, or reason. Good men could be hurt by institutions, which themselves were necessary to protect the larger rights of most individuals. There was, accordingly, almost constant paradox: the individual could not be fully tolerated, although toleration itself is good; and the institution could not be allowed to deteriorate, although institutions themselves can be evil. There was an acute awareness of the duality of man in a secular world, a mature acceptance of his allegiance to himself and to things outside.

Here, however, the man is no longer in question; he is merely a disembodied cause, someone to be saved and then discarded, as he is at the end of the novel. Snow is demonstrating a thesis: that a Marxist, even when opposed by everyone, must be afforded his rights in a democratic society. His rights, in fact, must perhaps be more carefully watched because he makes demands on men that test their sense of justice more than (say) a conformist would do. An outsider, according to this reasoning, must be afforded special treatment. As a political and social doctrine, this is just, Snow would of course argue, but embodied in a novel solely to illustrate this point, such material is weak.

The Affair, to digress for a moment, received as good a press as it did because several critics had awakened to *Strangers and Brothers* and found Snow to be an intelligent practitioner in the novel. Seen against the background of the whole series, however, *The Affair* does not have the complex qualities of *The Conscience of the Rich*, *The Light and the Dark*, or *The Masters*. More abstract than any of the others, it depends almost solely on that surefire device, a courtroom scene in which the case first appears lost only to be won back in the final minutes by new information that casts doubt in the mind of the jury.

The Affair seems to be paying the penalty of Snow's aims, and, paradoxically, it picks up its virtues from the same source. If anything, Snow wishes to show the place of reason, more often scientific reason, as it bridges the gap between the things that man has wished for himself over a period of time and the thing that man himself is. Often, in this scheme, reason is difficult to define; Snow shows us that reason does not rest all on one side or another, but can serve many masters and purposes. The strength of Snow's novels at their best was their ability to demonstrate how reason can be manipulated, and to suggest that even men of science, for whom reason should be a god, cannot judge reasonably when their own needs and prejudices are at stake. The reason of the laboratory, Snow admits, is not the reason of the world, and someone like Lewis Eliot, or Snow himself, must attempt to bridge the gap between the two worlds. That, patently, is Snow's aim in the long series: strangers must somehow become brothers. In *The Two Cultures and the Scientific Revolution*, his well-known essay on the same problem, Snow merely repeated in socio-political terms his life-long effort to connect the two cultures of science and the humanities.

Eliot's summation speech to the Court of Seniors indicates Snow's point: "Wasn't it the chronic danger of our time, not only practical but intellectual, to let the world get divided into two halves? Hadn't this fog of prejudice —so thick that people on the two sides were ceasing to think of each other as belonging to the same species— obscured this case from the beginning? Hadn't it done harm to the college, to Howard himself, and to the chance of a just decision?" (p. 329)

Here, Snow argues something that should be obvious to the intelligent man, but something, as he says, that is often obscure: that truth never rests on one side and that suspicion is a mutual affair. The political implications of the remark are clear. As Snow has argued in several symposia, the West and the Soviet Union are closer in general aims than the propagandists on both sides would have us believe. Just as the new man Snow foresees will be supra-science-and-humanities, so the new feeling must be supra-national, making reason and justice the touchstones of an ever-progressing world. Once again, strangers must become brothers.

Of course, Snow does not take into account that Cain and Abel were also brothers, and that fraternization can result in hate, even murder. Actually, what is missing is a real sense of evil. Snow's statement above assumes that men will change if they see that change is to their benefit, and that the change will be for the better. The latter part of the assumption, however, is questionable. Snow is optimistic that reason will somehow prevail, and yet history demonstrates that reason, except in the laboratory, is often merely a by-product of the need to survive. Only the Greeks believed that one could adjust oneself to a life of reason, and even they diverged from their theory in accepting furies, omens, and other abstractions untouchable by reason or logic. Their very notion of tragedy and the tragic hero recognized certain inexplicables, like the self-destructive qualities in each man which might topple him at his pinnacle of success and fame. His tragic flaw is a religious notion, not to be fathomed by reason, but to be accepted on faith, or as an explanation of phenomena that have no other explanation.

All this is by way of saying that Snow's reliance on reason—a dependence that varies in his work—is fine as a blueprint, but somewhat naïve when he accepts it as an actual mode of existence. As an alternative to Lawrentian blood consciousness, reason may, or may not, be suitable for a utopian society, but as a working plan for the present society, its limitations must be recognized. These limitations might in themselves become the basis of a tragic novel, but then the format and tone would have to be radically different from Snow's.

The Affair unfortunately demonstrates that reason, while it can be brought to the service of justice, does not in itself provide fiction of any great depth or persuasiveness, although it might provide light entertainment of an intelligent kind. *The Affair* suffers from an excess of reason, from the reasonably clear motives of the characters who support and attack Howard, to Eliot's own ability to analyze himself and realize, down to minute details, where he went right and wrong. There are few of the inexplicables which, previously, made both Roy Calvert and George Passant interesting—in the former a depression and death drift that reduced his powers, in the later an exuberant brilliance and sensuality that made lesser men reject him.

As I mentioned above, Snow's emphasis upon reason

circumscribes a real sense of evil, and any novel written against the background of twentieth-century life must somewhere indicate an awareness of evil. Here we mean real evil, not the kind that can be exorcised in daring trial scenes, or the kind which men resolve after they mend their ways. In life, there is evil that results simply from people coming together with mixed motives, even when they think that they are cooperating and acting like perfect gentlemen. There is evil present in any competitive society, communist or capitalist, which contains rewards and punishments. Even sensible men when pushed will lose their sense, or certainly be tempted to. Evil is a concomitant of life itself, as the major writers have always realized, not simply a by-product of error or mischance. It results from the collision of various motives, from the collapse of moral judgment when large issues are at stake. It is an ingredient of expedience and compromise, and it cannot, as Snow feels it can, be channeled and controlled.

A sense of evil in Snow's work would indicate that things happen even when no one wills them. It would indicate that a confluence of forces directly counter to what one wishes might result and be unsusceptible to reason. Melville's Captain Delano, when faced by impending doom, feels that nothing dreadful can happen to him; after all, he is Captain Delano, skipper of *The Bachelor's Delight*, and formerly known to his cronies as Jack of the Beach. Here is the innocence of the New World, the naturalness of the natural man, the faith and optimism of the Adam who has felt no real sense of evil and cannot conceive of anyone else feeling it. In reading Snow, one receives much the same impression: that he conceives his characters as Captain Delanos; only he is straightforward while Melville is ironic. When an "evil" circumstance does occur in Snow, it can be alleviated: Howard, despite the hopelessness of his position, can be exonerated by a court of his elders. Eliot, although shackled to Sheila Knight by choice, is suddenly rid of her when he seems to be breaking under the strain. Martin

Eliot wants the directorship of Barford and is eventually able to obtain it, although he rejects it once he knows it is his. The nature of the world is such that in the main it lends itself to the force of one's will; and even though happiness and joy may be elusive, nevertheless an ambitious man can obtain what he sets out to gain.

Snow's stress upon expedience and compromise, as well as his reliance upon reason, are all ways of channeling the evil within man. In his assumption that such control can be adequate lies the fallacy of the view. A novelist concerned with the whole range of reality, and not solely with one aspect of it, will create people for whom there are few resolutions. For Snow, there is always a tomorrow; the future counts; it portends something favorable; it can even be arranged. It is Snow's hope that in this "new world" the scientist will take the lead, and yet the scientists in *The Affair*, as well as those in *The New Men*, seem as confused and as calculating as their humanistic colleagues.

In his early novel *The Search*, Snow also showed his faith in scientists. From his childhood, Arthur Miles planned a scientific career, for in science he found religion and salvation. Yet midway in what promises to be a successful career, he stops, reconsiders, and then, like Snow himself, withdraws, becoming instead an historian of sorts. Here we have the shift from science to history, although Snow later reversed himself by slighting history and furthering science. In either use, it is illogical to expect the respective disciplines to carry over when personal feelings are touched, or to assume that the scientist transfers the method of the laboratory into his private and public decisions.

As a result of slighting real evil and relying upon the stabilizing power of the scientist, Snow tends to disguise or ignore the dislocations of the age despite his concern with contemporary problems. What could be more reassuring than the long court scenes in *The Affair*; a trial, as we saw in *Strangers and Brothers*, indicates a world of justice, stability, and decency: one has his day in court.

In the later novel, the trial indicates much the same. A spirit of decency is operating when "sensible" men get together, even though it is almost a fluke that Howard is saved. The argument for Howard's exoneration rests upon Francis Getliffe's testimony that one of the Fellows possibly stole the photograph. Suspicion falls on Nightingale, for he had the disputed Palairet notebooks first. Curiously, Getliffe's statement is simply speculative, and is in no way binding. Yet Snow would have us believe that the Court of Seniors is so awed by Getliffe's reputation that his word alone is enough to change their minds.

Winslow in his speech backing Howard's restitution rests his support upon Getliffe's statement. But the evidence is merely an expression of feeling, not the result of Getliffe's scientific knowledge. These are hardly the actions of sensible men, no less of logical men. There is little logic involved. On the basis of a technicality which should have been apparent at the first trial, Howard is freed. And Brown still has the last word, making it impossible for Howard to vote in the election by depriving him of his tenure, an act agreed upon by Winslow and Crawford, even though they both claim Howard should be exonerated. Once again, an indefensible position to be taken by sensible men.

Still, Eliot sincerely believes that they are sensible men; he is not being sarcastic or facetious. He believes Brown to be a good judge of men, although Brown has to be convinced by Jago's plea that common humanity should prevail. Snow finds Brown admirable, for he works within the rules set by a code of behavior, not by conscience. " 'Decent behavior,' for Brown, meant, among other things, not letting anyone interfere with one's integrity in a judicial process." (p. 194) Or again: "Brown . . . believed that he had to condemn Howard, and guided by his code, he was not tempted to examine either his own motives or any price he might have to pay." (p. 194) Most of this righteousness has nothing to do with judgment, and even less with logic or sense.

In most ways, Brown is despicable, more so as an ad-

ministrator than as a person. In his official functions, he
personifies what happens to virtually all institutions—
whether colleges, professional groups, or government
agencies—when they are run by someone with a "code of
behavior." Usually, this term disguises stodge, uninven-
tiveness, and, most of all, compromise and expedience.
A code of behavior means that a person need not be
right so long as he thinks he is just. The rationalizations
that result from this position are obvious. Brown typifies
all the worst in university presidents, government officials,
and professional people; he is usually one's own director,
chairman, or senator, against whom one has no recourse
except to run. Eliot, however, stays to praise. His Brown
makes the world go. But what a world it is! His Brown
makes institutions possible. But what institutions! His
Brown is the voice of reality. But what a reality we must
face in a world run by Browns! His Brown eventually decides on our futures. But what futures we have! No,
Brown is not adequate; he is a man who must be mocked
and rejected. Withal his fine wines and guiding hand, he
is self-righteous, complacent, inevitably contemptible. He
is the man the "angry young men" have relegated to their
dust bin; he is the Establishment at its worst, not its best.

Snow himself by this volume seems to be running with
the Establishment. His views on art and literature have
always been conservative, even though he did find many
of the so-called "angry novels" refreshing. But now as
honors are being heaped upon him—not the least of
which was a knighthood—he sounds increasingly as
though he believes in what the honors stand for, despite
his leftist political sentiments which put him out of step
with Macmillan and Company. Nevertheless, even his
leftism is safely contained within the respectability of the
Establishment, the kind of eccentricity that the English
political traditions permits.

Perhaps recognizing the situation, Snow attempts to
undercut the accusation by having this very charge
brought against Eliot after he has acquiesced to Brown's
decision to deprive Howard of his tenure. Young Tom

Orbell, although a reactionary himself, is bitterly opposed to the reigning powers and attacks Eliot for his complacence:

> "We've got the old men on the run, and this is the time to make them behave decently for once. I don't know what Lewis was doing not to make them behave decently, except"—his suspicions fixed themselves on me—"that's the way you've got on, isn't it, playing safe with the old men?"

> . . . .

> "Isn't that the whole *raison d'être* behind this precious bargain? I don't like the Establishment. But I'm beginning to think the real menace is the Establishment behind the Establishment. That's what some of you"— he looked with hot eyes at Martin [Eliot], at Francis [Getliffe], at me—"are specialists in, isn't it?" [p. 371]

Orbell is drunk, but that does not destroy the force of the charge. There is, of course, no answer to his attack. Snow, then, obviously recognizes the point, a serious one, indeed; but recognition and taking action upon it are two separate things. Eliot is not appreciably moved. He argues common sense. The move to have Howard's Fellowship continued would not stand a chance of being approved. Reality intervenes. The moment passes, and the Establishment with Eliot's acquiescence has won another round. He agrees with Crawford that sensible men make sensible decisions. Melville's Captain Delano has perceived the nature of the deception, but nevertheless agrees that things do work out for the best. The experience has not deepened or changed him.

Eliot retains his liberal political views, but for what purpose? How is he distinguishable from the conservatives? It is, after all, Skeffington, a rigid reactionary, who makes the retrial possible, a Skeffington who hates everything Howard stands for. The Establishment, we are led to assume, has room for its dissenters. Snow forgives all people their transgressions and allows that all behavior has its explanation. To understand all is to pardon all. His liberalism, in brief, is flaccid, being based more on compromise than on principle. This is not to say that Eliot is an evil man; on the contrary, Snow convinces us quite otherwise. But Eliot's views rarely have any ostensible bearing upon his action; he may as well be a principled conservative (like Skeffington) as a liberal (like Francis Getliffe) for all that his views mean in terms of his behavior.

Disallowing large distinctions between people—a liberal *is* different from a conservative—Snow falls into a kind of positivism. All we have to know, he claims, is the reason for a man's action, and then we can understand why he acts that way. It assumes, with the falsity involved in any simplification, that we can *know* why a person acts the way he does, that there is clarity in this difficult area of motivation and intention. It slides over the large inexplicables in human behavior, and, politically, it tends to place everyone in the same basket, an Eliot with a Skeffington, a Getliffe with an Orbell.

Of course, a great deal of the growing conservatism in the atmosphere—even Francis Getliffe is not immune—results from age. *The Affair,* as I noted above, is also about the passage of time, what happens to people when they grow old. Sixteen years have passed since we last saw the Cambridge Fellows, and generally they have become more complacent, more self-satisfied, less open to ideas than they previously were. They have aged as the College itself has aged; they have lived through a catastrophic period in man's history, and they have come through strangely untouched. Their world is not that of the outside but of their College; their problem is not that of atomic warfare, disarmament, or world disunity, but the relatively simple one of creating an atmosphere of justice in a small College.

On the whole, time has been kind to the Fellows. The terrible dislocations of the age have hardly affected them, and they have been able to continue along their courses. Only in one sense has time been ungenerous; that is, in their inability to have grown wiser as they have grown older. All the Fellows we see are now in old age, except

Luke, who is 42. Eliot himself is a stodgy 48. All have settled into harness, enjoying what they are and not attempting to break out or away. Dead are Despard-Smith, Pilbrow, Chrystal, and Calvert, the latter in the war. Crawford is 72 and ready to retire as Master. Gay is 94 and still communicative despite his senility. Brown is 63, Winslow 80, Jago (now retired) 68. Only Nightingale has radically changed; once tortured and eccentric, he is now, at almost 60, happily married, a less hateful man, although by no means a likable one. Among the younger Fellows, there is the impatient new generation waiting to fill the posts held by Brown, Jago, Chrystal, and Crawford: one like G. S. Clark is already a troublemaker, a defensive creature who has been crippled by polio, a reactionary who is as hard as nails. There is also Tom Orbell, another reactionary who wears his religion noisily, but nevertheless a man who despises authority and provides fair opposition to those who would temporize. Some of the other Fellows in the rapidly expanding College are only sketched in, men like Ince and Taylor, all of whom seem ready to become the nuisances that one usually expects in such a community.

The makings of the next clash are already present at the end of the novel. When Crawford retires at the mandatory age, the Mastership will once again be open, to be fought over by Francis Getliffe, now in his early fifties, and Brown, with other opposition in the form of Martin Eliot and even Clark himself, representative of one wing of the group. The struggle for power goes on; the jockeying for position continues. But what bores these men have become! Brown, as a typical insider and fixer, the prototype of the administrator, is as stodgy and stuffy as ever; Crawford, despite being a Nobel Laureate, is as unoriginal and complacent as expected, and so on through the others. Among the younger Fellows whom we met in *The Masters*, Francis Getliffe and Lewis Eliot, there has been a loss of energy and a corresponding loss of range. Getliffe, having made a name for himself in the scientific world—he is now Sir Francis—is anxious to be Master, although the steps leading to that post are of course demeaning. He has lost his sharpness of perception and his ability to see his own motives, even though he masochistically admits that he has become more conservative.

In this area, as Snow charts the process of growing old, we have one of the best parts of the book. Here, he approaches Anthony Powell's use of time in his *Music of Time* series, although Snow lacks Powell's urbane humor. Nevertheless, as a novel about aging, *The Affair* is better than as a story of suspense and courtroom drama. Gay himself, while still a colossal bore, provides humor, principally because he is so much himself at every moment. In his refusal to forgo what power he has, he rises to magnificent heights. Age has made him senile, but it has also given him Jove-like qualities.

Allied to the theme of age is the continuing theme of ambition and how it affects one's behavior. Snow is anxious to show that when justice is at stake even expedient men are willing to jeopardize their ambitions. Thus, Francis Getliffe, as well as Martin Eliot, somewhat compromises his chances as Master by coming to Howard's defense; Tom Orbell, in turn, hurts his chances of a College post, and Skeffington severely damages his hopes for a permanent Fellowship. All these people pick up Howard's cause because of some sense of abstract justice, while they all make it clear that they abominate Howard himself. The brunt of the case falls on Skeffington; as a man who originally reviewed the forgery and helped convict Howard of fraud, he is now as strongly convinced that Howard is innocent. Skeffington becomes a man obsessed with his cause, as only a man can who has no feeling for the person involved. Snow writes:

> For Howard's sake—or rather, for the sake of getting him fair play—Skeffington was prepared to quarrel with his natural associates in the college, the religious, the orthodox, the conservative. All this on behalf of a man whom Skeffington, not now able to bear him and not given to subtle political distinctions, had come to think of as the reddest of the red. The result of this was to

make Skeffington, in everything outside the Affair itself, more conservative than he had ever been before. He had taken on a rabid, an almost unbalanced, strain of anti-Communism. It was said, I did not know how reliable the rumour was, that he was even having doubts about voting for Francis Getliffe at the magisterial election— after all, Francis had been known to have a weakness for the Left. [p. 265–66]

This tightening of views in Skeffington is quite effective, for in every way except his defense of Howard, Skeffington is priggish and without imagination. Outside the discipline of his scientific training, his judgments are weak, even ill-considered, a curious point for Snow to be making when he wants the scientist to inherit the earth.

However, even in the generally successful portrait of Skeffington, Snow makes the man too consistent and his attitude toward Howard too neat. Certainly, Skeffington would have measured his future against his present actions, no matter how upstanding his views and how rigid his sense of justice. Once again, Snow accepts human behavior on the surface, at its own level of expression. The various psychological reactions implicit in a man like Skeffington as his innermost loyalties come under test would certainly be significant and of interest. After all, Skeffington as a man full of conflicts would be a richer character than a Skeffington who reacts to an abstraction and remains possessed until justice is done.

Part of the fault here—and we are talking about a basically effective characterization—is that Snow must sift everything through Lewis Eliot, and therefore the conflicts in others are smothered or only sketched in from the (disad)vantage of an observation post. Such a method worked well for James when the dramatic content of his novel took place in the growing awareness of his observer. Snow, however, does not work this way. His observer, Eliot, does not essentially grow, and accordingly there is little dramatic conflict implicit in his development. Dramatic tension is supposed to exist in those whom Eliot views, and yet the method tends to diminish this very tension. Consequently, we rarely know what really goes on in Skeffington; all we hear are his public pronouncements. Further, we rarely see or understand Howard himself, the center of the controversy. Every now and then, Eliot enters with a cryptic remark about this man whom he dislikes, such as: "One felt that, change his temperament by an inch, he would have made a good regimental officer." (p. 176) Here, for the sake of a point, Snow misses the nature of the communist sympathizer and falls into the trap of making easy generalizations. Such a comment about Howard is like the equally glib one that the non-believer is a believer turned around. Such statements do not create character so much as obviate it.

Snow falls into this same error again when he claims that extremes are linked: that Clark, the reactionary, and Skeffington, the defender of Howard, reach across to each other in a "curious accord." For the sake of symmetry, he simplifies patterns of behavior. More often than not, extremes despise each other, so dissimilar are they in basic attitudes. But such points are difficult to prove given Snow's development of character, for his technique suits the social novel, not the novel of characterization.

There is one more passage in which Snow's external view of character creates difficulty, when Eliot comments upon Clark's testimony before the court that character and opinion go hand in hand: that suspect opinions mean a suspect character. Eliot sums up: "Could the Court really give the faintest encouragement to the view that character and opinion went hand in hand? Wasn't this nonsense, and dangerous nonsense? Didn't we all know scientists—and I named one—whose opinions were indistinguishable from Howard's, and whose integrity was absolute?" (p. 329) What a simplification of human nature Eliot makes by separating character and opinion, and how irrelevant this argument really is! Of course, character and opinion go together, as much as form and content of a poem are inseparable. How does Eliot expect to disconnect them? Snow loads the dice by putting the attack against Howard in the words of Clark, who is him-

self an obnoxious creature; but Eliot cannot answer Clark
by dividing the human personality into water-tight com-
partments. What he means to indicate is that opinions
are relative to the individual and that Howard can be a
perfectly good scientist and College Fellow no matter
what his opinions. Opinions and character indeed go hand
in hand, but there is no indication that Howard is of bad
character *because of* his opinions. Logically, Eliot weakens
his argument by admitting that Howard's opinions are
reprehensible, for Eliot in several other places does not
find such ideas intolerable. However, Eliot's inability to
argue logically here is a natural outcome of Snow's
method, which does not probe into the individual: we
know so little of Howard's character that he may be quite
different from what everyone's opinion indicates.

These drawbacks are serious if the reader goes below the
surface of the novel. The point of view expressed here
narrows the range of the series. *The Conscience of the
Rich* showed a broadening of Snow's powers as a novelist,
for the people there reacted not to an abstract sense of
justice, but to conflict within themselves. Snow's novels
tend to be weakest when people react to something outside of themselves, strongest when they must come to
terms with the tortured man within. *The Masters* is a
powerful novel, albeit on a small scale and in a minor key,
because each character has to measure himself not against
issues but against what he is in relation to the issue. Whenever Snow must show characters who have lost this sense
of conflict with self, whenever he presents characters who
retain only their social functions, then he tends to present
cardboard characters who merely become symbols of their
functions.

Consequently, *The Affair*, number eight in the series of
eleven or so novels which will make up *Strangers and
Brothers*, adds little to the whole. It sets up no new terms
for the series. Even the moral decisions that remain to be
made have been faced in one way or another in the
earlier novels: decisions made by George Passant and
Charles March, for instance. *The Affair*, in fact, points

up the limitations of Snow's kind of novel. His attitude is akin to that of the naturalists who assume that behavior is composed of a stimulus and a corresponding effect, that a given environment generates a given behavior.

Snow is obviously closer to this group than to any other, but in his best work, as in the best work of naturalists like Zola, Bennett, and Galsworthy, he moved away from theory and let the human being within limitations determine his own course. Thus, we have a Charles March who must spite himself in many ways in order to survive, who must cut himself off from his ostensible roots in order to gain stability of a sort. Thus, reason is blocked off from its nourishment at nearly every turn and must constantly come to terms with certain inexplicables of character; in working out the conflict, Snow wrote what is perhaps the richest novel of the series. In the present novel, he provides a display of naked reason, almost completely cut off from the elements that would qualify it, and as a result wrote one of the weakest novels of the series, if nevertheless one of the most readable.

In this novel, the surface is all; the excitement the novel generates is the consequence of suspense, of courtroom drama. And yet even here, the defendant is so distant that the trial is devoid of human interest, becoming simply an exercise in justice. We feel suspense in *The Affair* not because Howard's case is compelling, but because we wish to see how Eliot can turn the pettiness of the Seniors into a reasonable verdict. We are more struck with the small-mindedness of these people than with their sense of justice. Their self-complacency, their feelings of rightcousness, their petty ambitions, their sniveling defenses—these are the elements of interest, and when Snow effectively seizes upon this side of them, he stresses what is of most significance in his mature work.

THE NOVEL AFTER SNOW

SNOW's work raises several interesting questions about the future direction of the English novel. F. R. Leavis's intemperate attack upon Snow in his farewell lecture at Downing College surely indicated, among other things, his fear that Snow might unduly influence the course of the novel. Leavis's remarks suggest that Snow, with his anti-Lawrentean emphasis upon reason and expedience, would drain both life and art of their imaginative content: that literature and science would somehow lose their sharp boundaries, to the detriment of literature and the advantage of science.

Leavis's fears are well grounded in part, although his attack often made the cause of the humanities seem more shrill and hysterical than need be. In his various comments upon the novel, Snow has, as we have seen, argued a conservative view of literature, picking out for particular attack the symbolists, the experimenters, the "irrationalists." If literature were to follow the course suggested by Snow, it would become an arm of social criticism; the "untruths" that literature should tell us would become transformed into social commentary. As soon as literature becomes involved directly with issues, it becomes newsworthy instead of creative. These points Snow has never fully admitted, for he argues for a literature along the lines of Chekhov, Tolstoy, and Dostoyevsky, while ignoring that the realism of the Russians would not be suitable for the American and English writer. With different experence, the Western writer must write differently, a contrast Snow tends to forget in his pursuit of common ground.

In politics, common ground is a good thing; in literature, it is impossible. In his vision of humanity in which all men are basically similar, regardless of their geography and history, Snow neglects the vast differences; and it is with differences, not similarities, that the serious novelist must concern himself. In Snow's very attempt to make strangers into brothers, we have an indication of his desire to cast aside distinctions in order to stress sameness.

In attacking the symbolists, Snow has a partially valid point, in that Symbolism, as practiced in the first third of this century, no longer seems practicable for the novel. It would, as Snow remarks, tend to lead fiction away from its larger social sense. Here there is no gainsaying Snow's anxiety about the novel. The quarrel arises when he presses for a kind of Naturalism which can deal directly with the issues of the day. In this area, Snow's position becomes dangerous. The best one can hope for in the novel of the future is that everyday events will not become too powerful for the novelist to resist. If he fails to withstand the temptation, then fiction will lose its imaginative thrust. An infusion of Symbolism into Naturalism would perhaps allow for social criticism on a large scale, without the descent into petty details that can frustrate a literary conception.

The novel needs some such merger, and in the best work of at least two of Snow's contemporaries, Iris Murdoch and William Golding, we do find attempts in this direction. What Snow himself has provided is an intelligent view of society, full of many mature judgments and an adult awareness of human nature. What he has failed to provide is the larger sense of the world in which details become symbolic of greater things, in which man not only is involved in doing his job or making an important decision, but is also concerned with the grander questions of his fate in a seemingly meaningless universe.

Chronology of Events in *Strangers and Brothers*

1905   (late summer or fall), Lewis Eliot born.

1921   Eliot takes the Senior Oxford.

1922   Eliot enrolls in the College of Art and Technology.

1924   Eliot first hears of Sheila Knight.

1925   Eliot falls in love with Sheila Knight.

1927   Eliot takes the final Bar examination in May, enters law chambers of Herbert Getliffe.

1929   Getliffe's shady business dealings, also Sir Philip March's.

1930   Eliot is stricken with what is diagnosed (falsely) as pernicious anemia.

1931   Eliot marries Sheila Knight. Katherine March marries Francis Getliffe. Charles March marries Ann Simon.

1933   Eliot is elected a Fellow of a Cambridge College with the aid of Francis Getliffe and Jago. George Passant's trial for fraud.

1936   (May), Leonard March is 70.

1937   (December 20), Crawford is elected Master of the Cambridge College where Eliot is a Fellow.

1939   Sheila Knight dies, a suicide. Martin Eliot marries Irene. Lewis Eliot enters government service.

1941   (September), Eliot meets Margaret Davidson.

1943   Roy Calvert dies.

1947   (late summer), Eliot and Margaret Davidson marry. George Passant is rejected for a permanent government position.

1952   Leonard March dies.

1953   Crawford is ready to retire as Master. Despard-Smith, Pilbrow, and Chrystal are dead.

1954   Eliot wins Howard's exoneration.

Chronology of Events in C. P. Snow's Life

1905   Charles Percy Snow born in Leicester, England, second of four sons.

1925   Entered University College, Leicester.

1927   Bachelor of Science, with First Class Honors in Chemistry.

1928   Master of Science in Physics. Awarded a Scholarship as a Research Student at Christ's College, Cambridge.

1930   Elected to a Fellowship at Christ's College.

1932   *Death Under Sail*, a detective story.

1933   *New Lives for Old*, a Wellsian science fantasy.

1934   *The Search*. Appointed Tutor of Christ's College.

1935   Idea for the series of novels that was to become, later, *Strangers and Brothers*.

1939   Asked by the Royal Society to assist in organizing university scientists for the war.

1940   *Strangers and Brothers*, first volume in the series of that name. Joined Ministry of Labor as a civil servant.

1942   Director of Technical Personnel in the Ministry of Labor.

1944   Personnel Advisor to the English Electric Company.

1945   Civil Service Commissioner.

1947   *The Light and the Dark*. Board of Directors of the English Electric Company.

1949   *Time of Hope*.

1950   Married Pamela Hansford Johnson, the novelist.

1951   *The Masters*.

1954   *The New Men*, winner of the James Tait Black Memorial Prize.

1956   *Homecoming(s)*.

1957   Knighted.

1958   *The Conscience of the Rich.*

1959   Rede Lecturer, Cambridge. *The Two Cultures and the Scientific Revolution.*

1960   *The Affair,* a Book-of-the-Month Club selection.

1961   *Science and Government* (the Godkin lecture at Harvard University, 1960). *Corridors of Power,* number nine in *Strangers and Brothers,* has been tentatively announced for spring, 1963, publication.

INDEX

CLEOPATRA'S DAUGHTER

FROM ROMAN PRISONER TO AFRICAN QUEEN

JANE DRAYCOTT

Liveright Publishing Corporation

A Division of W. W. Norton & Company
Celebrating a Century of Independent Publishing

B

Cleopatra Selene

For information about permission to reproduce selections from this book, write to Permissions, Liveright Publishing Corporation, a division of W. W. Norton & Company, Inc., 500 Fifth Avenue, New York, NY 10110

For information about special discounts for bulk purchases, please contact W. W. Norton Special Sales at specialsales@wwnorton.com or 800-233-4830

Manufacturing by Lakeside Book Company
Production manager: Louise Mattarelliano

Library of Congress Cataloging-in-Publication Data

Names: Draycott, Jane (Jane Louise), author.
Title: Cleopatra's daughter : from Roman prisoner
to African queen / Jane Draycott.
Description: First American edition 2023. | New York :
Liveright Publishing Corporation, 2023. | First published in the
UK in 2022 by Head of Zeus Ltd, part of Bloomsbury Publishing Plc
under the title Cleopatra's daughter: Egyptian princess, Roman prisoner,
African queen. | Includes bibliographical references and index.
Identifiers: LCCN 2023006613 | ISBN 9781324092599 (hardcover) |
ISBN 9781324092605 (epub)
Subjects: LCSH: Cleopatra, Queen, consort of Juba II,
King of Mauretania, 40 B.C.– | Mauretania (Kingdom)—
Kings and rulers—Biography. | Rome—History—Augustus,
30 B.C.–14 A.D.—Biography. | Cleopatra, Queen of Egypt, –30 B.C.—Family. |
Juba II, King of Mauretania, approximately 50 B.C.–approximately 24 A.D.
Classification: LCC DG59.M3 D73 2023 | DDC 932/.021092 [B] —dc23/
eng/20230307
LC record available at https://lccn.loc.gov/2023006613

Liveright Publishing Corporation, 500 Fifth Avenue, New York, N.Y. 10110
www.wwnorton.com

W. W. Norton & Company Ltd., 15 Carlisle Street, London W1D 3BS

1 2 3 4 5 6 7 8 9 0

32.50
5/23
DS

i 14629756

VG

For Amy, with thanks for the last seventeen years.
Here's to the next seventeen, and beyond!

CONTENTS

MAPS

THE ANCIENT MEDITERRANEAN IN THE MID-FIRST CENTURY BCE

Danube

MOESIA

Tomis

BLACK SEA

CASPIAN SEA

EDONIA

Byzantium

BITHYNIA-PONTUS

Amascia

ARMENIA

Ancyra

GALATIA

ASIA

Tigris

MESOPOTAMIA

PARTHIA

Ephesus

CILICIA

Antioch

Euphrates

HAEA

CRETE

RHODES

SYRIA

CYPRUS

NEAN SEA

JUDAEA

yrene

Alexandrla

ARABIA

EGYPT

RED SEA

KUSH

Meroe

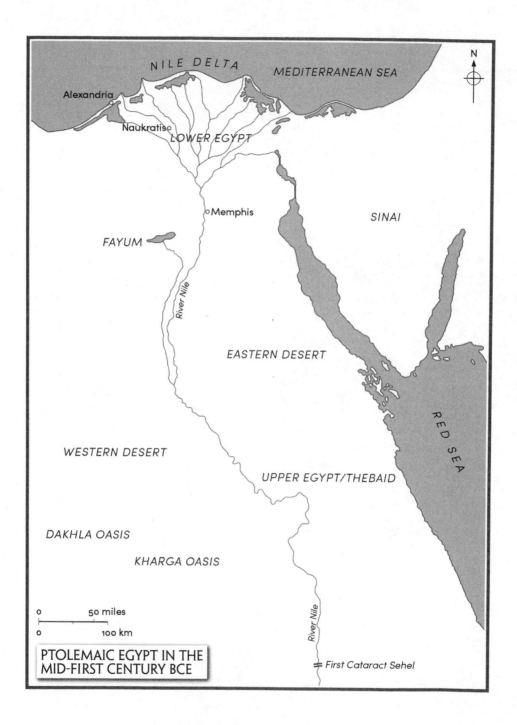

N

NILE DELTA

MEDITERRANEAN SEA

Alexandria

Naukratis

LOWER EGYPT

Memphis

FAYUM

SINAI

River Nile

EASTERN DESERT

WESTERN DESERT

RED SEA

UPPER EGYPT/THEBAID

DAKHLA OASIS

KHARGA OASIS

0   50 miles
0   100 km

River Nile

First Cataract Sehel

PTOLEMAIC EGYPT IN THE
MID-FIRST CENTURY BCE

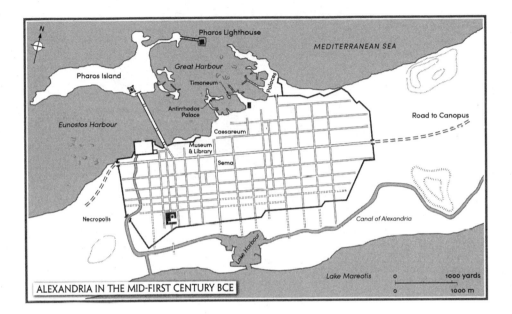

ALEXANDRIA IN THE MID-FIRST CENTURY BCE

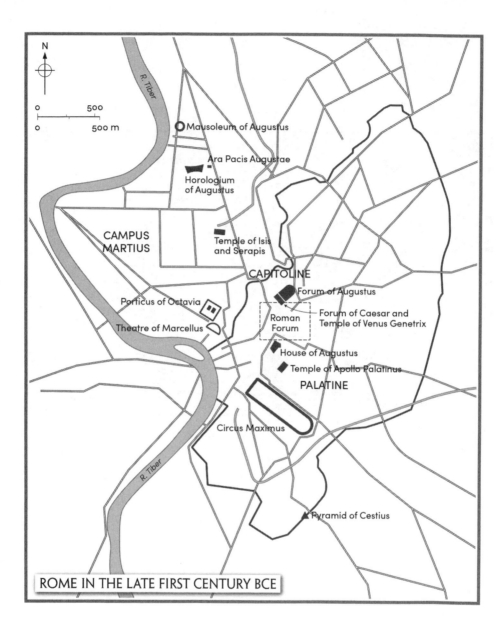

N

o ⊢━━━┥ 500
o ⊢━━━┥ 500 m

R. Tiber

○ Mausoleum of Augustus

Ara Pacis Augustae

Horologium
of Augustus

CAMPUS
MARTIUS

Temple of Isis
and Serapis

CAPITOLINE

Forum of Augustus

Porticus of Octavia

Roman
Forum

Forum of Caesar and
Temple of Venus Genetrix

Theatre of Marcellus

House of Augustus

Temple of Apollo Palatinus

PALATINE

Circus Maximus

R. Tiber

▲ Pyramid of Cestius

ROME IN THE LATE FIRST CENTURY BCE

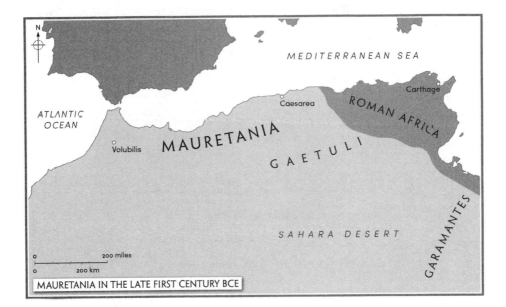

MEDITERRANEAN SEA

ATLANTIC
OCEAN

Carthage

Caesarea

ROMAN AFRICA

MAURETANIA

Volubilis

G A E T U L I

SAHARA DESERT

GARAMANTES

200 miles

200 km

MAURETANIA IN THE LATE FIRST CENTURY BCE

THE PTOLEMIES:
AN ABBREVIATED GENEALOGY

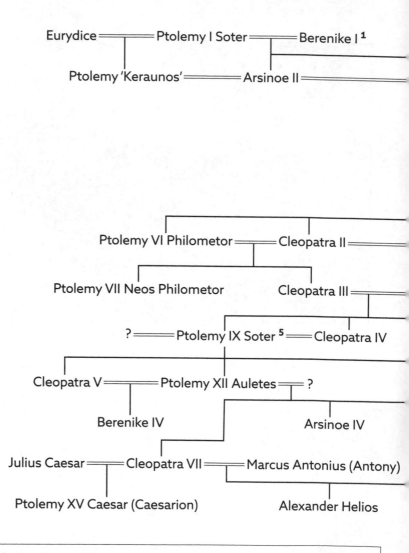

Eurydice ══════ Ptolemy I Soter ══════ Berenike I [1]

Ptolemy 'Keraunos' ══════ Arsinoe II ══════

Ptolemy VI Philometor ══════ Cleopatra II ══════

Ptolemy VII Neos Philometor   Cleopatra III ══════

? ══════ Ptolemy IX Soter [5] ══════ Cleopatra IV

Cleopatra V ══════ Ptolemy XII Auletes ══════ ?

Berenike IV   Arsinoe IV

Julius Caesar ══════ Cleopatra VII ══════ Marcus Antonius (Antony)

Ptolemy XV Caesar (Caesarion)   Alexander Helios

---

1 A Macedonian Greek noblewoman
2 Daughter of King Lysimachos of Thrace (Greece)
3 Daughter of the Greek King Magas I of Cyrene, the son of Berenike I
4 Daughter of the Greek King Antiochus III of Syria
5 It is possible that Ptolemy IX is actually the son of Ptolemy VIII and Cleopatra II
(see RdE 35. 1984:47–50)

══════ Married status

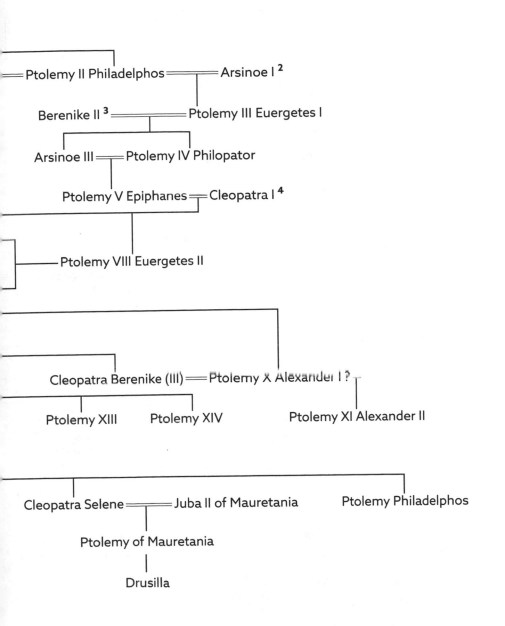

JULIO-CLAUDIAN FAMILY TREE

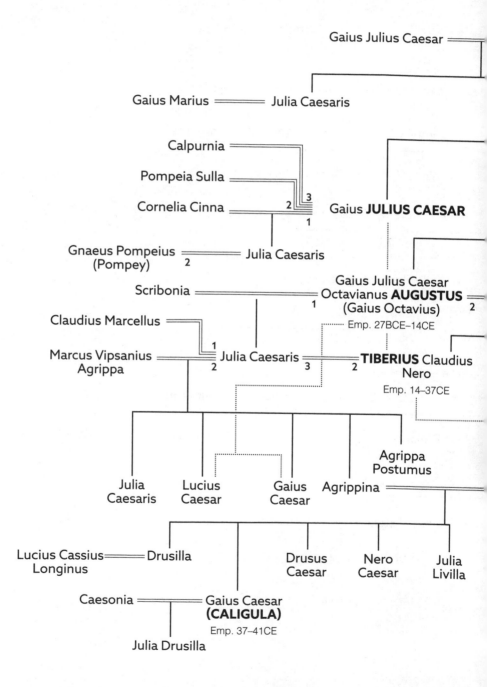

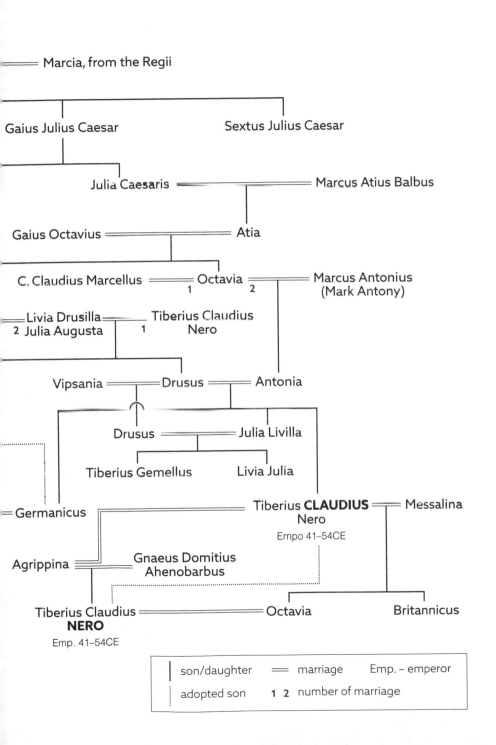

Marcia, from the Regii

Gaius Julius Caesar   Sextus Julius Caesar

Julia Caesaris ———————— Marcus Atius Balbus

Gaius Octavius ════════════ Atia

C. Claudius Marcellus ══ Octavia ══ Marcus Antonius
                        1   2   (Mark Antony)

Livia Drusilla —————— Tiberius Claudius
2 Julia Augusta   1   Nero

Vipsania ════════ Drusus ════ Antonia

Drusus ════════════ Julia Livilla

Tiberius Gemellus   Livia Julia

Germanicus   Tiberius **CLAUDIUS** ══ Messalina
                                      Nero
                              Empo 41–54CE

Agrippina ══ Gnaeus Domitius
             Ahenobarbus

Tiberius Claudius ════════════ Octavia   Britannicus
    NERO
Emp. 41–54CE

| son/daughter | ══ marriage | Emp. – emperor |
| adopted son | **1 2** number of marriage | |

FOREWORD

How does one dare to attempt to write a biography of any ancient historical figure, let alone an ancient woman? Unlike their medieval and modern counterparts, in the vast majority of cases ancient historians have no letters, certainly no diaries, and only very rarely the historical figure's own words, recorded verbatim, to rely on as source material. The literary, documentary, archaeological and even bioarchaeological evidence that one might attempt to use as source material is highly suspect. It is buried deep under thousands of years of chauvinism, sexism and even outright misogyny, and broad-brush stereotypes based on ideas about what women should or should not be, and what they should or should not do, not on detailed information about how they actually were or what they actually did.[1]

How well known is it today, for example, that many ancient women wrote works of literature, across all genres, that were extremely well received in classical antiquity? Starting with the most high-profile, the poet Sappho in the late seventh century BCE, but certainly not stopping there, we have evidence of around one hundred women writing and disseminating works written in Greek and Latin. There were surely many more, working in the numerous other languages in use around the ancient Mediterranean world, whose work unfortunately has not survived, or at least has not survived via manuscript transmission.[2] For at about the same time that Sappho was composing her poetry in Greek, an otherwise unknown woman named Asi Akarai was composing her own poetry in honour of the goddess Aphrodite in Etruscan, then engraving it onto an *aryballos*, a type of vase normally used to hold oils and perfumes.[3] Had archaeologists not recovered the *aryballos* from Caere (modern Cerveteri) in Italy, we would know nothing whatsoever about her literary endeavours. A fresco known affectionately as the 'Sappho' fresco dates from around 50 CE and was discovered in the Insula Occidentalis at Pompeii. Its depiction of a beautifully dressed woman, positively dripping in gold jewellery, chewing on a stylus as she composes her thoughts before preparing to write them down on her wax tablet, suggests that many ancient women were literate, and, just like men, used their literacy in creative ways, composing works of both poetry and prose, in addition to undertaking the types of writing required of them in their daily lives such as letters and household or business accounting.[4]

Nor is it widely known that ancient women produced magnificent works of art across all media. Another fresco, dating from around the same time but discovered in a different location, the House of the Surgeon, at Pompeii, depicts a woman painting a portrait while her peers look on in fascination. It indicates that women living at the time were artistically inclined, not just in private but also in public, and that some even worked as professional artisans.[5] Their work was exhibited in some of the most prestigious institutions in the ancient Mediterranean. According to the ancient Roman encyclopedist Pliny the Elder, from whom we know a considerable amount about famous ancient artists and their notable artworks, a panel painting of the goddess Artemis by the fifth-century BCE Athenian artist Timarete was displayed in Ephesus; a painting of a girl by another ancient Greek artist, Eirene, could be seen at

Eleusis; while a portrait of an elderly woman, plus a self-portrait – painted with the aid of a mirror – by the first-century BCE Roman artist Iaia of Cyzicus were exhibited in Naples.[6] While much of the fine work created by ancient women artists has been lost to the ravages of time, some of the more utilitarian work such as pottery has survived, complete with these women's palmprints and fingerprints set into the clay.[7]

The type of ancient women about whom someone might actually want to attempt to write a biography, or be interested in reading a biography about, are particularly difficult to come face to face with. Successful women – that is, women who were considered successful in the eyes of their male peers – are virtually invisible in the ancient historical record because, if all went to plan, and they discharged their duties appropriately, there was no need for anyone to mention them. Cleopatra Selene, who as an Egyptian princess, a Roman prisoner, and finally an African queen, lived her entire life in the public eye, is one such figure who is both visible and invisible. I knew, then, that when I embarked upon this adventure of writing the first modern biography of her, it was going to be a challenge.[8]

So, in addition to the literary, documentary, archaeological and bioarchaeological evidence that one might expect an ancient historian and archaeologist such as myself to use, I have also included a lot of contextual information in an attempt to fill in the inevitable gaps. This comparable material, sourced from the lives of other significant Hellenistic, Roman and Egyptian women, is reliable and it enables a qualified reconstruction of Cleopatra Selene's life as something more than just a glorified timeline.

I began researching Cleopatra Selene in 2009 as a PhD student at the University of Nottingham and started working on this biography in 2018 as a lecturer in Ancient History at the University of Glasgow. I had no idea then that current events would catch up with me to the extent that they have. It is only in the last couple of years that a sustained campaign of intimidation orchestrated and executed by members of the British media has driven the first biracial member of the royal family to leave not only the institution but also the United Kingdom; and that the Black Lives Matter movement has gained sufficient momentum as to cause the world to begin to reflect in earnest on its history and the actual rather than perceived place of Africa and people of African descent within that history.[9] And so, events transpired that made me even more certain that this biography was a project worth undertaking, and that Cleopatra Selene is an historical figure who should be much better known, particularly by young women of colour who look for someone they can personally identify and engage with in the historical record.[10] She will undoubtedly never reach the heights of fame, and infamy, and sheer name recognition of her mother, Cleopatra VII, but perhaps that is a good thing, as she can instead be judged on her own merits as an individual rather than as an idea or an archetype. And an individual with a trajectory like Cleopatra Selene's – who was born a princess of one of the most ancient kingdoms in the classical world, only to lose her entire family, her birthright and her rank and become a Roman prisoner, and succeed in being crowned queen of an entirely different and brand-new kingdom and rule it successfully for two decades – must have had merit indeed. What follows is her story.

INTRODUCTION

O NE DAY IN 1895 archaeologists were excavating at the site of what they had designated the Villa della Pisanella at Boscoreale, just outside Pompeii. It was one of many buildings around the Bay of Naples that had been buried under layers of ash and pumice in the wake of the eruption of Vesuvius on 24 August 79 CE.[1] The villa, a type known as a *villa rustica*, 'country villa', was a lavish but primarily agricultural establishment. As well as its luxurious living area, complete with a bathhouse that spread across two storeys, its rooms were decorated with fine frescos of which a few fragments such as one depicting an opulently dressed woman presenting fruit have been recovered. It also had facilities for producing wine and olive oil, a bakery and stables.[2] The villa was reburied once the excavations were complete and there is little sign of it today (the modern Via Settetermini actually cuts across the north-west corner of the site), but should you wish to get a sense of what life was like here prior to the eruption, items recovered during the excavation can be viewed in a range of museums including the Antiquarium of Boscoreale, the National Archaeological Museum of Naples, the Louvre and the British Museum.

Archaeologists were investigating the wine-pressing room when they made an incredible discovery. They had already come across the remains of two men and a woman, the woman having died as she covered her mouth with a cloth in a vain attempt to protect herself from the ashes in the air. But then they unearthed a trapdoor leading to a cistern underneath the floor. When they climbed down into the cistern, they found an additional set of remains, those of a man who had apparently died while desperately trying to find a place to hide. However, his physical remains were not all they found. He was lying on top of a selection of gold jewellery, including a ring, a necklace, a pair of earrings and some bracelets, and he was clutching a leather bag containing over one thousand gold coins – to date, one of the largest sums ever found in the Vesuvian region. And just beyond him, in a wider part of the cistern, was a vast hoard of more than one hundred pieces of silverware.

Scholars are divided over whether the man was a faithful retainer entrusted with the task of hiding and guarding his mistress's treasure – many of the pieces of silverware were engraved with the name 'Maxima' – or whether there is a more sinister explanation for his presence. Was he perhaps a thief, in the process of looting the villa after most of its occupants had either departed or died? Whatever his motivation, the hoard he was found with is spectacular. The Romans would have referred to this collection as a *ministerium*, a set of tableware comprising both *argentum escarium*, silver for eating, and *argentum potorium*, silver for drinking. It is one of the most important and prestigious sets of silverware surviving from the early imperial period, although some of the individual pieces date back almost four hundred years before then. Many were clearly already antiques and would have been family heirlooms. Of the 109 items, a significant number are particularly notable for their originality and quality. These are famous examples of Roman silversmithing, fit to grace the pages of glossy compendia of ancient art. Among them is a large, partially gilded, silver dish, currently on display in the Louvre.[3]

In the centre of the bowl of the dish is a bust of a female figure depicted in high relief. The technique used, known as repoussé, involved hammering the back of the dish to make the figure protrude, before engraving and gilding the fine details. She is a mature woman with thick, curly hair, deep-set eyes, a slightly hooked nose and a strong jaw. The imperfect and realistic nature of these facial features indicates that the subject was most likely a real person rather than a goddess or a personification. In the latter case, her features would have been portrayed in a more generic and idealised way, as we see on many thousands of familiar classical artefacts in museums around the world. The specific facial features depicted here suggest that this is a portrait of a particular woman, and that she was intended to be recognised as such by the people who would see the dish displayed on a sideboard in the *triclinium*, the dining room, during banquets.[4]

The woman is wearing an elephant's scalp headdress. In her right hand she holds an asp; in her left a cornucopia, the horn of plenty. The cornucopia is engraved with an image of the sun god Helios as a young man, accompanied by the two stars and pointed helmets that are commonly used to represent the twin gods Castor and Pollux, the Dioscuri. Mounted on top of the cornucopia is a crescent moon. At the woman's shoulder is a lion. Arranged below her is a series of religious and mythological symbols: the quiver and club of Hercules; the *sistrum*, or ceremonial rattle, of the Egyptian goddess Isis; the dolphin of Poseidon; the tongs of Hephaistos; the staff of Asklepios; the sword of Ares and the lyre of Apollo.

How might we interpret this surfeit of symbolism? I remember being immediately transfixed and fascinated by this dish the first time I saw it photographed in close-up in a glossy coffee-table book on ancient art. I have tried several times to see it in the flesh, so to speak, but on two separate trips to the Louvre in 2019 I was doomed to disappointment, as, despite the museum's website telling me that the Boscoreale treasure was on display in

Room 662 of the Sully Wing, it was not. On the first of these occasions, I had missed it by a matter of days! *C'est la vie.* Perhaps I shall meet with success on a future trip, third time lucky. In any case, I would go on to devote my first substantial academic journal article to trying to decode its meaning.[5] The fact that the woman is depicted in conjunction with so many political, religious and mythological symbols has led to much debate regarding her identity.[6] Suggestions have included Cleopatra VII, Queen of Egypt, even though the portrait does not resemble other images of her that have survived from antiquity. As explained above, the style seems too realistic for her to be a personification of Africa, the other most common suggestion. Then, in 1983, almost one hundred years after the dish was first discovered, a new interpretation was proposed. A German archaeologist, Andreas Linfert, suggested that this woman is Cleopatra Selene, the daughter of Cleopatra VII and Marcus Antonius, Roman general and triumvir.[7]

Cleopatra Selene was one of three children that Cleopatra and Antony had together; the others were her fraternal twin, Alexander Helios, and their younger brother, Ptolemy Philadelphos. Cleopatra and Antony have, of course, been immortalised in history and popular culture, and Cleopatra's eldest child Ptolemy Caesar, better known as Caesarion, whose father was Gaius Julius Caesar, is a relatively well-known historical figure. However, the three younger children have been all but forgotten. After their parents committed suicide in quick succession, Caesarion was executed at the age of seventeen by Octavian, soon to become the first Roman emperor Augustus. As Caesar's biological son – Octavian himself was merely an adopted son, and a posthumously adopted son at that – he represented too much of a threat to be left alive.[8] The others were taken to Rome and raised in the household of their father's wife (who was also Octavian's elder sister), Octavia. Alexander Helios and Ptolemy Philadelphos vanish entirely from the historical record shortly after their arrival in Rome, so the fact that they have been forgotten is perhaps understandable. While it was once thought that Octavian had them murdered, today it is assumed that they simply perished, like so many others, as a result of childhood illnesses.[9] Cleopatra Selene, however, does not vanish; quite the opposite, in fact. She not only survived her captivity in Rome, but she also seems to have thrived. At the age of fifteen, she married fellow royal African exile Gaius Julius Juba, more commonly known as Juba, the only surviving son of the deceased King Juba I of Numidia, who would go on to become King Juba II of Mauretania. Upon his ascension, she became Queen of Mauretania, and would rule there alongside her husband for the rest of her life.

Cleopatra Selene is an extremely plausible candidate for the subject of the silver dish from Boscoreale. As Queen of Mauretania, a Roman client kingdom that comprised much of modern Algeria and Morocco, the elephant's scalp headdress is entirely appropriate. Many ancient rulers of the parts of Africa and India where elephants lived chose to depict themselves wearing such headdresses. Alexander the Great, one of Cleopatra Selene's most famous ancestors, was depicted in this guise by his companion Ptolemy I Soter, the founder of the Ptolemaic dynasty, and Ptolemy subsequently depicted himself in the same manner.[10] Additionally, female members of the Ptolemaic dynasty were subsequently depicted wearing it on intaglios and seal impressions.[11] The Romans had particularly associated elephants with North Africa ever since the Carthaginian general Hannibal Barca had used them to cross the Alps during the Second Punic War in 218 BCE, and after which various other North African royal families followed suit in using these animals for military purposes. It may be no coincidence that the elephant's raised trunk here resembles the rearing cobra of the uraeus, often found incorporated into the headdresses gracing the brow of Egyptian monarchs.

The asp here not only reflects the means by which Cleopatra Selene's mother supposedly took her own life, but it is also the symbol of the Egyptian goddess Isis, with whom Cleopatra VII had always associated herself, even going so far as to declare herself the 'New Isis'. Furthermore, the crescent moon atop the cornucopia can be seen as a reference to her name, Selene, as she was named after the Greek goddess of the moon, while the images engraved on the cornucopia may refer to her brother Alexander Helios and the fact that, like the Dioscuri, they were twins. The lion, another symbol commonly associated with Africa, was also frequently employed by Juba II, Cleopatra Selene's husband.

Regarding the religious and mythological symbols that are arranged below the woman, the quiver and club of Hercules could allude to the fact that Antony claimed descent from one of the hero's sons, Anton – indeed, it was from this Anton that the family name supposedly derived. It was common for elite Roman families to claim divine ancestry and incorporate references to this into their material culture, such as the family trees painted on the walls in the *atria* of their houses. The *sistrum* is a reference to Isis, the goddess of whom the Egyptians believed Cleopatra VII to be an incarnation; Cleopatra was frequently depicted as Isis in works of art. Other elements of the iconography refer to Cleopatra Selene's patron, Octavian. The dolphin of Poseidon came to be associated with the Battle of Actium in 31 BCE, during which Octavian decisively defeated Cleopatra and Antony's navy, while the lyre of Apollo could be a reference to Octavian himself. He claimed Apollo as his patron deity, even building a temple to the god adjacent to his house on the Palatine Hill in Rome that was dedicated on 9 October 28 BCE, and featured motifs showing the struggle between Apollo, his patron, and Hercules, Antony's patron, over the Delphian Tripod.

If the silver dish from Boscoreale was intended to depict Cleopatra Selene, it was most likely commissioned by someone who not only wished to honour the woman herself, but also to recognise her Ptolemaic ancestry and pay tribute to her rule of Mauretania. Significantly, they also included references to the Roman imperial family, perhaps recognising her to be part of this, too, both through her descent from Antony and the years she spent in the household of Octavia.

Cleopatra Selene was raised alongside the emperor Tiberius, and was related by blood to the emperors Caligula, Claudius and Nero (ultimately her great-nephew Caligula would go on to execute her son Ptolemy, his first cousin once removed). The iconography of the dish is overwhelmingly positive, even celebratory. As such, it represents a departure from the generally negative and derogatory attitudes towards Egypt, the Ptolemaic dynasty and Cleopatra VII in particular that were prevalent in Rome at this time, and has more in common with the more positive ones found in the eastern Mediterranean in places such as Achaea, Cyprus and Syria. It was perhaps commissioned and produced in the wake of Cleopatra Selene's death in 5 BCE, by someone who wished to honour her and celebrate her relatively short but extremely eventful life. The family that owned the silverware does seem likely to have been connected to the imperial family, as one of its sets of salt dishes, also found at Boscoreale, was engraved with the name of the freedman Pamphilius, who was manumitted by Octavian at some point between 44 and 27 BCE (after manumission, freedmen and freedwomen often retained close links with their former masters and mistresses). One or more of the family members may have known Cleopatra Selene personally, perhaps encountering her during her time in Rome in the years between 30 and 25 BCE. Other items in the hoard feature laudatory portraits of the emperors Augustus and Tiberius, as well as Tiberius' brother Drusus, a successful general who died prematurely. Many of the pieces had seen better days. Perhaps they were keepsakes commemorating personal connections, which might explain why they were cherished for so long rather than being melted down so that the silver could be reused.

Discovering the dish led me to wonder if there were any other portraits of Cleopatra Selene lurking in public or private collections that I had previously overlooked in favour of the more prominently displayed and more frequently published portraits of mainstream ancient historical figures. I started to search. Sure enough, once I started looking, I found that a similar item was sold at auction in an antiquities sale in December 2011 at Christie's for just over two and a half million dollars. This unfortunately unprovenanced gilt and silver emblema would perhaps also have been set into a serving dish, and dates from between the late first century BCE and the early first century CE. Created from a single sheet of silver, this figure was sculpted in high relief, and again depicts a woman in an elephant's scalp headdress. She is wearing a standard female costume of the time, comprising a *chiton*, a draped and fastened tunic, with a *himation*, a mantle, on top. This figure has a scorpion on her right shoulder, a cobra on her left and a lion and lioness in the centre of her chest. A selection of fruit and wheat lies between them. This collection of symbols is simpler than that on the silver dish from Boscoreale. The figure could be interpreted as a personification of Africa, with the scorpion, snake, lion and lioness indicating the region's wildlife, and the fruits and wheat its agricultural produce. Yet once again there is an issue with such an explanation. We see a realistically rather than idealistically depicted mature woman with thick, curly hair, deep-set eyes, a long and slightly hooked nose, a small mouth with a rather full bottom lip and a prominent chin set in a strong jaw. Could this emblema be another representation of Cleopatra Selene in her guise as an African queen? Was this also intended to take pride of place in a wealthy family's collection of silverware? Perhaps. Unfortunately, we know too little about this artefact to do more than acknowledge this possibility. But if it is Cleopatra Selene, it could indicate that she may have had something of a following during her life and in the years immediately after her death. If so, these followers – perhaps her family's former subjects, disaffected members of the Alexandrian elite, or even religious devotees who worshipped her as the 'New Selene' just as they had worshipped her mother as the 'New Isis' – were dedicated, not to mention affluent, enough to commemorate her in such an elaborate manner.

There were strong links between the city of Rome and the Bay of Naples in antiquity and many elite Romans possessed country estates in the area. It is not surprising that these wealthy families might have chosen to honour the imperial family and their entourage in this way, just as people today might purchase memorabilia commemorating events in the lives of members of the British royal family. The Roman imperial family were the celebrity influencers of their day, setting empire-wide trends in hairstyles, beauty regimes and even medical treatments.[12]

Despite Cleopatra VII's rather ignominious end, she continued to be a source of fascination for the Romans, and over the following decades she appeared in histories and biographies, in poetry, and in works of art, both public and private. Some of these cherished her memory, while others ridiculed it, often by focusing squarely on her sex life. It seems likely that at least some of this fascination would have transferred to her daughter, not least because she also had her own claim to fame due to her proximity to the imperial family, now popularly known as the Julio-Claudian dynasty.

Cleopatra Selene's life included a series of reversals in fortune more dramatic than even her mother's. She was a princess who became a prisoner; a prisoner who became a queen; an Egyptian who became Roman; and a woman who became a powerful ruler in her own right at a time when women were officially politically marginalised throughout the Roman Empire. The more I learned about her, the more this trajectory fascinated and inspired me, and I realised that, as well as providing a new perspective on the legend of her famous (and infamous) parents, her story could also offer new insights into a range of other subjects with very contemporary resonances, such as the lives of ancient women, and of what we would today refer to as Black, Asian and minority ethnic individuals, or people of colour, living during the time of the Roman Empire. Her life story shines new light on the conflict between the politics, culture and history of Rome and Egypt, as well as the relationship between Rome and one of its most significant allied kingdoms (and the only one in Africa), Mauretania.

Cleopatra Selene's story also offers us a glimpse into an alternative Roman Empire, where women could be empowered and influential. It contradicts the overarching narrative created by ancient male historiographers – and perpetuated by generations of predominantly male scholars since – in which women did nothing of much significance but, rather, tended to stay indoors where they probably spent all their time weaving.[13] Cleopatra Selene was an Egyptian princess who was declared Queen of Crete and Cyrenaica (the eastern littoral of modern Libya) when she was just six years old. She was raised in the expectation of following in her mother's footsteps and one day being Queen of Egypt, reigning alongside her elder brother Caesarion in the Egyptian style, as both his sister and his wife.

While the debate regarding Cleopatra VII's ethnicity rages on with no sign of scholars ever reaching a definitive conclusion, we can potentially consider Cleopatra Selene, with her Graeco-Egyptian and Roman heritages, as having been multiracial. More pertinently still, since her husband was originally from North Africa, it is indisputable that her children were of mixed heritage, or biracial, as we would understand the term today. The Roman Empire, the imperial family and the social elite in particular were considerably more ethnically diverse than they are often assumed to have been. Cleopatra Selene's Greek, Roman and Egyptian heritages would each have profoundly influenced her life and her identity. These influences are clearly visible in the literary, documentary and archaeological records and they can be of considerable use to us as we embark upon our quest to reconstruct Cleopatra Selene's life.

Admittedly, for an ancient historian and archaeologist like myself, the trouble with attempting to reconstruct the life of any woman from the ancient world is that most writers of the surviving literary sources, particularly the 'canonical' ones, were men who, perhaps unsurprisingly, were mainly interested in writing about other men. Generally speaking, when these writers do refer to women it is either because those women were, in their opinions, paragons of virtue (such as Octavia) or the opposite (such as Cleopatra VII). They tend to write about women in order to make a point about the men in their lives, rather than out of any interest in them as individuals. So Octavia is written about in relation to Octavian or Antony, and Cleopatra VII is written about in relation to Caesar or Antony. For the most part, when we hear about Cleopatra Selene from these writers, the references are short and to the point, and tend to be more concerned with her father, her husband, or her son. By far the most information about her comes from the *Antony*, Plutarch's biography of her father, an instalment in his sequence of parallel lives of famous Greeks and Romans written as tools to instruct the reader about morality. There are other references in histories of the period of the Late Republic and Early Principate, but they are few and far between.

More illuminating are sources from other literary genres such as poetry. Works like this can give us an indication of how Cleopatra Selene was seen by her peers as well as a degree of insight into her personality. Her marriage to Juba and her untimely death are both commemorated in epigrams by the court poet Crinagoras of Mytilene, and there are other epigrams that may well refer to her.[14] Unfortunately, though, Cleopatra is an unhelpfully common name. One such epigram discusses the commissioning of a ring made of amethyst, which was thought to ward off drunkenness. While we cannot be sure that this refers to Cleopatra Selene, when taken in conjunction with her desire to avoid sharing her parents' bibulous reputation and her fondness for engraved gems it is certainly suggestive. Fortunately, her husband, Juba, was a prolific scholar and polymath, and much of his writing survives. It is often possible to identify Cleopatra Selene's influence in these, such as in his descriptions of Cleopatra VII and his investigation into the source of the Nile. He seems suspiciously well informed about a woman he had met only rarely, if at all, and a land he had never visited in person, and it is far from unusual for a writer to make use of their spouse's superior expertise.

Much more useful and informative, in my opinion, are documentary sources such as inscriptions on stone and archaeological sources such as coinage that I have found, particularly those which Cleopatra Selene was directly responsible for commissioning. Honorific and commemorative inscriptions can help us fill in the gaps for periods when Cleopatra Selene is otherwise missing from the historical record and give us insights into what she was up to. For example, many funerary inscriptions have been recovered from the site of her and Juba's capital city, Iol Caesarea, modern-day Cherchell in Algeria. These commemorate members of her court who had also been in Antony's, indicating that she had inherited (or been permitted by Octavian to inherit) her father's household.

In the two decades that I have been studying the ancient world, I have looked at a lot of ancient coins, and I have never seen anything like the coinage that Cleopatra Selene designed, commissioned and issued during her reign. It is strikingly innovative, using a unique fusion of Greek and Egyptian text and images. At the University of Glasgow, the Hunterian Coin Cabinet has a wonderful selection of these coins that I have been lucky enough to hold and examine up close. Not only are they beautifully crafted miniature works of

A coin depicting Juba with the Latin legend REX IUBA on the obverse face, and the *sistrum* of Isis and the Greek legend BASILISSA KLEOPATRA on the reverse face.

art, but they are also highly informative about their commissioners and designers. Whereas Juba uses Latin text ('REX IUBA' – King Juba) and a fairly standard royal portrait, Cleopatra Selene always uses Greek text ('BASILISSA KLEOPATRA' – Queen Cleopatra), accompanied sometimes by a royal portrait and others by a variety of symbolic imagery, including the sun and the moon, the *sistrum* of Isis, the royal crown of Egypt, and the occasional crocodile.[15]

Many surviving works of art from the early imperial period tend towards the generic. The portraits of Juba and their son Ptolemy on display in the Louvre, for example, are very much in keeping with the standards set by Augustus in his official portraiture. Conversely, those suggested to be of Cleopatra Selene are rather more interesting and informative, as we can see in the public marble sculptures that have survived from Mauretania, and the private portraits produced in precious metals that have survived from other places around the Roman Empire, such as the one in silver from Boscoreale and the emblema in silver and gilt discussed above. These tantalisingly human glimpses of Cleopatra Selene inevitably raise questions about her day-to-day life, and I have sought out these artefacts and examined them to find the answers.

Recent archaeological surveys have brought to light a huge amount of information about life in the Royal Quarter of Alexandria in the mid-first century BCE. And in Rome, the imperial family's houses on the Palatine Hill, and outside the city, have been excavated and found to be well preserved and richly decorated with frescos and mosaics. Other architectural remains attest to the Romans' enthusiasm for Egyptian culture at the time. There are temples dedicated to Egyptian deities like Isis, and obelisks transplanted all the way from Egypt, many of which are still standing in Rome today. All of this can give us a sense of the places where she lived. Finally, buildings and monuments built by Cleopatra Selene during her reign can be found in Cherchell and other sites in Algeria and Morocco. I have travelled to most of these places, breathed the air and retraced her steps, to try and imagine what she would have seen and experienced in these locations.

Cleopatra Selene succeeded where her mother and other allied queens – such as Cartimandua of the Brigantes and Boudicca of the Iceni in Roman Britain – failed. Cartimandua ruled the Brigantes tribe based in what is now northern England from around 43 to 69 CE. She sided with the Roman Empire and ruled with its interests in mind – surrendering the rebel Caratacus, King of the Catuvellauni tribe, to the Romans in chains – but was overthrown by her subjects and exiled.[16] Boudicca ruled the Iceni tribe based in what is now East Anglia. She was ambivalent about Rome at best, even before her lands were seized, her daughters were raped and she was flogged by Roman soldiers, which motivated her to lead a revolt against the Roman occupation. She was eventually defeated by the Romans in around 61 CE and forced to commit suicide.[17] Cleopatra Selene on the other hand, from an extremely young age, successfully wielded power over a large, influential and prosperous allied kingdom during a period when women were marginalised in most areas of life and monarchic rule was regarded with suspicion and unease. Considering that she came to Rome as the illegitimate daughter of a man declared a public enemy and a woman deemed his rapacious paramour, this was an immense achievement. How did she manage it? Perhaps she inherited her mother's considerable personal charm as well as her intelligence. These abilities, combined with her unique position at the intersection of three ancient cultures, allowed her to adapt to the rapidly changing circumstances of her eventful life, and to thrive where others may have struggled. I believe this makes her simultaneously an historical and a contemporary role model, one who we can learn from and be inspired by in equal measure.

1

Alexandria:
Cleopatra Selene's Birthplace

I F WE ARE TO understand Cleopatra Selene, we must first
understand where she came from. Many of the things that
she did in her adult life as Queen of Mauretania were rooted
in her desire both to live up to a family legacy dating back three
hundred years and to ensure that that family continued, albeit in a
slightly different form. This legacy, and the sense of responsibility
that came with it, was a weighty one indeed. The founder of the
Ptolemaic dynasty, Ptolemy son of Lagos (hence another name
by which the family was sometimes referred to in antiquity: the
Lagids, or the Lagidae), later known as Ptolemy I Soter, came to
power in Egypt in 323 BCE after the death of Alexander the Great,
King of Macedonia, who had seized the kingdom from the
Achaemenid Persians in 332 BCE. Though he died nine years later,
Ptolemy Soter's direct descendants ruled with varying degrees of
success and competence for the next three centuries.

Thanks to the strenuous efforts of Ptolemy I Soter (367–283
BCE) and his immediate successors, the Ptolemaic Empire was
at its height over the course of the third century BCE, during the
reigns of Ptolemy II Philadelphos (285–246 BCE) and Ptolemy
III Euergetes (246–222 BCE). It comprised not just Egypt but

also parts of modern-day Libya, Israel, Jordan, Lebanon, Syria and Cyprus, as well as numerous overseas territories in modern-day Turkey, Thrace and the Peloponnese in Greece. This pre-eminence would not last, however, and over the course of the second century BCE the Ptolemaic kingdom was whittled away by its neighbours, the Antigonids of Macedon and the Seleucids of Syria, and the rising Roman Empire. Indeed, in time all these successor kingdoms would fall victim to Rome, until, by the reign of Cleopatra VII, only Egypt would be left. As a result of her father Ptolemy XII Auletes's previous dealings with Rome, Cleopatra would find herself forced to cultivate good relationships with a series of influential Romans.[1]

Macedonian women (such as Alexander the Great's mother Olympias (375–316 BCE), who worked hard to ensure the succession of her son and, after his death, her infant grandson) seem to have been much more visible and influential than their Athenian counterparts, the Classical Greek women about whom we have the most ancient surviving evidence. The female members of the Ptolemaic dynasty certainly continued in this vein. These trailblazing women include Arsinoe II (316–270 BCE), who instituted brother-sister marriage as a defining feature of the dynasty, acted as co-ruler alongside her brother-husband, and was deified upon her death; and Cleopatra Syra (205–176 BCE), who married into the Ptolemaic dynasty from the neighbouring Seleucid dynasty, a vast territory comprising modern-day Turkey, Syria, Iraq, Iran, Jordan and Israel. Cleopatra Syra served as regent for her young son Ptolemy VI, and so became the first Ptolemaic queen to rule without her husband. And there was also the first Cleopatra Selene, who ruled Egypt alongside two of her brothers in succession. She then left Egypt to marry into the Seleucid dynasty and became queen consort to Antiochus VIII of Syria, later queen regnant, ruling in conjunction with her son Antiochus XIII.[2] These powerful women established a template for female rule in the

Hellenistic and Roman periods that Cleopatra VII would follow and that Cleopatra Selene, in turn, would adapt as Queen of Mauretania. They demonstrated how queens – whether regnant, regent, or consort – could wield considerable power politically, militarily and culturally over extended periods of time.

The power, influence and sheer importance of the women of the Ptolemaic dynasty is made clear in a mosaic from Thmuis, a city in Lower Egypt, created by the artisan Sophilos in around 200 BCE (the Greek text in the top left corner says 'Sophilos made this'; clearly, he was proud of his artistic achievement and wished to advertise that fact), that is now housed in the Graeco-Roman Museum in Alexandria.[3] Probably based on a painting, its emblema is thought to depict Berenike II, the wife of Ptolemy III, in the guise of the personification of Alexandria. This queen's headdress is in the form of the prow of a ship with sea creatures painted on the sides, her red, purple and gold robes are gathered at the collar with a brooch in the shape of an anchor, and she carries the flagstaff of a ship festooned with ribbons, all symbolising Egypt's naval prowess during her and her husband's joint reign.

Alexandria was the political capital of Egypt while Memphis was its religious and administrative capital (Ptolemy I Soter had actually transferred the seat of government from Memphis to Alexandria). This complementarity was widely recognised in antiquity and we can see it visualised in a Byzantine mosaic from the Church of Saints Peter and Paul in the ancient city of Gerasa (modern Jerash in northern Jordan) that illustrates them side by side.[4]

Alexandria, the city in which Cleopatra Selene was born and spent the first decade of her life, was founded by Alexander the Great on 7 April 331 BCE, after the poet Homer appeared to him in a dream and inspired him to do so, although he did not live to see it completed.[5] In classical antiquity, its Egyptian name was, amusingly, 'Building Site', while its official Graeco-Roman name was 'Alexandria Next To Egypt'. It is fair to say that the city, deliberately situated on the Mediterranean coast and facing outwards towards Greece rather than inwards towards Egypt, always remained somewhat aloof from the rest of the kingdom. The *Oracle of the Potter*, a piece of anti-Ptolemaic propaganda originally written in Demotic Egyptian and later translated into Greek, written in the third century BCE but in circulation for several centuries after that, makes it clear how separate and different Alexandria and its population were from the rest of Egypt, referring to it as 'the city by the sea', 'the city of the foreigners' and 'the city of the Girdle-Wearers', in reference to the Greek style of dress.[6] By the time of Cleopatra Selene's birth, although Egypt was nowhere near as powerful as it had been and the Ptolemaic Empire nowhere near as extensive, Alexandria was still the largest and most important city in the eastern Mediterranean. It was a political, cultural, intellectual and economic hub that had links with places including Juba's patrimony of Numidia and the kingdoms that would one day be amalgamated into Cleopatra Selene and Juba's kingdom of Mauretania. It attracted people from all over the ancient world, and its population included not just Macedonians and other types of Greeks, but also Egyptians, Jews, Syrians and Persians.[7] These heterogenous ethnic groups seem to have lived together in relative harmony.[8] The Greek intellectual Strabo of Amasia (modern Amasya in Turkey) described the city as an intellectual and commercial powerhouse.[9] Later in Cleopatra Selene's life, the city would serve as inspiration for the renovation of Iol Caesarea, the capital of the kingdom of Mauretania, that she and her husband Juba undertook.

Alexandria covered an area of thirty stades long by seven or eight stades wide, approximately twenty-five and a half hectares, and this was divided into five distinct areas.[10] These seem to have been named after letters of the Greek alphabet (although we only know the names of three of these five areas, we can infer the other two). Alpha contained the courts of justice, Beta contained the

Square Stoa and a number of granaries, and Delta was where the Jewish population of Alexandria predominated. What Gamma and Eta contained is unknown. According to the Greek historian Diodorus Siculus, who lived in Alexandria during the middle of the first century BCE, during his time there the city contained 300,000 free inhabitants, although since this figure does not include the enslaved, in reality the number of occupants would have been far higher.[11] There are indications that the city was modelled after Athens, a city where Alexander the Great and many other prominent figures in Alexandria's early history had spent significant and formative periods of their lives.[12]

Strabo arrived in Alexandria shortly after the Roman conquest and annexation of Egypt in 30 BCE, in the entourage of the second Roman governor of the new province, Gaius Aelius Gallus, between 26 and 24 BCE. Thanks to him, we have a detailed description of the city as it would have been during Cleopatra Selene's childhood, many aspects of which have been confirmed by underwater archaeological surveys undertaken over the last three decades.[13] At this point in time, it was a far finer city than Rome, although sadly little of its ancient magnificence is visible today because of a series of natural disasters – such as earthquakes and tsunamis, as well as gradual subsidence – which submerged large parts of it. By the eighth century CE most of Cleopatra Selene's Alexandria had disappeared beneath the waves of the Mediterranean, where it would remain inaccessible and unknown until the early 1990s, when rival teams of underwater archaeologists, led by Jean-Yves Empereur and Franck Goddio respectively, started exploring the seabed. They proceeded to uncover wonderful things, not just the remains of magnificent ancient buildings and monumental honorific statues of pharaohs and deities, but also minuscule objects once in the possession of the city's long-dead inhabitants, such as coins and jewellery.

Strabo begins with the Pharos lighthouse, designed and

constructed from white marble by the Greek architect and engineer Sostratus of Cnidus at a cost of 800 talents of gold during the third century BCE. This was situated on Pharos island overlooking the city's Great Harbour, which was connected to the city proper by a causeway known as the Heptastadion because it was seven stadia long.[14] This lighthouse was one of the seven wonders of the ancient world, but its purpose was primarily practical as it was visible from 300 stadia away.[15] It comprised four storeys, with the ground floor square, the first floor octagonal, the second floor circular; the third was where the fire – and the mirrors that were used to reflect it and project it to the ships out at sea – was located. (A tomb located in the necropolis at Taposiris dating to the second century BCE is modelled after it at one quarter of the size, and gives a sense of what the lighthouse would have looked like.) Numerous depictions of the lighthouse in its prime have survived from antiquity, particularly on the reverse faces of coins issued in Alexandria, such as this bronze hemidrachm issued in the reign of the Emperor Hadrian in 134–135 CE.[16] Although it was destroyed and plundered for its building materials long ago, some of the original blocks of marble can still be seen in its vicinity lying discarded on the seabed. The lighthouse was extremely influential, inspiring not only the lighthouse that Cleopatra Selene and Juba built at Iol Caesarea but also others around the Roman Empire such as the one at the harbour of Ostia, the port of Rome itself.[17]

According to Strabo, the royal palace complex, the 'Brucheion', constituted a quarter or even as much as a third of the entire city, as successive Ptolemaic rulers had added to the original construction, building palaces of their own and leaving those of their predecessors untouched.[18] Archaeological excavations in the area have uncovered signs of occupancy dating back to the fourth century BCE: a house, decorated very much in the Macedonian style of the houses in Alexander the Great's hometown of Pella, was uncovered in the garden of the former British consulate.[19]

A coin depicting the Pharos lighthouse.

The Brucheion covered the Lochias peninsula in the north-eastern part of the city, and the northern part of the city proper. This is where Cleopatra VII and her family lived and spent most of their time when they were in residence. Aulus Hirtius, one of Caesar's legates, observed that Alexandria's buildings were virtually fireproof as they were built of stone, the use of wood minimal.[20] All the palace buildings within the complex – each one consisting of many colonnaded courts, each one a different size and set of dimensions to the others – were linked. If someone with access to them felt so inclined, they could make their way from the most recent construction all the way back to the original one, the palace of Alexander the Great at the Acropolis, or Akra.[21] Thus there was plenty of room to accommodate important visitors such as Caesar, Antony, and finally Octavian. Caesar's suite of rooms seems to have been close to the Theatre of Dionysos and conveniently equipped with access to the royal port and dockyards.[22]

Also belonging to the complex, and as internationally renowned and influential as the lighthouse, were the Museum and Great

Library. Just as Alexandria was modelled on Athens, so was the Museum modelled on Aristotle's Lyceum.[23] The Museum was not exactly what we would recognise as such today, but, rather, a temple dedicated to the Nine Muses of Greek mythology, the divine patronesses of the arts: Clio (history), Urania (astronomy), Calliope (epic poetry), Euterpe (lyric poetry), Polyhymnia (sacred poetry), Erato (erotic poetry), Melpomene (tragedy), Thalia (comedy) and Terpsichore (dance). The Museum comprised an exedra (a place, such as an arcade, with recesses and seating where the scholars could sit and listen to lectures and discuss their work), and public walkways through landscaped gardens in which they could stroll, just as Aristotle and his fellow Peripatetic philosophers had done back in Athens. It was decorated with beautiful paintings and statues of eminent philosophers.[24] It contained an aviary of birds including pheasants, a menagerie of exotic animals (including, at one point, a huge snake captured in Ethiopia) and a botanical garden planted with specimens sourced not only from North Africa but also from places as far afield as Arabia and India.[25] The royal children undoubtedly spent a considerable amount of time here, and it may even have been here that Cleopatra Selene developed the fondness for crocodiles that she would retain for the rest of her life.

The scholars whom the Ptolemies selected and bestowed their patronage upon were able to live the academic dream, albeit in a marble temple rather than an ivory tower, receiving a generous stipend, immunity from payment of taxes and full-board accommodation. In keeping with the Museum's possession of an aviary, one ancient satirist, Timon of Phlius, jokingly referred to the Museum as a bird cage, because the scholars ensconced within were kept and fed like birds in a netted enclosure: 'Numerous cloistered papyrus-warblers are fattened in Egypt with its many peoples, quarrelling endlessly in the Muses' bird-cage.'[26] This gives the impression of the scholars swarming around the buffet table and taking full advantage of the all-inclusive nature of their lodgings (a phenomenon that anyone who has been to a work event with decent catering will recognise). Another ancient commentator, the playwright Antidotus, was more mean-spirited, sneering that the scholars were parasites.[27] One of Strabo's contemporaries, Aristonikos of Alexandria, wrote a treatise focused on the Museum, which presumably went into considerable detail about its day-to-day workings, but it unfortunately has not survived.

It was common in classical antiquity for temples to include libraries, and there was an even longer tradition of this combination in Egypt, where archaeological remains of the temples and their libraries are still visible, and significant parts of their collections have been discovered and translated.[28] Alexandria's Great Library was the largest library in the ancient world and contained the most extensive collection of works, the full tally being somewhere between 500,000 and 700,000 titles.[29] The early Ptolemies were clearly bibliophiles. Ptolemy II Philadelphos (309–246 BCE) was in the habit of purchasing the substantial personal libraries of notable book collectors, and in this way sourced books from Pergamum, Athens and Rhodes.[30] Ptolemy III Euergetes (284–222 BCE) worked even harder to stock the library. He sent letters to all the ancient sovereigns that he was aware of, asking for donations of books.[31] He received a huge donation from Syracuse, transported to Alexandria on board the enormous ship *Syracusia* that the inventor Archimedes had built for Hieron II (tyrant of Syracuse from 270 to 215 BCE).[32] He borrowed manuscripts of the tragedians Sophocles, Aeschylus and Euripides from Athens, and refused to return them. The polymath and physician Galen tells us that he even instituted a policy that ships docking in Alexandria were to be searched and, if there were any books on board, these books were to be copied and added to the collection, with the copies being returned to the owner rather than the originals.[33] Bilingual people who could translate the works of literature written in their native languages to Greek were employed to do precisely that. However, in 48 BCE, during the civil war between Cleopatra and her younger siblings, Caesar fired the ships in the harbour that were blockading the city and, because of the direction that the wind was blowing, the fire spread to the part of Alexandria containing the Library.[34] Just how badly the Library and its collection was damaged is a subject much debated by scholars, as the ancient sources that refer to this event are contradictory: one claims that the Library was completely destroyed, others that only some additional book storage facilities burned.[35] But it is probable that repair and restoration work was ongoing throughout Cleopatra Selene's childhood. Antony allegedly presented Cleopatra with 200,000 books looted from the Royal Library of Pergamum, the Great Library of Alexandria's main rival as far as grandiose Hellenistic libraries were concerned, by way of recompense. This was a gesture that, if it actually occurred, must have been met with considerable enthusiasm by the book-loving royal family.[36]

Also significant was the Sema, or Soma, the mausoleum containing the mummified remains of the individual to whom the Ptolemaic dynasty owed its possession of Egypt in the first place, Alexander the Great.[37] Ptolemy I Soter had intercepted Alexander's body on its way home from Syria to Macedon for burial, stolen it and brought it back to Egypt with him, originally interring it at Memphis, the religious capital city of Egypt, but his son Ptolemy II Philadelphos relocated it to Alexandria, where he had built a sacred precinct worthy to house it.[38] While originally Alexander's mummy had been interred in a golden sarcophagus, by the time of Cleopatra Selene's birth it had been replaced by one made of glass, or perhaps alabaster, the gold having been plundered by an earlier cash-strapped Ptolemy. This desecration made no difference to the esteem in which Alexander, his body and his tomb were held: Octavian reportedly spared Alexandria from the predations of his army out of respect for the deceased king, an idol of his adopted father Caesar.[39]

A more recent addition to the city came in the form of the Caesareum, the temple dedicated to Caesar that was begun by Cleopatra VII and completed by his adopted son, the Roman emperor Augustus. While Strabo does not mention it (and, in fact, during his tenure in the city it was probably largely unfinished), the Jewish intellectual Philo, who was himself born in Alexandria in around 20 BCE and lived there until his death in the middle of the first century CE, provides a detailed description of the temple precinct in its entirety.[40] According to Philo, the Caesareum was without parallel in the Roman world. It was situated opposite the best harbour, was the largest and most beautiful temple complex in the city, decorated in silver and gold, augmented with porticoes, libraries, groves, terraces and open-air courtyards, and was full of offerings made by worshippers. In fact, the two obelisks known today as 'Cleopatra's Needles', one of which is located on Victoria Embankment in London, the other in Central Park, New York, were once situated on either side of the entrance. They had originally been erected in the ancient city of Heliopolis during the reign of the Pharaoh Thutmosis III (c.1504–1450 BCE), but were relocated to Alexandria on the order of Augustus around 13–12 BCE.

Finally, there was the mausoleum of Cleopatra herself. This was another building project that was started by Cleopatra and completed by Octavian. Cleopatra seems not to have wished to be interred alongside her ancestors and Alexander the Great, but, rather, to have a funerary monument all to herself. Attached to a temple dedicated to Isis, it was a two-storey structure, and the second floor possessed windows large enough for Antony to be hauled through following his attempted suicide in 30 BCE, and for Octavian's soldiers to gain entry.

Memphis was Egypt's second city after Alexandria, its location a crucial strategic point on the Nile. It was to Memphis that Alexander the Great had travelled upon first arriving in Egypt, and it was there that he made sacrifices to the Apis Bull and other Egyptian gods, indicating his respect for them. His successor Ptolemy I followed suit. When Cleopatra VII and her children travelled to Memphis, sailing up the Nile on the royal barge, it is possible that they stayed in the Palace of Apries, originally built to accommodate a pharaoh in the sixth century BCE but still in use centuries later under the Ptolemies. Memphis was where the Temple of Ptah and the cult of the Apis Bull were located.[41] Although Egypt had a number of bull cults (one of Cleopatra's earliest acts as queen was to consecrate the Buchis Bull at Hermonthis, and a stele commemorating this occasion has survived and is on display in the New Carlsberg Glyptotek in Copenhagen), the Apis Bull was the most important and most famous. The Apis Bull was a black bull with a specific set of white markings: a triangular spot on its forehead, a likeness of an eagle on its back, and crescent-shaped spot on its right flank. Once selected from among the calves, the bull was identified with Osiris and worshipped as a god during its lifetime, living in the lap of luxury within the Temple of Ptah.[42] Upon the Apis Bull's death, it was embalmed and interred in the catacombs beneath the Serapeum in the necropolis at Saqqara. The embalming beds used to do this, made from alabaster and decorated with carvings of lions, can still be seen today.[43] Unlike Alexandria, which was a Greek city decorated with Egyptian artefacts requisitioned from across the kingdom, Memphis was a true blend of earlier Egyptian and later Greek construction. But like Alexandria, it also had a multicultural population, with people from the Levant, Syria, Persia, Caria and Ionia (the last two locations being neighbouring regions on the western coast of Anatolia/Asia Minor). In addition to the Egyptian temples, there was one dedicated to the Phoenician goddess Astarte, and one to the Greek goddess Aphrodite or perhaps Selene, Cleopatra Selene's namesake.

As we proceed through the story of Cleopatra Selene's life, it will become abundantly clear just how important her ancestors and her heritage were to her. How she honoured them informed the decisions she made and the things that she did, throughout her time not just as an Egyptian princess, but also a Roman prisoner, and an African queen. She would be driven by her desire to continue the Ptolemaic dynasty and live up to the standards set by her ancestors both male and female. It is time to meet her parents.

2

Antony and Cleopatra: West Meets East

WHILE EVERY PERSON IS, to a greater or lesser extent, influenced by their parents, the impact of the Roman statesman Marcus Antonius and the Queen of Egypt Cleopatra VII on Cleopatra Selene's life was extreme and profound. This impact commenced from the circumstances of her conception, for Antony and Cleopatra's connection was not a private matter but, rather, a public one and represented something far larger in scope than a simple romantic relationship. It had huge political implications – and symbolic resonance – for both the Roman and Egyptian polities. For the Romans, it was reconfigured as a meeting of West and East, an encounter that recalled the legendary Helen of Sparta and Paris of Troy, which ultimately resulted in the Trojan War. Indeed, on occasion Roman authors go so far as to explicitly link Cleopatra with Helen.[1] This meeting of Antony and Cleopatra would have similar ramifications, as once again the peoples of West and East would ultimately find themselves at war and, once again, the West would – rightly, in the Romans' view – triumph over the East. The meeting of Antony and Cleopatra was a story with which Cleopatra Selene was no doubt extremely familiar, having been told one version of it by her mother and another by her father, before being bombarded with elaborate albeit highly fictionalised recreations in Latin and Greek poetry and prose, and even art.

By early 41 BCE, Antony would have had every right to feel extremely pleased with himself. The previous year he had defeated Marcus Junius Brutus and Gaius Cassius Longinus – the ringleaders of the conspiracy that had assassinated Antony's friend and mentor Gaius Julius Caesar in 44 BCE – at the Battle of Philippi in Macedonia (modern Filippoi in Greece). With the civil war that had raged across the Roman Empire in the wake of Caesar's death concluded to his satisfaction, he was now the most powerful man in the ancient Mediterranean, the senior member of a triumvirate consisting of himself, Caesar's adopted son Gaius Julius Caesar Octavianus and Marcus Aemilius Lepidus. The three men had divided the Roman world up between them, with Antony receiving the prime cut: the wealthy eastern provinces of Macedonia, Asia, Bithynia-Pontus, Syria and Cilicia. Now he was heading east to take this territory in hand and deal with any problem individuals who had taken advantage of the upheaval caused by three years of intermittent civil warfare between powerful Romans and their legions, the Caesarian faction on one side and the so-called Liberators on the other. His approach was simple: he would expand the pre-existing system in which territories that were adjacent to the Roman provinces but not themselves under the control of Rome would be ruled by allied kings and queens. These individuals, with the exception of Cleopatra VII, queen regnant of Egypt, were not members of existing royal dynasties but were appointed by him personally, thus ensuring their loyalty not just to Rome but also to him. As part of this process, he would undertake a certain amount of territorial reorganisation and redistribution. He would also begin preparations for an extended military campaign against Rome's old enemy, Parthia. Ancient authors considered the Roman and the Parthian empires to be the world's largest known domains, and the world to have been divided between the two, but the precise nature of the division was up for debate and saw a considerable amount of jostling, since both empires laid claims to world domination.[2] The Arsacid dynasty's Parthian Empire (modern north-east Iran) is little known today, and most of what we do know about it derives from ancient Greek and Roman sources. These were not generally positive, as there was a long history of hostilities between first the Greeks and then the Romans, and their eastern rivals. The most recent expression of these hostilities had resulted in Parthia gaining the upper hand after the total annihilation of Roman forces under the command of the general Marcus Licinius Crassus at the Battle of Carrhae in 53 BCE. It was this catastrophic defeat and the resultant humiliating loss of military standards that Antony was seeking to avenge.[3]

But alas Antony was destined to fall prey to the aphorism 'history is written by the victors'. Owing to a combination of carefully organised and orchestrated character assassination and sheer random chance, the ancient literary evidence that has survived from his lifetime is that written by his enemies rather than his friends or even himself (and the members of the wealthy and educated ancient Roman elite tended to write *a lot*, in both prose and poetry). The famous orator Marcus Tullius Cicero loathed him. This was in part due to their diverging political views, emblematised by Antony's friendship with Cicero's arch-enemy and nemesis, the populist rabble-rouser Publius Clodius Pulcher (indeed, after Clodius' death, Antony would marry his widow Fulvia), and in part due to Antony's support for Caesar and his actions in the wake of the dictator's death. Consequently, Cicero wrote a series of fourteen speeches that have come to be known as the *Philippics* (after the famous Athenian orator Demosthenes' speeches against Philip of Macedon) over the course of 44 and 43 BCE, which set out in considerable detail exactly what he thought of his colleague, and none of these thoughts were remotely positive. To be fair,

Antony had his own reasons for loathing Cicero, as Cicero had had Antony's stepfather Publius Cornelius Lentulus Sura executed for participating in the Catilinarian Conspiracy in 63 BCE, an act for which Cicero would subsequently be exiled from Rome for a year – but the *Philippics* were the last straw. By way of revenge, Antony resorted not to character assassination but to actual assassination, and had Cicero proscribed and murdered, publicly displaying his head and hands on the rostra in the Forum in the centre of Rome.[4] While this may sound like an extreme overreaction, to be fair to Antony, Cicero considered him a 'noxious creature', and openly bemoaned the fact that the assassins of Caesar had not managed to finish off Antony as well. He went so far as to claim that if he had been involved in the planning and execution of the 'splendid feast on the Ides of March', there would have been no 'leftovers'.[5] And in later years, once the Caesarian faction had started to fight among itself, Octavian waged a propaganda campaign against Antony for almost a decade that was so successful that most of Antony's achievements have either been forgotten or attributed to Octavian himself.[6] Antony's speeches, pamphlets and letters written in his own defence have regrettably not survived. A case in point: Antony was famous for his drinking, and the personal and political consequences of this for him were ultimately severe – he had once humiliated himself in public by having to vomit into the folds of his toga when hungover from a wedding he had been to the night before, and Cicero used this and other similar episodes to facilitate his character assassination in the *Philippics*. As a result he had been moved to write a treatise entitled *On His Own Drunkenness* in defence of himself.[7] Since the work does not survive, we have no idea of its contents.[8] All we can surmise is that it was not a particularly convincing defence, as this hard-drinking reputation would endure. Much later, moralising philosophers such as Seneca the Younger would acknowledge Antony as a great man ruined by drinking, which sapped his abilities and made him cruel, with a tendency to ramble on in graphic detail about the men such as Cicero that he had proscribed and executed.[9]

While most of the accusations levelled at Antony – that he spent money like water, went in and out of debt, ate, drank and socialised to excess, had a taste for the company of his social inferiors, bedded unsuitable women and men, and let his wives and mistresses boss him around – are fairly stereotypical ways by which Romans attempted to smear each other's good names, there is presumably more than a grain of truth in them.[10] But it must be borne in mind that for every rather puritanical Roman like Cicero or Octavian who disapproved of this sort of behaviour, there were plenty of others who approved and readily participated in it with him. And, in point of fact, while Cicero may have been quite the prig, Octavian was rather a hypocrite in this regard, being very much a proponent of 'do as I say and not as I do'. He had a taste for the finer things in life such as expensive furniture and bronze vessels, was a degenerate gambler and an enthusiastic adulterer, cutting a swathe through the wives of prominent senators, particularly those who were his political adversaries, apparently ably assisted in his activities by his wife Livia Drusilla and his friends, a fact which was not lost on Antony as he raised the issue during one of their many bitter exchanges.[11] On one occasion, Octavian even threw a banquet in which he dressed as the god Apollo and the other guests likewise appeared in the guise of Olympian gods and goddesses, despite there being food shortages and famine in Rome at the time.[12] In any case, however Antony may have behaved, for most of his life he does seem to have been an able politician and a competent general.[13] He was certainly extremely popular with his soldiers.

Identifying portraits of Antony is challenging because Octavian encouraged the Roman Senate to subject him to *damnatio memoriae*, 'damnation of memory', after his death, which led to the destruction of all representations of him in portraiture and

A white marble portrait
bust of Antony.

references to him in inscriptions. However, this yellowish marble bust dating from the late first century CE, originally found near the Porta Maggiore in Rome in the nineteenth century and now in the collection of the Vatican Museums, is thought to be a rare surviving portrait of him since it bears similarities to the depictions on his coin issues. It gives us a sense of what Antony may have looked like in the prime of his life and at the peak of his career.[14]

So, in 41 BCE Antony travelled east, making his leisurely way through allied kingdoms where kings and queens sought to curry favour with him in various seemly and, on occasion, unseemly ways. During his sojourn in Cappadocia, for instance, he had an affair with the courtesan Glaphyra, and since he subsequently appointed her son Archelaus as king of Cappadocia, clearly her strenuous efforts on his behalf met with success.[15] Octavian used this affair as ammunition against Antony's wife Fulvia, with whom he had a fraught relationship, as he had been briefly married to her daughter Claudia until he had divorced her in order to marry another woman while insisting she remained a virgin.[16] He wrote a deliberately inflammatory and rather crass poem about the love triangle that only survived his subsequent attempts to rehabilitate his image because it was included by the satirist Martial in one of his own poems over a century later:

> Because Antony fucks Glaphyra, Fulvia has arranged
> This punishment for me: that I fuck her too.
> That I fuck Fulvia? What if Manius begged me
> To bugger him? Would I? I don't think so, if I were sane.
> 'Either fuck or let's fight', she says. Doesn't she know
> My prick is dearer to me than life itself? Let the trumpets
>   blare![17]

Like any Roman male citizen of consequence, Antony was accompanied on his travels by an entourage composed not just of staff for business but also staff for pleasure, and its members included musicians such as Anaxenor of Magnesia, an internationally famous cithara player and singer, Xouthos, a flute player, Metrodoros, a dancer, and an entire troop of Asiatic entertainers.[18] No doubt rather inappropriately to Roman onlookers, but perhaps more in keeping with the Eastern way of doing things, Antony blurred the lines between business and pleasure, allocating Anaxenor the responsibility of exacting tribute from four cities, and gave him his own bodyguard of soldiers.[19]

Antony eventually settled in Tarsus, the capital city of the province of Cilicia (modern southern central Turkey), in the summer of 41 BCE, and prepared to get down to business. On his agenda was a meeting with Queen Cleopatra VII of Egypt. The pair were already reasonably well acquainted, having met on numerous previous occasions. The first of these meetings took place during Cleopatra's childhood when Antony was serving as a soldier in Egypt in 55 BCE, when Rome intervened to restore Ptolemy XII Auletes to the Egyptian throne after a revolt – an intervention that was so costly it virtually bankrupted the kingdom

A white marble portrait
bust of Cleopatra.

and created a debt that ensured Rome's future interference in
Egyptian affairs. The second meeting occurred a few years later
during Cleopatra's visits to Rome as a guest of Caesar in the period
between 46 and 44 BCE.[20] It would subsequently be claimed that
Antony had been enamoured of her since their first meeting and
had been biding his time. This may well be true, but equally this
may simply be retrospective romanticising of their relationship.[21]
However, despite Cleopatra having been Caesar's mistress and the
mother of his only recorded biological son, she had reportedly
rendered aid to the assassin Cassius, supposedly providing him
with money and resources with which to continue his campaign
against the Caesarean faction. Antony was decidedly not amused
by her apparent perfidy and summoned her to Tarsus to explain
herself.[22]

Just as portraits of Antony are difficult to identify with certainty,
so are portraits of Cleopatra, and for much the same reason. This
Parian marble portrait, discovered in the ruins of the Villa of the

Quintillii on the Via Appia (Appian Way) in Rome and now part of the collection of the Museo Gregoriano Profano in the Vatican Museums, is considered by art historians to be the one most likely to depict her, on account of its clear resemblance to the portraits of her featured on her coinage.[23] This woman wears a broad diadem, the symbol of a Hellenistic monarch, and has her hair arranged in Cleopatra's signature 'melon' coiffure. If it is indeed the queen, it was probably sculpted during one of her visits to Rome during Caesar's dictatorship in the period 47–44 BCE, and is perhaps a copy of the golden statue of her that he set up in the Temple of Venus Genetrix in the Forum of Caesar, a singular honour that was probably inspired by her bearing his son, Caesarion.[24] And if so, this gives us a sense of what she may have looked like in the years immediately before her liaison with Antony began.

This first time Antony summoned Cleopatra to meet him in his capacity as governor of the Roman East, she had been ruling Egypt as an ally of Rome for almost ten years. She had reigned first in conjunction with her father, Ptolemy XII Auletes, then after his death she had fought her brothers and sister for control of the kingdom, eventually winning the civil war and regaining her throne with the help of Caesar and his army. She had ruled with Ptolemy XIII Theos Philopator (62–47 BCE), the elder of her two brothers, until 47 BCE, then with Ptolemy XIV Philopator (61–44 BCE), her youngest brother, until 44 BCE. After 44 BCE she reigned with her son, Ptolemy XV Caesar, known as Caesarion, 'Little Caesar', until Octavian's invasion of Egypt and their subsequent deaths in 30 BCE.

Although Cleopatra was never officially the sole ruler of Egypt, she was significantly older than both of her brothers and was also personally supported first by Caesar and then by Antony – so in reality her word was law. The alliance between Egypt and Rome was both embodied and personified in Caesarion. Egypt was extremely wealthy. The annual inundation of the Nile covered the land on either side of the river in a layer of thick black silt so agriculturally fertile that it was possible to harvest multiple crops each year. The Eastern Desert contained fabulous mineral resources that were mined for gold and precious stones, and the eastern coastline boasted ports such as Berenike (named after the famous early Ptolemaic Queen Berenike I) and Myos Hormos that connected Egypt not only with southern Africa but also with India and China, thus facilitating the Red Sea trade routes that brought exotic luxuries into Europe, also known as the Silk Road. In addition to the natural advantages provided by the environment of Egypt, the city of Alexandria was a major centre of trade in the Mediterranean and considered by some to be the greatest emporium in the world.[25] The Ptolemies had the monopoly on trading with India and the Far East. As a result, despite the debts left by Ptolemy XII Auletes' misadventures, Cleopatra was not only powerful, but she was also inordinately wealthy, too, and her power and wealth made her a desirable ally.[26]

The assumption that is often made about Cleopatra is that to attract the attention and support of two prominent Roman generals, two of the most powerful men in the ancient world, both of whom were notorious for their sexual misadventures with both women and men, she simply *must* have been beautiful and sexy. In fact, Plutarch tells us that it was not so much her physical attributes that made her so attractive, but, rather, her mental ones.[27] She spoke many languages, an impressive feat even by ancient Roman standards, when most educated people spoke both Latin and Greek. She therefore seldom resorted to using an interpreter in her dealings with foreign administrations and could take full control of negotiations; this undoubtedly gave her an edge.[28] Owing to the hot and dry Egyptian climate which preserves organic remains particularly well, thousands of papyri and ostraca (pot shards used as writing material just as we would use a piece of paper) have survived which demonstrate what a multilingual society Egypt was, with people writing, reading and speaking a range of languages including Egyptian, Greek, Latin and Aramaic.[29] In addition to the importance of language-learning, the necessity of seeking the advantage at all times, not just for yourself but also for your kingdom and subjects, was undoubtedly something she would have imparted to her children – indeed, they may well have been present for many of these embassies and had the chance to see her in action. In later life Cleopatra Selene would have been wise to follow her mother's example and take pains to learn the African languages and dialects, such as Punic, that were in use in Mauretania so that she could do the same.

According to Plutarch, Cleopatra, as well as being a polyglot was extremely intelligent, highly educated and endowed with considerable personal charm and charisma. She was able to gauge exactly what the person she was speaking to would best respond to and act accordingly, so when she saw that Antony was more comfortable interacting on an informal basis rather than a formal one, behaving more like a rank and file soldier than a lofty general, she adapted her own behaviour and unleashed a charm offensive.[30] This must have been refreshing for Antony, who had frequently been on the receiving end of criticism from his Roman peers such as Cicero for behaving crassly and crudely, and in a manner not in keeping with his status as a consul.

As queen of a nominally autonomous kingdom, Cleopatra was not inclined to answer such a peremptory summons – at least, not at first. She ignored Antony's letters and did not acquiesce until Antony's friend and representative, Quintus Dellius, travelled to Alexandria and requested her presence in person, going out of his way to reassure her about the positive nature of Antony's motivations.[31]

Once Cleopatra arrived in Tarsus, what might, under different circumstances, and with different participants, have been a routine meeting between an influential Roman and a Roman ally, instead became something extraordinary. It initiated a partnership that was both a strategic political alliance and a passionate romantic relationship, a combination that was virtually unprecedented in Roman political history. Antony, of course, had a well-deserved reputation as a sexual adventurer, and a tendency to mix business with pleasure, so it was not entirely unexpected that he might attempt to seduce Cleopatra in an attempt to sweeten any deals the pair made. And Cleopatra had already indicated that she was not averse to overtures from Romans that she considered worth her while. Nor was she averse to bearing their children. So, there was an element of inevitability in their professional and personal alliance. What was unexpected, however, was that their relationship would endure for the rest of their lives, and even into the afterlife. A marble relief currently housed in the British Museum, dated to the late first century BCE or the early first century CE., depicts a couple having sex on board a boat, and has been tentatively identified as a caricature of Antony and Cleopatra owing to the presence of a hippopotamus, representing Egypt, and dolphins, representing the Mediterranean, with this merging of Egypt and the Mediterranean symbolising their alliance.[32]

Having received Antony's summons from his messenger Dellius and having been reassured that Antony was well disposed towards her, Cleopatra sailed from Alexandria to Tarsus on board her royal barge with no great sense of urgency. No full and detailed description of Cleopatra's barge has come down to us, but we do have a surviving account of a barge belonging to her ancestor Ptolemy IV Philopater (c.240s–204 BCE). This gives an indication of just how extravagant these vessels were, and the impression they would have made on someone coming aboard for the first time.[33] Such pleasure barges were distinct from warships and merchant vessels, and Ptolemy IV Philopater's was half a stade long, thirty cubits wide at its broadest point and just under forty cubits high, although the mast that bore the purple sails was

A fragment of a relief, which
may depict Antony and
Cleopatra having sex on a boat.

seventy cubits high. It contained everything one would need to
travel in fine style, including bedrooms, dining rooms, covered
walkways, peristyle courtyards and closed courtyards. To gain
entrance to these living quarters, one walked through an entrance
made of ivory and scented citronwood, with fittings of gilded
bronze. The columns were made of cypress wood, their capitals of
ivory and gold. The boat even contained a shrine to the goddess
Aphrodite, occupied by a marble cult statue, and another to
the Ptolemies themselves, filled with portraits of members of
the dynasty fashioned from translucent marble. The interior
decoration incorporated elements of Greek and Egyptian styles.
Thus, we should envisage a craft somewhat akin to the super-
yachts favoured by the super-rich today.

Although archaeological evidence of any of the Ptolemaic barges has yet to be discovered, in 1929, two ships built during the reign of Antony's grandson, the emperor Gaius, better known as Caligula, were excavated from the bed of Lake Nemi in Italy. These ships are thought to have been inspired by those of Cleopatra, so although the ships themselves were destroyed in 1944, when United States Army shells hit the Museo delle Navi Romane they were housed in and started a fire, some of their trappings survive in a dedicated room in the Museo Nazionale Romano, Palazzo Massimo alle Terme in Rome. Viewing these beautifully cast bronze human and animal faces makes it clear that the ancient authors who wrote about these crafts were not exaggerating their luxuriousness.[34]

It is important to remember that, according to Plutarch, Cleopatra's previous introduction to a prominent Roman citizen with whom she was seeking an alliance, Caesar, in 48 BCE had necessitated her being smuggled into her own palace in Alexandria in a linen sack (not, as many popular representations have insisted, rolled up in a carpet) and being dumped on the floor at his feet.[35] Some years before, her father Ptolemy XII Auletes, himself deposed and seeking an alliance and assistance from Rome, had had to endure an even more degrading encounter. He was admitted into the presence of the senator Cato the Younger, who had just taken a laxative and, unable to stand up to greet Auletes in a manner befitting his status as a king, proceeded to defecate uncontrollably for the duration of their discussion.[36] Under the circumstances, it is no wonder that on this occasion Cleopatra wished to engineer a meeting in which she had the upper hand and could use every one of the considerable resources at her disposal, perhaps envisaging being the dominant partner in the relationship for a change. There was, after all, only one of her, whereas there were three Roman triumvirs who might attempt to seek her favour: she held all the cards.

One account of the meeting at Tarsus that circulated in antiquity but has since been lost was written by Dellius, who continued to serve as a go-between for Antony and Cleopatra and was involved in organising the logistics of the encounter. He would later be responsible for publishing salacious love letters that he claimed were written by Antony to Cleopatra, as part of Octavian's propaganda campaign against the lovers, the ancient equivalent of the contemporary 'revenge porn' and 'slut shaming'.[37] The version that survives today was included by Plutarch in his biography of Antony and would itself be used 1,500 years later by William Shakespeare. Since this account contains detailed and plausible information that is not featured in any other contemporary historical sources, it is possible that it was based on Dellius' eyewitness account. Dellius, however, was not Plutarch's only witness: his source for other details of Antony's life with Cleopatra was a friend of his grandfather Lamprias, the physician Philotas of Amphissa who lived in Alexandria at that time and was acquainted with Cleopatra's servants.

There is certainly no doubt that Cleopatra carefully orchestrated every single detail of her arrival in Tarsus: she was not only performing for Antony; she was also performing for the crowds that flocked to see her. The importance of such pageantry was another aspect of monarchical rule that she no doubt made clear to her children, and in later life Cleopatra Selene would have had the advantage of experiencing not just Egyptian and Greek but also Roman versions of public spectacles, all of which she could have drawn on for inspiration in Mauretania. Tarsus was both a major port and an important city. Caesar had awarded Tarsus such generous privileges that it had been temporarily renamed Juliopolis, while Antony himself decreed the city a *civitas libera*, a 'free state', meaning it was able to govern itself and could therefore elect its own magistrates, pass its own laws and even issue its own coinage. Tarsus was linked by Roman roads to the equally important cities of Ephesus, Corinth, Antioch and Jerusalem, allowing news to spread quickly. To the west of the city, the gate through which Antony and Cleopatra reportedly entered Tarsus still stands and is even known as the Cleopatra Gate in her honour.

According to eyewitness accounts of Cleopatra's arrival in Tarsus, the stern of the ship was covered in gold, the oars in silver and the sails were purple, probably dyed with Tyrian purple, the most valuable dye in the classical world, painstakingly harvested from the mucus of the murex snail.[38] Cleopatra had planned her entry into the city carefully, aiming to make as triumphant and eye-catching an entrance as possible. As the barge sailed up the Cydnus River, she posed hard, reclining beneath a golden canopy in a tableau designed to resemble a painting of the Greek goddess of sex Aphrodite, flanked on both sides by beautiful young male attendants dressed as Erotes (winged gods associated with love and sex, the antecedents of the modern Cupids) and female ones dressed as Nereids and Graces. Musicians playing flutes, pipes and lyres provided a suitably sensual soundtrack, and thuribles pumped out wave after wave of heady incense. It is hardly surprising that the inhabitants of Tarsus flocked down to the riverbanks to witness the spectacle, leaving Antony sitting alone on the rostrum (the speaker's platform) in the city's forum, waiting, growing increasingly embarrassed and impatient as time passed. When it finally became apparent that Cleopatra had no intention of coming to him, he was forced to acquiesce and issue her with a dinner invitation which she promptly refused, suggesting instead that he come to her. What that moment may have looked like is captured neatly by Sir Lawrence Alma-Tadema in his evocative 1883 painting *The Meeting of Antony and Cleopatra, 41 B.C.*, in which Antony hesitantly boards the vessel as Cleopatra insouciantly lounges, not even bothering to turn her head to greet him. This composition exemplifies the concept of *tryphé*, an enthusiastic and (as far as the Romans were concerned) somewhat excessive level of luxury and extravagance. It had originally developed out of the cult of the god Dionysos and the celebrations associated with it, and was enthusiastically adhered to by all the Ptolemaic monarchs.

A detailed account of what followed was recorded by Socrates of Rhodes, a Greek historian who wrote about the civil war between Antony and Octavian in the late first century BCE. This has survived thanks to the efforts of Athenaeus of Naucratis, who wrote a compendium that covered all aspects of ancient banqueting (and contains extensive material harvested from ancient treatises that are now lost) in the late second century CE. That first evening Antony was hosted by Cleopatra, presumably in one of the dining rooms on board the barge, which was decorated with a multitude of lights, suspended and arranged to cast their illumination in intricate patterns. Initially, she threw what she described as a royal drinking party, a small and intimate occasion, before inviting him, his friends and his commanders to dine with her the following evening.[39] At this initial soirée, the drinking vessels were made of solid gold, elaborately worked and set with precious stones, the walls of the dining room were covered in purple tapestries worked with gold thread and the couches were covered with sumptuous throws. When Antony expressed amazement at the expensive display before him, she merely smiled and said it was all a gift for him. The following evening, Cleopatra hosted a second banquet and the setting was extravagant to the point of making the previous evening's events seem insignificant by comparison, and once again, at the end of the night, she made a gift of everything to Antony and his companions.[40] Additionally, she provided litters and litter-bearers to transport the guests of the highest ranks back to their quarters, horses weighed down with silver trappings to the others, and enslaved Ethiopians to accompany them, carrying torches to light their way. On yet another occasion, she spent a talent of gold on roses, which florists braided into a mesh and spread across the floor like a carpet a cubit deep.[41] Roses were the most popular flower in the ancient Mediterranean, appreciated for their scent not just when freshly cut and worked into garlands but also when processed into perfume and scented oils. Antony was no stranger to spectacle himself – he had once driven a chariot pulled by lions through the streets of Rome, and had the distinction of being recorded as the first person in Roman history to do so.[42] But on this occasion he simply could not compete: when it was finally his turn to host her, his banquet suffered considerably in comparison with hers, a fact that he freely admitted.[43]

In response to Antony's accusation that she had aided the assassin Cassius in the civil war, Cleopatra patiently explained that she had provided troops to Caesar's ally Publius Cornelius Dolabella and that these troops had defected to Cassius upon Dolabella's death, which was hardly her fault. Additionally, she elaborated, she had personally sailed her fleet to the Ionian Sea fully prepared to participate in the hostilities, but it had been damaged by a storm and she had fallen ill and not recovered until after the civil war was over. Antony accepted her explanation with good grace, and he also accepted an invitation to spend the winter with Cleopatra at the royal court in Alexandria. Since Antony had spent much of the last three years on campaign and living out of a tent, he presumably jumped at the chance to spend a few months enjoying rest and relaxation in one of the wealthiest and most luxurious courts in the ancient world. While he was there – because he was staying in Egypt in an unofficial rather than an official capacity – he dressed as a private citizen, wearing a Greek *himation* rather than a Roman toga, and a style of shoe known as a *phaecasium* that was particularly favoured by Athenian priests.[44] He worshipped in temples, attended lectures and seminars given by the scholars at the Museum and Library, and socialised with the Alexandrian citizens.

The Ptolemaic dynasty's approach to interior decoration, as with so many other things, was entirely maximalist. So Antony found himself pottering around the Brucheion, a complex that made the barge look like a hovel in comparison. The walls and ceilings were richly decorated with marble, agate and porphyry panelling, the supporting beams were covered with gold, the floor was tiled with onyx, the doorposts were made of ebony and the doors were inlaid with ivory and tortoiseshell.[45] Off-white, rich red and deep purple fabrics and plush animal skins were hung from the ceiling, fragrant myrtle and laurel branches were placed strategically, and the floors were either strewn with flowers, even those that would be out of season and thus unavailable anywhere else in the ancient Mediterranean, such as roses and snowdrops, or covered with Persian carpets embroidered with representations of animals.[46] Marble statues carved by famous sculptors and paintings crafted by the finest artists, such as Pamphilus of the Sicyonian school, lined the walls.[47] For a man who in his formative years was permanently strapped for cash (his father had so many debts that Antony was forced to refuse his inheritance), and who spent much of his adult life out in the field on military campaigns, this must have been a disorienting experience.[48] It may have been at this point in his life that he began using a golden chamber pot to relieve himself, much to his contemporary Marcus Valerius Messalla Corvinus' disgust: his opinion was later recorded by Pliny the Elder, who in the process huffed that it was a shame that the rebel gladiator Spartacus had no longer been alive to call him to account for doing so at the time.[49] The descriptions of Cleopatra's palace written by later authors such as Lucan and Athenaeus go out of their way to emphasise the sheer luxuriousness of the complex in comparison with more restrained Roman interiors, almost to the point of parody. However, underwater exploration of the site off the coast of the modern city of Alexandria that was once occupied by the palace has supported these accounts. Divers have even brought some of the palace's fine decorations, ranging from monumental stone sculptures to pieces of gold jewellery, to the surface, and they have been displayed in exhibitions all over the world, including one held at the British Museum that I was lucky enough to visit in 2016.[50]

Cleopatra was renowned for the quality and quantity of her banquets, one of the most important ways that a Hellenistic monarch could display their immense wealth and luxurious style of living. The dinner service was gold, and she was such an obliging host that she would often send guests home with pieces of it.[51] Attendants offered guests crystal pitchers of Nile water to wash their hands before and after each course, anointed them with oils scented with cinnamon and cardamom, and adorned them with crowns of woven flowers, that, if worn, were believed to have medicinal properties that would prevent drunkenness and, better still, hangovers. Pliny the Elder recounts that, on one notable occasion later in their relationship, Cleopatra, aware that Antony feared death by poisoning and employed tasters to sample his food, apparently indulged in a spot of erotic terrorism. She ordered poisoned blooms to be included in his crown then, during the banquet, removed some and dipped them into his wine,[52] suggesting that they drink. As Antony prepared to oblige, she stopped him, saying: 'Look, I am she, Mark Antony, of whom you are wary with your new wish for tasters. If I could live without you, this is the extent to which I lack opportunity and motive!' She then summoned a condemned prisoner to the banqueting hall, ordered them to drink the wine, and she and Antony watched as the hapless convict died.

A variety of homegrown and imported food and drink was served, even when the banquets were small and the guests were few. One eyewitness account from the palace kitchens recounts that they saw eight wild boars being spit-roasted and assumed a sizeable feast was in the offing, only to be informed by the palace staff that, on the contrary, only Cleopatra, Antony and a handful of guests would be present.[53] However, multiple boars were necessary as the staff could never be certain of what time the group would finish drinking and talking, and actually commence dining, so they started roasting each one at a different time in the hope that there would always be one ready to go the second either Cleopatra or Antony sat down and called for food.

They ate. They drank. They drank so much that they even founded a drinking society named the 'Association of the Inimitable Livers'. A basalt statue base bearing an inscription referencing the society set up by a man named Parasitos, one of Antony's clients, that is now housed in the Graeco-Roman Museum in Alexandria, confirms its existence, and it confirms something else, too, as it refers to 'Antony, the Great, lover without peer'. So not only was he an inimitable liver, but he was also an inimitable lover.[54]

They gambled. They not only played games of chance such as dice but also made extravagant wagers against each other. On one memorable occasion, Cleopatra bet Antony that she could host a banquet that cost ten million sesterces, roughly equivalent to sixty thousand pounds of gold.[55] Antony, of course, took that bet. Cleopatra happened to own two of the largest pearls in history, that had been handed down to her as family heirlooms and which she had set into earrings. The following evening, she hosted a banquet that, while very fine, was certainly not worth ten million sesterces, causing Antony to laugh and claim that he had won their bet. Cleopatra laughed in turn, stating that the banquet was a mere fraction of the amount. Then she requested a cup of vinegar be brought to her. As Antony looked on, curious and perplexed, she removed one of her pearl earrings and dropped it into the cup. Once the pearl had dissolved in the vinegar, she drank it.[56] The adjudicator, Antony's friend Lucius Munatius Plancus, a former Roman consul, judged in Cleopatra's favour, and then personally intervened with the queen to prevent her from destroying the second pearl in the same manner.[57] This event has been immortalised and celebrated in art countless times since, such as in Jacob Jordaen's *Cleopatra's Feast*, Giambattista Tiepolo's *The Banquet of Cleopatra* and Guido Reni's *Cleopatra Dissolving the Pearl*, the latter fortuitously saved from destruction by Rosamond

Warren Gibson in the Great Fire that raged through Boston in 1872. Cleopatra was apparently not the first to perform this trick. Some years earlier in Rome, a gentleman named Clodius, the son of the most celebrated tragic actor in Rome, Clodius Aesopus, had been left a fortune by his successful father and wished to know what pearls tasted like.[58] Dissolving one set from an earring belonging to his mistress Caecilia Metella in vinegar, he enjoyed it so much that he invited his friends to a banquet and served them each a pearl of their own, encouraging them to follow suit and swallow theirs. Cleopatra may have heard this story while staying in Rome a few years before and waited for an opportune moment to put her own spin on it. She may also have been aware that Caesar's sumptuary law, passed in 46 BCE, restricted the wearing of pearls to mothers alone, and forbade them to unmarried women or women under the age of forty-five. Although as queen of an autonomous kingdom Cleopatra was not subject to Roman laws, she still may have delighted in the fact that, while a mother, she was neither married nor over forty-five (she may even have enjoyed flaunting her pearls upon her earlier visits to the city, well aware that while people might not have approved, there was nothing that they could do or say about it). According to Pliny the Elder, pearls were relatively rare in Rome prior to the annexation of Egypt in 30 BCE, and those that were in circulation were small and of relatively low value; Cleopatra's pearls would have been considerably larger. Much later, Octavian would take Cleopatra's remaining pearls as spoils and use them to adorn the ears of a statue of Venus set up in the Pantheon built by Agrippa between 27 and 25 BCE.[59]

They were entertained. They watched the performances put on for them by members of Cleopatra's entourage, including one by a monkey that had been trained to dance in perfect time with the music made by singers and flautists. The monkey, however, was easily distracted by treats such as figs and almonds, which would lead him to pull off his mask and tear it up.[60]

They dressed up in all sorts of costumes. Antony was keen on cosplay throughout his life, at various points dressing up as his ancestor Hercules or the god Dionysos, but at this point in time he liked to dress as an enslaved person, so Cleopatra sought to match him, quite a departure from her normal garb of Sidonian silk, a fabric that was thin, figure-hugging and rather sheer.[61] They roamed the city together in disguise, although of course everyone they encountered knew exactly who they were – the citizens of Alexandria reportedly loved Antony precisely because he did not put on airs and graces but, rather, was happy to let his hair down and act the fool; they said that he wore his tragic mask in Rome and his comic mask in Alexandria.[62] It would appear that this sort of behaviour was infectious: on one memorable occasion, Antony's companion Plancus painted his entire naked body blue and dressed up as the sea god Glaucus, complete with a headdress made of reeds and a fish tail, and spent the evening writhing around on the floor and dancing for their amusement.[63]

Cleopatra provided Antony with an abundance of other entertainments.[64] She watched and admired him while he exercised and trained with weapons, no doubt preening and flexing his muscles for her appreciation. They went hunting (hunting lions was a royal prerogative and doing so would have given Antony the opportunity to follow in the footsteps not only of Alexander the Great but also of his divine ancestor Hercules in his pursuit of the Nemean Lion). They also fished – on one occasion Antony found himself unable to catch anything while Cleopatra looked on. Embarrassed, he ordered some fishermen to dive underwater and attach a previously caught fish to his hook so he could pretend to have caught it. No fool, Cleopatra realised exactly what he was up to but pretended to be impressed with his fishing prowess, so much so that she invited her friends to watch him in action the following day. While everyone was watching Antony, and he was preparing to cast his line, she ordered one of her servants to dive underwater and attach a smoked fish from the Black Sea to his hook. Antony, believing that he had, at last, caught a fish, pulled up his line only to be flummoxed by what was attached to it, and embarrassed as his audience laughed merrily. Cleopatra consoled him and stroked his deflated ego, saying: 'Leave the rod to those who rule Pharos and Canopus [i.e. fishermen]; your prey is cities, kingdoms, and continents.'[65]

Finally, since Romans had been visiting Egypt to see the sights for over a century, and Cleopatra had taken Caesar on a cruise all the way up the Nile, it is likely that she offered the same opportunity to Antony, albeit on a smaller scale.[66] Her original trip with Caesar had been designed as a way of communicating her restoration to the throne to her subjects, to cement her rather less than secure position by emphasising the fact that she enjoyed the support of the might of Rome, and her barge had been accompanied by 400 additional craft. Her trip with Antony would have been more understated – although she would still have wanted to indicate that she was a force to be reckoned with, and now in possession of even more powerful friends. Popular sites were the sacred crocodiles of the god Sobek, who, adorned with jewels, ate offerings from the hands of their cult's priests; and the colossal temple nicknamed 'Labyrinth' after the one supposedly designed and built for King Minos of Crete by Daedalos to house the Minotaur.[67] It may have been a trip such as this that led to them being accused of attending orgies in the Nile Delta's pleasure resorts of Canopus and Taposiris Magna.[68]

In return for all this hospitality, Antony assisted Cleopatra in securing her position as Queen of Egypt once and for all. He arranged to have her sister Arsinoe assassinated. She had been living in the Temple of Artemis at Ephesus since her appearance in Caesar's quadruple triumph, and had been slowly amassing support and influence.[69] The Ephesian high priest Megabyzus had apparently recognised her claim to the throne of Egypt and addressed her as queen, for which Antony and Cleopatra sought to punish him.[70] He was saved from their displeasure by the supplications of the Ephesians, and forgiven for his transgression. Arsinoe was dead, and no longer a threat to Cleopatra and her child, and that was the important thing.

Unfortunately, Antony's Egyptian sojourn could not last for ever. Early in 40 BCE, he received word from Italy that his wife, Fulvia, and brother, Lucius Antonius, had gone to war, first with each other and then, settling their differences, with his fellow triumvir Octavian. While Fulvia insisted that she was representing Antony's interests in Italy in his absence, others were less convinced, claiming that she had acted entirely out of a desire to get Antony's attention, distract him from Cleopatra and win him back. Antony departed Egypt and headed back to Italy. Following this, he would not see Cleopatra again for three years, but by the time they were finally reunited, much had changed for them both and they were now inextricably linked by virtue of their shared parentage of the twins Cleopatra Selene and Alexander Helios.

3

The Birth of a Queen

IN ANTIQUITY, EGYPT WAS renowned for its seemingly boundless agricultural fertility, the result of the annual inundation of the Nile. Authors as far back as Aristotle in the fourth century BCE recorded the belief that Egyptian women were likewise exceptionally fertile, and prone to multiple births, so it would not have been entirely surprising to onlookers when Cleopatra VII gave birth to fraternal twins, a boy named Alexander and a girl named Cleopatra, in the spring of 40 BCE. Pregnancy and childbirth were the most dangerous experiences a woman would have in the ancient world, and maternal and infant mortality were extremely high, even when the woman in question was wealthy and attended by the best physicians and midwives that money could buy, as Cleopatra VII certainly would have been. She had already been through pregnancy and childbirth at least once, having given birth to Caesarion in around 47 BCE, although some oblique references in Cicero's correspondence around the time of Caesar's death in 44 BCE suggest that it is possible that she was pregnant again in 44 BCE but suffered a miscarriage, perhaps as a result of the stress of Caesar's assassination and her subsequent dramatic departure from Rome and flight back to Egypt.[1] So, by the time she became pregnant with twins, she had likely already experienced both the highs and the lows of pregnancy and childbirth and would have been well prepared for all eventualities.

We know nothing about Cleopatra Selene's birth and next to nothing about her childhood prior to her arrival in Rome at the age of ten or eleven in 29 BCE, just as we know next to nothing about the childhoods of any of her brothers, including her half-brother Caesarion, despite his particularly illustrious paternity. Ancient authors were simply not interested in children or childhood, and even those who wrote the ancient equivalents of biographies such as Plutarch or Suetonius only included anecdotes about their subjects' youths if they considered it relevant to the men they would become, no matter how blatantly falsified and retroactively inserted those anecdotes might have been (e.g., prophecies and omens foretelling future greatness). For what follows, I have combined the surviving scraps of information we have about Cleopatra Selene specifically with more general information regarding pregnancy, childbirth and childhood in Ptolemaic Egypt during the mid-first century BCE.

It would have been sensible for Cleopatra VII to engage some of the physicians from the Museum in Alexandria, who were well versed in the theory and – more importantly – the practice of the various contemporary schools of medicine, to oversee her pregnancy and labour. Alexandria was the only place in the ancient Mediterranean where someone wishing to study medicine could not only dissect the bodies of condemned criminals but also live ones.[2] Herophilus of Chalcedon, a physician living and working in Alexandria in the early third century BCE, was one of the earliest recorded anatomists in Graeco-Roman medicine. He was particularly interested in gynaecology and obstetrics, and wrote a treatise entitled *Midwifery*, which discussed the duration and stages of childbirth. His fame was such that he inspired many tall tales: he was apparently responsible for dissecting up to 600 live prisoners, and he was named as a mentor to the first female physician of classical antiquity, Agnodike.[3] Although none of his works have survived, he is referred to repeatedly by the second-century CE

74

author Soranus in his treatise *Gynaecology*. Through Soranus, we can reconstruct some of his research findings and infer from them aspects of his medical practice. Given her fondness for the Egyptian goddess Isis, Cleopatra may have looked to other Egyptian deities closely associated with pregnancy, childbirth and the protection of mothers and babies for support, such as Taweret, the hippopotamus goddess, and Bes, the dwarf god. Many amulets and statuettes of these deities have survived, showing how much the women of ancient Egypt valued them at this most difficult and dangerous of times in their lives. A different type of insight into this experience can be found in the form of a set of mummified human remains dating from the first century BCE that are currently in the possession of the University of Warsaw. They belong to a woman aged between twenty and thirty years old who died and was mummified between the twenty-sixth and thirtieth weeks of pregnancy – the only known example of a pregnant mummy.[4] Acquired by the university in 1826 and said to have been found in a royal tomb at Thebes in Upper Egypt, she was clearly a member of the Theban social elite, as her mummification was expertly done, she was equipped with a rich set of amulets and she was carefully wrapped in fabrics.

It was just as well that Cleopatra VII's resources as Queen of Egypt were virtually limitless, because gestating and giving birth to fraternal male and female twins was considered especially risky by ancient physicians as they believed that the foetuses did not develop at the same rate.[5] But as far as we know, the delivery of the twins was unproblematic, and both mother and babies were healthy: indeed, Cleopatra VII would go on to have another child, Ptolemy Philadelphos, in 36 BCE. In Egypt through the Pharaonic, Hellenistic and Roman periods the preferred method of childbirth was for a woman to be sitting upright on a birthing stool, with someone or something behind her offering support.[6] Even the gods were believed to have laboured in this way: the Alexandrian

A terracotta figurine depicting
a woman in the process of
giving birth.

poet Callimachus, based at the Museum in Alexandria during the reigns of Ptolemy II Philadelphos and Ptolemy III Euergetes, described the Titan Leto loosening her girdle and birthing the twin deities Apollo and Artemis while leaning against a palm tree on the island of Delos.[7] Many images of birthing stools in use have survived in the archaeological record, such as a terracotta figurine dating from the first century BCE and discovered in Alexandria that depicts a pregnant woman straddling one in a Greek *chiton* tied with a girdle and the *himation* draped over her hair.[8]

Cleopatra's birthing stool would probably have been a beautiful and luxurious object, like everything else she owned, carved from gleaming ebony, or scented citrus wood, inlaid with precious metals, ivory or tortoiseshell, a fitting way to bring the next generation of the Ptolemaic dynasty and Egypt's future into the world.

A bronze figurine depicting the goddess Isis nursing the god Horus.

Given Cleopatra's consistent self-identification with the goddess Isis, she may have chosen to imitate Isis, one of whose guises was Isis Lactans, 'Breastfeeding Isis', and to breastfeed her children herself. This depiction of Isis was certainly extremely popular around the ancient Mediterranean, judging by the number of statuettes that have survived from antiquity, such as this solid bronze example from Egypt now housed in the Cleveland Museum of Art.[9] Here the goddess, identifiable because she is sporting her unmistakable headdress comprising the solar disc flanked on either side by cow's horns, sits with her son in her lap, carefully supporting his head with one hand and guiding her breast to his mouth so he can suckle with the other.

However, it was standard practice for wet nurses to be engaged to feed and care for newborns, in place of birth mothers. While

Cleopatra Selene and Alexander Helios' wet nurses were probably enslaved women who were already members of the royal household, a number of papyrus employment contracts for wet nurses have survived from Ptolemaic and Roman Egypt, giving us an idea of what such a position entailed.[10] A wet nurse was expected to be clean, hygienic, of good moral character and habits, often required to refrain from drinking alcohol or having sexual intercourse. She would nurse an infant for the first eighteen to twenty-four months of its life before weaning it onto solid food. She was also responsible for taking care of it using techniques such as swaddling to encourage its body to form and grow in the correct way, bathing to keep it clean and bestowing affection such as cuddles and kisses, rocking it to sleep and singing it lullabies. Strong bonds formed between wet nurses and their charges, and in elite households the wet nurse was often retained as a caregiver, remaining with their charge for the rest of their life.[11] Two famous examples of wet nurses taking their duties seriously well beyond their charges' childhoods can be found in the biographies of the emperors Nero and Domitian. In the case of Nero, his wet nurses Egloge and Alexandria deposited his ashes in his family tomb on the Pincian Hill. Likewise, Domitian's wet nurse Phyllis cremated his body at her suburban estate on the Via Latina, then sneaked into the temple he had built and dedicated to his family on the Quirinal Hill, which housed the remains of his brother Titus, his niece Julia and his own infant son, and mixed his ashes with those belonging to Julia, to whom she had also served as wet nurse.[12] Not for nothing, according to Publilius Syrus, an ancient author who was himself once enslaved, writing at around this time in the mid-first century BCE, was a common ancient saying 'the grief of a wet nurse is second only to that of a mother'.[13] There was believed to be a particularly close and ongoing relationship between a wet nurse and her female charge, as it would often be the wet nurse who would advise about female matters such as puberty, menarche, contraception, pregnancy and childbirth. In Greek and Roman literature, it is regularly the character of the nurse who is responsible for arranging her charge's romantic liaisons. So, although we do not know her name, it is probable that Cleopatra Selene's wet nurse remained a significant figure in her life for many years, and may have been something of a comfort and confidante to the young princess.

While we know that the twins were born in 40 BCE, we do not know the precise date that they were born, nor the order in which they were born, nor what sort of celebrations accompanied their birth beyond the possibility that the fortieth day after the birth marked the point at which Cleopatra would be considered pure and permitted to enter temples again. However, we do know that after the birth of Caesarion she built a *mammisi*, a chapel of birth, dedicated to him at the Temple of Montu in Hermonthis.[14] This chapel was executed entirely in the traditional Egyptian style, consisting of an outer courtyard, outer and inner halls and a birth room. It survived largely intact until 1861, when it was destroyed so its stone could be requisitioned and repurposed to build a sugar refinery for Ismail Pasha, Khedive of Egypt and Sudan, as part of his programme to modernise the country, its industry and its economy. Thankfully, many early European travellers made drawings and paintings of it, and some even took photographs (those that have survived were taken in 1857, a mere four years before the building's destruction, by an English traveller named Francis Frith). To date, no similar chapel for the twins has been identified, although Cleopatra may well have dedicated one.

Or perhaps she augmented existing temples: in 1918, a monumental sandstone sculpture was discovered near the Temple of Hathor at Dendera. Now housed in the Egyptian Museum in Cairo,[15] the sculpture depicts two naked children, a girl and a boy, standing with their arms around each other, encircled by the coils of two snakes. The girl, whose hair is dressed in the so-called

The ruins of Caesarion's chapel of birth at the
Temple of Montu in Hermonthis.

'melon' style favoured by Cleopatra VII, bears a crescent and a
lunar disc on her head (a reference to the goddess Selene), while
the boy, whose hair is dressed in the traditional 'side-lock' style
favoured by Egyptian boys, bears a sun disc on his (a reference
to the god Helios). Based on its stylistic likeness to a statue of
Pakhom, the governor of Dendera in the period 50–30 BCE, this
unique sculpture has been dated to the same period and identified
as Cleopatra Selene and Alexander Helios, making it the only
surviving representation of the twins together, and the only
confirmed surviving representation of Alexander Helios.

A sandstone statue from the Temple of Hathor at Dendera,
which may depict Cleopatra Selene and Alexander Helios.

The birth of twins was considered a joyous occasion in classical
antiquity, and for Cleopatra VII it was confirmation of her
fecundity. It was also entirely in keeping with her practice of *tryphé*
and its accompanying excessively luxurious lifestyle: after all, if
something is worth doing, it is worth overdoing.[16] It did, however,
play into pre-existing negative stereotypes and opinions about her
morals held by conservative Romans such as Cicero, as it was often
assumed that the birth of twins was indicative of the mother having
had sex with two different men, with a twin being fathered by
each.[17] However, in Graeco-Roman mythology the birth of twins

A coin depicting Cleopatra VII and Caesarion on the obverse face, and the Ptolemaic double cornucopia on the reverse face.

was often indicative of the mother having had sexual relations (either consensual or non-consensual) with a god, and Cleopatra VII had certainly claimed to have done so previously. Upon the birth of Caesarion, she presented herself as Isis and Caesarion as Horus to her Egyptian subjects, and herself as Aphrodite and Caesarion as Eros to her Greek ones, as is demonstrated on a bronze coin that circulated in Cyprus, a territory given to her by Caesar in 48–47 BCE.[18] Almost too neatly, Caesar's death in 44 BCE meant that he could be presented as Osiris, and she went so far as to inaugurate a monumental temple complex dedicated to him in the centre of Alexandria.

While the truth of Caesarion's paternity was repeatedly questioned in antiquity, the fact that Antony was the father of Cleopatra Selene and her twin was never doubted. On the contrary, during the 30s BCE, Octavian's propaganda made much of the fact that Antony had not only indulged in a shameful liaison with a foreign woman that had resulted in him rejecting his legal Roman wife, but that he had also fathered a number of illegitimate foreign children. According to Plutarch, Antony responded to these accusations by claiming that his actions were not only entirely justified, but also in the interests of the Roman people and their empire.[19] He took the opportunity to remind everyone that his ancestor Hercules had not restricted himself to one woman, but, rather, had founded many great families.

The twins were initially named Alexander, presumably in honour of Alexander the Great (the name had appeared occasionally in the Ptolemaic family tree prior to this, presumably for the same reason), and Cleopatra, presumably in honour of Cleopatra herself.[20] The other two female names normally used for women born into the Ptolemaic dynasty, Berenike and Arsinoe, were evidently deemed inappropriate in this instance. After all, Cleopatra VII's sisters Berenike and Arsinoe had both proved disloyal: Berenike had attempted to depose their father Ptolemy XII Auletes, and Arsinoe had tried to depose Cleopatra VII herself. However, upon their introduction to Antony at his and Cleopatra VII's second meeting, this time in Antioch in Syria in 37 BCE, when they were around three years old, the twins gained additional monikers. These were simultaneously loaded with celestial significance and rather whimsical, the ancient equivalent of the modern practice of giving twins names that begin with the same letter, or names that rhyme. It is possible that an eclipse coincided with Antony's introduction to his children and gave him the idea, or perhaps male and female twins simply reminded him of the Titan siblings Helios and Selene, the god of the sun and the goddess of the moon. He had previously shown an interest in the god Helios, issuing silver denarius coins depicting himself dressed for religious ritual, veiled, togate, and wielding a *lituus* (a curved wand that was used by Roman augurs in their divinations), on the obverse face, and the radiate head of Helios (or Sol, as he was known to the Romans) on the reverse face. This has been interpreted as him attempting to connect himself, the supreme Roman, with the sun, the supreme deity.[21] There were also several prophecies circulating in the eastern Mediterranean about a forthcoming child and their bright future.[22] Just as parents today sometimes like to give their twins complementary names that mark them as a pair, so, too, did the Romans. Within Antony's lifetime, the Roman consul Lucius Cornelius Sulla had named his male and female twins Faustus Cornelius Sulla and Fausta Cornelia, the male and female versions of the adjective 'joyful' in Latin, complementing his own nickname Felix, the adjective 'lucky' in Latin. However, antithetical names such as those borne by the Gallic senators Sextus Coelius Canus, 'white', and Sextus Coelius Niger, 'black', were also used.

In any event, Alexander Helios and Cleopatra Selene's names were both complementary and antithetical in addition to being of significance in both the Greek and Roman divine pantheons. A few years later, Octavian would use the fact that Antony chose these particular names to criticise him for his overinflated sense of self-importance.[23] Since Cleopatra Selene and her mother shared the same first name, it is possible that during her childhood she was known by her second name to avoid confusion, at least in private. However, once she reached maturity, it is clear from her coinage that she was known, publicly at least, as Cleopatra. At that point, with her mother long dead, there would have been no cause for confusion, and the additional authority imparted by the ancient and venerable name would have been extremely useful to her in establishing herself. The name Cleopatra, or Kleopatra, as Cleopatra Selene spelled it on her coin issues, had the added benefit, in the original ancient Greek, of being an amalgamation of the words *kleos*, 'glory, honour', and *pater*, 'father, ancestor', or *patris*, 'country, fatherland'. It meant, quite literally, 'the glory of her father/ancestors' or 'the glory of her country/fatherland'.

Traditionally, a Roman child was placed at the feet of its father immediately after birth and it was up to the father to decide whether the child lived or died. If he decided the former, he would pick the child up, thus formally acknowledging it and subsequently naming it; if he decided the latter, the child would be exposed (i.e. left somewhere for someone else to claim or, if nobody did, to die). Considering her love of dramatic spectacle, Cleopatra may well have gone through the motions of placing Cleopatra Selene and Alexander Helios at Antony's feet, although, of course, in the event that he had chosen not to acknowledge the twins, there would have been no danger of them subsequently being abandoned.

However, Antony was not a significant presence in Cleopatra Selene's childhood. He did not spend any extended time in Alexandria with his Egyptian family until 34 BCE, when Cleopatra Selene was six years old. The fact that Antony was an absent father probably did not strike Cleopatra Selene as strange; after all, her elder brother Caesarion's father had been equally absent prior to his death while Caesarion was still a toddler, and it is unlikely that he had any genuine memories of the man. The royal children would have grown up being told tall tales of their fathers, and so would have been familiar with them as legends rather than as mortal men.

While Cleopatra Selene and Alexander Helios were out of Antony's sight, they were not necessarily out of his mind. It was perhaps due to their presence in his thoughts that he became intrigued by twins, and purchased a pair of exceptionally handsome twin boys from a slave dealer named Toranius Flaccus.[24] However, despite the boys' identical appearance, it transpired that they were not, in fact, twins, nor were they even related: one was from Asia, the other from north of the Alps. Upon realising that the boys could not possibly be twins, as they did not speak each other's languages, Antony returned to Toranius, complaining bitterly and feeling that he had been cheated out of the 200,000 sesterces that the boys had cost. Toranius merely shrugged and responded that the reason the price was so high was precisely because the boys were identical without being twins. After all, what was so remarkable about children born of the same parents looking alike? Seeing his point, Antony was mollified.

For the first ten years of her life, Cleopatra Selene was raised in Egypt as an Egyptian princess at an Egyptian court; the fact that her father was a Roman citizen, former consul and triumvir was almost irrelevant at this stage of her life. Since Antony was largely absent, particularly during her formative years, Cleopatra was the dominant influence. Still, it is unlikely Cleopatra Selene saw very much of her mother from one day to another. Although Cleopatra was technically ruling Egypt and her other territories in conjunction with Caesarion, the boy was too young to have anything other than a nominal role in ruling the region. Thus, Cleopatra would have been far too preoccupied with the business of government to have much to do with the regular care of any of her children.

Cleopatra Selene's childhood was spent predominantly in Alexandria, at the royal court in the palace quarter of the city. We can get an impression of her during this period of her life from a sardonyx cameo currently housed in the State Hermitage Museum in St Petersburg in Russia, which, dating from the first century BCE and found in Alexandria, has been identified as a depiction of her.[25] The portrait shows a solemn child with her hair swept back from her face, perhaps arranged at the nape of her neck in the 'melon' coiffure, and topped with a diadem. Behind her is a crescent moon, a reference to her divine namesake. It may originally have been one of a pair, partnered by a sardonyx cameo of Alexander Helios accompanied by the rays of the sun, a combination that his namesake Alexander the Great had often favoured in his own portraiture.

Although based predominantly at the royal court in Alexandria, from time to time Cleopatra Selene would have accompanied her mother around the ancient Mediterranean on diplomatic trips, such as the one to Antioch to meet Antony in 37 BCE. Although the primary purpose of that meeting was to discuss political and military matters in advance of Antony's planned eastern campaign, it was in Cleopatra's interest to show off her burgeoning family and emphasise the security of her dynasty. She had, after all, accompanied her own father Ptolemy XII Auletes to Rome for an extended stay as a child.[26] At this time, Alexandria was one of the largest and finest cities in the ancient world, a commercial hub for trade with the Far East, including India and even China, and with a large multicultural population. However, Cleopatra Selene would also frequently have travelled up the Nile to other cities within Egypt, such as Memphis, where she and her family would participate in religious festivals like those that celebrated the Apis and Buchis bulls, overseen by their close friends and, potentially, their relatives the High Priest of Ptah and his family.

Although Cleopatra Selene was not able to spend much time with either of her parents, it is unlikely that any of the royal children were ever lonely; they would have been constantly attended by a variety of enslaved persons and eunuchs, ranging in role from wet nurses to personal attendants to tutors as they grew and matured. Additionally, many Hellenistic royal courts included extraordinary individuals such as people of unusually large or small stature, or other distinctive features, with dwarfs having been particularly popular and prominent in Egypt since the Pharaonic period. (In the Hellenistic period, during one of his public appearances, Ptolemy IV Philopator was even followed by a retinue of dancing dwarfs.) It seems unlikely to be a coincidence that one member of Antony's entourage in this period was a dwarf named Sisyphus, who may have been acquired during Antony's time in Egypt, as he was apparently the first notable Roman to take up this practice.[27]

Cleopatra Selene and her siblings would have been highly educated, as befitted members of the Ptolemaic dynasty. Many of Cleopatra VII's predecessors had been scholars and authors as well as kings and queens, and she herself was a lover of literature, to the degree that her enthusiasm was described as 'sensuous pleasure'. Cleopatra VII was also so interested in botany, pharmacology and toxicology that treatises on those subjects purported to have been written by her circulated in antiquity and were used by later generations of medical practitioners such as Galen of Pergamum.[28] Unsurprisingly for a woman who had borne four children, including one set of fraternal twins, she was also interested in gynaecology, and was rumoured to have experimented on pregnant women.[29]

The scholar Nikolaos of Damascus, perhaps hired by Cleopatra VII during her trip to Antioch in 37 BCE, was one of the royal children's tutors. Three others are known by name, and they were Euphronios, Rhodon and Theodoros, although nothing is known about their academic credentials. Since the internationally renowned Museum and Library were located within the palace quarter, it is likely that Cleopatra Selene had access not just to the holdings, but also the scholars in residence there. Unlike the Romans, the Macedonian royal families had a long history of educating their daughters just as they educated their sons. Therefore, it is probable that Cleopatra Selene was educated by the same tutors and in the same manner as her brothers, perhaps even simultaneously. She certainly seems to have been comfortable around scholars and interested in intellectual pursuits, as she put her education to good use later in life, assisting Juba with his literary works, fragments of which have survived, and show a clear interest in Egypt as well as knowledge about the region.

Cleopatra Selene may not have been aware that she had other half-siblings; apart from his three children with Cleopatra VII, Antony had at least five other children with three other wives, and there was an early marriage to another woman that may have resulted in yet more children, but this is obscure.[30] We only know about it because the woman in question, Fadia, was the daughter of an emancipated enslaved person, and Cicero used her status as a way of criticising Antony.[31] At the time of Cleopatra Selene's birth, Antony already had a daughter, Antonia Prima (so known because she was the first of Antony's three daughters named Antonia after him in the Roman fashion) by his second wife, Antonia Hybrida Minor, and two sons, Marcus Antonius Antyllus and Iullus Antonius, by his third wife, Fulvia.

Since Antonia Prima was much older than Cleopatra Selene, having been born in 50 BCE and married in 36 BCE, it is possible that the sisters never actually met, and Antonia Prima played a minimal role in Cleopatra Selene's life. Yet it is also possible that Antonia Prima travelled in Antony's entourage on his journeys around the eastern Mediterranean. Her marriage to Pythodoros of Tralles was arranged primarily so that Antony could convince his wealthy son-in-law to invest in his planned military campaign in Parthia, so she may have been a feature of Cleopatra Selene's life as early as her first meeting with her father in Antioch in 37 BCE. Antonia Prima's daughter Pythodoria, born in either 30 or 29 BCE, went on to marry King Polemon Pythodoros of Pontus around 14 BCE, which made her Queen of Pontus and the Bosphoran Kingdom, two of the Roman Empire's eastern allied kingdoms. Pythodoria may have sought the advice of her aunt (who, only ten years her senior, was almost her contemporary) on various aspects of queenship over the years.[32] Antony's decision to marry his daughter, a Roman citizen, to a foreigner was an extremely unusual one for a Roman consul to make. No matter how highly ranked, wealthy, politically useful and influential foreigners could be, they were still seen as inferior to Romans, particularly members of Roman senatorial families, and Romans did not normally engage in these sorts of dynastic games.[33] It gives us an insight into his pragmatism and indicates that he was putting down a variety of familial roots in the East.

Antyllus, however, certainly *was* part of Antony's entourage and was resident in Alexandria in the period from 34 to 30 BCE, when he was murdered on the steps of Cleopatra VII's Caesareum during the Roman occupation of Alexandria. As his father's oldest acknowledged son, he was Antony's heir, his status made clear on a series of gold aureus coins issued by Antony from 34 BCE.[34] Antony's portrait is on the obverse face accompanied by an abbreviated Latin legend which reads as follows: 'Marcus Antonius, son of Marcus, grandson of Marcus, Augur, Imperator for the third time, consul for the second time, consul designate for the third time, triumvir for the ordering of the state'. Antyllus' portrait is on the reverse face accompanied by an abbreviated Latin legend which reads as follows: 'Marcus Antonius, son of Marcus'.

It was this status that made Antyllus' death inevitable; no doubt Octavian thought back to himself at the age of eighteen, posthumously adopted by Caesar and made his heir, determined to avenge his murdered father, and considered him too dangerous to

A coin depicting Antony on the obverse face, and Antyllus on the reverse face.

be allowed to live. Since Antyllus and Caesarion were the same age and of roughly equal status – one the son of the Roman triumvir, the other the son of the Egyptian queen – it is likely that they were friends, or at least comrades. They were probably encouraged by their parents to forge a bond that would be politically useful to both over the coming decades, much stronger than the normal patron–client relationship normally enjoyed by Romans and client rulers. A key reason why Egypt was the last remaining Hellenistic kingdom to be ruled by a descendant of one of Alexander the Great's generals was that its rulers had managed to maintain good relations with Rome. Cleopatra had enjoyed the patronage first of Caesar, then of Antony, while her father had enjoyed the patronage of Gnaeus Pompey, also known as Pompey the Great. It would be a boon to Caesarion as King of Egypt to have a powerful friend in the Roman Senate, one who, if not related to him by blood, was certainly related to his siblings.

Cleopatra Selene, her brothers and her half-brothers were not the only youngsters in residence at the Egyptian royal court. It was common practice for influential families to send their children to foster with others, where they would be raised and educated but also serve as a living guarantee of their own family's good intentions and trustworthiness. So, Cleopatra VII's court contained many children who were members of the royal families of the surrounding kingdoms, including, from 33 BCE onwards, Princess Iotape, the daughter of King Artavasdes I of Media Atropatene (part of modern Iran).[35] In 35 BCE, her father made an offer of an alliance to Antony to assist him with his planned campaign against the Parthian Empire to which Antony agreed, and in 34 BCE their partnership was formalised by the betrothal of Iotape to Alexander Helios.[36] This betrothal was dissolved in 30 BCE and Iotape was returned to her father. Eventually she married her cousin King Mithridates III of Commagene (another part of modern Iran), and as Queen of

Commagene she may have stayed in touch with her childhood playmate.

As for Cleopatra Selene herself, it is likely that she was betrothed to her older half-brother Caesarion. He had technically been Cleopatra VII's co-ruler since the death of his uncle Ptolemy XIV in around 44 BCE when he was a toddler, after Cleopatra VII reportedly poisoned her second brother-husband to clear Caesarion's path to the throne. In reality Cleopatra VII ruled alone until Caesarion was old enough to assist her and have some agency. But it was very clear that Caesarion was his mother's chosen successor, and monumental sculptures and reliefs of his image proliferated around the kingdom. There are even some indications of Caesarion's autonomous activities in the archaeological record.[37] Yet while Cleopatra VII and Caesarion may have ruled together, and parent–child alliances were not unknown in the Ptolemaic dynasty, the obvious stumbling block to this arrangement – despite its convenience while Cleopatra VII was still young and Caesarion still a child – was that it would not produce any heirs that could succeed Caesarion upon his death. So Caesarion needed a wife and, eventually, a co-ruler: who better than Cleopatra Selene?

The Ptolemaic dynasty had practised sibling marriage for three centuries, since Ptolemy II Philadelphos had married his sister Arsinoe II.[38] While incest is distasteful, not to mention illegal, today, in classical antiquity it was practised legally in various ways and in many places around the ancient Mediterranean. For the Ptolemies, brother–sister marriage not only had practical benefits in that it concentrated power within the family, but also symbolic ones in that it equated the individuals who practised it not only with the Greek but also the Egyptian gods, who were themselves frequently married to their siblings and half-siblings. In the case of Caesarion and Cleopatra Selene, it would have an additional political benefit: although the Romans found incest repulsive, the couple were both half-Roman, and through their fathers both members of ancient, powerful and influential Roman families. This would give them a significant advantage over other allied kings and queens, who could not say the same regarding their own more humble genealogies.

4

Death of a Dynasty?

EARLY IN 40 BCE, the year of Cleopatra Selene's birth, Antony's wife Fulvia died suddenly at Sicyon, a Greek city-state, on her way to reunite with him at Athens, from where he was overseeing the eastern part of the Roman Empire. While this was unfortunate for Fulvia, it was, it must be said, rather convenient for Antony.[1] As a result, Antony was able to blame Fulvia for everything that had recently occurred in Italy, thereby exonerating himself. It suited Octavian to let him do so; their friends encouraged them to reconcile and reunite in the interests not only of themselves but also of the Roman Empire. Consequently, in the September of 40 BCE they met at Brundisium (modern Brindisi in Apulia), a port city on the Adriatic coast in the south of Italy that was conveniently located for trade not only with Greece but also with the Middle East, as Antony was in the early stages of planning his military campaign against the Parthian Empire. The agreement that they came to there would have significant ramifications for Cleopatra VII and her family, and particularly significant consequences for Cleopatra Selene that would define the course of her adult life, although that would not become clear for quite some time.

The two men entertained each other lavishly in their separate camps. Octavian's banquet was of the traditional Roman sort while

Antony, perhaps inspired by his experiences in Alexandria, chose to entertain in the Egyptian style.[2] He may even have used the gifts that Cleopatra had given him at the banquet she had hosted in Tarsus. Depending on the nature of Octavian's feelings towards Cleopatra and Egypt at this time, this may not have gone well. The Pact of Brundisium, as the agreement that Antony and Octavian came to is now known, saw them reaffirm their territorial grants, with Antony allotted the east, Octavian the west, and Lepidus Hispania and Africa. They also each chose a man to hold the consulship for the duration of the following year, since neither of them were inclined to take the office at that time. As a means of indicating to everyone that they were genuinely reconciled, Antony agreed to marry Octavian's older sister Octavia, who, like him, had recently lost her spouse (Gaius Claudius Marcellus, a former consul in 50 BCE and by whom she had two children, one daughter and one son).[3] A senatorial decree allowing the marriage had to be issued because Octavia was actually pregnant with her deceased husband's child, another daughter, at the time, and under normal circumstances a widow was required to wait until ten months after her husband's death to remarry, to avoid any uncertainty surrounding the paternity of a child she might bear during this time. But this was clearly not considered taboo as Octavian would do something similar (albeit considerably sleazier) himself the following year, divorcing his wife Scribonia the day that she gave birth to his only biological child, his daughter Julia, and then marrying Livia Drusilla, the wife of his political ally Tiberius Claudius Nero, despite the fact that she was six months pregnant with her first husband's second child. Nero even gave Livia away at the wedding and allowed his two sons, one of whom was the future emperor Tiberius, to be raised in Octavian's household. This was a startling reversal of the usual Roman practice whereby fathers were the parents who automatically possessed the legal rights to their children and could even completely forbid mothers' access if they felt so inclined.

A coin depicting Antony on the obverse face,
and a bust of Octavia on the reverse face.

Antony issued numerous coins celebrating the marriage (his
fourth) from the eastern mints that were under his control. On
one rather evocative type, a silver tetradrachm that circulated in
Ephesus in Asia Minor in 39 BCE, he is depicted on the obverse
face, while a bust of Octavia atop a *cista* (a box or a basket used
for practical and ritual purposes) and flanked by entwined snakes
is depicted on the reverse face.[4] It is worth noting that this coin
depicts a bust of Octavia, rather than a portrait, as living Roman
women were not typically depicted on coins, no matter who their
husbands were.

Although marrying Octavia was politically expedient in the
short term, and the marriage itself seems to have been happy
prior to their divorce in 32 BCE, it was a disaster for Antony in the
long run. By marrying Octavian's sister, Antony blurred the line
between political and personal, and ensured that Octavian could
use his treatment of Octavia for political purposes, making it all
about himself if he felt so inclined – which, of course, he did.

Around the time that Antony was marrying Octavia, on the
other side of the Mediterranean Cleopatra was preparing to give

birth to his twins. While she would have been delighted that Antony's control of the eastern half of the Roman Empire had been reaffirmed, her feelings regarding Antony's new marriage may have been less enthusiastic. The fact that Antony was married was probably not a concern: after all, both Caesar and Antony had been married to Roman women at the times of their liaisons with her – Caesar to Calpurnia Pisonis and Antony to Fulvia – and neither marriage had made any material difference to Cleopatra or her children's circumstances. But Antony's marriage to Octavia would potentially be rather different in this respect because Octavia was Octavian's sister, and she was from the outset more present in Antony's life than her predecessor had been. Fulvia had stayed in Rome whereas Octavia had already come east and settled in Athens, a city in which Cleopatra herself was well known, having spent time in exile there with her father as a child. Certainly, it was not long before Octavia gave birth to the first of her daughters

A white marble portrait of Octavia.

by Antony, Julia Antonia Major, known as Antonia Major, in 39 BCE.[5] While Cleopatra Selene would have been too young to know or care about this, it is probable that Cleopatra spent some time worrying about how Octavia's daughter, so close in age to her own, might affect Antony's feelings and leave her and Cleopatra Selene at a disadvantage.

By all accounts, Octavia seems to have been a lovely woman. She was universally praised, lauded, in fact, by ancient authors for her intelligence, dignity and loyalty, as well as for her beauty, which is on display in many surviving marble portraits, such as the one currently on display in the Palazzo Massimo alle Terme museum in Rome, which dates from around 39 BCE.[6] She was presented to ancient readers as a paragon of virtue and an example of a sort of *ultimate* Roman woman. While this conveniently allowed ancient authors to contrast Octavia with both her predecessor Fulvia and her rival Cleopatra, to Octavia's clear advantage, there must have been some truth to this overwhelmingly positive characterisation. She seems to have been an entirely supportive and faithful wife to Antony, uprooting herself and her young family to travel east and settle with him in Athens, where she spent the majority of the period 40–36 BCE raising not only her own three children by Marcellus, and the two daughters that she would go on to have by Antony, but also taking responsibility for his two sons by Fulvia. It seems highly likely that Juba, too, grew up in her household, since, after Caesar's death in 44 BCE, Octavian's military campaigning meant she was the family member with the more stable home life.

While based in Athens in order to oversee the eastern part of the empire in his role as triumvir, Antony seems to have taken his fondness for the Greek god Dionysos to new extremes. He built a rustic hut in a conspicuous spot above the Theatre of Dionysos on the south slope of the Acropolis, covered it with brushwood and hung Dionysiac paraphernalia including drums and fawnskins up inside it.[7] He and his friends would laze around, drinking, entertained by a troupe of musicians summoned from Italy especially for that purpose, and essentially perform for the citizens of Athens. Antony even requested that he be proclaimed as Dionysos throughout the Greek East.[8] He decreed that statues erected to him be inscribed with the name of the god rather than his own, and he even began to dress himself like the god, and his entourage, like the god's attendants.[9] He had, perhaps, been inspired by Cleopatra in this, in the way that she presented herself publicly as Isis, Venus and Aphrodite, seemingly to great acclaim from her subjects. The Athenians were happy enough to play along and address him as Dionysos, going so far as to request that he marry their patron goddess Athena.[10] Antony agreed, but requested a dowry of one thousand talents of gold, which the citizens provided; however, they also proceeded to graffiti his statues with messages directed at Octavia and Cleopatra, advising both women to divorce him.[11]

The five-year term of the triumvirate expired in 38 BCE, and so in 37 BCE Antony and Octavia returned to Italy to renew it for another five years.[12] Octavia arranged a meeting between Antony and Octavian at Tarentum in Italy (she is frequently presented acting as an intermediary and peacemaker between the two in this period), and one of the agreements they reached there was that Antony's younger son by Fulvia, Iullus Antonius, would marry Octavian's daughter Julia, in an attempt to solidify the bond between the two men.[13] It was agreed that now was the time for Antony to undertake his military campaign against the Parthian Empire, and he left Italy having been gifted two legions by his brother-in-law and a thousand soldiers by his wife, in exchange for all of his ships (this loss of his navy would, ironically, come to make him more reliant on Cleopatra and her considerable resources when he sought to replace it). On this occasion, rather than accompanying Antony on his military campaign, Octavia remained in Italy.[14] This proved convenient when Antony summoned Cleopatra to

Antioch in 37 BCE to request that she provide resources for the campaign, and she arrived toting their three-year-old twins and seeking his recognition of their paternity. This he was happy to give, and he may even have been the one responsible for coming up with their whimsical second names. He was also happy to resume his sexual relationship with Cleopatra. She left Antioch with him, accompanied him as far as the Euphrates, and then returned to Egypt pregnant again. Her third child by Antony, a son she would name Ptolemy Philadelphos, after her illustrious ancestor Ptolemy II Philadelphos, was born in 36 BCE. It is unlikely to have been a coincidence that around this time Cleopatra started double-dating the coinage that she issued. It was traditional practice for Egyptians to date things according to the year of the ruler, so 37 BCE was Year 16 of the reign of Cleopatra. However, at this point she began a new chronology, so Year 16 was also Year 1. What was she marking by doing this? Perhaps, in her eyes, the reconstitution of the original Ptolemaic Empire, as it had been during the reign of her finest predecessor.

While Cleopatra was celebrating, Antony was marching. His intended military campaign was one that Caesar had been planning prior to his death, an attempt to avenge the death of his friend and ally Marcus Licinius Crassus, Crassus' son Publius Licinius Crassus, and the loss not only of his legions but also their standards at the Battle of Carrhae (modern Harran in Turkey) in 53 BCE. Crassus' humiliation, and by implication Rome's, was total when, after his death, the Parthians poured molten gold into his mouth in reference to his unquenchable thirst for wealth. They also used his severed head as a prop in a performance of Euripides' *The Bacchae* given to mark the wedding of King Orodes II's son and heir Pacorus, and dressed the Roman prisoner who most resembled Crassus in women's clothing.[15]

So, in early 36 BCE, in an attempt to make things right (from the Roman perspective) and, at the very least, recapture the lost Roman standards, Antony and his army travelled east. Unfortunately, his campaign did not go to plan. Like many Roman attempts to invade the Parthian Empire, it proved to be a costly and resounding failure. On the way there, Antony lost 24,000 men, and on the way back, another 8,000. In December, he asked Cleopatra to meet him at Leukokome, a Nabataean port on the coast of the Red Sea, and to bring with her equipment for his troops and money to pay them. He then returned with her to Alexandria. Plutarch is very clear in his assignment of blame for the debacle: Antony's failure was caused by his longing for Cleopatra, which caused him to linger overlong with her in Alexandria, and set out on campaign far too late in the year, leaving his army at the mercy of harsh winter conditions.[16]

In the spring of the following year, Antony planned a new military campaign, this time travelling via the kingdom of Armenia to set up a permanent base from which the campaign could be co-ordinated.[17] At this point, Octavia, who had spent the previous year in Rome, where she had given birth to her second daughter by Antony, Julia Antonia Minor, wrote to Antony to tell him that she was travelling to Athens with 2,000 troops and supplies with the blessing of her brother. Since Antony's first campaign had floundered so spectacularly, he was in no mood to be patronised by either sibling, so he wrote back and asked her not to travel any further than Athens. In turn, Octavia wrote back and asked him what he wanted her to do with everything that she had brought for him. Antony responded that he was prepared to accept the resources, but not her.

Upon Octavia's return to Rome, Octavian ordered her to leave Antony. Octavia, however, refused to do so, and furthermore refused to allow her brother to use her husband's poor treatment of her as a pretext for war. She remained living in Antony's house, taking care of his Roman children, administering to his business affairs and mediating between him and Octavian.

Ancient authors lay the blame for Antony's treatment of Octavia squarely at Cleopatra's feet. According to them, she was jealous and possessive, saw Octavia as a rival and refused to tolerate her presence, afraid that Antony would compare the two women and find her wanting.[18] So, in order to ensure that Antony was not given the opportunity, she went out of her way to manipulate and emotionally blackmail him, dieting to give the impression that she was wasting away; not-so-surreptitiously weeping where he could see her and, when he asked what was the matter, drying her eyes and replying that nothing was; and swooning whenever he attempted to leave her presence. She allegedly engaged some of Antony's companions to support her in this, and they reproached him for his treatment of her, and told him he was a harsh, unfeeling man, all on her behalf. They even compared the two women to Cleopatra's advantage, pointing out that Octavia had married Antony at the behest of Octavian, and she would always put his interests first, whereas Cleopatra, a powerful queen in her own right, was dismissed and disrespected, referred to only as Antony's mistress. These criticisms, they continued, Cleopatra was prepared to tolerate, so long as she had the benefit of Antony's presence. If there is any truth in these allegations, it is probable that she enlisted the children in her crusade, parading them around in front of him, encouraging them to be as winning and endearing as possible. After all, she had borne Antony three children while Octavia had only produced two, and two of the three were sons. Moreover, her three children were royalty, something that Octavia's two children could never be.

After Antony's departure from Alexandria, and while he was staying in Antioch in preparation for further travels east, Cleopatra's minions convinced him that she was on the brink of taking her own life, so he turned around and travelled back to Alexandria. This would have been an interesting experience for Cleopatra Selene, an object lesson in how to wield soft power in the face of an equally matched or perhaps even overmatched adversary, and achieve one's goals by undertaking a calculated, prolonged and sustained campaign of emotional manipulation, rather than attempting to force the issue and showing one's hand.

In 34 BCE, Antony set out on campaign once more but on this occasion he only travelled as far as Armenia. Initially, relations between him and Armenia's king Artavasdes II were cordial, and Antony's intermediary Dellius even offered Artavasdes a betrothal between Alexander Helios and Artavasdes' daughter, indicating he was already making plans for his Egyptian children's futures. Artavasdes was not convinced by this. Sure enough, Antony occupied the kingdom, seized Artavasdes and his family and dragged them back to Alexandria in golden chains.[19] This manner of display turned the royal family into just another piece of plunder, albeit plunder of the highest quality.[20]

Once in Alexandria, Antony marked his victory with a celebration that seems to have been purposely designed to resemble a Roman military triumph, which his critics back in Rome did not appreciate. The Ptolemies were renowned for their lavish public festivals, and a detailed description of one event celebrating the god Dionysos and held during the reign of Ptolemy II Philadelphos, written by the eyewitness Callixeinus of Rhodes, has survived. This account can be used to imagine how Antony, who was a dedicated follower of the same god, may have been welcomed back into the city.[21] Antony, dressed as Dionysos in a saffron robe with an ivy wreath atop his head and a *thyrsus* – a fennel staff that was tipped with a pinecone – in his hand, rode in a chariot through the city and into the Gymnasium. Here Cleopatra – dressed as the goddess Isis – Caesarion, Cleopatra Selene, Alexander Helios and Ptolemy Philadelphos were waiting for him, seated on golden thrones atop raised silver platforms.[22] This must have been a thrilling occasion for Cleopatra Selene, as she was now six, old enough to understand that this was a special day, and that she had an important role to play in it. She was probably very excited at the thought of seeing her father and celebrating what was being presented as a magnificent victory, even if that was not precisely the truth. Antony disembarked from his chariot and presented Artavasdes and the royal family, all bound in golden chains, to Cleopatra.[23] The royal captives, however, refused to pay obeisance to her, remaining standing rather than prostrating themselves on the floor and kissing her feet in the traditional *proskynesis* posture; the ritualised manner in which inferiors greeted their superiors had been introduced to the Macedonian royal court by Alexander the Great following his victory over the Persians.[24] Little did Cleopatra Selene know that in a few short years she would be in their position.

In addition to the presentation of the Armenian spoils to his Egyptian family, Antony also made extensive territorial grants to them, an action that has come to be known as the Donations of Alexandria. These grants were a combination of real and imaginary, comprising not only territory that the Roman Empire already possessed, but also that which Antony wished and planned to acquire. He proclaimed Cleopatra to be Queen of Kings, the Queen of Egypt, Cyprus, Libya and Syria, with Caesarion, King of Kings, as her co-ruler. He also made sure to acknowledge Caesar's paternity of Caesarion, and state that Cleopatra had been Caesar's wife at the time, making Caesarion Caesar's legitimate son.[25] This decision was guaranteed to enrage Octavian when he heard about it, as it set Caesarion up as his rival for the affections of Caesar's supporters. Alexander Helios was proclaimed King of Armenia, Media and Parthia (once Antony had managed to conquer it). The boy was dressed in a traditional Median costume complete with ceremonial headdress and flanked by Armenian bodyguards. It has been suggested that two bronze statuettes dating to the second half of the first century BCE, found in Egypt and currently housed in the Metropolitan Museum of Art in New York and the Walters

Art Gallery in Boston, are portraits of him made to commemorate this occasion.

If the statuettes do depict Alexander Helios, and they were commissioned by either Cleopatra or Antony to commemorate the occasion, this raises the possibility that the other children were commemorated in a similar way, but their statuettes simply have not survived, or, if they have survived, not been recognised as such. For Ptolemy Philadelphos was likewise granted territories – Syria, Cilicia and Asia Minor – and was especially dressed up for the occasion, in a Macedonian military uniform, and flanked by Macedonian bodyguards. No mention is made of Caesarion's or Cleopatra Selene's clothing on this occasion, so perhaps they were dressed in their usual Egyptian royal garb. Since Caesarion was already King of Egypt, and Cleopatra Selene was proclaimed Queen of Crete and Cyrenaica, territories adjacent to Egypt, this lends credibility to the theory that she was ultimately intended to reign as Queen of Egypt and co-rule with Caesarion after Cleopatra's death.

Cleopatra Selene's new kingdom of Crete and Cyrenaica had once been Ptolemaic territory, but Cyrenaica's king, Ptolemy Apion (c.150–96 BCE), had died without heirs and bequeathed the kingdom to Rome in his will. The fact that Cleopatra Selene was allotted the Roman territories of Crete and Cyrenaica is potentially significant for another reason: Antony had a particular relationship and history with Crete. In 74 BCE his father, also named Marcus Antonius, had been tasked with combatting pirates in the Mediterranean that were based on the island, but had met with spectacular failure and was defeated by the Cretans in a naval battle, forcing him to make a peace treaty with them.[26] Ancient authors are unanimously scathing about his behaviour and competence during this time.[27] Yet he was awarded the *cognomen* Creticus, and was subsequently known as Marcus Antonius Creticus.[28] Was this a way of publicly humiliating him as punishment for his failure, and making sure neither he nor anyone else forgot it? If so, it was a snide inversion of the usual Roman practice of awarding geographical *cognomina* to military commanders who had successfully overcome foreign enemies and captured foreign territory, such as Publius Cornelius Scipio, awarded the *cognomen* Africanus because of his victory over the Carthaginian general Hannibal Barca at the Battle of Zama in 202 BCE. Since Antony's father had died shortly after the Cretan debacle, Antony may have felt a certain sense of satisfaction at being able finally to get the better of Crete on behalf of his family, and to impose his daughter as a ruler over the Cretans whose ancestors had so embarrassed his father. It was around this time that bronze coins with a crocodile motif began to be issued on Crete and in one of the Cyrenaic cities by Antony's lieutenant Publius Canidius Crassus, and it is possible that this was done to honour the new young queen.

In the wake of the ceremony, Antony wrote to the Senate in Rome, requesting that they confirm the territorial grants. The two consuls, both of whom were loyal to Antony, intercepted his letter and refused to do so. They were attempting to protect him because they recognised, as he did not, that his apparent giving away of Roman territory would be received very poorly by his peers back in Rome.[29] Antony's lengthy stays in the eastern half of the Roman Empire had made it easy for Octavian to present him as out of touch and out of step, and put a negative spin on even the most sensible and reasonable actions. Although, admittedly, Antony had not helped himself in this regard.

Despite the consuls' efforts, immediately following the Donations of Alexandria, with Antony based in the east and Octavian in the west, relations between the two became increasingly strained. They hurled accusations at each other across the Mediterranean, and their propaganda war began in earnest. Things cannot have been helped by the apocalyptic prophecies that were now circulating around the empire and which had distinctly pro-Greek and anti-Roman sentiments. Cleopatra was being proclaimed as the Woman or the Widow, a mighty queen who would rescue the east from Roman subjugation.[30] One such oracle refers to Cleopatra cutting Rome's hair, a rather whimsical reference to the territories that she and her children had acquired at Rome's expense.[31] Unlike the rest of the sources from this period that have survived, these present us with the eastern perspective on Antony, Cleopatra and their children, and enthusiasm for the possibilities that their supremacy could bring.[32]

Early in 32 BCE, Antony and Cleopatra travelled to Ephesus and summoned the Eastern Empire's allied kings, many of whom owed Antony their positions and kingdoms.[33] Caesarion probably remained in Egypt, as he was just beginning to have some agency as king. The younger children may have been present for this event, especially if there was some sort of ceremonial aspect to it, in which Antony and Cleopatra emphasised their hopes for the future, hopes that rested on their dynasty and the roles that had been outlined for them by the Donations of Alexandria. Upon the conclusion of the meeting, Antony and Cleopatra travelled first to Samos and then to Athens. Antony had spent a considerable amount of time in the city over the course of his life, first studying there as a young man and subsequently using it as his base of operations as a triumvir. Additionally, the city had long been favoured by the Ptolemies who had favoured them in return, and on this occasion its citizens honoured Cleopatra. This may have endeared Athens and the Athenians to Cleopatra Selene, and them to her in turn, and she would visit the city and patronise it with Juba later in her life. Epigraphic evidence indicates that there was at least one Athenian woman in residence at Cleopatra's court; perhaps she had been engaged on one of Cleopatra's previous visits.[34]

Around this time, Antony finally divorced Octavia. She left his house in Rome and either moved in with Octavian at his house on the Palatine Hill or moved to her own residence nearby. She took all of the children with her, although in the eyes of Roman law she had no right to Iullus, Antonia Major or Antonia Minor, as, legally, Roman children were considered the property of their father rather than their mother. Perhaps in retaliation for Antony's divorcing his sister, and to further blacken Antony's name in Rome, Octavian took this opportunity to seize the copy of Antony's will that he had deposited at the Temple of Vesta with the Vestal Virgins prior to his departure from Rome.[35] He had been informed of its presence there by Antony's former friends Titius and Plancus, both of whom had witnessed the document but had subsequently defected from Antony's faction to Octavian's. He read it, marked particularly incriminating and inflammatory passages, and then read these aloud in the Senate. In it, Antony clearly favoured his Egyptian family, reiterating that Caesarion was the son of Caesar, leaving substantial legacies to his children borne by Cleopatra, and requesting that, after his body had been processed through Rome and into the Forum, it be sent to Cleopatra and he be interred in Alexandria.[36] Whether Antony's will was legally valid rather depends upon the status of Cleopatra and of her children, as Roman citizens could only leave legacies to other Roman citizens. Certainly, the smear campaign waged against Cleopatra by Octavian and his cronies emphasised her foreignness and intrinsic otherness, referring to her as 'the Egyptian woman' and 'the Egyptian whore'. But Antony's will implies that either Cleopatra possessed Roman citizenship, probably granted either by Caesar or Antony, and her children had inherited it from her, or Antony had granted it to them himself. Failing that – and it was this interpretation that Octavian put on the document – Antony had become so alienated from Rome that he was no longer following traditional Roman law or custom.[37] Yet one thing to take away from this is that Antony viewed his children by Cleopatra as equal to his children by his Roman wives; no matter how little time he had actually spent with her, he saw Cleopatra Selene as being no different from her three half-sisters.

A letter written by Antony to Octavian from this time has survived. In it, he tries to determine exactly what his former brother-in-law's problem with the relationship is while needling him in sexually blunt language for his hypocrisy: 'What has made such a change in you? Because I'm fucking the queen? Is she my wife? Am I just beginning this, or was it nine years ago? What then of you – do you fuck only Livia Drusilla? Good luck to you if when you read this letter you have not been in Tertulla or Terentilla or Rufilla or Salvia Titisenia, or all of them. Does it matter where or in whom you have your stiff prick?'[38] Here he makes the point that both he and Octavian have made a habit of cheating on their Roman wives, but asks, ultimately, what does it matter if they are philanderers? Legally, Roman men could sleep with whomever they wanted, female or male, the only exception to this being another Roman man's wife. The only person of whom marital fidelity was expected, and basically demanded, was the wife; this expectation would subsequently be made legally enforceable in 18 BCE when Augustus passed the *Lex Julia de adulteriis coercendis*, the 'Julian Law for the Repression of Adultery', which criminalised adultery, penalising not only the adulterous wife and her lover, but also the cuckolded husband if he did not take action and divorce his wife, which would lead him to risk being prosecuted as a pimp.

Following the expiration of the Second Triumvirate at the end of 33 BCE, relations between Antony and Octavian deteriorated swiftly and the two men's mutual distrust of each other's ambitions was loudly voiced by their respective supporters in the Senate. The climax to more than a decade of rivalry arrived in 31 BCE, when Octavian formally declared war on Cleopatra, on the grounds that she had not behaved appropriately as an allied monarch.[39] In response, Antony and Cleopatra gathered their forces in the spring of 31 BCE in the Gulf of Ambracia on the north-western

A bronze fitting from one of the ships destroyed during the Battle of Actium.

coast of Greece.[40] Plutarch recalled his great grandfather Nicarchus complaining that all the residents of his hometown of Chaeronea near Delphi had been forced to transport wheat down to the coast to provision Antony's forces, and they were whipped if those responsible for overseeing felt they were doing so too slowly.[41] Throughout the summer, the omens went from bad to worse. Finally, on 2 September, the two fleets engaged off the promontory of Actium. A bronze fitting from the prow of a ship has been recovered from the seabed at Prevesa Bay, near the site of the battle, and is thought to have come from one of the ships sunk during the battle, probably a minor one due to the relatively small size of the fitting.[42] The fitting depicts a figure dressed for battle in a helmet and an aegis, usually interpreted as a representation of the goddess Athena.

Octavian's victory at Actium became the foundation of his personal authority and, as such, it was relentlessly hyped by promoters and propagandists of his regime both during and after his reign.[43] Augustan poets such as Horace and Virgil wrote lengthy screeds presenting the battle as a magnificent clash of civilisations, with Virgil going so far as to rework Homer's famous description of the shield of Achilles in the *Iliad* as a description of Octavian's ancestor Aeneas' shield in the *Aeneid*, with this second shield bearing a depiction of the battle that showed it to be the culmination and defining moment of the entire Julian dynasty.[44] One veteran of the battle, a man named Marcus Billenius, a soldier in the eleventh legion who subsequently settled in the Roman colony set up at Ateste and ended up as a decurion (a type of local councillor), even adopted the name Actiacus in honour of his participation.[45] In reality, however, it was a relatively minor skirmish and militarily underwhelming. Cleopatra may initially have had thoughts of following in the footsteps of the famous and renowned Queen Artemisia I of Caria, immortalised by one of her subjects, who happened to be the Greek historian Herodotus, for fighting as an ally to King Xerxes in the first Persian invasion of Greece and commanding five ships at the battles of Artemisium and Salamis in 480 BCE. However, Cleopatra left the battle early, presumably realising that it was more important for her to be in Egypt with her children than in Greece with Antony. She captained her purple-sailed flagship, *Antonias*, away, and her actions concerned Antony enough that he sailed after her and boarded the ship to ask what was happening, only to find himself being taken south. Their departure was seen as surrender, demoralising the rest of their fleet.[46]

For the duration of the journey on *Antonias* Antony sat alone in the prow, despairing, ignoring Cleopatra completely until her handmaidens Eiras and Charmian convinced him to speak to her.[47] They travelled to the coast of Egypt and there went their separate ways, Cleopatra returning to Alexandria as if victorious, her ship decked out in garlands and with triumphant music blaring, so as not to alarm the populace, and Antony heading west to Cyrene in an attempt to acquire more forces by taking control of the legions that were based there. Unfortunately for Antony, however, the legions were not inclined to join him. At this point, with his final hope of military victory over Octavian dashed, he attempted to take his own life and was only prevented from doing so by loyal friends who had stayed by his side. Even so, he plunged into a deep depression and upon his return to Alexandria isolated himself from everyone, including, presumably, his children. He went down to the Poseidium, an elbow of land projecting out from the Great Harbour, upon which there was a Temple of Poseidon, and here built a hermitage that he called his Timonium, as he was choosing to follow the example of Timon of Athens, who lived during the time of the Peloponnesian War (431–404 BCE).[48] This man had been nicknamed 'the misanthrope', as he felt that he had been wronged and treated with ingratitude and, as a result, hated all men.[49] Perhaps, like Timon, Antony spent some of his time attempting to commune with Poseidon, asking the god of the sea why, exactly, he had been forsaken.

Antony and Cleopatra responded very differently to the situation in which they now found themselves. While Antony struggled with his depression, Cleopatra was galvanised, and worked hard to salvage the situation for herself and her children. She wrote to Octavian and offered to abdicate in favour of her children, presumably meaning Caesarion and Cleopatra Selene.[50] After abdicating, she said, she intended to travel to India, but this plan was forestalled when Antony returned from the Poseidium to the palace. Still, in preparation for what Cleopatra must have presumed would be Caesarion's imminent assumption of power, she enrolled him as an *ephebe*, marking his assumption of citizenship and the start of military training, and Antony exchanged Antyllus' *toga praetexta*, the purple-bordered toga worn by Roman children, for a *toga virilis*, the plain white toga worn by Roman adult men. These actions confirmed that both young men were now considered to be adults. It is at this point that we start to see signs of Caesarion acting independently of Cleopatra in the archaeological record, perhaps in anticipation of his mother's abdication and departure from Egypt. An unfinished sandstone stela found at Coptos in Upper Egypt can be dated precisely to 19 January 30 BCE. It records an agreement between a guild of thirty-six linen manufacturers, their families and two high-ranking priestly officials of Coptos regarding the expenses of the local Apis Bull, and on it Caesarion is depicted as an adult male pharaoh making offerings to a group of Egyptian deities including Min, Isis, Geb and Sobek.[51]

Upon elevating their children, Antony and Cleopatra seem to have taken a step back. They changed the name of their drinking club to 'The Partners in Death', and Cleopatra apparently began testing poisons.[52] Yet Cleopatra, rather than thinking emotionally about her own sorry situation, was still thinking strategically about how she might salvage her dynasty, prioritising the political survival of the Ptolemaic house and Egypt above all else. To that end, she sent all four of her children away from Alexandria: Caesarion to India by way of the Red Sea trade routes, and Cleopatra Selene, Alexander Helios and Ptolemy Philadelphos up the Nile to Thebes.[53]

Finally, in the summer of 30 BCE, Octavian headed to Egypt. On 1 August, the remainder of Antony's forces deserted to Octavian. Cleopatra barricaded herself and her treasure inside her mausoleum and sent a messenger to tell Antony that she had taken her own life.[54] This seems to me an indication that, however much she might have loved Antony, she had finally chosen her children, dynasty and kingdom over him, prioritising their survival over his, and perhaps even hers. Ultimately this would prove to be the right choice. Upon receiving this message, Antony reacted precisely as she predicted he would, which is why she sent the message in the first place. He attempted to take his own life with the assistance of a slave named, ironically, Eros. Unfortunately, he only succeeded in seriously injuring himself, and he was at this point informed that Cleopatra was not, after all, dead, and demanded to be taken to her. Because Cleopatra was locked inside her mausoleum, Antony could not enter through the main entrance, and a sort of farcical street theatre ensued, with the haemorrhaging Antony hoisted up through a first-floor window on ropes by Cleopatra, Eiras and Charmian. Antony died in Cleopatra's arms. Eventually, Octavian's allies gained entrance to the mausoleum and succeeded in apprehending Cleopatra, although not before she had attempted to take her own life by stabbing herself in the chest.

Once back in the palace, patched up by her personal physician Olympus and under house arrest, Cleopatra attempted to take her own life again with the only means available to her, this time refusing food as a means of starving herself to death. In response, Octavian sent soldiers to Thebes to take Cleopatra Selene, Alexander Helios and Ptolemy Philadelphos hostage and threatened to harm them if she did not eat. How much the children knew about this is debateable. They had presumably been informed that their father was dead, although they may have been spared the more gruesome details, and were probably grieving his passing, despite his irregular presence in their lives. While Ptolemy Philadelphos, at the age of six, was perhaps too young fully to understand their situation, Cleopatra Selene and Alexander Helios, at the ages of ten (the same age their uncles Ptolemy XIII and Ptolemy XIV had been upon acceding to the throne), were probably more cognisant of the precarious position they were in. They knew their circumstances were grievous enough that their two older half-brothers Caesarion and Antyllus had been sent away from the royal court for their own protection, Caesarion on his way up the Nile to the Red Sea ports to take a ship to India, Antyllus in hiding somewhere out in the city. They must have feared for their own lives.

Relieved of all the duties commensurate with her position as Queen of Egypt, Cleopatra had nothing to do with her time in captivity but ruminate. She was determined not to be led through the streets of Rome in Octavian's triumph, ogled and jeered at by hostile crowds as her sister Arsinoe had been sixteen years earlier, prior to being either executed or exiled from Egypt. Another aspect of her younger sister's fate may have weighed heavily on her: the fact that she herself had had to eliminate Arsinoe after she had been recognised as Queen of Egypt in exile. Assuming that Octavian permitted Cleopatra to abdicate in favour of her children, which was by no means certain since he had not yet agreed to her proposition, there might come a day when Caesarion and Cleopatra Selene felt that their mother was sufficiently dangerous to order her execution, just as she had ordered her sister's. She still had some small amount of influence: a spy told her that Octavian did, in fact, intend to take both her and her children to Rome and include them all in his triumph. Once the reality of her situation became clear, she hatched a plan.

On 10 August 30 BCE, cognisant of the fact that the success of her plan hinged upon Octavian not realising anything was amiss, she asked to be allowed to visit Antony and make the customary funerary libations.[55] She was, after all, a bereaved widow. For Cleopatra to be able to visit Antony at this time implies that he had been cremated according to Roman practices and his ashes placed in an urn or an ash chest rather than mummified according to Egyptian practice, since the mummification process took weeks. Octavian had no interest in returning Antony's remains to Rome, so they were probably interred in Cleopatra's own mausoleum. She may have been permitted to take the children with her, or they may have been taken to the mausoleum separately, to allow them to pay their respects to their father, as *pietas* was an extremely important concept to the Romans.

Cleopatra dined, bathed and dressed herself in her full regalia. Then, in a manner which remains a mystery to this day but probably involved some sort of poison, she took her own life. Her loyal handmaidens Eiras and Charmian took theirs in quick succession, one of their last acts being to straighten Cleopatra's royal diadem.[56] A beautifully painted but unfortunately fragmentary fresco dating from the early first century CE from the House of Giuseppe II at Pompeii in Italy, was once thought to depict the suicide of the Carthaginian noblewoman Sophonisba, the lover of King Massanissa of Numidia. It has more recently been suggested, by the historian Duane W. Roller, as a depiction of the suicide of Cleopatra.[57] There are certainly details in the painting that support this interpretation. The male attendant on the left of the painting is holding the muzzle of a crocodile, either a real one, or, more realistically perhaps, part of a tray in the shape of a crocodile. The positioning is right for the woman at the centre of the painting holding a bowl to have picked it up from there. There are also two female attendants in discussion, one dark-skinned and one light, and these could be Eiras and Charmian.[58] The woman reclining and raising the bowl is wearing a diadem, and it is she who has been identified as Cleopatra, while the man standing directly behind her, leaning close and also wearing a diadem, has been identified as Caesarion. Of course, Caesarion was not actually present at the moment of Cleopatra's death, as he was on his way to India, but he was certainly the next in line for the throne, so his inclusion may be an acknowledgement of this position.

After her death, Cleopatra would have been mummified and interred in her mausoleum. The location of the mausoleum has been lost; to date neither the tomb of Alexander the Great nor any of the tombs of the Ptolemies have been discovered by archaeologists excavating in Egypt. It is thought, based on the ancient literary accounts of first Antony's and subsequently Cleopatra's deaths, that the mausoleum was situated in Alexandria, although recently the theory that it was actually situated in Taposiris Magna, thirty miles east of Alexandria, has received considerable attention.[59]

So, in the space of just over a week, Cleopatra Selene found herself deprived of both of her parents, and it was not long before she was deprived of both of her older half-brothers, too. Antyllus, who had gone into hiding in Alexandria, fearing, correctly, that as Antony's eldest son and heir, he would be a target, was betrayed by his tutor Theodorus. Octavian's soldiers dragged him out of the Caesareum, where he had been trying to claim sanctuary, and ignominiously beheaded him on the temple's front steps. Not content with betraying his young charge, to add insult to injury, Theodorus robbed his decapitated corpse of a precious stone that Antyllus had worn on a chain around his neck. He did not get away with it, however, and Octavian had him crucified as a punishment. Caesarion was likewise betrayed by his tutor Rhodon, who told him that if he returned to Alexandria Octavian would accept him as King of Egypt. He was either intercepted and executed on the spot or brought all the way back to Alexandria and executed there.[60] There is no record of what was done with either of the young men's remains; perhaps they, too, were interred in Cleopatra's mausoleum along with their parents.

It may be that Octavian had genuinely considered permitting Caesarion to succeed Cleopatra and reign as King of Egypt, albeit a much smaller and weaker Egypt relieved of all the territorial grants and special benefactions that Antony had made to Cleopatra over the course of the last decade. He had, after all, on his way to Egypt confirmed the titles of other kings who had been elevated by Antony, such as Herod of Judea. However, Octavian's companion, the philosopher Areius, apparently advised him that 'too many Caesars is not a good thing' and encouraged him to rid himself of his rival.[61] But even with Caesarion out of the way, there were still three other members of the Ptolemaic dynasty who could occupy the Egyptian throne, if not necessarily now, then at some point in the future. This is where Cleopatra Selene was in a slightly stronger position than her brothers: after all, while there were two remaining possible kings of Egypt, there was only one remaining possible queen.

5

The Aftermath of Actium

I T IS CLEAR FROM Octavian's actions while he was in Egypt that, if he had ever considered allowing Alexander Helios and Cleopatra Selene to succeed Caesarion and Cleopatra VII as King and Queen of Egypt, he certainly did not entertain that possibility for very long. For Cleopatra Selene, Alexander Helios and Ptolemy Philadelphos, grieving their mother, father, half-brothers and cousin under heavy guard in the Brucheion, this must have been a strange and disturbing time indeed. Since Octavian classed Rome's rule of Egypt as beginning on the first day of the new Egyptian year 29 August 30 BCE, the kingdom was nominally under the rule of the children from Cleopatra VII's death until that time, but under the circumstances they cannot have felt much like monarchs.[1] They were perhaps permitted to visit their mother's mausoleum and pay their respects to their deceased parents and siblings, but they were unable to do likewise to their cousin Imhotep Petubastes IV, the much anticipated and adored only son of Pasherenptah III and Tayimhotep, who had died mysteriously, perhaps assassinated, just as the Romans had entered Alexandria. This was because Imhotep Petubastes IV was not buried immediately and would not in fact be interred for another seven years.[2] His embalmed body finally received its funerary rites in 23 BCE, long after Cleopatra Selene and her brothers had left Egypt, never to return.[3]

Octavian and his legions remained in Egypt for some time, settling affairs in the wake of the invasion and annexation. He may have been considering whether to install Alexander Helios and Cleopatra Selene as the new King and Queen of Egypt; Alexander Helios' betrothal to Princess Iotape of Media had been dissolved and she was on her way home to her father so this prior arrangement was no longer an impediment. However, at around the age of ten, the children were too young to rule independently, and their uncle Ptolemy XIII's dependence upon the nefarious advisers Pothinus, Theodotos and Achillas offered a salutary warning of what could happen when child rulers were poorly served by those who were supposed to guide them. Additionally, since Caesarion had been betrayed by Rhodon, and Antyllus by Theodoros, two individuals in whom their family had placed considerable trust only to see it betrayed with fatal consequences, it is unlikely the children were feeling particularly well disposed towards their own tutors. Indeed, Nikolaos of Damascus hurried to distance himself from Cleopatra and her offspring in a most unseemly manner, ingratiating himself with Octavian and Cleopatra's rival King Herod of Judea. Nikolaos would later write a biography of Octavian, of which some rather obsequious extracts survive. Since Egypt was both strategically and economically important to the Roman Empire, it needed to be carefully managed. One solution was for Octavian, or someone loyal to him, to oversee the kingdom until Alexander Helios and Cleopatra Selene were old enough to return and be installed as allied rulers answering directly to Octavian, in five to ten years' time. In any case, the death of Cleopatra had not changed Octavian's plans for the children: they were to be taken to Rome and led in his triumph, and to remain there for the time being so that he, and people he trusted such as his sister Octavia, could keep an eye on them.

While in Egypt, Octavian visited the Sema/Soma to pay his respects to Alexander the Great.[4] He apparently reached inside the glass sarcophagus to touch Alexander's face and in the process broke off a piece of the mummified corpse's nose.[5] He declined to pay his respects to the Ptolemaic kings and queens, however, saying somewhat contemptuously, 'I wished to see a king, not corpses'.[6] He also declined to pay his respects to the Apis Bull at the Temple of Ptah in Memphis, saying, even more contemptuously, 'I worship gods, not cattle'.[7] Perhaps this is why the Apis Bull is recorded as having bellowed in lamentation and burst into tears.[8] This behaviour was unlikely to endear him to Cleopatra Selene and her brothers. Nor would it have endeared him to the staff at the Temple of Ptah. Their High Priest was dead and had no direct descendant to take up his mantle, which meant that a significant religious role would go unfilled for the time being – the Egyptians must have wondered what would happen if the Apis Bull died, and a new one needed to be installed before a replacement High Priest could be appointed.

He also agreed not to remove any statues of Cleopatra after Archibius, one of her loyal retainers, offered him 2,000 talents of gold to leave them in situ.[9] Octavian may have been relieved by this offer, as, since Cleopatra was perceived as a living goddess in Egypt, there may have been some religious opposition and the possibility of accusations of impiety had he removed all evidence of her from the kingdom. Perhaps this is why the fine monumental relief of Cleopatra and Caesarion making a sacrificial offering has survived on the wall at the Temple of Hathor at Dendera; Octavian chose to leave it in situ and intact, but did make sure to add his cartouche to it, thereby drawing viewers' attention to the fact that the relief remained untouched only because he had determined it should be so. In the process, he not only rewrote Egyptian history but also redefined Egypt's position in the ancient Mediterranean, making this ancient kingdom a small part of the much larger Roman Empire.

Octavian was merciful to the citizens of Alexandria, and the inhabitants of the rest of Egypt, even though there was, unsurprisingly, a degree of civil unrest in the wake of the invasion and the deposition and death of the queen and king. Regarding his clemency, he gave particular credit to the influence of his friend Areius, a philosopher from Alexandria, although he probably neglected to mention to the citizens of Alexandria that it was on Areius' advice that he had had Caesarion executed.[10] He was also merciful to Antony's rank-and-file soldiers and sailors: now that he was the undisputed master of the Roman world, he could afford to be magnanimous, and this was cited as an example of his clemency by Seneca the Younger some years later in a treatise he wrote to guide the young emperor Nero in 55–56 CE.[11] He instructed his forces to undertake maintenance work on the irrigation system, clearing drainage channels that had become clogged up with silt.[12] Perhaps these practical actions gained him the support of the inhabitants of the kingdom, despite the troubling omens that were said to be proliferating: it rained both water and blood, mysterious music could be heard, a huge serpent appeared, comets streaked across the sky, the ghosts of dead men walked the streets and statues frowned.[13] Accounts of these omens passed on to Cleopatra Selene and her brothers by their staff may have given them hope that the gods had not completely abandoned them after all, although these hopes were likely short-lived.

Like their former subjects, Cleopatra's children were now at the mercy of Octavian. We must ask, why did Octavian put the older children to death yet keep the younger children alive? Caesarion, as the biological son of Julius Caesar, was his main rival, as Octavian was merely adopted, and posthumously at that. Additionally, since Caesarion had been enrolled as an *ephebe*, he was legally an adult and so able to hold a position of political and military power. The same was true of Antyllus. If the pair had joined forces, linked as they were by their half-siblings, they would have been able to do what Octavian and Antony had themselves done to the assassins of Caesar, and they would have attracted the loyalty of disaffected supporters of both Caesar and Antony, not to mention anyone else alienated by Octavian over the years; they could have proved formidable adversaries. The other children were not merely younger but much younger, nowhere near the Roman understanding of adulthood, which was around fourteen years old. Alexander Helios and Cleopatra Selene were ten and Ptolemy Philadelphos was six, and so were much less dangerous and much more sympathetic, still young enough to be re-educated and repurposed in favour of the Roman Empire, and in favour of Octavian himself, since they owed their lives to him specifically. And it must be borne in mind that there was nothing to stop him from having them killed later if they stepped out of line, just as he would ultimately do with their surviving half-brother, Iullus Antonius.

At some point, Octavian decided to take responsibility for raising Cleopatra Selene, Alexander Helios and Ptolemy Philadelphos. This may have been his own idea, or it may have been Octavia's: she was, after all, raising Antony's other surviving children – her two daughters and his son by Fulvia, Iullus – and it made a sort of sense to keep all of them together, despite the fact that they had not yet met. Since Octavian only had one biological child, taking Antony's six surviving children under his wing along with his wife's two children offered him an opportunity to present himself as the ultimate Roman *pater familias*, simultaneously a stern patriarch and a congenial family man. It may have been born out of practicality, since the three surviving members of the Ptolemaic dynasty and the heirs to the throne of Egypt were a precious resource and could not be entrusted simply to anyone. Equally, it may have been born out of affection, the children may have been endearing: ancient authors record that he raised them as carefully as if they were his own kin.[14]

There were other royal children living at the court in Alexandria, and while some, like Princess Iotape, were sent home, others, such as the brothers of Artaxes of Armenia, he retained and brought to

Rome. This meant that Cleopatra Selene and her brothers were not alone in their new situation, and they may have been grateful for this as they travelled from Egypt to Greece, and from Greece to Italy. They finally arrived in Rome in the summer of 29 BCE, almost a year after the deaths of their parents, half-brothers and cousin, and the loss of everything they had ever known. But fate had one more blow in store: Ptolemy Philadelphos disappears from the historical record at this point, and it is assumed that he died either on the journey to Rome or soon after his arrival, perhaps unable to cope with the rigours of travel or the change in climate or environment. Alexandria, situated on the Mediterranean coast, was known in antiquity for its salubriousness, whereas Rome, a much more densely populated city sprawling across marshy plains and straddling a river that frequently burst its banks, was known for quite the opposite. Malaria, to name but one disease, was endemic, and since it also exacerbated any pre-existing health problems, newcomers to the city were prone to succumb to it, with children particularly vulnerable, especially during the hot summer months.[15]

Cleopatra Selene's grand entry into Roman public life took place at Octavian's triple triumph in the summer of 29 BCE, an honour that he was awarded by the Roman Senate for the three victories that made him the undisputed master of the Roman world: Illyricum (35–33 BCE), Actium (31 BCE) and Egypt (30 BCE). A military triumph comprised a parade that set out from the Campus Martius, the 'Field of Mars', outside of both the ancient city walls and the *pomerium*, the sacred boundary of the city that separated the centre from its environs, and wound its way through the centre of the city, past the Circus Maximus, up the Via Sacra, 'Sacred Way', and culminated in a sacrifice at the Temple of Jupiter on the Capitoline Hill. (This route was used until the construction of the Forum of Augustus and its Temple of Mars Ultor, 'Mars the Avenger': from then on, most Julio-Claudian triumphs would instead culminate there, at the temple where Octavian had vowed to avenge the assassination of Caesar.) It served as the means by which a victorious general could present himself, his soldiers and all the prisoners and plunder from his campaigns to the Roman people. Octavian's was somewhat unusual in that it celebrated three victories across three days, with Illyrium on the first day (13 August), Actium on the second (14 August) and Egypt on the third (15 August) as the grand finale.[16] In this, he was following his adoptive father, who had celebrated a quadruple triumph across four days. Octavian's, however, was the first Roman triumph to take place over consecutive days rather than across a longer period of time with breaks in between.[17]

A military triumph was also the only chance the majority of Romans ever had to put faces to the names of figures of historical significance, those notorious enemies of Rome that they had been hearing so much about for weeks, months, potentially even years, or to experience the exotic and mysterious far-off peoples and places that had been subjugated by the empire. They were assisted by placards depicting these peoples and places, complete with explanatory labels and captions. Geographical features such as rivers were particularly popular, and it is likely that the Nile, renowned throughout the ancient Mediterranean for being a river that behaved in an utterly unique and, to the Romans, entirely bizarre way, was represented in this manner (it certainly soon became a popular subject in Roman public and private art). Notable landmarks were often featured, and it is almost certain that an image of the Pharos graced a Roman triumph for the second time in twenty years, probably accompanied by images of the Brucheion, the Museum and the Library, Alexandrian assets that were all now under Roman control. Rams, weapons and armour confiscated from the defeated forces of Antony and Cleopatra, objects plundered from Egypt's temples, and exotic animals requisitioned from the royal menagerie would also have been prominently displayed. It would have been a riot of noise and colour, a feast for the senses of the hundreds of thousands of spectators thronging the streets of the city and leaning out of windows and over balconies, desperate to obtain a decent view.

As anyone who has participated in any sort of parade can appreciate, it would have been simultaneously tedious and terrifying for Cleopatra Selene and Alexander Helios. They would have had to wait in formation, with the sun beating down on them on the Campus Martius, for hours until it was their turn to move, and then they would have had to trudge at length through an unfamiliar (and, no doubt in their eyes, used as they were to Alexandria, much inferior) city. They had probably never walked so far or for so long before in their lives. As the guests of honour, they were situated at the very end of the parade of booty, images, placards and prisoners, immediately before the chariot bearing Octavian, impossible for the spectators to miss.

Had Cleopatra lived, Octavian would have paraded her through the streets of Rome in golden chains, just as she had paraded the members of the Armenian royal family five years before. From her perspective, suicide, which the Romans viewed as a positive, honourable and ultimately heroic course of action, would certainly have been preferable to such public humiliation; Antony's friend Horace makes precisely this point in the poem he wrote about her death.[18] This seems to have been a common attitude among defeated enemies of Rome, with famous historical personages such as Perseus of Macedonia and Mithridates IV of Pontus likewise taking their own lives as one last defiant act, thus depriving the Romans of the ultimate spectacle. It did not make much of a difference to the occasion: Plutarch and Cassius Dio tell us that, in the absence of a living Cleopatra, either an image or an effigy of her dead body being embraced by a snake took her place in the parade, with Alexander Helios and Cleopatra Selene walking alongside it.[19] The twins were dressed as the sun and the moon, their costumes referencing their second names. There was no way the thousands of Roman spectators could fail to identify them. A brief eyewitness account of this part of the triumphal procession has survived in one of the poems written by the Roman elegist Propertius, in which he gives his response to the effigy of Cleopatra that was displayed: 'Your hands received Romulus' [i.e. Rome's] chains. I watched your arms bitten by sacred serpents and your limbs draw in the hidden course of sleep.'[20] While Cleopatra Selene and Alexander Helios would have been familiar with the sensation of being on public display, this appearance before the inhabitants of Rome was something more akin to Princes William and Harry walking through central London in the wake of their mother's hearse on the way to her funeral. It must have been excruciating.

The cruelty and humiliation of being forced to take part in such a spectacle so soon after her parents' deaths must have been hard for Cleopatra Selene to reconcile with the demands of her new life in Rome. It may have been comforting for her to realise that, whereas adult participants in triumphal processions were greeted by spectators with scorn, child participants tended to inspire sympathy. On occasion their plight even moved spectators to tears: it was understood that they were entirely innocent of their relatives' crimes. Additionally, it would not have been lost on many of the spectators that these specific children were in the unique position of being half-Roman themselves. They may even have physically resembled their father, bringing him to the forefront of the spectators' minds. Since it was not considered appropriate for Romans to be awarded military triumphs for defeating other Romans, or to celebrate the deaths of other Romans, Antony and his followers did not feature in the second and third days of the triumph, celebrating the Actian and Egyptian victories, respectively. Instead, Cleopatra was presented as the sole enemy throughout.

While walking in the procession, Cleopatra Selene would have seen many reminders of her former home and life, as all the spoils from Egypt, including the treasures of the Ptolemies and Cleopatra's fine possessions, were on display alongside herself and her brother. After the triumph, these spoils were distributed to temples around the city for display and would remain there for decades. One of these was the Temple to the Deified Julius Caesar in the Roman Forum, the foundations of which can still be seen today, often decorated with offerings left by visitors.[21] This temple, had been vowed in 42 BCE and was finally dedicated on 18 August 29 BCE, the entrance decorated with some of the gleaming bronze rams captured at the Battle of Actium. An illustration of it can be seen in the background of a later relief of the emperor Trajan, which is currently on display in the *Curia Julia*, the Senate House, in the Roman Forum. The games that accompanied the dedication incorporated wild beast hunts which included a rhinoceros and a hippopotamus presumably sourced from Egypt, potentially only the second time these exotic creatures had ever been seen in Italy.[22] Before being killed in the arena, the rhinoceros was exhibited on the Campus Martius.[23] Rome acquired so much wealth from the conquest and annexation of Egypt that interest rates and property prices rose dramatically.[24]

Even once the triumph was over and done with, Cleopatra Selene would not have been able to escape the Battle of Actium and the conquest of Egypt. Octavian's victories over Antony were the foundation of his personal authority and status as the *princeps civitatis*, the first citizen of Rome. Consequently, reminders of both were set up everywhere, in public and in private, across the Roman Empire. The Senate voted to erect an honorific arch in the centre of the Roman Forum, spanning the Via Sacra between the Temple of Castor and Pollux and the Temple of the Deified Julius Caesar.[25] It was the first permanent three-bayed arch to be built in Rome and, although only the foundations remain today, we can get a sense of what it would have looked like from the depictions of it on Octavian's coinage.[26] Copies of the arch were set up around the empire; part of one survives as the Arch of Augustus at Rimini. According to a medieval description of the original arch, it included a relief depicting Octavian's ship in pursuit of Cleopatra's, meaning that Cleopatra Selene would have encountered a scene from the battle that depicted her mother in action as a naval commander. It may also have included scenes from Octavian's triumph, so that she may have had the odd experience of viewing a scene depicting her mother's effigy, herself and her brother.[27]

Elsewhere, lavish monuments commemorating the battle were set up in prominent locations, their decorative reliefs depicting scenes from the battle. A marble relief, currently in the Duques de Cardona Collection in Córdoba in Spain, is particularly faithful to one of the fictionalised literary accounts of the battle that circulated afterwards. In this poem written by Propertius, Octavian's patron god Apollo addresses him prior to the battle, reassuring him upon his first glimpse of Antony and Cleopatra's enormous fleet: 'Do not be afraid because their fleet is propelled on oars by a hundred wings; the sea on which it sails will not abide it, and though their fearsome prows bear rocks such as Centaurs throw, you will find them hollow planks and painted terrors'.[28]

It is notable that the ship in the foreground at the centre of the relief has a substantial centaur figurehead. This same motif appears on a terracotta lamp that was found in the Fayum in Egypt and has been dated to between 10 BCE and 50 CE, which perhaps indicates continuing interest in Antony and Cleopatra, and regret at their defeat and deaths, among the residents of the former kingdom.[29]

A marble frieze, found in the necropolis of Colombella at Praeneste (modern Palestrina in Italy) and currently housed in the Vatican Museums at Vatican City in Rome, is slightly different however.[30] The relief depicts a bireme warship carrying Roman soldiers armed with shields and spears, ready for action. Once

A white marble relief depicting the Battle of Actium.

again, the crocodile is used to indicate Egypt; this relief may have originated on the funerary monument of someone who participated in the battle and wished to emphasise their role in such a significant moment in contemporary Roman history. Praeneste was a city that was more inclined toward Antony than Octavian, so this could have come from the tomb of someone who had fought on the losing side in the battle but remained loyal to his commander.

Octavian also lavished attention on the Actian peninsula in north-western Greece, close to the site of his victory. He rebuilt the Temple of Apollo, constructing ship sheds in which he dedicated one of every type of ship that had been used in the battle, and dedicated an enormous victory monument at the city he founded there, which was named Nikopolis ('Victory City'). The monument was set with thirty-five bronze rams, taken from the ships of Antony and Cleopatra's navy that had been captured by his forces.[31] It may have become something of a tourist destination, viewed by the Romans much like the Western Front is by Europeans today. He also instituted the Actian Games, a series of competitions that would be celebrated every four years, an addition to the pre-existing Greek circuit of sacred games which included the Olympics. The Actian Games encompassed athletic, equestrian and musical competitions, along with occasional boat and chariot races. The male competitors were divided into three age classes (boys, youths, adults), and victors were awarded crowns woven from reeds, a reference to the god Poseidon. When the Actian Games were first inaugurated, they were celebrated not only at Nikopolis, but also in Rome on 2 September 27 BCE, the fourth anniversary of the Battle of Actium, and it is probable that Cleopatra Selene was in attendance, along with the rest of the imperial family. While the now teenage girl undoubtedly found some, maybe all, of the competitions exciting and the competitors engaging, her constant awareness of the occasion that they were commemorating must have made the experience bittersweet.

Finally, Octavian issued a series of coins in gold and silver celebrating his achievement that were put into circulation around the Roman Empire. On the obverse face of the coin is a portrait of Octavian, on the reverse a crocodile, an animal often used as a shorthand for 'Egypt' in ancient art, and the Latin legend AEGYPTO CAPTA, 'Egypt Captured'.[11] This practice of using an image of a crocodile to represent Egypt would be resurrected later.

A widely circulated coin depicting Octavian, victor of Actium, on the obverse face, and a crocodile (symbol of defeated Egypt) and the legend AEGYPTO CAPTA on the reverse face.

A coin depicting Octavian and Agrippa on the obverse face, and a crocodile
chained to a palm tree on the reverse face.

Additionally, a bronze coin was issued in the Roman colony of
Nemausus (modern Nîmes in the South of France) in the province
of Transalpine Gaul between 10 and 14 CE.[33] On the obverse face is a
joint portrait. On the right-hand side, it depicts Augustus wearing a
laurel crown, the prize awarded to a military victor and worn during
his triumph. On the left-hand side, it depicts Marcus Vipsanius
Agrippa, his best friend, son-in-law and father of his grandsons and
heirs Gaius and Lucius, wearing a rostral crown (a crown decorated
with representations of the prows of ships, *rostra* in Latin). This was
the prize awarded to the person who was first to board an enemy's
ship, and was intended to honour Agrippa's role as the admiral
of the Roman fleet at the Battle of Actium. On the reverse face, a
crocodile weighed down in chains is positioned in front of a palm
tree. These direct references to the Battle of Actium and the conquest
of Egypt suggest that some of the veterans from the campaign were
settled at Nemausus. This was a fitting place for them, as previously
veterans of Caesar's Egyptian campaign had been settled there, and
no doubt the two groups had much to say to each other about their
experiences in the region and many war stories to exchange.

While Cleopatra Selene could try to avoid these tangible reminders of the Battle of Actium and the conquest of Egypt such as the public monuments set up and the coins issued to celebrate these events, there was little she could do about the intangible ones. Octavian, for example, eventually named the calendar month 'Sextilis' after himself, having chosen Sextilis because it was the month in which he had defeated Antony and Cleopatra, first at Actium and then, the following year, at Alexandria. In January 27 BCE, the Senate bestowed a new name and title upon Octavian, and he was subsequently known as Augustus, 'Revered One'. Hence the new name of the month, August, which remains in use to this day.

Over forty years later, and long after the death of Cleopatra Selene and her brothers, Augustus, for all intents and purposes now the first emperor of Rome, was still reminding people of his Egyptian victory. He would go so far as to write an account of his achievements that he had engraved in bronze and set up on the doors of his mausoleum in the centre of Rome (the mausoleum survives; the engraved bronze does not), stating tersely, 'I added Egypt to the empire of the Roman people'.[34] This account was also inscribed on stone and set up in many other places around the empire (the surviving copies have all come from sites in Turkey). Yet Cleopatra Selene would have taken some comfort in knowing that she was not the first in her family to have endured this experience. After all, Arsinoe, Cleopatra's younger sister, who in many ways served as both a role model and a cautionary tale for Cleopatra Selene, was a Roman prisoner, albeit one locked inside a gilded cage. And, Juba, Cleopatra Selene's soon-to-be husband, had participated in this same triumph as an infant, yet his experience had been very different from that of Arsinoe. As we shall see in a later chapter, as a foster child of Caesar, he had been raised as a Roman citizen.

6

When in Rome...

THERE IS A BEAUTIFUL fresco on the wall of the House of Marcus Fabius Rufus in the Insula Occidentalis at Pompeii.[1] Painted in the middle of the first century BCE, it depicts a woman holding a child. She wears a pair of snake bracelets on her wrists, a transparent tunic, a purple mantle and a white veil topped with a gold diadem decorated with a serpent or – perhaps – the Egyptian uraeus. The child clings to her face and neck. Yet at some point this lovely work of art was covered up, and a false wall was constructed in front of it.

Why did the owners of the house do this? At the time that the painting was produced, the house belonged to two freedmen of the Julian family named Euplus and Pothinus, and this Pompeian branch of the Julian family may have been related to the Roman branch of the Julian family, which included Caesar and Octavian (Pompeii received a significant amount of patronage from Augustus and his immediate family over the course of the Julio-Claudian dynasty). The woman and child depicted in the painting have been identified as the mother goddess Venus Genetrix and her son Cupid. Venus Genetrix was particularly dear to Caesar, and he dedicated to her the temple he built adjacent to the Forum in the centre of Rome. However, Caesar also set up a gilded statue of Cleopatra VII in this temple; she was, after all, the mother of his only biological son.[2] So is it possible that this fresco depicts not just Venus Genetrix and Cupid, but also Cleopatra VII and Caesarion? The woman certainly bears some similarities (particularly the large diadem and hairstyle) to the portrait recovered from the Villa of the Quintilii on the Via Appia in Rome and now housed in the Vatican Museums, and marks on the bust's cheek indicate that something – perhaps a child, representing either Eros or Caesarion – was once pressed up against it, so it may have looked like the woman and child depicted in the fresco. If so, it can perhaps provide insight into what a visitor to the Temple of Venus Genetrix might have seen in the late first century BCE,[3] and more specifically, what Cleopatra Selene would have seen had she visited the temple during her time in Rome in the period 30–25 BCE, in an attempt to honour, and perhaps feel close to, her deceased mother and older brother.

This proposed identification of the figures in the fresco could explain why they were covered up. After Octavian's conquest of Egypt, and the deaths of Cleopatra and Caesarion, it would have been politically expedient to renounce them. Yet, on the off chance that the figures might become less problematic in the future, the fresco was not obliterated but, rather, disguised, leaving Euplus and Pothinus with the option of reinstating it later. We cannot blame them for hedging their bets in this way: while Cleopatra and her oldest son were beyond the pale in Rome at this time, somewhat contradictorily her daughter was not. Quite the opposite, in fact.

Cleopatra Selene was now ensconced at the heart of the family that held the most power not only in the city of Rome but in the whole of the Roman Empire. She moved into her father's former wife Octavia's home atop the Palatine Hill in the centre of the city and found herself living alongside a trio of half-siblings: her older half-brother Iullus and two younger half-sisters, Antonia Major and Antonia Minor. Antonia Major was very close to her and her twin brother Alexander Helios in age, and Antonia Minor was of a similar age to her now deceased younger brother Ptolemy Philadelphos, so the sibling dynamics would have taken some getting used to.

Unfortunately for Cleopatra Selene, she did not have an ally in her twin brother for very long. Alexander Helios' appearance at Octavian's triple triumph dressed as the sun is the last time he appears in the historical record, and it is assumed that, like Ptolemy Philadelphos, he sadly failed to adapt to his change in circumstances.[4] In fact, Octavia's son Marcellus, Octavian's nephew and closest male blood relative who was, for a time, considered his likely successor, died only a few years later in the autumn 23 BCE at the age of nineteen after a short illness contracted at the holiday resort of Baiae in Campania.[5] Octavia's grief for her only biological son was recorded by the biographer Suetonius, who writes of her listening to Virgil recite a scene from the *Aeneid* that named Marcellus.[6] Upon hearing the poet mention his name, she fainted and could be revived only with difficulty.[7] No doubt this succession of deaths of promising young boys and men was difficult and disheartening for everyone in the family, but it would have had a particular impact on Cleopatra Selene. She had now lost her entire Egyptian family but unfortunately her lingering grief over Ptolemy Philadelphos and Alexander Helios was undoubtedly overshadowed by that of Octavia and her own children, who had lost their son, brother and half-brother, not to mention that of Augustus, who had lost his heir and received a significant blow to his nascent dynastic plans. It is highly unlikely that Ptolemy Philadelphos and Alexander Helios received a grandiose state funeral or had substantial monuments like the Theatre of Marcellus, the beautiful remains of which can still be seen in Rome today, dedicated to them like Marcellus did.[8] Her brothers may have been interred with far less fanfare in Augustus' mausoleum, or their remains may have been added to their father's family's mausoleum, but it is improbable they received the funerary rites that were

customary for members of the Egyptian royal family. This was
yet another indication of the enormous change in circumstances
the children faced upon the death of their mother and the loss of
their patrimony. (It was extremely rare for Romans to undergo
mummification; the embalming of the empress Poppaea Sabina,
the wife of the emperor Nero, Cleopatra Selene's great-nephew, was
sufficiently unusual as to be considered noteworthy of recording
by the historian Tacitus.)[9]

While Octavian (and perhaps Octavia as well) had been born in
a house in the Ox-Heads area on the Palatine Hill in Rome, later
in life he purchased another house in the neighbourhood from
a man named Quintus Hortensius Hortalus, a famous Roman
lawyer. It was in this house that he and his family would live for
the remainder of his life, and over the next few years he acquired
the adjacent properties. This building was the nucleus of what
would become, over the course of several decades, the imperial
palace.[10] At some point, part of the house was struck by lightning
and, after receiving advice from soothsayers, in 28 BCE Octavian
erected a temple to his patron god Apollo on that spot, the Temple
of Apollo Palatinus ('Apollo on the Palatine'), the remains of the
podium of which are visible today.[11] The temple was attached to
two libraries, one Greek, one Latin, by colonnades (how Octavian
obtained the volumes necessary to stock this library is not recorded,
but it is possible that he appropriated items he considered suitable
from the Library in Alexandria).[12] As compensation for Octavian
converting part of his residence into a temple, the Senate voted to
give him a house paid for by public funds.[13] So the remainder of
his residence was enlarged, and on 13 January 27 BCE the Senate
voted that a *corona civica*, the 'Civic Crown', a wreath woven from
oak leaves, should be placed above the door.[14] The *corona civica*
was a military donative traditionally awarded to a Roman citizen
who had saved the lives of their fellow Roman citizens by killing
an enemy combatant in battle on a spot held by the enemy that

same day, and Octavian was judged to have done so on numerous occasions.[15]

Part of what may have once been Octavian's house has been identified, preserved and can be visited today in the form of venues advertised as the 'House of Augustus' and the 'House of Livia'. While – despite what tour guides may tell you – this identification is not certain, the house, whomever it originally belonged to, can at least offer us a glimpse of how Roman aristocrats lived during the Late Republic and Early Principate. The walls are covered with beautifully painted frescos, such as those in the 'Room of the Masks' and the 'Room of the Pine Festoons'.

The 'Aula Isiaca', an apsed chamber decorated with frescos that include numerous visual references to Egypt and the goddess Isis – motifs such as lotus flowers, snakes, ritual vases and garlands of roses – gives an indication of how fashionable Egypt and Egyptian motifs were in interior decor at this time. Cleopatra Selene may therefore have felt particularly at home surrounded by them, although it would have been a poignant reminder of a life that she was no longer living. Furthermore, as Roman interpretations of Egyptian motifs rather than the genuine article, they may have seemed rather odd to her.

However, while the aristocratic residences on the Palatine Hill that Octavian and his family occupied were undoubtedly very fine by Roman standards, decorated with elaborate frescos and mosaics that are still in situ today, they were no match for the ancient palace on the waterfront in Alexandria that Cleopatra Selene was used to. A significant part of Octavian's personal brand involved him presenting himself as being no better than any other citizen, despite his preeminent position. Consequently, he made a show of presenting himself as being relatively simple in his tastes. His furniture and household goods were plain and unadorned, and he preferred to decorate his homes with rare and ancient objects, natural curiosities such as animal bones and fossils, rather than fine works of art.[16] (Apparently the only one of Cleopatra's many possessions that he retained for himself was a murrhine drinking cup, which must have bothered Cleopatra Selene every time she saw him use it.[17]) The contrast between this and the Brucheion, with its richly decorated walls and ceilings, its golden beams, its gleaming marble, agate, porphyry and onyx panelling, its ebony woodwork, its ivory, tortoiseshell and emerald inlay, and its couches upholstered in Tyrian purple and golden cloth, could not have been starker. An episode recounted by Athenaeus details how Cleopatra used to refer to her gold and silver plate as 'earthenware', since that was what the Romans used for their meals, and to gift it to her guests at the end of every meal. Consequently, it is not hard to imagine Cleopatra Selene being slightly confused upon sitting down to her first Roman banquet and being presented with genuine earthenware, which then remained the property of the host![18] Since Athenaeus sourced the anecdote from Juba's writings, it is probable that he heard it from Cleopatra Selene herself, a charming family story that she shared with her husband and children about the family they had not had the chance to know.

Since both of Cleopatra Selene's parents were dead and she was underage, she needed a guardian. Although guardians were normally appointed by a child's father and named in his will, it is unlikely that Antony had ever thought that it would be necessary for him to make such an arrangement for Cleopatra Selene, although he may have done so for her half-siblings Iullus Antonius, Antonia Major and Antonia Minor. Antony had had two younger brothers, Gaius Antonius and Lucius Antonius Pietas, who would normally have been expected to fulfil such a role. However, Gaius had died during the civil wars in 42 BCE, his death ordered by Marcus Junius Brutus, one of the assassins of Caesar, and nothing is known of Lucius' activities after he took up the governorship of Spain following his participation in the Perusine War against Octavian in 41 BCE. He may have died shortly afterwards, or he may simply have had his fill of getting caught in the middle of Antony and Octavian's feuding and decided to live quietly away from Rome. In any case, once Octavian had gained control of Cleopatra Selene and her brothers, he was leery of letting anyone else get too close to them. People with ambitions had often set their sights on royal children and sought to get into a position where they could exercise influence over them: after all, their uncle Ptolemy XIII and aunt Arsinoe IV had been targeted in just such a way by their tutors, and the result had been a civil war necessitating Roman intervention. In these early years after Actium, Antony did still have some friends and supporters who might have been inclined to reignite his war against Octavian, given sufficient motivation and belief in the likelihood of success. So, Octavian seems to have formally assumed the role of guardian over Cleopatra Selene, which gave him wide-ranging responsibilities including her upbringing, education, property management and even the arrangement of her betrothal and marriage. While Antony's property had been confiscated upon his being declared a public enemy, Octavian seems to have restored some of it to Iullus Antonius, Antonia Major and Antonia Minor, so he may have made donations to Cleopatra Selene as well.[19] She does, at some point, seem to have acquired some of Antony's household staff, and many of them would remain with her for the rest of their lives, dying at Iol Caesarea and being buried or cremated and then commemorated there.

Cleopatra Selene's appearance in Octavian's Triple Triumph was probably the last occasion that she was permitted to dress in the style of clothing that she was used to, unless it served Octavian's purposes to allow her to do so, at least until she moved to Mauretania and was in a position to decide how she wished to present herself. Gone were the purple and gold robes and the cloaks lavishly embroidered with portraits of members of the Ptolemaic dynasty and mythological figures.[20] For a sense of what these garments looked like, we can refer to the painted and gilded cartonnage mummy cases that have survived from the first century BCE, such as that of Taminis, the daughter of Shepminis from Akhmim, currently housed in the British Museum, whose tunic is decorated with vignettes of domestic activities such as the preparation of food and hunting scenes.[21]

From one extreme to the other, Roman girls normally sported their hair long and loose, pushed back from their faces with ribbons woven through it, and were covered from their necks down to their feet by a tunic and a *toga praetexta* with a purple stripe thought to be apotropaic and therefore protective, around the edge on top of it.[22] Also thought to be protective was the *lunula*, an amulet shaped like a crescent moon, which would protect its wearer from evil forces, such as the evil eye, like this one hanging from a necklace strung with agate dating to the first century CE.[23]

While Roman children were normally given their protective amulets – the *lunula* for a girl and the *bulla* for a boy, shortly after birth when they were formally recognised and accepted into the family by their father – Cleopatra Selene would obviously not have received one then. It is possible that Antony had bestowed amulets on Cleopatra Selene and Alexander Helios when he first met and acknowledged them at Antioch in 37 BCE, or perhaps they had to wait until 29 BCE, when they arrived in Rome and were admitted into Octavian's household and extended family. Some Roman children were kitted out with other protective charms, such as the phallus, often engraved on golden rings.[24] Perhaps, as Cleopatra's sole surviving child, Cleopatra Selene was thought to warrant an extra level of protection.

As Cleopatra Selene grew older, she would have needed to wear a breastband in an attempt to restrict the growth of her breasts.[25] According to ancient Roman poets, the ideal body type for a Roman woman was considered to be slim, with small breasts and large hips to facilitate childbearing, as all Roman women were

A necklace bearing an apotropaic *lunula* charm.

expected to marry and bear children. During Cleopatra Selene's time in Rome, laws would be passed that made bearing children mandatory, and rewarded women who successfully bore three or more with certain desirable legal privileges.[26] Ancient doctors recommended a diet and health regime intended to ensure that women were in the best possible condition for childbearing. They referred to medical writings such as Rufus of Ephesus' *Regimen for Girls* which promoted exercise as a means of helping the female body overcome its intrinsic excessive moisture, but his exercise needed to be carefully calculated, monitored and controlled, as the heat generated by exercise was thought to have a drying effect on the body that would prevent the accumulation of excess blood. Too much exercise could lead to the development of masculine qualities. Rufus prescribes healthy activities such as long walks, running, singing and dancing in a chorus, and ball games – all appropriate activities for girls – and in this way we see the replacement of childhood games with exercises specifically designed to prepare girls for marriage, and the resulting pregnancy and childbearing that was expected to result.[27] Cleopatra Selene's health regime is likely to have been overseen by Octavian's personal physician Antonius Musa, or his brother Antonius Euphorbus, both of whom had originally been part of her father's household; Euphorbus would later travel to Mauretania with her and serve as her physician there.

Another part of the socialisation that Roman girls went through in order to prepare for their lives as Roman women involved dolls. Depending on the wealth and status of a Roman girl, she might play with dolls made from rags, bone or even ivory.[28] These dolls generally took the form of adult women and often came with clothing and accessories that little girls could dress them up in, much like the contemporary Barbie. An elaborate example that belonged to a little girl named Crepereia Tryphaena, who died sometime in the middle of the second century CE, can be viewed in the Centrale Montemartini museum in Rome.[29]

This ivory doll, recovered from Crepereia Tryphaena's sarcophagus along with many other fine possessions, seems to have been modelled after one of the female members of the imperial family at that time, either Faustinia the Elder or Younger. It has articulated limbs that facilitate movement and is in possession of a whole suite of gold jewellery including a ring, bracelets and pearls, as well as an ivory box to store them in, a mirror and a comb. When the time came for young girls to be married, they would

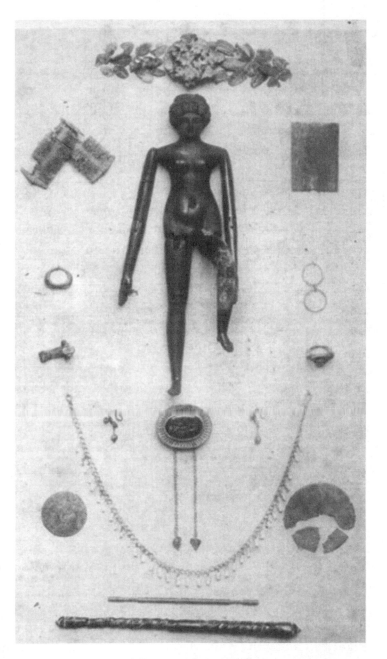

A Roman girl's ivory doll.

dedicate their childhood possessions such as their *toga praetexta* and their toys to their household gods.[30] Upon Antony's death, his household gods, most of which were probably stored in the household shrine located in the atrium of his house in Rome, would have passed to his surviving Roman son Iullus Antonius. It may be that Cleopatra Selene was encouraged to worship them in the traditional manner in the company of her three half-siblings, a subtle form of indoctrination.

Cleopatra Selene would have needed to continue her education. She undoubtedly knew how to read and write, most likely in more than one language. While she would have spoken, read and written Greek in Alexandria, she probably spoke, read and wrote Latin in Rome: although members of the Roman aristocracy were generally bilingual, Octavian was something of an exception in that while he could speak Greek, he did not feel comfortable writing it, despite his interest in Greek culture, so it may have pleased Cleopatra Selene to learn that she had the advantage of him there.[31] Both Greek and Roman education were based on canonical works of ancient literature, and Cleopatra Selene would have been well acquainted with all manner of ancient literature found in the Great Library at Alexandria. Living next to the Temple of Apollo Palatinus' Greek and Latin libraries would have been a boon, as she could benefit from the literary riches they held. Octavian had delegated the task of organising the new libraries' collections to a young man named Pompeius Macer. As a priority, he asked Macer to ensure the removal from public circulation of the youthful literary attempts of Caesar (who had at one point fancied himself a playwright). Once this was done, the family tutors and other intellectuals undoubtedly made good use of both libraries.[32] The library was later run by Gaius Julius Hyginus, one of Octavian's freedmen who was either a Spaniard or an Alexandrian brought to Rome by Caesar, and while in post he took on many students and wrote many works of scholarship himself.[33] If he did originally hail from Alexandria, he and Cleopatra Selene would have had much to talk about.

The extent to which aristocratic Roman women were educated depended very much on the inclinations of their parents or guardians, but many were renowned for both their learning and their employment of it. One such woman was Hortensia, daughter of the famous orator Quintus Hortensius Hortalus, Cicero's rival. She studied rhetoric and oratory and put her studies to good use in 42 BCE to argue against a tax imposed on Rome's 1,400 wealthiest women by the members of the triumvirs to fund their war against the assassins of Caesar. She marched into the Forum and argued her case against Antony, Octavian and Lepidus, and although the men were outraged at being upbraided by a woman, she did ultimately get her way: only Rome's 400 wealthiest women had to pay the tax.[34] The ability to speak well in public would have been a crucial skill for a former princess and future queen to acquire (and perhaps Cleopatra Selene had even heard stories of Hortensia's intervention). Antony's preference for the so-called 'Asiatic' style of oratory, which was characterised as bombastic and emotional and employing a lot of wordplay, was not one that Octavian shared He preferred the so-called 'Attic' style, which was more austere and formal, and he went so far as to publicly criticise Antony for it, so if Cleopatra Selene did study oratory it was likely to have been with practitioners of the latter style rather than the former.[35] Her stepbrother Marcellus and her half-brother Iullus Antonius were tutored by intellectuals, the Platonic philosopher Nestor of Tarsus and the grammarian Lucius Crassicius respectively, so she may have shared some of their lessons.[36]

However, there were also things that Cleopatra Selene may not have learned, or ever thought she would need to learn, prior to arriving in Rome. For example, the women of the imperial family were taught the traditional Roman domestic crafts of spinning and weaving.[37] They were charged with making articles of clothing worn by other members of the household.[38] This may have been an odd experience for someone more used to silk from Cos than wool from Campania.

Roman children were encouraged to follow the examples set for them, not only by people of their immediate acquaintance but also famous historical figures. Cleopatra Selene would have been expected to look to Octavia and her sister-in-law, Livia Drusilla, and model her behaviour after theirs. They would, in turn, have been expected to influence her and mould her behaviour. They would have taught her how to manage a household and undertake the religious duties required of a Roman wife and mother. Qualities that were particularly prized in Roman women were purity, modesty, discretion and self-control, and undoubtedly Cleopatra Selene would have found the example set for her by her mother difficult to reconcile with the examples set for her by her stepmother and step-aunt. The presentation of Octavia in particular as a role model for Roman women, and the comparisons made between her and Cleopatra, both implicitly and explicitly, went on for years, essentially offering Cleopatra Selene two competing visions of how to be a powerful woman in the Roman world. Should she follow her mother's example, and aim to be an independent and assertive woman in the manner of a Ptolemaic woman, or Octavia's, and aim to be a dependent and submissive woman in the manner of a Roman woman? Or could she, perhaps, incorporate elements of both into something new? Figures from Rome's distant and recent past would also have been used and presented to her as suitable role models. One likely example was Claudia Quinta, a Roman matron who had proved her chastity and piety by pulling *Salvia*, the ship that was transporting the statue of the goddess Cybele, from her shrine in Asia Minor to Rome during the Second Punic War, off a sandbank and up the River Tiber. She reportedly did so using only her girdle, thereby proving herself a paragon of virtue as well as the saviour of her city.[39]

At this point in time, in the Late Republic and early Augustan Principate, Rome was full of strong women. One of those who may have played a significant role in Cleopatra Selene's life during her years in Rome was her paternal grandmother, Julia. Julia had been particularly close to her eldest son and, like Antony's brothers Lucius and Gaius, had often worked on his behalf during his long absences from Rome. It may have been her example that fostered Antony's appreciation for strong and dynamic women such as Fulvia and Cleopatra later in life. And it was through her that Antony was able to claim kinship to Caesar, as she was his third cousin (their great-grandparents Gaius and Sextus Julius Caesar had been brothers). This family tie, and the connection that it gave Cleopatra Selene to Octavian, would not have been lost on her. Plutarch described Julia as a virtuous and dignified woman, and it seems that she spent a considerable amount of time and energy cleaning up the messes made by her rather ineffectual husband and, later, her sons.[40] She and Octavian had had a rather fraught relationship: she had been primarily responsible for preventing the Senate from declaring Antony an outlaw in 43 BCE, had saved her brother Lucius Julius Caesar from being proscribed in 43 BCE, and had even fled from Octavian to his enemy Sextus Pompeius in 41 BCE, although she did not trust Pompeius and simply used him as a means of getting to her son. She did, however, help to broker the peace between Antony and Octavian that became known as the Pact of Brundisium in 39 BCE. This is the last historical reference to her; she, like Antony's brothers, may have died soon after but, having been born in 104 BCE she would have been around seventy-five in 29 BCE, when Cleopatra Selene and her brothers arrived in Rome, so it is not beyond the realm of possibility that she lived long enough to meet her Egyptian grandchildren.

The fact that we know so little for certain about Cleopatra Selene's time in Rome tells us one thing about her, at least: she behaved herself, lived quietly and did what was expected of her in her new situation. Owing to her celebrity – or perhaps we should say notoriety – as the daughter of Antony and Cleopatra, people were undoubtedly watching her, waiting for her to put a foot wrong and behave as inappropriately as her parents were considered to have done. That none of the Roman authors whom we might expect to discuss her, had she transgressed, do so, even though they readily and gleefully discuss the misadventures of other members of the extended imperial family, such as Octavian's daughter Julia, is informative.

While in Rome, Cleopatra Selene may have found comfort in visiting Roman buildings which reminded her of her own family, such as the Temple of Isis and Serapis on the Campus Martius, a temple that had been built on the orders of her father in 43 BCE.[41] As mentioned previously, the Temple of Venus Genetrix in the Forum of Julius Caesar housed a golden statue of her mother in the guise of Isis, and the Temple of the Deified Julius Caesar, in the Forum, was sacred to her older brother's father. Octavian was unlikely to have objected to her visiting the latter two as it would have appeared that she was honouring his divine father rather than her mother and brother. And, of course, there were Egyptian spoils held in other temples around the city. Seeing them was probably bittersweet, on the one hand reminding her of home, on the other, a sharp reminder of why she was no longer there. We shall explore the presence of Egypt in Rome in the next chapter.

7

Egyptomania!

FOR SIGNS OF THE Egyptian presence in Italy, and Egypt's influence on Roman culture, during Cleopatra Selene's lifetime, we do not have to look very hard. A short distance from Rome to the south-east lies the city of Praeneste (modern Palestrina). The National Archaeological Museum of Palestrina is housed in the Palazzo Barberini, a Renaissance palace that was erected on top of the ancient sanctuary of Fortuna Primagenia, a monumental complex built on multiple levels of terraces that was one of the most impressive sites in Roman Italy during the Late Republic. I first visited with a group of students almost a decade ago after a particularly ferocious snowstorm. The snowdrifts were so deep that we were lucky that the museum was even open, but despite the horrible weather the views from the terraces of the Sacco Valley and the Alban Hills, all the way to the Mediterranean, were spectacular. Despite the dramatic setting, the museum's main attraction is an ancient artefact known as the 'Palestrina Mosaic', a huge piece of work (20 x 13 feet/6 x 4 metres) that originally graced the floor of a nearby Roman building, perhaps part of the Temple of Fortuna Primagenia, at some point from the late second century BCE onwards, although most of it is now displayed on a wall in a hall on the third floor that it has all to itself.[1]

It is an enigmatic mosaic and numerous suggestions regarding its date, place of production and how it should be interpreted have been made over the years since its initial discovery by the Barberini family in the seventeenth century. It is not in its original state, having been damaged and restored a number of times, most recently during the Second World War when it was dismantled to prevent it from being damaged by bombs dropped during air raids. It is currently labelled as having been commissioned by local businesspeople with interests in Egypt, and certainly Praeneste was well connected with Egypt and the Ptolemaic dynasty at this time (and its citizens would go on to support Antony and Cleopatra during their war against Octavian). The mosaic is thought to have been created by an artisan of Alexandrian origin – it is significant that the labels are written in Greek rather than Latin – and it is thought to show the course of the Nile from the Delta up to the First Cataract, with anecdotal vignettes illustrating what one might see and do at different points on the journey. No firm date has been agreed upon: it has even been suggested that Cleopatra VII commissioned it herself, with Caesar's agreement, to commemorate her trip up the Nile with him, perhaps as a thank offering to the goddess for her successful pregnancy and the birth of Caesarion.[2] This notion is perhaps a little far-fetched.

The scenes on the mosaic can give us an insight into what exactly the Romans knew about, or thought they knew about, Egypt in this period. Ancient authors had been writing about Egypt since Herodotus, known as 'the Father of History', visited the region in the fifth century BCE, and devoted an entire book of his *Histories* to it and its culture.[3] He considered Egypt and its inhabitants to be different from everywhere else: 'As the Egyptians have a climate peculiar to themselves, and their river is different in its nature from all other rivers, so have they made all their customs and laws of a kind contrary for the most part to those of all other men.'[4] He went into considerable detail about these differences, and this is something that other ancient authors such as Hecateus and Hippocrates

1. The so-called 'Sappho' fresco, which depicts a woman carrying a stylus and a set of wax tablets, from the Insula Occidentalis in Pompeii.

2. A fresco of a woman painter at work from the House of the Surgeon in Pompeii (below).

3. A fragment of a fresco of a woman presenting fruit from the Villa della Pisanella at Boscoreale.

4. A gilded silver dish from the Villa della Pisanella at Boscoreale, which may depict Cleopatra Selene.

5. A gold and silver emblema, possibly depicting Cleopatra Selene.

6. A mosaic showing the cities of Alexandria and Memphis from Jerash (in modern Jordan).

7. A sardonyx cameo, possibly representing Cleopatra Selene.

8. A bronze statuette, which may depict
Alexander Helios.

9. The Battle of Actium depicted in a white marble relief of the first century CE.

10. The so-called 'Palestrina' mosaic, illustrating the course of the Nile.

11. A fresco depicting Isiac rites from the Temple of Isis at Pompeii.

13. The Pyramid of Cestius in Rome.

2. The mausoleum of Juba II and Cleopatra Selene in northern Algeria, between Cherchell and Algiers.

4. The demi-god Hercules and Omphale a fresco of the first century CE.

15. A fragment of a decorative terracotta plaque from the Temple of Apollo Palatinus, which depicts Hercules and Apollo arguing over the Delphic tripod.

16. A black marble portrait of a Nubian.

17. A carnelian intaglio, which may depict
Cleopatra Selene, and its impression in wax.

18. The 'Severan Tondo' depicting the Emperor
Septimius Severus, his wife Julia Domna, and
their children Caracalla and Geta, with Geta's
image obliterated.

also highlighted.[5] During the middle of the first century BCE, the historian Diodorus Siculus spent a significant amount of time living and working in Alexandria, just as the geographer Strabo would do a few decades later, immediately after the Roman conquest and annexation of Egypt. Their writings offer an extensive account of the region as it would have been during Cleopatra Selene's lifetime.

Of course, Romans were aware of the Nile and its annual inundation, and the agricultural fertility that resulted, so different from the Tiber and the other rivers with which they were familiar. Once Octavian had succeeded in annexing Egypt, the former kingdom and new province became the breadbasket of the Roman Empire, with the city of Rome in particular receiving five million bushels of grain per year, around one-third of the total supply. The Roman grain supply was known as the *Cura Annonae*, after the goddess Annona, and was of such political import that the Roman poet Juvenal sarcastically remarked that all a ruler had to do to ensure the support of the people was provide them with 'bread and circuses'.[6] There was more than a grain of truth in this remark, as grain shortages inevitably led to riots, notably in 22 BCE. The significance of Egypt's grain for the city of Rome is made explicit in a relief carved into a marble sarcophagus that is currently on display in the Museo Nazionale, Palazzo Massimo in Rome, and is my personal favourite of all the sarcophagi I have seen.[7] Thought to have belonged to someone involved in the transport of grain from Alexandria to Ostia, on the right-hand side we see the personification of Africa and the Roman goddess of agriculture Ceres, on the left-hand side we see the personification of Ostia, with its lighthouse built in imitation of Alexandria's Pharos, and the Roman goddess of luck Fortuna.

The Romans were also aware of Egypt's exotic and intriguing flora and fauna, most notably crocodiles and hippopotami, and its wealth of natural mineral resources such as granite, porphyry marble, gems, gold and silver, and the access that it permitted to

The so-called 'Annona' sarcophagus, depicting a personification of
the Roman grain supply.

the Red Sea trade routes and goods from Arabia, India and China,
all of which they were very keen on acquiring. The popularity
of these items was such that the encyclopaedist Pliny the Elder
complained bitterly that in his day, the mid-seventies CE, millions
of denarii were being spent on them.[8]

It is fair to say that regarding Egypt itself, the Romans were
enthusiastic and enamoured, but they were rather less keen
on the new province's inhabitants. No real effort was made to
differentiate between Alexandrians, Greeks or Egyptians. Even
though the population was legally differentiated, and each group
had very different statuses and rights, to the Romans they were
all simply Egyptians. They were subjected to crude stereotyping,
orientalising, and the discourse surrounding them was peppered
with what we would today refer to as racist dog whistles. The
prevailing stereotype was an extremely negative one, and the insults
directed at Egyptians were both considerable and considerably
varied.[9] From Suetonius we learn that the Egyptians – like many
other easterners – were believed to be weak, effeminate, servile
and dishonest, and given to excess in all things.[10] And they were
not only considered shifty, they were also lustful, lazy and prone
to arrogance, despite their undoubted cowardice.[11] According to

Cicero, speaking in 54 BCE, Alexandria was 'the home of every sharp practice, every deceit; it is from its inhabitants that writers of farces draw all their plots'.[12] According to Caesar, the Alexandrians were 'a deceitful race, always pretending something different from their real intentions'.[13] In line with Herodotus' observation of the unique nature of Egypt, its people were considered to be not only different from everyone else, but also perverse, particularly regarding gender roles, as women in Egypt had more autonomy and agency than virtually anywhere else in the ancient Mediterranean.[14]

This xenophobia and racism was particularly prevalent in the 30s BCE, the years of Octavian's propaganda war against Antony and Cleopatra. It suited Octavian to make use of these existing stereotypes to smear Antony and undermine him in the eyes of his peers with accusations of him having 'gone native', so to speak, and been contaminated by his association with Cleopatra. How else to explain his adoption of Egyptian ways in preference to Roman ones? His self-identification with the god of wine and pleasure Dionysos? His wearing purple robes encrusted with gems, his wielding a golden sceptre, the Persian dagger thrust through the right-hand side of his belt?[15] His desire to move the government of the Roman Empire from Rome to Alexandria? As a result, during these years, Roman authors had various negative things to say about both Antony and Cleopatra. Antony was described as having become enslaved to Cleopatra, addressing her as 'Mistress', following her around in the company of eunuchs and even massaging her feet in public.[16] On one notable occasion, he was listening to a speech delivered by Gaius Furnius, a famous Roman orator, yet upon seeing Cleopatra pass by in her litter, jumped up and ran off after her, leaving Furnius open-mouthed and speechless at the loss of his audience.[17] According to the historian Cassius Dio, in the speech that Octavian delivered to his forces immediately prior to the Battle of Actium, he reiterated all of the ways in which Antony had cast aside his Roman pedigree in favour of Egypt and Egyptian ways, and culminated in referring to him as 'one of the cymbal players from Canopus'.[18] In the eyes of the Romans, Cleopatra had completely emasculated Antony, transforming him from a hale and hearty general into a coddled and cringing reprobate thoroughly under her thumb, and she aimed to do the same to them.[19]

While Cleopatra Selene would have been ignorant of Octavian's propaganda campaign against her parents prior to her arrival in Rome, once she was living in the city and circulating in Roman society she could not have failed to become aware of its lingering after-effects. It would not have been lost on her that when her mother was described as Egyptian, the adjective was used only in a negative sense: 'Egyptian wife', 'Egyptian queen', 'Egyptian whore' and so on. Since many of the authors writing at this time were members of Octavian's close friend Gaius Maecenas' salon, their literary output was disseminated among the Roman social elite. This literature set the tone for the new regime and it is highly probable that Cleopatra Selene would have been familiar with it. She may have been placed in the unenviable position of having to sit and listen, during public and private recitals, to poetry and prose that excoriated her parents, which would have been read and sung aloud to rapturous applause and critical praise. She may also have read it herself, as seminal and influential works such as Virgil's *Aeneid* were circulated among the Roman literati with Octavian's blessing, if not outright encouragement, and became touchstones of Roman culture. When Virgil described Antony and Cleopatra approaching, he wrote, 'there follows him (oh the shame of it!) his Egyptian wife'.[20] Propertius also emphasised Antony and Cleopatra's 'shameful union'.[21] Additionally, he accused Cleopatra of fornicating with her slaves, and referred to her as 'the harlot queen of licentious Canopus'.[22] Cleopatra's apparent promiscuity is a recurring theme in invective directed against her. The historian Florus accused her of prostituting herself to Antony in return for territorial grants.[23] Her long-time rival and enemy King Herod of Judea claimed that she made sexual advances towards him, with her desire to acquire some of his territory again a significant factor.[24] Antony's minion Dellius wrote her obscene love letters.[25] The lyric poet Horace emphasised Cleopatra's drinking, painting her as an out-of-control lush, and described her army as comprising 'disgustingly perverted men' and 'shrivelled eunuchs'.[26] The historian Livy emphasised that Egypt had ruined the once impressive Lagid family, turning them from hardy Macedonians into degenerate Egyptians.[27] This belief in the dynasty's gradual degeneration is echoed by his contemporary Strabo, who is particularly scornful of Cleopatra's flute-playing father, Ptolemy XII Auletes.[28] As the final member of the dynasty to rule in Egypt, and thus perceived to be its lowest point, Cleopatra was referred to as 'a singular stain branded on Philip's blood'.[29] This obviously had serious implications for Cleopatra Selene and her own personal prestige and reputation.

One accusation that seemed to pick up steam over the years was that Cleopatra had used witchcraft to attract and control Antony.[30] Ancient authors frequently state that she bewitched him. Antony was not the only Roman she attempted to use her wiles on. Towards the end of her life, when she was being held under house arrest in her palace in Alexandria, she apparently attempted to ensnare Octavian, too.[31] He, however, despite being tempted, was strong enough to resist her.[32] In Roman discussions of witchcraft, particularly in the first century BCE, love spells cast by unsuitable women on unwitting men are a recurring theme. Documentary and archaeological evidence in the form of curse tablets and voodoo dolls support the suggestion that a prominent purpose of ancient magic was to inspire feelings of love, passion and sexual attraction.[33] No doubt suspicious eyes watched Cleopatra Selene to see if she showed any signs of familiarity with the dark arts.

The components of this character assassination will no doubt be familiar to contemporary readers as the nature of misogynistic invective has not really changed over the course of the intervening two millennia. This depiction of Cleopatra as a drink- and drug-addled nymphomaniac made its way into material culture and was exaggerated to the point of absurdity, as in an image of her engaging in sexual activities with a crocodile on a terracotta oil lamp dating from around 40–80 CE.[34] The Romans called this sexual position the *pendula* and it can be seen in various works of erotic art (although normally bestiality was not involved). Nevertheless, they still considered this particular sexual position abnormal and perverse, as it involved the woman dominating, conquering and, in the process, humiliating her male partner, who in the natural order of things was always supposed to be the dominant partner in the sexual act. Considering the prevailing narrative about Cleopatra dominating, conquering and humiliating Antony in front of the entire world, it is not surprising that she would be portrayed in this manner. The fact that the sexual act is taking place outdoors and potentially in public, rather than behind closed doors and in private, is another indicator of Cleopatra's wild and unrestrained sexuality and shamelessness. Lamps bearing this image have been found not only around the Mediterranean basin but also in northern Italy, southern France, Switzerland and as far north as Germany, so it clearly had widespread appeal.

During her years in Rome no aspect of Cleopatra Selene's background was safe from criticism. Beyond the work of Herodotus and Diodorus Siculus, no serious neutral or objective attempts to understand Egyptian history or culture were made, and certain aspects of Egyptian religion, such as its human–animal hybrid deities, made many Romans, particularly those who wrote at any length on the subject, extremely uncomfortable. The Romans believed that men were superior to animals, and gods were superior to men, so the idea of animal gods was a deviation from the natural

Cleopatra as nymphomaniac: a
Roman terracotta lamp displays an
image of a woman having sex with
a crocodile.

order of things and the accepted hierarchy. Cicero considered
Egyptian animal worship not just superstitious but also depraved
and a form of insanity.[35] Virgil described the Egyptian pantheon
as comprising of 'monstrous gods of every form' and set 'barking
Anubis' against the Roman gods Neptune, Venus and Minerva.[36]

The anthropomorphised goddess Isis and her consort the god
Serapis, on the other hand, were extremely popular outside Egypt,
even if their presence in Rome was extremely contentious. In
58 BCE, the Senate ordered that altars dedicated to Serapis, Isis,
Harpocrates and Anubis located inside the *pomerium* should be
destroyed, while members of a political faction with an alternative
view on the matter ordered that they be re-erected.[37] In 53 BCE,
the Senate declared that Egyptian cults could not be worshipped
inside the *pomerium*, and ordered that temples to Serapis and Isis
be torn down.[38] Similar prohibitive measures were also taken in
50 and 48 BCE.[39] Yet in 43 BCE, the Second Triumvirate of Antony,
Octavian and Lepidus had dedicated a temple to Isis in the city of
Rome in an attempt to benefit from the goddess's popularity in
the city, although it is not clear if they ever actually succeeded in
building it.[40] During Cleopatra Selene's sojourn in the city, there

was a Temple of Isis situated on the Campus Martius, and it either adjoined or was located opposite a Temple of Serapis. Whether or not Cleopatra Selene would have been permitted to visit it to participate in the rites and worship the goddess is debatable: according to the poets Tibullus and Ovid, also in residence in Rome at this time, the temple was frequented by prostitutes.[41] That does not seem to have affected the cult's appeal to women, as both Catullus and Ovid wrote about their girlfriends worshipping the goddess, but it is questionable as to whether either woman, or any women like them, would have been considered suitable acquaintances for Cleopatra Selene.[42] Octavian cracked down on the cult in 28 BCE and forbade its worship for a time; Agrippa did likewise in 21 BCE, so we know that it became operational again at some point between those two dates, and this may have enabled Cleopatra Selene to participate in the rites once again.[43] Perhaps her participation was one of the factors that motivated Octavian and Agrippa's restrictions, as Roman religion was frequently politicised and there seems to have been a connection between certain popular religious practices and civil unrest.

There were several festivals held throughout the year that would have been of considerable importance to someone like Cleopatra Selene, who was raised to see religious worship as both a private matter and a public act, an important responsibility with potential ramifications for kingdom and subjects if not taken seriously and undertaken properly. One key festival was the *Navigium Isidis*, celebrated on 5 March to mark the beginning of the shipping season, another was the *Inventio Osiridis*, which took place in November and commemorated how Isis found Osiris' dismembered body parts, reunited them and resurrected him, symbolising the annual inundation of the Nile and renewed growth of crops. A fresco from Herculaneum that depicts an Egyptian festival can give us a sense of what Isiac rites would have involved at this time.[44] Unusually, ancient priests of Isis shaved their heads, and the rest of their body hair, in the pursuit of purity, and the rites included pouring water from golden ritual vessels and shaking the *sistrum*, the sacred rattle, to musical accompaniment.

Additionally, a marble relief from a funerary monument dating to no later than the first century CE and reused in a grave dating from the second century CE on the Via Appia, just outside Rome, depicts ecstatic worshippers participating in a dance in honour of the goddess, perhaps at the Temple of Isis in Rome.[45] Some priests of Isis would dress up as the jackal-headed god Anubis, who had guided Isis on her search for the pieces of Osiris' body, as depicted in a fresco from the Temple of Isis at Pompeii.[46]

Such a costume made one completely unrecognisable, as is attested by the story of the plebeian aedile Marcus Volusius, who was proscribed during the civil war between the assassins of Caesar and the triumvirate. He borrowed his friend's linen robes and jackal mask and used them to escape Rome in disguise, an act that was praised

A marble relief depicting devotees of the Egyptian goddess Isis performing ecstatic rites in her honour.

for its cleverness.[47] That this tactic could also be used for more nefarious schemes is made clear by an episode that occurred during the reign of Augustus' successor Tiberius, when a man named Decius Mundus used it to seduce a married woman named Paulina.[48] With the help of a freedwoman called Ida, he bribed the priests of Isis to tell Paulina that they had had a vision of her with the god, and when she visited the Temple of Isis on the Campus Martius to worship him, Mundus impersonated the god and succeeded in seducing her. Sometime later, Mundus informed Paulina of what had really occurred, she informed her husband and he in turn informed the emperor. Tiberius had Mundus exiled and Ida and the temple priests crucified, then razed the temple to the ground and threw the cult statue of Isis into the River Tiber. Occurrences such as this, which were no doubt much talked about at the time, bolstered negative stereotypes of Egyptians, their temples and their cults.

In the wake of Octavian's annexation of Egypt, and Cleopatra Selene's sojourn in Rome, we see certain aspects of Egypt and Egyptian culture being reviled while simultaneously, and somewhat contradictorily, others were being enthusiastically promoted. We see a huge influx of what has been designated as 'Aegyptiaca' into Rome and Roman Italy – that is, objects imported from Egypt, objects produced outside Egypt that visually allude to aspects of Egyptian styles or prototypes and objects that depict people, places and deities typically associated with Egypt.

Octavian appropriated certain symbols of Egypt for his own personal use. He used a sphinx motif on his seal for a time.[49] He also incorporated sphinxes into the design of his armour, decorating the epaulettes of his cuirass with them. This can be seen on the famous statue recovered from the empress Livia Drusilla's villa, known as the Villa ad Gallinas Albas ('Villa of the White Chickens', also known as 'the Hennery', because of the chickens that were bred there) at Prima Porta just north of Rome. He even issued coins stamped with a sphinx.[50] He also, although neither

Cleopatra Selene nor anyone outside Egypt may have known this, made a concerted effort to co-opt Cleopatra's building projects, either finishing them, as with the Caesareum in Alexandria, or augmenting them with his own additions, like his cartouche or reliefs of him in action as Pharaoh on the shrine of Geb at Koptos or the Temple of Hathor at Denderah.

Octavian's insistence on displaying his Egyptian loot continued throughout his reign, and he filled the city's temples with choice pieces of it.[51] This process continued throughout his reign: for example, in 10 BCE, to celebrate the twentieth anniversary of the conquest and annexation, he ordered the transportation of two immense obelisks from Heliopolis in Egypt to Rome.[52] Since the obelisks weighed 230 and 260 tonnes apiece, gigantic ships needed to be specially constructed to transport them. One was set up on the Campus Martius, near the Mausoleum of Augustus, and dedicated to the sun. It was put to use as a gnomon – the part of a sundial that casts the shadow – of an enormous meridian constructed from marble and inlaid with strips of gilt metal, some of which has been uncovered and is visible today in the basement of a shoe shop.[53] The other was likewise dedicated to the sun and erected on the *spina* of the Circus Maximus, although it was transferred from there to its present location in Piazza del Popolo in the late sixteenth century.

And in turn we see what has been described as 'Egyptomania', a process of cultural appropriation whereby Egyptian motifs were reworked for this newfound Roman audience and became extremely fashionable as a result. Numerous aristocratic houses, not just in Rome but further afield in Italy in locations around the Bay of Naples such as Pompeii, display Egyptian-themed decor, from the so-called 'Aula Isiaca' in the 'House of Augustus' on the Palatine Hill, to the Villa of Agrippa Postumus at Boscotrecase, to the garden fresco in the House of the Golden Bracelet at Pompeii. Quintessential Egyptian architectural forms such as obelisks and pyramids were enthusiastically adopted by the Romans. The pyramid tomb of Gaius Cestius Epulo was set up prior to 12 BCE at the junction of the Via Ostiensis – the road than runs from Rome to the port Ostia Antica – and a road running along the south-west side of the Aventine Hill towards the River Tiber. Later subsumed by the city's Aurelian walls, it can still be seen today near the Porta San Paolo, adjacent to the Non-Catholic Cemetery where the poets John Keats and Percy Bysshe Shelley are buried.[54] Constructed from brick-faced concrete and covered with slabs of white Luna marble, quarried from nearby Carrara, the story of the erection of the monument, which took less than a year, was inscribed on it, and on the bases of two bronze statues set up in front of it. Perhaps Gaius Cestius Epulo had participated in Octavian's Egyptian campaign in 30 BCE, or even the subsequent Roman expeditions into Nubia in the 20s BCE.

Another pyramid, known as the 'Pyramid of Romulus', was located across the the city, but it was dismantled in the sixteenth century and its marble was appropriated for the construction of St Peter's Basilica.

It must have been a strange experience for Cleopatra Selene to witness this dissonant mixture of revilement, appropriation, dissemination and celebration of her native Egyptian culture and its symbols. She may have been encouraged by her Roman family to set aside her Egyptian tendencies and proclivities in favour of Roman ones and behave in the manner of her half-sisters. Alternatively, the fact that she was part Egyptian may have made her somewhat fashionable, an object of fascination to her peers. But it seems that she used her time in Rome wisely, learning exactly which aspects of Egypt and Egyptian culture the Romans found the most appealing, knowledge that she would use to her advantage during her reign as Queen of Mauretania.

8

A Queen in the Making

WITH HER BROTHERS ALEXANDER Helios and Ptolemy Philadelphos dead, Cleopatra Selene was the last surviving member of the once mighty Ptolemaic dynasty and the last living link to the legendary Alexander the Great. So, what was Octavian to do with her?

Regarding Antony's other surviving young children, the solutions were simple.[1] They were Roman citizens, the products of Antony's marriages to Roman women. Iullus Antonius (43–42 BCE), the son of Antony's third wife Fulvia, was raised and educated in the traditional manner befitting a young man of the senatorial class, in preparation for his embarking upon a political career and joining the Senate. He would climb the Roman *cursus honorum* (the 'ladder of offices'), taking on roles comprising a mixture of political and military administration in order of increasing seniority as he reached the age threshold for each title. In this way, he became praetor in 13 BCE, consul in 10 BCE and Asian proconsul in 7 BCE. He would later marry his stepsister Claudia Marcella Major, the daughter of Octavia and her first husband Gaius Claudius Marcellus Minor, and the marriage would produce two sons and a daughter. He would even write suitably tactful and sycophantic poetry in praise of Augustus.[2] However, he would ultimately come to a sticky end, dying by suicide at the age of forty-one in 2 BCE after an adulterous liaison with Augustus' daughter Julia, and involvement in some sort of conspiracy against Augustus and his stepson (also, by this time, Julia's husband), Tiberius.[3]

Antonia Major and Antonia Minor, the daughters of Antony's fourth wife Octavia (and therefore also Augustus' nieces), were raised and educated in the manner befitting young women of the senatorial class, in preparation for advantageous marriages. The former would marry the consul Lucius Domitius Ahenobarbus in 22 BCE and bear him three children: a son who would go on to father the emperor Nero, and two daughters. The latter would marry the consul Nero Claudius Drusus, the younger son of Augustus' wife Livia Drusilla, in 16 BCE and bear him three children: two sons – one the famous general Germanicus and the other the emperor Claudius – and a daughter. In other words, any potential threats that they might have posed to Augustus and his fledgling dynasty were thoroughly neutralised. Augustus clearly liked to keep his friends close and his enemies (or the children of his enemies) closer. Two marble portrait busts dating from the years of the Augustan Principate have been tentatively identified as Antonia Major and Antonia Minor, and are displayed as such in the Musei Capitolini and Palazzo Massimo museum in Rome respectively; they do indeed resemble more securely identified marble portraits of their mother Octavia.[4]

Regarding Cleopatra Selene, though, the solution was neither quite so simple nor so neat. Her father had been a Roman citizen, and it is entirely possible that her mother had been gifted Roman citizenship by one of the many influential Romans she had known, as was a common occurrence when members of the Roman elite developed close working relationships with allied kings and queens. There was no getting away from the fact that, as a queen in her own right, she was in an entirely different class to her Roman half-brother and half-sisters, let alone her numerous newly acquired stepbrothers and sisters, and foster brothers and sisters, who all

Marble portrait busts of Antonia Major and Minor,
daughters of Antony and Octavia the Younger.

lived alongside her on the Palatine Hill in the years between 29 and
25 BCE.[5] As a young man, Octavian had owned a house near the
Forum on the northern slope of the Palatine Hill. It had formerly
been owned by Gaius Licinius Macer Calvus, an orator and poet
who wrote in a similar vein to the more famous Catullus, loathed
both Caesar and Pompey the Great with equal intensity and was
particularly famous for his short stature.[6] Later in life, however,
once Octavian was both more affluent and more influential, he
purchased a house on the summit of the Palatine Hill, one formerly
owned by the renowned orator Quintus Hortensius Hortalus,
and it was here that he lived for the rest of his life.[7] Octavia lived
in an adjoining house, and this compound gradually became not
just a home to Augustus and his extended family but also, when

the princeps was in residence, the political centre of the Roman Empire. Later emperors would gradually transform it into an elaborate palace complex that reflected this, and it is the remains of this that survive today and are visited by millions of tourists each year, including, from time to time, myself and groups of students.[8] Consequently, it also came to serve as a sort of finishing school for wealthy young Romans and Roman allies, not just educating these individuals but also training them for their bright futures as ambassadors of the Roman way of life, assuming that they returned to their places of origin.[9]

As the daughter of Antony, Cleopatra Selene would have been considered a member of an ancient family attested in Roman historical records as early as the fifth century BCE. The family was exceedingly proud to be able to trace its lineage back to Anton, a son of Hercules.[10] Indeed, when he was young, Antony would emphasise his physical resemblance to his divine ancestor as much as possible, even appearing in public dressed in his distinctive style.[11] This relationship and resemblance did not always work in his favour, however. One of the myths that circulated about Hercules was that after the completion of his twelve labours he had entered the service of Omphale, the Queen of Lydia. She completely dominated him, forcing him to wear women's clothes and spin wool while she wore his Nemean lionskin and wielded his club. Analogies were made between Hercules' enslavement by Omphale and Antony's apparent enslavement by Cleopatra.[12] In the years after the deaths of Antony and Cleopatra, this mythical role reversal and the historical figures it alluded to became a popular subject in ancient Roman art. It appeared in various guises, some of which can be seen decorating the residences of Pompeii and Herculaneum, such as a fresco now housed in the National Archaeological Museum of Naples.[13]

Another of the myths that circulated about Hercules concerned his battle with the god Apollo for the Delphic Tripod. Hercules had travelled to the Oracle at Delphi to consult with the Pythia, the priestess, in the hope that she could advise him about how to cure a disease that he was afflicted with. When she was unable to provide an answer to his question, he took out his frustration on the temple and attempted to steal the Delphic Tripod in order to establish an Oracle of his own. At this point Apollo (who was, in fact, Hercules' half-brother as they shared a father, the god Zeus) intervened and the pair wrestled for the Tripod. Apollo won and the Tripod remained at Delphi. Since Apollo was Augustus' patron deity, this tussle served as a convenient visual stand-in for Antony and Octavian's struggle for supremacy. As a result, it was prominently represented in public art during this period, such as on the brightly painted terracotta plaques decorating the Temple of Apollo on the Palatine, dedicated by Augustus in 28 BCE, the remains of which can be seen today occupying an entire wall of the Palatine Museum in Rome.[14] These images would have been visible to Cleopatra Selene every time she passed through the Temple of Apollo on her way to its libraries, and their double meaning was unlikely to have been lost on her.

Cleopatra Selene could not only also claim descent from the demigod Hercules but also from her deified mother, who had been venerated in her own lifetime as the 'New Isis', as well as Cleopatra's predecessors, a long line of deified Ptolemaic kings and queens. Augustus' adoptive father Gaius Julius Caesar had not been deified until after his death, so Cleopatra Selene's divine ancestry put the emperor's to shame. (Antony, for one, had enjoyed making pointed comments about how lowly Augustus' human ancestry was, and frequently referred to him disparagingly by his birth name Gaius Octavius Thurinus rather than his adopted name of Gaius Julius Caesar Octavianus; Octavian had airily insisted that this repeated slight was of no consequence to him.)[15] Additionally, Cleopatra Selene was also distantly related to Caesar through Antony, as his mother Julia, her grandmother, was Caesar's third cousin (the cousins' great-grandparents were brothers). Antony had emphasised this relationship in his choice of name for his second son by Fulvia, Iullus, as Iullus was another name for Ascanius, the son of Aeneas who had travelled with him from Troy to Italy or, in some versions of the myth, Ascanius' son. By our contemporary standards this is an extremely tenuous connection, but it would have mattered to the Romans, as it accounted for Antony's closeness to Caesar and his family, including his nephew Lucius Pinarius Scarpus, who, despite his family ties to Octavian, remained Antony's ally until his defeat at the Battle of Actium in 31 BCE.[16] Thus this relationship would have been clearly marked in Cleopatra Selene's genealogy.

Even more threateningly from Augustus' point of view, the founder of the Ptolemaic dynasty, Ptolemy Soter, was reportedly the bastard son of King Philip II of Macedon, the father of Alexander the Great, and there had been frequent intermarriage between the Ptolemaic dynasty and the neighbouring Seleucid dynasty. This meant that Cleopatra Selene's mortal pedigree was every bit as exalted as her divine lineage. The icing on the cake was the fact that she had been declared Queen of Crete and Cyrenaica in her own right in 34 BCE as part of the Donations of Alexandria. Cleopatra Selene presented both a challenge to the emperor's security and an extraordinary dynastic opportunity. Neither could be easily dismissed.

Perhaps if Augustus had had a son of his own, he might have arranged to marry him to Cleopatra Selene, with the intention that she would reign alongside him as empress at some point in the future. At the very least she might have borne children who would have made the future course of the Julio-Claudian dynasty look very different.[17] But he did not and marrying Cleopatra Selene to one of his stepsons or nephews would probably have upset the delicate balance of his household, which was full of volatile individuals with strong personalities and even stronger senses of entitlement. There were enough plots and accusations of attempted murder and murder circulating as it was without throwing what would inevitably be perceived as favouritism into the mix. Yet Cleopatra Selene was too dangerous to be left alone, potentially amassing influence in the imperial court at the heart of the Roman Empire, a possible rallying point for any disaffected Egyptian expatriates whose dreams of restoring their traditional joint monarchy had been dealt a blow by the deaths of Alexander Helios and Ptolemy Philadelphos yet still lingered. Luckily, a solution seems to have presented itself, or at least Octavia seems to have presented it: she apparently played matchmaker between Cleopatra Selene and another member of North African royalty exiled in Rome, a young man who had come to be named Gaius Julius Juba.

Known to posterity as King Juba II of Mauretania, Gaius Julius Juba was the son of the deceased King Juba I of Numidia, who had been a casualty of the civil war between Caesar and Pompey the Great. Ruler of a relatively autonomous and extremely wealthy kingdom, Juba I had sided with Pompey and died by suicide after being defeated at the Battle of Thapsus in 46 BCE, his chosen method a dramatic yet simultaneously rather pitiable single combat with the Roman general Marcus Petreius, in which both men sought to kill the other simultaneously in order to ensure that their deaths were honourable.[18] In the wake of Juba's death, Caesar stripped the extremely wealthy Numidian royal court of its assets, which included the infant prince, and returned to Rome. The infant Juba was exhibited in a Roman triumph as a proxy for his deceased parent, just as Cleopatra Selene would be seventeen years later. Although Juba was only a baby at the time, he would presumably have found the experience far less impactful and potentially traumatising than she. Indeed, according to Plutarch, recording Caesar's epic triumph for posterity in his biography of the dictator, Juba was 'the happiest captive ever captured'.[19] Juba's birth name may not actually have been the same as his father's, but since it meant 'flowing hair on the back of the head' in Latin, and the Numidians were renowned for their voluminous hair and elaborate hairstyles, such a stark contrast to the neatly trimmed hair of the Romans, it may have amused Caesar to bestow it on the infant. It would also have made his identity obvious to those who may otherwise have looked at him in bemusement and seen just another baby. Following the triumph, Juba was raised in Rome as a Roman citizen, probably in Caesar's own household until his assassination in 44 BCE. By the time Cleopatra Selene arrived in Rome, Juba was one of a number of young foreign royals voluntarily or involuntarily living with Octavia, while Augustus attempted to stabilise the empire and its relationships with its neighbouring territories. He was close enough in age to Octavia's son Marcellus and Livia's son Tiberius, both born in 42 BCE, for the three of them to share many experiences during their childhood and youth, including their first experience of military life when they joined Augustus on his campaigns in Hispania (modern Spain) in the period 27–25 BCE, and witnessed first-hand how to conquer recalcitrant indigenous peoples who were understandably reluctant to submit to Rome.[20]

Cleopatra Selene and Juba had a great deal in common in addition to their North African heritages. Both had parents who had died ignominious deaths as enemies of Rome and continued to be excoriated in public discourse. In the wake of her death, Cleopatra was known variously as 'the whore queen', 'the doomed destructive monster', 'the licentious queen of impious Canopus' and 'the woman whom her own servants used to grind', while Juba's father was repeatedly denounced for his greed and savagery, equally stereotypical slurs that had been hurled at previous African kings who had had both the temerity to face off against Rome and the misfortune of not managing to do so successfully. Cleopatra Selene and Juba had both, in the absence of those parents, suffered the consequences of their parents' actions in their places. They had both lost not only their entire families but also their kingdoms. They were cut off from their societies and cultures and had been publicly humiliated as captives paraded in Roman military triumphs. However, things were not necessarily all bad for the pair: they may well have been able to share more than just the nature of their exile. Juba, for instance, may have met Cleopatra VII and Caesarion during one of their trips to Rome as guests of Julius Caesar in the years between 46 and 44 BCE. Even if he did not remember them himself (he would have been aged between two and four years old at the time), he may have heard stories about the visit that he could share or been able to suggest people whom Cleopatra Selene could approach for their reminiscences. He would certainly have known Antony and may even have lived in his household during the years of his marriage to Octavia, between 40 and 32 BCE. Perhaps in addition to bonding over the heavy weight of responsibility that came with having to live up to ancient and prestigious yet recently disgraced lineages, they would also have forged more personal and intimate connections.

What did Cleopatra Selene make of this potential suitor? Juba's surviving portraits, several examples of which are on display in the Glyptotek in Copenhagen and the Louvre in Paris, depict a serious and thoughtful young man. Ancient Roman portraiture, particularly that of members of the imperial family, can be problematic. It is not entirely trustworthy as a true likeness as subjects often chose to be depicted as though they physically resembled their predecessors – even when they were not related to them – to help create the illusion of continuity. Yet while Juba's portraiture follows stylistic precedents set by Augustus and replicated by his successors, the facial features they depict are significantly different from those of Tiberius and other young Julio-Claudian males, which does suggest a degree of personalisation. His curly hair is thick, his face is rounder and his lips are fuller.

Juba II of Mauretania,
sober and reflective
in a white marble
portrait bust of the
first century CE.

Juba's surviving literary output shows that he was an intelligent individual with an enquiring mind, a polymath who was interested in history, archaeology, the arts and geography. Indeed, in later life, he would become something of an explorer and adventurer, and after his death he was venerated for both the quantity and quality of his scholarship. Juba was also clearly held in high regard by his foster family. If there had been any doubts about his character or his capabilities, Augustus would never have entrusted him with the responsibility of ruling the vast kingdom of Mauretania at the relatively young age of twenty-three. Had his loyalty to Rome and the emperor's dynasty ever been in question, Augustus would not for a moment have entertained the notion of aligning him with such a potentially powerful threat as Cleopatra Selene, and then sending the couple so far from his sphere of influence.

While the marriages of the Roman senatorial and equestrian elite were generally arranged according to political and financial considerations rather than emotional ones, the Romans did idealise the institution of marriage. Many prominent authors, including Plutarch, wrote guides for couples, with advice tailored for both bride and groom on how best to fulfil their roles as husband and wife. While a Roman wife was expected to subordinate herself to her husband, a Roman husband was expected to treat his wife with respect and consideration. A Roman marriage was supposed to be a true partnership, a genuine meeting of minds. During the period that we are concerned with, the Late Republic and Early Principate, the Roman poet Sulpicia wrote a series of elegies to the object of her affections, a young man she calls Cerinthus. These are the only lyric poems written by a woman in Latin to have survived from antiquity, and thus the only ones to give us the female perspective on ancient Roman love affairs. Sulpicia was extremely well connected, her uncle the highly influential politician and military man Marcus Valerius Messalla Corvinus, a peer of both Antony and Octavian, as well as being an important literary patron who sponsored poets such as Ovid and Tibullus, making Sulpicia herself an exact contemporary of Cleopatra Selene.

Cleopatra Selene had grown up with her father largely absent from her life, but whenever he had actually been resident at the Ptolemaic court in Alexandria the relationship she would have witnessed between her parents would have appeared rather different from that of typical married couples at the time. In their political alliance of Egyptian queen and Roman triumvir, they represented the meeting of the Hellenistic east and the Roman west, and they depicted this meeting in physical form on the joint coinage that they issued. On these, it is often difficult to tell who is on the obverse face, the primary position, and who is on the reverse face, the secondary position, such as in a silver denarius issued in Alexandria in 34 BCE to celebrate the Donations

An example of the joint coinage issued by
Cleopatra VII and Antony, dating from 34 BCE.

of Alexandria and Antony's Armenia conquest.[21] They offered
each other not only love and affection but, more importantly
considering their respective positions, political, military and
financial support.

To Cleopatra Selene, marriage to Juba offered the very real
possibility of replicating this arrangement. The idea of regaining
her lost status and effectively reconstituting the Ptolemaic dynasty,
thus fulfilling her mother's most cherished ambitions, must have
been satisfying indeed.

Their wedding took place in 25 BCE, presumably with a significant
amount of ceremony. It is commemorated in an epigram written
by Crinagoras of Mytilene, the unofficial Augustan court poet
who was responsible for writing many poems about members of
the imperial family (he also wrote a poem celebrating the marriage
of Cleopatra Selene's half-sister Antonia Minor, referring to the
roses that the bride wore in her hair).[22] He writes of the union
between Cleopatra Selene and Juba representing the unification of
the neighbouring regions of North Africa, although his historical
and geographical knowledge is impressionistic rather than exact:

Great bordering regions of the world which the full stream of Nile separates from the black Aethiopians, you have by marriage made your sovereigns common to both, turning Egypt and Libya into one country. May the children of these princes ever again rule with unshaken dominion over both lands.[23]

With the conquest of Egypt in 30 BCE, the entirety of coastal North Africa had finally come under Roman control. Early on in his Principate, Augustus tried to come up with a solution to the pressing problem of how to manage this huge expanse of territory and protect the southern frontier of the Roman Empire, which had already seen some troublesome incursions from the Kingdom of Kush, south of Egypt. Strabo writes of Queen Candace, a warrior woman who was blind in one eye, and how she took advantage of the diversion of the Roman legions from the border region up to Arabia to invade Egypt, sack territories and towns including the Thebaid, Syene, Elephantine and Philae, enslave the inhabitants and pull down all the statues of Octavian that had been set up.[24] Part of one of these, a larger than life-sized head from a bronze statue, has been recovered through archaeological excavation in Nubia. The eyes are inlaid with glass, with pupils set in metal rings and irises made of calcite, which gleam in the light and appear almost lifelike.[25]

It was taken back to Meroe, the Kushite capital, and buried beneath the steps of a temple dedicated to Victory, to be permanently subjugated beneath the feet of its Kushite captors. The temple also contained frescos depicting Roman prisoners of war before the Kushite ruler. The incursions were swiftly dealt with by the new Roman governor of the province, Petronius, who invaded Kush, razed Candace's royal residence at Napata to the ground and enslaved the inhabitants, although Candace's son managed to escape. Petronius returned to Egypt and, while

Candace and her army initially pursued him, eventually the situation was resolved diplomatically.

In his account, Strabo mistakenly and repeatedly uses the title Kandake, which tends to be Latinised as Candace, as the queen's name: her name was in fact Amanirenas, and she ruled Kush from around 40 to 10 BCE. These dates mean that the first ten years of her reign coincided with the last ten years of Cleopatra VII's reign. It is highly probable that these queens of neighbouring kingdoms were well acquainted and sought each other's support and advice on some of the more challenging aspects of ruling over the course of that decade. After all, we know from ancient Roman historiography that Cleopatra was in frequent contact with her fellow allied kings and queens around the Mediterranean, so it follows that she was also in frequent contact with her fellow African rulers. It only goes unmentioned by Roman authors because Kush was not part of the Roman Empire and so its day-to-day business was not part of their remit. Amanirenas may well have been inspired to invade Egypt's southern border to discourage any Roman designs on her kingdom as a direct result of her witnessing Rome's treatment of Cleopatra, her children and her kingdom, and her desire to avoid such an outcome for herself and hers. Cleopatra Selene would certainly have been aware of Amanirenas, who had acceded to the throne the year that she and her brother were born (the pair may even have met, assuming Cleopatra VII and Amanirenas had undertaken the sort of diplomatic embassies to each other's kingdoms that Cleopatra had taken to Rome and other Roman cities). Amanirenas' position as queen regnant would have been yet more proof, if any were needed, that women could wield power in their own right, and not simply exist as ornamental appendages of men. Although far away, first in Rome and then in Mauretania, Cleopatra Selene undoubtedly followed the political and military developments in Egypt, Nubia and Kush with close attention until hostilities ceased when a peace treaty between the Roman Empire and the kingdom of Kush was agreed in 21–20 BCE.

So much upheaval in the only recently annexed and still potentially unstable province of Egypt made the necessity of placing the rest of North Africa in steady hands both obvious and pressing. As the Roman Empire had expanded, acquiring foreign territories through a combination of military conquest and political manoeuvring, it had sought to manage these territories in two different ways. Provinces were part of the empire and overseen by provincial governors appointed by the Roman Senate: Caesar, for example, had been the provincial governor of Gaul (modern France), Antony of Asia Minor (modern Turkey). However, the Roman Empire also had interests in territories that were not technically part of the empire, at least not at first, but were adjacent to it. These territories are traditionally called 'client kingdoms', although the term 'allied kingdoms' or even 'friendly kingdoms', has been suggested as a more accurate alternative.[26] These kings and queens had patrons situated within the Roman aristocracy who personally supported them and represented their interests in Rome: for example, Cato the Younger and Pompey the Great were heavily invested in the kingdom of Egypt during the reign of Cleopatra Selene's grandfather Ptolemy XII Auletes. The formal designation 'friend and ally' was a coveted status that neighbouring kings or queens might angle after for years before it was granted. In return for Rome's friendship, client monarchs were expected to provide Rome with material support, often in the form of financial aid or access to the kingdom's natural resources as a means of funding military activity. Cleopatra VII's aid, for example, was sought by both sides in the civil war that followed Caesar's assassination, and then later by Antony in the lead-up to his Armenian and Parthian campaigns. Rome did not tend to interfere in the day-to-day running of its client kingdoms unless serious problems arose that compromised the authority of the client king or queen. If that happened, and the situation became unsalvageable, either the king or queen could be replaced with someone more competent or, as a last resort, the kingdom could be formally annexed and turned into a province. While the Hellenistic kingdoms ruled by the descendants of Alexander the Great's successors in the Near East had gradually disappeared over the course of the second and first centuries BCE, absorbed by the burgeoning Roman Empire, there were many other client kingdoms that succeeded in retaining their independence for centuries.

What better person to appoint as a client king than someone who, while technically a member of a foreign royal family, had spent most of their life in Rome and been raised and educated according to Roman values – like Juba? And what better person to be his client queen than someone who was both a member of a foreign royal family and a member of a Roman one – like Cleopatra Selene? Both had a combination of positive and negative examples of predecessors to follow: while Juba's father's reign had ended as a result of him choosing the wrong side in the conflict between Caesar and Pompey the Great, prior to that he had acquitted himself well as a client king. Furthermore, Juba's ancestor Massinissa was a prime example of how to rule successfully as a client king for decades. And, of course, Cleopatra Selene had witnessed first-hand her mother's political machinations, both successful and unsuccessful.[27] Like Juba I, Cleopatra VII had fulfilled all her obligations as a client monarch entirely competently; she just had the misfortune of her patron being the loser rather than the winner in a Roman civil war.

In view of the volatility and instability of North Africa, Augustus created the allied kingdom of Mauretania out of two pre-existing North African kingdoms and appointed the newly wed Juba and Cleopatra Selene as king and queen, dispatching them across the Mediterranean to the Mauretanian capital city of Iol forthwith. Mauretania protected the Roman Empire from incursions by nomadic African tribes, such as the famously aggressive Gaetulians from the south. It also historically served as a source of wild animals for the Roman games, luxury goods such as citronwood furniture and purple dye, and staple goods such as a variety of agricultural produce of which grain was first and foremost. It was understood that Mauretania was to be an extremely important trading partner which needed to be competently ruled and safeguarded. The previous rulers, the kings Bocchus and Bogudes, had been absent for many years owing to their participation in the civil war between Octavian and Antony, so many things had been neglected and needed to be set right by the new royal couple. Under their rule, Mauretania would become a powerhouse client kingdom, the only one in the west of the Roman Empire. As to what they did and how they did it, we shall see in the next chapter.

9

A Fresh Start:
The Kingdom of Mauretania

To ROMANS WHO HAD not actually been to North Africa, which is to say most Romans, it was a mysterious land where numerous dramatic mythological episodes had taken place. It was here that Hercules had wrestled with the giant Antaeus – immortal as long as he was in contact with his mother Gaia, the Earth – finally lifting him up and crushing him to death. It was also here that Hercules had undertaken his eleventh labour, searching for the paradisiacal Garden of the Hesperides (three nymphs who were associated with the evening and the golden light of sunset), and slaying the Hesperian Dragon who was guarding the treasure of the tree bearing the golden apples at the Garden's centre.[1] Frescos depicting these mythological episodes were popular interior decorations, particularly in *triclinia*. Banqueters would have reclined, sipped wine and nibbled canapes while feasting their eyes upon the sight of Hercules, clad in his famous cloak (made from the skin of the Nemean Lion), and wielding his famous club, sidling up to the Hesperides and their Dragon, his eyes on the prize of the golden apples hanging from the tree behind them.

It was in North Africa that the mysterious and beautiful Aethiopian people lived, and they were also a popular subject in ancient Greek and Roman art, one example being a marble portrait of a Nubian dating from the late second century BCE and originally part of a larger sculpture on display in Ptolemaic Egypt.[2]

North Africa was believed by the Romans to be a vast desert that was home to strange flora and fauna, notably lions and other big cats, elephants, rhinoceroses, hippopotami and crocodiles that were displayed infrequently at *venationes* ('beast hunts') that were a popular part of the Roman games.[3] At one point, it had been forbidden to import wild animals from Africa to Rome, but the tribune of the people, Gnaeus Aufidius, had passed a law repealing this ban in the late second or early first century BCE.[4] Consequently, such displays were relatively new innovations. Lions were first included in 186 BCE by Marcus Fulvius Nobilior, and elephants in 169 BCE. According to Pliny the Elder, it was not until much later that rhinoceroses were first featured by Pompey the Great at the dedication of his Theatre in 55 BCE, and hippopotami and crocodiles by Marcus Aemilius Scaurus during his tenure as aedile in 58 BCE, so as far as Roman spectators were concerned these African beasts were still a relative novelty.[5]

Today, our knowledge of pre-Roman North Africa and its Berber, Phoenicio-Punic and Greek inhabitants is rather scanty. We are reliant upon classical literary sources that mention the region – in which the information provided is not necessarily accurate – and piecemeal archaeological investigation, the results of which have been appropriated by those with vested nationalist interests.[6] Additionally, some of the archaeological evidence for indigenous material culture, such as the rock art carved into the Atlas Mountains, is difficult to date with any precision. Even so, it is clear that this romanticised idea of North Africa promulgated by ancient authors was somewhat simplistic. There were indeed vast swathes of arid desert occupied predominantly by prides of lions, and sinister venomous creatures that slithered and scuttled, but there were also areas of considerable agricultural fertility that supported intense human productivity. The poet Silius Italicus, writing in the latter part of the first century CE, stated 'where Africa spreads her untilled plains, the burnt-up land bears nothing but the poison of snakes in plenty; though, where a temperate strip blesses the fields, her fertility is not surpassed'.[7] African farmers were responsible for contributing a sizeable portion to Rome's annual grain supply, with Cicero describing it as one of Rome's 'three granaries', along with Sicily and Sardinia.[8] Along with grain, other staples of the Roman diet produced by North Africa were olives, fish (particularly tuna, passing through on their seasonal migration from the Mediterranean to the Atlantic and back again), and garum, that famous Roman condiment comprising fermented fish sauce that went with everything. Other important exports were timber, horses – the Mauritanian and Mazacian breeds that, while not much to look at, with their misshapen (by Roman standards) heads and bellies, were incredibly hard-working – and dogs.

More renowned still were North Africa's exotic exports.[9] Factories on islands known as the Purple Islands, of which Mogador was one, just off the Atlantic coast (near modern Essaouira in Morocco) processed the predatory sea snail, the murex. They crushed its shell to access the secretions within that produced the Tyrian purple dye that was used to colour the edges of the togas worn by Roman senators, and other fine clothing worn by the aristocratic members of Roman society.[10] The remains of these factories, including heaps of discarded shells, can still be seen today. Forests on the slopes of Mount Atlas were a source of citronwood, a species of cypress, that was not only beautiful to look at but also scented, smelling of citrus or lemon. Homer described the witch Circe as burning cedar and citronwood and using the lovely aroma to entice the hero Odysseus to her home on the island of Aeaea.[11] It was believed to be durable, if not indestructible, and since its scent was believed to repel insects it was also a favoured material for writing tablets and cases used to store papyrus scrolls.[12] It was frequently coupled with ivory, and the contrast between the dark gleaming wood and the pale, glowing ivory must have been incredibly pleasing to the eye. Only the wealthiest of Romans possessed tables with citronwood tops, which were often round and sliced from the width of the entire trunk. The knotted appearance of the wood was much admired, particularly when joined to a set of ivory legs, which were often elaborately carved into mythical creatures such as sphinxes. These pieces sold for eye-watering sums of money.[13] The orator Cicero paid 1,200,000 sesterces for one, Gaius Asinius Gallus Saloninus, the emperor Tiberius' arch enemy and romantic rival, 1,100,000 for another.[14] Juba himself owned two which were sold at auction, and one of them sold for 1,200,000 sesterces, the other slightly less.[15] Cleopatra Selene and Juba's son Ptolemy apparently owned the largest one ever made at four and a half feet in diameter and a quarter of a foot in thickness.[16]

Such tables were so popular that there was something of a craze for them in the latter part of the first century BCE and early first century CE, and possession of them by influential members of ancient Roman society, including members of the imperial family and their royal relatives, would undoubtedly have increased the cachet of owning one. It may have been believed that the citron tree was a version of the species that grew in the fabled Garden of the Hesperides, and its fruit, the citron, was similar, in appearance at least, to the fabled Apples of the Hesperides, although citron fruit was considered to have a bitter taste and an unpleasant scent.[17] By the middle of the first century CE, the forests that produced the most esteemed citronwood had been considerably depleted. Thus, we might imagine the rooms of Cleopatra Selene and Juba's palace to have been draped with richly dyed purple cloths and populated with elaborate items of furniture intricately carved from citronwood, which would have been fitting not only because these luxuries originated in their kingdom but also because of their prestige. It would have undoubtedly impressed visitors who arrived expecting a primitive backwater.

Neither the land nor its peoples were very well known in Rome. The term 'Libya' was used to refer to the entirety of North Africa between the Atlantic Ocean and the border of Egypt, the area that we refer to today as the Maghreb. Beyond the cities and towns of the Mediterranean littoral that had been inhabited by Carthaginians, Greeks and Romans in turn, the indigenous peoples were predominantly nomadic, and the Romans relied upon antiquated ethnic stereotyping that dated from the days of Homer to conceptualise them. Virgil imagined Libyan shepherds tending their flocks far and wide across the desert, travelling from hut to hut, carrying all their possessions with them on their backs.[18] Romans differentiated – not necessarily accurately, it must be said – between different groups using the names Maurusians, Massylians, Masaesylians, Numidians, Cyrenaeans, Carthaginians, Gaetulians and Garamantes, and today we tend to refer to them collectively as 'Berbers'. To Roman eyes, these different groups presented themselves in similar ways and went to considerable lengths to beautify themselves.[19] They braided their hair into complicated arrangements that they were very careful not to disturb, taking pains to clean their teeth and pare their nails, and ornamenting themselves with gold. Unlike the Romans in this period, the men grew beards and presumably tended to these as equally carefully as they did their hair. Virgil also commented on the looseness of their robes, worn without girdles.[20] Those who rode horses did so bareback, leading their mounts with bridles made from rushes and controlling them with small rods. They armed themselves with javelins and daggers, while those who went on foot bore shields made from elephant leather and dressed in wide-bordered tunics topped with the skins of lions, leopards and bears.

The amorphous borders between different parts of North Africa meant that frequently there was armed conflict between members of these groups and the Romans who had colonised, immigrated to and settled in the region. During the last years of the Republic and the early years of the Augustan Principate, the bellicose indigenous population presented an irresistible challenge to members of the Roman senatorial elite looking to make names for themselves as successful generals in the hopes of being awarded military triumphs and all the associated privileges; just as Carthage had been Scipio Africanus' destiny, many Roman senators saw North Africa as theirs.[21] Indeed, the last military triumph celebrated by someone who was not a member of the imperial family, Lucius Cornelius Balbus' in 19 BCE, was in recognition of his African victories achieved at the expense of the neighbouring Garamantes.[22] Unlike the Roman legionaries, North African warriors fought from horseback, and wielded javelins and bows from which they shot poisoned arrows.[23] The only experience most Romans would have had of these individuals would have been watching professional Gaetulian beast hunters – who were believed to be able to charm lions – engaging with wild animals in the arena, and this is perhaps true of Cleopatra Selene herself, prior to her move to Mauretania, as the imperial family and its associates did make a point of being seen to attend, pay attention to and enjoy the spectacles. This was partly an exercise in public relations, a response to the fact that Caesar had been universally criticised for attending the games yet not paying sufficient attention to them, preferring instead to work throughout the proceedings, reading and answering letters for the duration.[24] Sometimes the imperial family watched the games from the imperial box, other times from conveniently located homes of close friends, and it is highly likely that Cleopatra Selene accompanied them.[25]

While Cleopatra Selene may not have been personally familiar with North Africa beyond Egypt, she had undoubtedly experienced first-hand the difference between what Romans believed of Egypt and Egyptians, and what was actually the case, so it is likely that

she took the tall tales she was told about her new kingdom prior
to her arrival with a sizeable grain of salt. While Juba had been
taken from Numidia as a baby and would have had to rely upon
second-hand accounts of what his early life had been like while
in residence at his father's palace at the Numidian capital city of
Zama, he may have had the opportunity to undertake short visits
to Mauretania while on campaign with Augustus, Marcellus and
Tiberius in Hispania in the years 27–25 BCE. Both Cleopatra Selene
and Juba would have undoubtedly availed themselves of all the
considerable resources at their disposal in familiarising themselves
with the land and peoples they were tasked with ruling. These
resources would have included prominent Romans who had spent
time in North Africa, not just on military endeavours during the
civil wars but also on commercial ventures, as well as works of Latin
and Greek literature concerning the region, such as the history
written by Antony and Octavian's peer Gaius Asinius Pollio, who
had spent a considerable amount of time there on campaign with
Caesar. Pollio would have been a person of considerable interest
to Cleopatra Selene, as he had been close friends with her father
and had initially sided with him during his conflict with Octavian.
He had facilitated the Pact of Brundisium between the pair in 40
BCE, before refusing a request from Octavian to participate in the
Battle of Actium because of that friendship. While Pollio's history
of the civil wars no longer survives, it was a significant source for
the later writers Appian, Dio, Plutarch and Suetonius, whose works
indicate that Pollio placed considerable emphasis on eyewitness
testimony, especially his own.[26] The couple would also have had
access to works of Punic literature that had been seized from the
royal library of Hiempsal I of Numidia (died c.117 BCE) and the
state library of Carthage by Gaius Sallustius Crispus, known to
posterity as Sallust, during his military service in the region with
Caesar and subsequent governorship of Africa Nova in 46 BCE.
These collections included works on the geography and inhabitants

of the region. Juba continued to use them as research material for his own writings on North Africa some years later.[27]

What would soon become the allied kingdom of Mauretania was an immense territory encompassing modern-day Algeria and Morocco, and the royal court of Mauretania was based at the kingdom's capital city Iol. Since the allied kingdom had been created from the amalgamation of two separate kingdoms, one ruled by Bogudes II and one ruled by Bocchus II, there were actually two capital cities: Bogudes' Volubilis, in the far west, in what is now Morocco, and Bocchus' Iol, on the Mediterranean coast. Cleopatra Selene and Juba would choose the coastal city as their permanent residence, since this allowed them to remain connected to the rest of the Roman world, rather than being isolated on what was effectively the southern frontier of the Roman Empire. In the case of an emergency, they could sail from Iol to Rome, or send a messenger to someone in the empire's capital in just under nine days, whereas to do so from Volubilis would take as many as twenty-three.[28] In so doing, they were following in Alexander the Great's footsteps, as his choice of site for Alexandria in Egypt was predicated on its proximity to the Mediterranean and the rest of the Greek world, a fact of which Cleopatra Selene was no doubt aware, and probably informed Juba. Mauretania's connection to the rest of the Roman world is made clear in the number of sherds of a particular type of pottery that have been recovered from excavations in and around Cherchell: *terra sigillata* tableware ranges from pale orange to bright red in colour, has a glossy surface and is often covered with relief decoration in a wide range of designs. It was manufactured on an industrial scale in Italy (Arretine ware) and Gaul (Samian ware) and then shipped all over the empire. It is so ubiquitous that it would not be an exaggeration to say that there is probably some tableware on display in almost every museum in the world with a Roman collection.

Soon after taking up residence at Iol, Cleopatra Selene and Juba would, rather diplomatically, rename the city Iol Caesarea, after their benefactor, Augustus.[29] They were not the only allied rulers

to make a gesture like this: Herod of Judea built a grand city that
he named Caesarea Maritima (modern Keisarya, or Qaysaria, in
northern central Israel), while Archaelaos of Cappadocia founded
Cappadocian Caesarea. Despite being located far to the west of
Rome, during the reign of Cleopatra Selene and Juba, Iol Caesarea
became a highly sophisticated and multicultural court, populated
by well-educated and prolific Greek, Roman, Egyptian and African
scholars and talented and creative artisans. Perhaps unsurprisingly,
the royal couple made a concerted effort to model their court at
Iol Caesarea on that at Alexandria, although they were aiming to
imitate Cleopatra Selene's distant rather than immediate relatives.
Ptolemy II Philadelphos and his sister-wife Arsinoe II had, after
all, transformed the fledgling city into the cultural capital of the
Hellenistic world through their creation of the Museum and the
Great Library, and their patronage of scholars and artists. It is
possible that at this point in his life Juba had not yet had the
opportunity to visit Alexandria (assuming he had not accompanied
Octavian on campaign there in 30 BCE), so Cleopatra Selene would
have been primarily responsible for directing and realising their
shared vision.

The capital city was one of the largest metropoles in the western
part of the Roman Empire and both it and the rest of the kingdom
seem to have been very ethnically and culturally diverse.[30] The
architecture and art of the city proudly promoted Greek, Roman,
Egyptian and African history in a manner unique in the ancient
Mediterranean. Cleopatra Selene and Juba's first responsibility
as allied monarchs was renovating the city, making it a fitting
capital for an allied kingdom. Augustus was himself an enthusiastic
builder and was famously described as having found Rome a city
of brick and left it a city of marble in his quest to make it as fine
as cities such as Alexandria that he had seen in the eastern part
of the Roman Empire. The couple undoubtedly communicated
with him regarding their plans.[31]

Iol Caesarea's harbour was endowed, like Alexandria, with a small island (interestingly, the name Iol has Semitic origins and means 'sandy island' in Hebrew), and on it the couple built a lighthouse, a practical step but perhaps also as an homage to the harbour and the Pharos of Alexandria.[32] This would not have seemed strange: many ancient Roman cities had imitated the famous lighthouse and its innovative octagonal design. Nearby, they built a grand royal palace for themselves to live in, which they decorated with glorious works of art in Greek, Roman and Egyptian styles, including many portraits of themselves, members of their respective families, and friends.[33] Perhaps they even referred to their palace between themselves as the Brucheion.

Every Roman city needs a Forum, where public business, not only political but also social and economic, could take place. While the Forum that survives today was built later, in the reign of the Severan emperors of the second and third centuries CE, it seems that Cleopatra Selene and Juba's Forum was located somewhere nearby. Columns resembling those of the Temple of Mars Ultor in Rome and carved from Luna marble, the white and grey marble that was a favourite building material of Augustus, have been found in the vicinity, having been reused in the construction of the Severan Forum and its basilica.

To the south of the Forum, they built a Greek-style theatre according to the recommendations made by the Roman architect Vitruvius, and we know that Roman artisans were involved in its construction because one of the capitals is inscribed with the name Publius Antius Amphio, presumably a freedman of the Antistii, perhaps a member of the workshop that produced the capital or a worker on the building site.[34] These artisans could have been hired and sent as a gift to the couple from their family and friends back in Rome. One of Juba's surviving poems is an epigram criticising a performance of a play that took place there, a version of *Hypsipyle* staged by Leonteus of Argos, a member of the Mauretanian court.

This may have been the play of that name written by the Greek tragedian Euripides, or possibly an original work by Leonteus himself. In either case, Juba was not impressed with Leonteus' performance, which had apparently been ruined by his overeating:

> When you behold me, the cardoon-eating voice of the
>   tragic actor
> Leonteus, do not believe that you look upon Hypsipyle's
>   ugly heart.
> For I was once Bacchus' friend, nor did his gold-spangled
>   ears
> Get as much pleasure from any other voice.
> But now earthenware pots and dry frying-pans
> have taken away my voice, since I paid more attention to
>   my belly.[35]

Juba was himself something of a theatre buff, having written a work entitled *Theatrical History* while still quite young, and *Hypsipyle* may have been chosen to flatter Cleopatra Selene as its subject matter would probably have resonated particularly with her. The play is about the eponymous Queen of Lemnos who was exiled from her kingdom, captured by pirates and sold as a slave to Lycurgus, the priest of Zeus at Nemea. There, she works as a nursemaid until one of her charges suffers a tragic accident under her care and his mother insists upon her death as recompense, although thankfully she is rescued and so escapes this fate. It may have been that the source of Juba's irritation with Leonteus was that he knew the play would resonate with his wife and he had wanted her to enjoy it. In addition to the performance of comic and tragic plays, Iol Caesarea's theatre would have provided a venue for concerts, poetry recitals and dance performances. They also built an amphitheatre in which to host other types of entertainment, such as wild beast hunts, for which purpose it would undoubtedly have been kept well stocked with local fauna. The couple seem to have planted trees, set up and decorated an altar, and created a sacred grove that they called the Lucus Augusti.

The couple was also responsible for renovating old temples and dedicating new ones to the gods and goddesses that they felt particularly close to. The indigenous religion revolved around cults dedicated to ancestral worship, including the deification of deceased monarchs. Judging by the surviving architectural remnants this seems to have continued, but it seems likely that Cleopatra Selene was responsible for the promotion of Egyptian gods and goddesses in Mauretania, and the promotion of her namesake, the Greek goddess of the moon Selene, in particular. There was a Temple of Isis in Caesarea, the building of which Cleopatra Selene perhaps instigated in honour of her mother, although considering the abundant Isis-related imagery she included on her coinage, the goddess does appear to have been a favourite of hers, too.[36] Juba consecrated a crocodile to the temple, which he took as proof that the Nile originated in Mauretania, another concrete link between himself and Cleopatra Selene, and their kingdom of Mauretania and her rightful inheritance of the kingdom of Egypt, just as Crinagoras' wedding poem for them had said. This was perhaps also an attempt by the couple to institute a cult practice comparable to the sacred crocodiles of Sobek found in temples in the Fayum in Egypt.[37] These crocodiles were famous throughout the ancient world, and there is papyrological evidence of Roman tourists visiting Egypt to see them as early as 5 March 112 BCE in the form of an itinerary that includes a visit to Petesouchos and the sacred crocodiles of Arsinoe, known as Crocodilopolis, 'Crocodile City'.[38]

Since there is literary, documentary and archaeological evidence of members of the Ptolemaic dynasty worshipping Egyptian deities as well as Greek ones within Egypt, including living animal deities such as the Apis Bull, the Buchis Bull and the crocodiles of Sobek, it is likely that Cleopatra Selene had done so herself as a child living in Egypt. She would not, however, have been able to do so while living in Rome, where – as we have seen – Egyptian cults were carefully monitored and frequently subjected to disciplinary measures such as temporary bans on their activities. She may have attempted to introduce the practice to Mauretania, albeit on a small scale. And there is certainly some archaeological evidence of worship of the goddess Selene in the kingdom at this time: when I visited Volubilis a few years ago, I came across several dedications to the goddess in the site's compact yet well-curated museum. The emphasis placed upon the goddesses Isis and Selene in Mauretania, and their promotion by Cleopatra Selene, during this period may account for the unusual design of an intaglio currently housed in the National Soares dos Reis Museum in Oporto in Portugal.[39] This pale orange oval carnelian gem has been dated to the second half of the first century BCE, therefore during Cleopatra Selene's lifetime, and is decorated with a draped bust of the goddess Isis/Selene in profile and facing to the left. She wears her hair styled in long Libyan-style locks with a fillet passing over her head and a lotus bloom on her forehead, and below her is a crescent moon. Although the intaglio is unprovenanced, four of the six intaglios in the museum's collection that depict Isis originated in the south of Portugal, so it is not implausible that the Mauretanian presentation of Isis/Selene had spread north, considering the close links between Mauretania and Hispania Lusitania (as this region was known) during the Roman period.

At the same time, Cleopatra Selene and Juba undertook the expected glorification of Augustus and the imperial family. This culminated in Juba issuing coins late in his reign with portraits of himself on the obverse face accompanied by the Latin legend REX IUBA, and depictions of a temple accompanied by the Latin legend AUGUSTI, 'Of Augustus', on the reverse, indicating that he had built at least one temple and maybe even two temples dedicated to his benefactor, presumably after Augustus' death and deification in 14 CE.[40] One of the temples depicted is in hexastyle design with a pediment decorated with the figure of an eagle

A coin issued by Juba II, in which he is depicted wearing the lionskin of the demi-god Hercules, accompanied by the Latin legend REX IUBA. On the reverse face is a temple dedicated to Augustus.

and flanked by a Victory on either side; the other is a tetrastyle temple with a pediment decorated with a star, perhaps a reference to Augustus' ascension into the heavens. Despite Juba's clear expression of loyalty to Augustus, and his acknowledgement of Augustus' peerless position, it is worth noting that on one of these coins Juba took pains to depict himself wearing the lionskin and bearing the club of Hercules – his and Cleopatra Selene's shared divine ancestor – making it clear that he had his own claim to sovereignty in Africa.

Finally, with an eye to the future of the dynasty that they were intent on founding, Juba constructed a large mausoleum, which can still be seen today on the road between Cherchell and Algiers in Tipaza Province in Algeria.[41] The mausoleum resembles other significant funerary monuments located in North Africa and the East, so Juba was clearly aiming for continuity. But simultaneously, it is very similar to the Mausoleum of Augustus in the centre of Rome, the construction of which was begun in 27 BCE, before Cleopatra Selene and Juba left the city. Juba could easily argue that this resemblance was deliberate, another attempt to link his family with the imperial family in which he had grown up.[42]

Unfortunately, the mausoleum was looted and relieved of its contents long ago, so no trace of the royal family or their remains survives. Iol Caesarea was also an intellectual and cultural centre. The royal library included Latin, Greek and Punic works of literature, and scholars working in a variety of academic disciplines spent time there, including Juba himself.[43] Many Hellenistic monarchs, including a number of Cleopatra Selene's ancestors, had combined kingship with scholarship, and prior to their marriage Juba had already published works on Roman history and/or archaeology, Greek and Latin terminology, theatrical history and art.[44] The scholarship that he produced during their marriage seems to have been influenced by Cleopatra Selene, and she may even have contributed to it. He wrote about his mother-in-law, and the information that he included would in all likelihood have been provided by his wife, and he may well have sought her approval on his drafts that mentioned her: it was the considerate thing to do, after all.[45] He also wrote an in-depth treatise on North Africa entitled *Libyka*, in which he continued their joint project of laying claim to the entire continent, and included extensive sections on the Nile and the Red Sea trade routes.

There was a longstanding association between women of the Ptolemaic dynasty and poets: Arsinoe II had been a patron to Theocritus, and Berenice II had been a patron to Callimachus, so it would not have been untoward for Cleopatra Selene to foster poetic talent in Mauretania. Crinagoras of Mytilene, the poet who wrote the grandiose epigram celebrating Cleopatra Selene and Juba's wedding, may also have been invited to Iol Caesarea to commemorate other key events in the couple's reign, an ancient version of the contemporary poet laureate (he certainly wrote an epigram on the occasion of Cleopatra Selene's untimely death).[46] It has recently been proposed that Cleopatra Selene served as a patron to a circle of poets with a very specific interest, the precious stones owned by the early Ptolemies, particularly the Ptolemaic queens.[47] Hellenistic rulers had long been enthusiastic collectors of precious stones and these collections were known as *dactyliotheca*: King Mithridates VI of Pontus' immense collection passed to Pompey the Great upon his defeat, and Pompey dedicated it to the Temple of Jupiter, Juno and Minerva on the Capitoline Hill in Rome, a benefaction which started a craze for pearls and gemstones among elite Romans.[48] His rival Caesar went one better and dedicated six sets to the temple of his ancestress Venus Genetrix in the centre of his Forum. Cleopatra Selene would have witnessed Marcellus dedicate a collection to the Temple of Apollo on the Palatine Hill, and Livia dedicate a sardonyx set in a golden horn to the Temple of Concord and the largest piece of rock crystal ever seen to the Temple of Jupiter, Juno and Minerva on the Capitoline Hill. She could, potentially even have learned of Antony's enthusiasm for opals.[49] She would also perhaps have been inspired by Augustus and the imperial family's interest in and use of cameos to communicate their preferred ideology – surviving examples of which include the famous Gemma Augustea ('Gem of Augustus'), and the Blacas Cameo, both possibly carved by Augustus' favourite gem cutter Dioskourides. If so, it encouraged her to commission various epigrams and even some gems in an attempt to communicate hers, presenting herself as the descendant and successor of historical heavyweights rather than lightweights.

Certainly, one of the most renowned artisans in residence at Iol Caesarea was Gnaios the gem cutter. Gems were key markers of wealth, culture and status – every Roman citizen of consequence had a signet ring set with an intaglio. These were engraved with an image specific to them that they would use to seal, authorise and verify all their documentation. Augustus, for example, used first a sphinx, then an image of Alexander the Great, and then finally an image of himself as his seal during the course of his long life, all carved by Dioskourides.[50] Gnaios carved cameo portraits of some of the most powerful people in the ancient Mediterranean into precious stones, and two of the three works of his that have survived from classical antiquity can be associated with the Mauretanian royal court.

During his residence at Iol Caesarea, Gnaios carved a red carnelian intaglio bearing a portrait of Cleopatra Selene, perhaps for Juba himself, in which she wears her hair in the so-called 'melon' coiffure, and bears a sceptre, the symbol of her royal authority, at the nape of her neck.[51] This portrait resembles those found on her coinage: Gnaios may have been responsible for producing what amounts to a formal likeness of Cleopatra Selene for use in official capacities, just as the sculptor Lysippos' portraits of Alexander the Great so pleased the king that he decreed that no other ancient sculptor could reproduce his image.[52]

He also carved a blue beryl intaglio bearing a portrait of a youthful Hercules, with his club propped up behind him and Gnaios' signature below the portrait.[53] Sadly, at some point, the intaglio was damaged, but the missing piece has been restored to it in gold.

Unsurprisingly, considering Hercules was not only Cleopatra Selene and Juba's shared ancestor but was also associated with specific sites in North Africa, he was a prominent figure at the royal court in Iol Caesarea and a significant part of the royal family's branding; Cleopatra Selene and Juba's son Ptolemy seems to have been especially enthusiastic about his heroic ancestor, featuring him and his club on his coinage with regularity.

While we know a reasonable amount about the celebrity members of Cleopatra Selene and Juba's entourage and what they were up to at various points during the couple's reign, it is important to remember that from the moment she was born, Cleopatra Selene would have seldom, if ever, been alone. As an Egyptian princess, then a member of the extended Roman imperial family, and finally an African queen, she would always have been surrounded by people who were at her beck and call at all hours of the day and night. Her household staff would have comprised enslaved individuals, formerly enslaved individuals and potentially even freeborn individuals from all around the ancient Mediterranean. While we do not know the names of any of her Egyptian staff apart from her tutor Nikolaos of Damascus, we are better informed about her Roman and Mauretanian households owing to a combination of literary and documentary evidence, such as funerary monuments set up in honour of their members that have been discovered in Rome and Iol Caesarea.

Since it was Roman custom for enslaved individuals to take on the family names of their enslavers once they had been officially manumitted and regained their freedom, we can see that Cleopatra Selene seems to have inherited several members of her father's household staff, such as her personal physician Antonius Euphorbos, the brother of Augustus' personal physician Antonius Musa.[54] The pair were Methodists – that is to say members of the Methodist medical sect – and disciples of the Late Republican physician Asclepiades of Bithynia. They followed in his footsteps in popularising innovative cold water medical treatments, and Euphorbos seems to have been dear enough to Cleopatra Selene and Juba for the latter to name a plant, known today as *Euphorbia resinifera* Berg, a type of resin spurge, that he discovered growing in the Atlas Mountains, after him.[55] This was quite an honour, as Juba went on to devote an entire treatise to the plant, and this is in fact the only reason that Euphorbos' name has survived, as, unlike his brother, his therapies do not seem to have become famous.[56] By way of consolation, however, the plant genus *Euphorbia*, which contains a range of plants including the poinsettias with which we decorate our homes at Christmas, still bears his name today. There are also epitaphs for Aischinos Antonianus and Cleopatra, the daughter of Gaius Antonianus, who died at the age of twenty-three years and seven months old, from Iol Caesarea, and their names indicate their connection to Antony's family.[57]

Members of Cleopatra Selene's staff seem to have died and been commemorated in Rome, and this supports the theory that she had a residence in the city – perhaps her half-brother Iullus had made Antony's house, bought from Pompey the Great, in the heart of the city near Pompey's Theatre, available to her – and spent extended periods there over the years.[58] One such staff member was Ecloga the mime who, at the relatively young age of eighteen, may have performed in the theatre at Iol Caesarea and proved so proficient in her craft that Cleopatra Selene took her to Rome to share her talents with her family and friends.[59] If her name is any indication of her approach to her art, she would select short sections from long pieces, the edited highlights of plays and poems, and perform them for her audience. Other known members of Cleopatra Selene's staff include Chios Jubatianus, a host responsible for not just laying the table but also serving food, and Julia Prima Jubatiana.[60]

By this time, the fashion for displaying unusual individuals such as dwarfs had spread from Egypt to Rome, and many elite households boasted them as a feature of their staff. Cleopatra Selene may have been in a position to offer her father's dwarf companion Sisyphus a home at the Mauretanian royal court. The freedom to do so would have been especially gratifying for her since Augustus was not a fan of this trend.[61] It would also have been another way that she and Juba could attempt to model their burgeoning royal court on the Ptolemaic one in Alexandria.

However, the royal family do also seem to have imitated Augustus, who founded the Praetorian Guards in 27 BCE, in their use of bodyguards. They formed their own version of the organisation, the *corporis custodes*, as inscriptions set up by some of the cohort's members, such as Hyacinthus, Crestus and Gaius

Julius Dapnus, the latter presumably, judging from his name, a former member of the royal household, attest.[62] Iol Caesarea is the only place in the Roman world apart from the city of Rome itself that attests such an institution. Additionally, the royal family seem to have formed and made use of a company of urban cohorts, the *cohors urbana*, and an epitaph set up to commemorate one of its members, Aebutius Rufus, who died while on active duty, has survived.[63] Iol Caesarea coming to boast these two institutions indicates that Cleopatra Selene and Juba ruled in grand style, making a concerted effort to simultaneously flatter and imitate the imperial cult at Rome.[64] It indicates the sheer size of the city and its population, and perhaps implies that the inhabitants were somewhat unruly, necessitating a degree of crowd control, with the members of these companies ensuring acquiescence by wielding the ancient equivalents of nightsticks with relative impunity.[65] It is also possible that these companies served to safeguard the kingdom's method of supplying grain to the city of Rome.[66]

When in residence at the royal palace in Iol Caesarea, one of the more varied duties undertaken by Cleopatra Selene and Juba would have been the reception of embassies and exotic goods from elsewhere in the ancient world. At around the time that Cleopatra Selene and Juba were establishing themselves in Mauretania, Augustus was receiving embassies from destinations as far flung as India and China, and accepting all manner of exotic gifts, including a tiger that he presented at the dedication of the Theatre of Marcellus in honour of his nephew and Juba's foster brother, now deceased.[67] Cleopatra Selene and Juba may have received similar delegations. They certainly commissioned expeditions of their own, including one to an archipelago off the western coast of Africa that they identified as the fabled Islands of the Blessed (the modern Canary Islands), and these returned with intriguing souvenirs. All these islands were charted, recorded and given classical names considered appropriate, one of them called Canaria because of the numerous species of very large dogs that were found living there (and from which the modern name 'Canary Islands' originates). Two of these dogs were captured and brought back to Cleopatra Selene and Juba at Iol Caesarea and presumably they remained there, probably put on display for the inhabitants of the city to see, the beginnings of a royal menagerie like the one that Cleopatra Selene's ancestors had founded at Alexandria. Depending upon the extent to which they could be tamed and controlled, they may have become something akin to pets of the royal household. Another expedition was sent out to search for the source of the Nile and it reached a lake called the Nilides, in which crocodiles were found, a discovery taken as proof that the source of the Nile was in Mauretania, despite the fact that the actual source of the Nile lies thousands of miles away on the other side of the continent.[68] One of these crocodiles was captured and, like the dogs, brought back to the capital. This particular gift undoubtedly delighted Cleopatra Selene, not just because it was a reminder of her homeland but also because the crocodile was to all intents and purposes her personal symbol. The creature was subsequently kept in the Temple of Isis: it was common practice in this period for temples to serve as repositories of all manner of treasures, including rare and unusual objects, and there was often a special significance, usually a programmatic or ideological one, to the temple chosen by the dedicator as the repository for their treasure.[69] In this case, the Temple of Isis was the obvious choice for the crocodile due to its Egyptian nature and its special significance to Cleopatra Selene herself.

Like any married couple, Cleopatra Selene and Juba would have exchanged gifts between themselves on special (and perhaps not so special) occasions. One of Juba's predecessors, King Bogudes, once presented his queen with a rather unconventional bouquet, a bundle of giant reeds and asparagus that he had discovered while on campaign in the west of Africa. Since Juba was himself an intrepid explorer and travelled all over the realm, it is likely that he brought Cleopatra Selene many similarly intriguing souvenirs throughout their marriage, conceivably even recreating Bogudes' present of a bouquet when he discovered the species of spurge he named Euphorbion.

Over the course of their reign, Juba and Cleopatra Selene oversaw the gradual urbanisation of Mauretania, founding new towns that followed the Roman precedent of being carefully planned and laid out, and occupied by Roman citizens allocated parcels of land. The extent to which the indigenous population relocated to these towns remains debatable, however, as does the extent to which the indigenous population accepted their new rulers. It is notable that in the years after Cleopatra Selene's death Juba's hold on the kingdom became increasingly precarious: without her, her unique heritage and her unmatched prestige, he did not have quite the same clout.

Throughout the Hellenistic period, the role of queen was never as clearly defined as the role of king.[70] A king's duties were clear: he was expected to operate in the political, judicial and military spheres, and act as a patron and benefactor to his subjects. A queen's duties were less so, and somewhat dependent on the individual occupying the role. Juba was an active and highly competent king – he would not have been able to maintain stability within Mauretania for almost five decades had he not been – but how much of his activity and competency was a result of him having an equally active and competent partner to share the burden of rule? Cleopatra Selene had, after all, borne witness first to her mother's rule of Egypt and later to Octavia and Livia's less overt but equally significant contributions to Augustus' rule of the Roman Empire. It is notable that much previous scholarship on the Roman client kingdom of Mauretania has focused on the kings, first Juba and then Ptolemy, because of the traditional understanding of male power, but new approaches to the subject are starting to consider female power and its somewhat different manifestation. Thus, it would not be an exaggeration to describe Juba and Cleopatra Selene as co-rulers rather than as a king and his consort, as is so often the case with ancient husbands and wives. She played an active rather than passive role in the joint project that was their reign; solidifying their hold on the newly established kingdom required the enthusiastic and sustained participation of both.[71] In the following chapter, we shall examine Cleopatra Selene's role within the Mauretanian royal family.

10

Wedded Bliss?

CLEOPATRA SELENE'S TWENTY-YEAR reign in Mauretania was characterised by her attempts to fuse her past and present and create something new and distinctive in the Roman Empire. She was uniquely capable of this because of her complex ancestry and multicultural heritage. After all, she was, through her mother, descended from Macedonian and Syrian royalty as well as Egyptian. She was, through her father, a member of an ancient Roman family and related to the Pontic and Cappadocian royal family. She was married to a member of the Numidian royal family. She had been in her relatively short life a princess of Egypt, queen of Crete and Cyrenaica, and was now Queen of Mauretania. Aspects of all these different identities must have been clearly apparent during her lifetime and immediately afterwards, as traces of them are still visible today in the ancient literary, documentary and archaeological records of both the Roman Empire and Mauretania itself.

It is notoriously difficult to identify specific individuals depicted in ancient portraiture. Unless, that is, those individuals happen to have been prominent enough to have a stable portrait type depicted across many examples produced in different media (such as, for example, Alexander the Great or the Roman emperors), or their portraits were labelled (such as those of ordinary people's funerary monuments, which are often accompanied by epitaphs relating their names and information about their lives, such as their significant achievements). In the case of many notable ancient individuals, the only securely identifiable portraits of them are those that appear on their coin issues, although even these are not entirely naturalistic or realistic owing to ancient ideological artistic conventions used by many monarchs. These include modelling themselves after Alexander the Great, depicting themselves with divine attributes like the ram horns of the god Zeus/Jupiter/ Ammon, or the appearance of fleshiness as an indicator of what the Greeks (and the members of the Ptolemaic dynasty in particular) defined as *tryphé*. And so it is with Cleopatra Selene. Her Mauretanian coin portraits indicate that she followed the example set by her mother and presented herself in the manner of a Hellenistic queen, with her hair styled in the 'melon' coiffure and held in place by a diadem, the traditional headwear of a Hellenistic king and, sometimes, even a queen. Originally, a diadem was a strip of white cloth, knotted at the back of the wearer's head, with the ends left dangling below. An alternative ancient headdress that was used to indicate the elevated status of its wearer was the stephane, a circlet with a pediment at the front that stood upright from the head. The early Ptolemaic queens who featured on coins such as Arsinoe II were depicted wearing the stephane topped by a veil rather than the diadem, indicative of their divine status. Despite her identification with the goddess Isis, Cleopatra VII preferred to portray herself wearing the diadem, perhaps meant to indicate her position as queen regnant rather than queen consort, and it seems that Cleopatra Selene followed her example in this, emphasising that she ruled alongside Juba as his equal, not as his subordinate. This was made explicit in one particular design, issued during the sixth year of their joint reign, which depicted Juba on the obverse accompanied by the Latin legend REX IUBA REGIS IUBAE F (King Juba, son of King Juba), and Cleopatra Selene on the

A coin depicting Juba and Cleopatra Selene.

reverse, accompanied by the Greek legend BASI KLEO KLEOPA THUGA (Queen Cleopatra, daughter of [Queen] Cleopatra).[1]

Art historians use these coin portraits as a reference and a guide when attempting to identify portraits of her produced in different media.[2] If we are to accept these as a reasonable reproduction of her features, it is clear that she inherited the distinctive nose of her maternal ancestors!

Portraits that have been tentatively identified as Cleopatra Selene have been recovered from various sites around Mauretania, although art historians are often tempted to identify them as her famous – or, more accurately, infamous – mother rather than her.[3] One such portrait is a marble bust, dating from 10–1 BCE, currently housed in the Cherchell Museum and labelled as Cleopatra Selene, yet when it appears in publications it is often misidentified.[4]

The woman it depicts is mature, wearing her hair in the 'melon' coiffure held in place by a large diadem, but her facial features are somewhat different from the handful of surviving marble portraits that art historians tend to agree depict Cleopatra. Since we do not have written physical descriptions of either Cleopatra Selene

The mature Cleopatra Selene in this white marble portrait bust, *c.* 10–1 BCE.

or her mother, and the only securely identified portraits of either that have survived from classical antiquity are the portraits on their coin issues, and these only depict them in profile, it is hard to say whether they looked at all alike (apart from their prominent noses). Based on its findspot, it seems fair to say that this is likely to be a portrait of the adult Cleopatra Selene, a queen at the height of her powers, and that she chose to represent herself in the style favoured by her mother and her Ptolemaic ancestors. Since the royal court at Iol Caesarea was far from Rome, and it was usual practice for allied monarchs to attend on members of the imperial family wherever they happened to be based rather than the other way around, and there is no record of any member of the imperial family ever visiting Mauretania, it was relatively safe for her to present herself in this manner there.

Both Cleopatra Selene and Juba commemorated their parents in the cities of their new kingdom. Antony had initially been subjected to certain aspects of the process of *damnatio memoriae* after his death, his statues torn down, his birthday declared a *dies nefas*, an 'unlucky day', in the Roman calendar, and the Antonii forbidden from ever again naming a son Marcus, so it is unlikely that Cleopatra Selene felt able to commemorate him openly and publicly.[5] However, since Octavian had permitted statues of Cleopatra VII to remain in situ in Egypt, thanks to the political manoeuvring and timely donation of 2,000 talents of gold from her loyal courtier Archibius, and since there was even a statue of Cleopatra in Caesar's Temple of Venus Genetrix in the Forum of Caesar in the heart of Rome, Cleopatra Selene probably felt on safer ground when it came to commemorating her mother.[6] A marble bust that was found in Cherchell and is now housed in the Cherchell Museum may represent the deceased Queen of Egypt.[7] Perhaps this was displayed alongside a marble bust that was likewise found in Cherchell but is now housed in the Louvre and is thought to represent Juba's father, King Juba of Numidia, due to its unusual hairstyle in combination with a beard. This was an aspect of the elder Juba's appearance that Cicero had commented on and Caesar had mocked, once actually pulling on it during a physical altercation that occurred between the pair.[8] Additionally, the man is portrayed wearing a diadem, indicating his royal status.

It is very similar to the portraits of himself that Juba of Numidia included on his coinage. The obverse face depicts a portrait of Juba accompanied by the Latin legend REX IUBA, 'King Juba', while the reverse face depicts a representation of a temple that is classical in style accompanied by a Punic legend that translates to the same.[9] It was perhaps these coins that inspired the royal couple's own bilingual coin issues.

The portrait's likeness to representations of Zeus/Jupiter is intriguing, and suggests that Juba attempted to glorify his father

King Juba I of Numidia, resplendently bearded
and coiffed in this white marble bust.

An example of Juba I's coinage: Juba I and the Latin legend
REX IUBA on the obverse face, and a temple on the reverse.

in the manner that Antony and Cleopatra had glorified themselves in their lifetimes by linking themselves to the Greek god Dionysos and the Egyptian goddess Isis.[10] A red glass intaglio engraved with what has been identified as a portrait of Juba of Numidia dating from the middle of the first century BCE has also survived and is currently housed in the British Museum.[11] Perhaps like Cleopatra Selene, Juba was forced to commemorate his disgraced father privately.

Once their rule was established, Cleopatra Selene and Juba aimed to establish a dynasty of their own to secure their possession of the kingdom. The precise number of children that they had is unknown, as is often the case with ancient families. However, there is no mention in the ancient literature of any internecine strife, as seems to have been common in other Hellenistic kingdoms and was certainly going on across the Mediterranean in Judea around this time. Because this was often so serious and toxic that it resulted in matricide, patricide, fratricide and uxoricide, all of which tended to have serious political ramifications, it is the sort of thing that Roman authors would have paid attention to and recorded, had it occurred. This indicates that the family was a stable one, and this stability was probably one of the reasons that Juba's reign was secure, lasted so long and culminated in a straightforward handover of power to his son upon his death.

During the two decades of their marriage and joint rule, while Juba spent a considerable amount of time on the frontiers of the kingdom dealing with incursions from hostile tribes, it is probable that Cleopatra Selene was based in Iol Caesarea, overseeing the kingdom during his absence. She was, after all, the one of the royal pair with the more prestigious ancestry, the closer ties to the imperial family, the higher status and, as a result, the greater personal authority. She would certainly have been in constant contact with a network of powerful women around the Mediterranean including the empress Livia, her foster mother

Octavia, her half-sisters Antonia Major and Minor, and the women of the Herodian dynasty and other eastern kingdoms, in addition to Augustus himself.[12] That this was a standard feature of the lives of client queens and other powerful women in the ancient Mediterranean is made clear, and some tantalising hints about these networks can be found in the writings of ancient historians such as Tacitus and Josephus. For example, Cleopatra VII corresponded with Queen Aba of Olbe (modern southern central Turkey) and Alexandra, the matriarch of the Hasmonean dynasty, and Livia corresponded with Salome of Judea (the sister of King Herod the Great), Queen Dynamis of the Bosporan Kingdom (modern eastern Crimea and the Taman Peninsula), Queen Pythadoris (also known as Pythodorida) of Pontos and her daughter Antonia Tryphaena, and the latter pair even stayed with her during their visits to Rome.[13] It is also likely that Cleopatra Selene visited Rome for significant historical occasions such as the funerary rites staged upon the death of Octavia in 11 BCE and the dedication of the Ara Pacis in 9 BCE.

While ancient historians tend not to devote much space to client queens, or at least not to successful ones, it is worth considering what they say about them when they do include them.[14] Take, for example, Berenice, the daughter of King Herod Agrippa I and sister of King Herod Agrippa II, a Jewish client queen who is today famous for her lengthy love affair with the future Roman emperor Titus.[15] A variety of ancient sources detail how scandalised the Romans were with her not only cohabiting with Titus in the imperial palace, but making interventions in the government of the Roman Empire and in the judicial system. She reportedly entreated her brother to commute death sentences to life imprisonment and even went so far as to preside as a judge over legal proceedings.[16] The opprobrium culminated in the couple being heckled by Diogenes and Heras, two Cynic philosophers, at the theatre, and Titus, recognising how unpopular the relationship was with the Roman people (and how it was inspiring comparisons with Cleopatra VII's relationship with Antony), promptly sent Berenice away.[17] Yet it needs to be borne in mind that while this behaviour may have been scandalous at the very heart of the Roman Empire, where women were expected to wield soft power (if they wielded any power at all) and do so discreetly, client queens, particularly those who ruled alone or autonomously, would have been much more visible in their own kingdoms out on the periphery. They would have been involved in all aspects of the day-to-day running of their kingdoms as a matter of course, to the point where their subjects may have been aggrieved had they not participated!

Cleopatra Selene spent her entire adult life as a successful allied queen. Since she would only have been about thirty-five upon her death, it is possible, perhaps even probable, that like so many other women, both famous and unknown, in classical antiquity, she died in childbirth. This was a fate from which no amount of prestige or power could protect her. The danger of pregnancy and childbirth to both mother and baby was well known, and numerous deities were invoked in an often vain attempt to protect them at every stage of the process. Crinagoras of Mytilene, the imperial court poet who had commemorated Cleopatra Selene and Juba's wedding in 25 BCE, also wrote a poem addressed to Cleopatra Selene's half-sister Antonia Minor. She had married Octavian's stepson and Livia's son Drusus, and Crinagoras composed the following poem while she was pregnant, calling on the King and Queen of the gods, Zeus and Hera, and Hepione, the wife of the god of healing Asclepius, to bring her safely through her delivery:

Hera, mother of the Eleithyiae, and you, Hera Teleia, and Zeus, the common father of all who are born, hear my prayer and grant that gentle pangs may come to Antonia in the tender hands of Hepione, so that her husband may rejoice and her mother and her mother-in-law. Her womb bears the blood of great houses.[18]

This poem has been associated with Antonia Minor's first pregnancy in around 15 BCE and the birth of a child who died in infancy or early childhood, for while she was pregnant many times, only three of her offspring survived into adulthood (Germanicus, Livilla and the future Roman emperor Claudius).[19] It is notable that Crinagoras acknowledges Antony's paternity here, however obliquely. He may have written one or more similar poems for Cleopatra Selene; after all, her womb bore the blood of great houses too, arguably more, and greater, than her half-sister's. Moreover, when it came to such highly placed individuals, the death of a mother and child could be politically as well as personally catastrophic (years earlier, Caesar's daughter Julia had been married to his political ally Pompey the Great, and upon the death of Julia and her baby their alliance had dissolved, and civil war had soon followed). Whatever the cause of Cleopatra Selene's early death, Crinagoras wrote another poem to serve as a eulogy:

> The moon herself, rising at early eve, dimmed her light,
> veiling her mourning in night, because she saw her namesake,
> pretty Selene, going down dead to murky Hades. On her she
> had bestowed the beauty of her light, and with her death she
> mingled her own darkness.[20]

Since Crinagoras' words refer to a lunar eclipse that seems to have occurred at around the time, it is possible to use astronomical information to get a sense of when her death could have occurred. During the period in which he was composing his poems, and the period in which Cleopatra Selene lived, there were four years in which lunar eclipses that were visible in both Iol Caesarea and Rome took place: 5 BCE, 1 BCE, 3 CE and 7 CE.[21] However, based on the specific descriptive details about the lunar eclipse that he provides, it has been proposed that her death can be dated precisely to one of two eclipses, occurring on either 23 March 5 BCE or 4 May 3 CE (an extremely rare achievement when it comes to an ancient historical figure), with the former date preferred.[22] In Iol Caesarea, the moon would have been completely covered by the shadow cast by the earth, while in Rome the moon would have been half-covered upon rising and then completely covered around a quarter of an hour later, and the phenomenon would have lasted for almost two hours. Eclipses were viewed as portents of impending doom by their ancient observers, and they were often associated with imminent death; additionally, lunar eclipses were seen as the result of witchcraft, with witches being renowned and reviled for their supposed power to 'draw down' the moon. This poem also helps us gain some idea of the impact of Cleopatra Selene's death on those who knew her, as it was clearly considered an event worth recording for posterity.[23] Crinagoras evokes a touchingly beautiful amalgamation of Cleopatra Selene and her divine namesake, the poetic equivalent perhaps of this depiction of the moon goddess on an altar from Italy dating from the second century CE (currently on display in the Louvre).[24]

Cleopatra Selene was perhaps the first member of the family interred in the royal mausoleum that Juba had built for himself, his wife and their descendants, although, assuming they had a child or children who predeceased her, such as the little boy depicted on the Ara Pacis, their remains would soon have been recovered from their initial place of interment and placed in the mausoleum alongside hers.

Cleopatra Selene and Juba's joint rule of Mauretania seems to have been successful enough to have cemented their hold on the kingdom to such a degree that three years after her death, in 2 BCE, Juba felt sufficiently confident of his grasp on power to leave his kingdom in the hands of advisers. He accompanied

A marble altar depicting the goddess Selene, second century CE.

Augustus' grandson and adopted son, and acknowledged heir, Gaius Caesar, on an expedition to Arabia. Possibly he was still grieving the loss of his wife and partner to the point where he felt a complete change of scene would be beneficial. It was the following year, in 1 BCE, while still on this trip, that he would visit the court of King Archelaus of Cappadocia and there encounter Archelaus' daughter Princess Glaphyra. She was distantly related to Cleopatra Selene by marriage and even connected to Antony through his affair with her grandmother, also named Glaphyra (it was supposedly this liaison that had resulted in Archelaus being crowned King of Cappadocia several decades previously).[25] Juba married Glaphyra, and although this marriage may initially have been conceived as a way of linking these western and eastern client kingdoms, it did not pay off; within a year or so he had divorced her, left the expedition and returned to Mauretania.[26] She does not seem ever to have set foot in Mauretania and attempted to rule the kingdom in the manner of Cleopatra Selene; she certainly did not issue her own coinage in the manner of her predecessor. In fact, her marriage to Juba (her second) rates barely a mention in ancient sources, in comparison to the amount of detail we have about her first and third marriages.

In the years that followed, Cleopatra Selene was not forgotten by either Juba or Ptolemy, as a hoard of coins deposited in around 17 CE at Alkasar near Tangier makes clear. This hoard contains coins that can be dated to the period 11–17 CE and consists of those not only issued by Cleopatra Selene and Juba together, but also those issued by Cleopatra Selene alone, indicating that her coinage was not taken out of circulation upon her death and was still in use by her former subjects over two decades after her death. The problem with coin hoards is that it is very difficult to date them precisely; without any corroborative evidence the best you can do is conclude that they were deposited at some point after the latest dateable coin was issued. This frequently lacks precision, particularly when it comes to classical antiquity when coins might remain in circulation for decades, if not centuries (a case in point: coins issued by Antony have been found in Britain, despite the territory not becoming part of the Roman Empire until 43 CE, under the auspices of Antony's grandson the emperor Claudius). This has led some scholars to question whether Cleopatra Selene did in fact die in 5 BCE, or if she lived for at least another twenty-two years, ruling Mauretania in Juba's absence and continuing to issue her own coinage.[27] There are, however, no other traces of her in the historical or archaeological records during this time, or at least none that have been recognised to date. The fact that

Juba married another woman, however briefly, while he was away suggests that he was not still married to Cleopatra Selene at that time, since Roman citizens did not practise polygamy and men who juggled multiple committed relationships that were either classed as marriage or equated with marriage (such as Antony, for example) were subject to considerable criticism.[28] Juba would have been foolish indeed to invite comparisons to his deceased father-in-law. It is not entirely impossible that the couple separated for a time, even divorced, thereby allowing us to envisage a scenario in which Cleopatra Selene remained in Mauretania and ruled independently and competently, while Juba had something akin to a midlife crisis and went travelling, remarried, divorced, and then returned home to reconcile with and subsequently remarry her. Despite the enmity between Augustus and Cleopatra VII, Augustus was not averse to female allied rulers provided that they recognise his and Rome's supremacy; in this same period, he appointed Queen Dynamis, the granddaughter of King Mithridates VI of Pontus, Rome's great enemy, to rule the Bosporus.[29] Yet this seems like the sort of complex domestic arrangement that would have had serious diplomatic ramifications and resulted in considerable political instability, thereby catching the attention of ancient commentators, and leaving some trace in the historical record.

Another potential issue with the historical sources for this period and what they record (or, rather, do not record) involves Alexander Helios and Ptolemy Philadelphos. As discussed previously, the scholarly consensus today is that Cleopatra Selene's brothers died in childhood, Ptolemy Philadelphos dying sometime in either 30 or 29 BCE prior to Octavian's triple triumph, and Alexander Helios at some point after the triumph in 29 BCE but before 20 BCE since he is not included in any of the sources that discuss the composition of the imperial family or the workings of the extended imperial household in the 20s or 10s BCE. The only ancient author to mention the boys in this period is Cassius

Dio, who was writing in the late second and early third centuries CE, so around 250–300 years after the events he was recounting, but he only mentions them in passing in relation to Cleopatra Selene and Juba's marriage. According to Dio, '[Octavian] gave both the maid and the kingdom of his fathers [to Juba], and as a favour to them spared the lives of Alexander and Ptolemy'.[30] Since Cleopatra Selene and Juba were married in around 25 BCE, five years after Octavian assumed control of the three siblings, it seems odd that he would wait five years to make a decision about their futures, especially since Ptolemy Philadelphos had already disappeared from public view by 29 BCE. It seems equally odd that none of the other ancient authors who record the fates of Antony's children over the course of the decades following his death, referencing not only the marriages they contracted and the children they had but also the careers they forged, mention either Alexander Helios or Ptolemy Philadelphos. We would expect to hear about them marrying and having children, or undertaking the political or military careers that would be expected of men of their rank and proximity to the imperial family and seat of government. It is theoretically possible that Octavian was willing to maintain the boys while they were minors with a view to disposing of them once they reached adulthood and became potential threats (as he had, of course, with their older half-brothers Caesarion and Marcus Antonius Antyllus in 30 BCE). And it is likewise theoretically possible that he then decided not to follow through on that course of action after extensive negotiations with Cleopatra Selene and Juba, and their assurances that, if allowed to live, the brothers would see out their lives in relative obscurity in Mauretania and would not seek to marry or father children who had the potential to become threats in their turn. Yet their half-brother Iullus Antonius, as Antony's fully Roman son and the bearer of his name, the product of a legitimate marriage between Antony and his third wife Fulvia, was surely more of a threat, and he was not only spared and maintained until he reached adulthood, but also encouraged to pursue a political career, progressing all the way up to the rank of consul. So while it is appealing to envisage Augustus taking Cleopatra Selene and Juba into his confidence and trusting them enough to give them custody of Alexander Helios and Ptolemy Philadelphos, and to imagine the brothers living out their lives as pampered princelings under a sort of indefinite luxurious house arrest in the royal palace at Iol Caesarea, this seems unlikely. Surely if Augustus was so concerned about their potential for malfeasance, he would have either had them executed or kept them under house arrest in Rome where he could keep an eye on them? This latter scenario has, in fact, been suggested recently, with the point made that, unlike their half-brother Iullus, the boys were not able to follow traditional Roman political or military careers. Yet nor could they be used for diplomatic purposes in the eastern half of the empire, just in case any of the client kings or queens based there started to get ideas about availing themselves of the still potent mystique of either Antony or Cleopatra, through a marital alliance such as the one that had long ago been planned by Antony between Alexander Helios and Princess Iotape of Media.[31] This course of action had the added benefit of discouraging potential claimants to the Egyptian throne from asserting themselves: after all, how could their claim have any veracity or hope of success if one, two, or even all three of Cleopatra's children were still alive?[32] Yet if this gilded cage was the ultimate outcome for Alexander Helios and Ptolemy Philadelphos, it is surely even more ironic that, in the unambiguously patriarchal society that was the Roman Empire, it was Antony and Cleopatra's female child rather than either of their male ones that wielded power and came the closest to realising the Eastern prophecies that had circulated in advance and anticipation of their births, and their parents' hopes and dreams.

Whatever date we choose for Cleopatra Selene's death, it is

clear that she died somewhat prematurely. Despite this, it is also clear that her reputation lived on long after her death, aiding her husband and her son in their attempts to legitimise their rules and ensure the survival of their kingdom and their dynasty. It is to the members of that dynasty that we shall now turn our attention.

11

Family Matters: The Second Ptolemaic Dynasty

ONSTRUCTING A FAMILY TREE for the Ptolemaic dynasty starting with Ptolemy I Soter and his various wives and mistresses in the late fourth century BCE, and working down to Cleopatra Selene in the late first century BCE is relatively straightforward. While there are certainly gaps (for example, the names of Cleopatra VII's mother and grandmother are unknown and this has resulted in much speculation by ancient historians), we do at least have a sense of the members, both male and female, of each generation and their connections. Unfortunately, the same cannot be said for the generations following Cleopatra Selene.

Cleopatra Selene and Juba certainly had at least one son who was named Ptolemy, thought to have been born sometime between 13 and 9 BCE, who would rule alongside Juba after Cleopatra Selene's death in around 5 BCE.[1]

The choice of the name Ptolemy rather than Juba, or a name from further back in Juba's family such as Hiempsal, the name of his grandfather, raises questions. Did he have an older brother who was named after his father who died in childhood, leaving Ptolemy to succeed their father, or did Cleopatra Selene and

A white marble bust of Cleopatra Selene's son Ptolemy of Mauretania.

Juba deliberately choose to emphasise her royal connections at the expense of his, and was their goal to either continue or re-found the Ptolemaic dynasty in the west? If the latter, she would not have been the first woman of Macedonian descent to emphasise her maternal lineage: Philip of Macedon's wife Audata, an Illyrian princess, passed on her family traditions to her daughter Cynane, and Cynane in turn passed them on to her daughter Adea Eurydice.[2] And, of course, Cleopatra Selene had herself been named according to her maternal rather than her paternal lineage. As mentioned already, it is likely that Cleopatra Selene visited Rome for significant historical occasions such as the dedication of the Ara Pacis Augustae, the Altar of Augustan Peace, in 9 BCE.

It has been suggested that she and one of her children appear in the processional frieze on its side alongside members of the Julio-Claudian family, an indication of how highly she was thought of by Augustus and his family.[3]

The Ara Pacis survives virtually intact today in a purpose-built museum, the Museum of the Ara Pacis Augustae, designed by the architect Richard Meier in the centre of Rome next to the Mausoleum of Augustus, although this was not its original position on the Campus Martius in antiquity. Upon its rediscovery under Palazzo Peretti, next to the Basilica of San Lorenzo in Lucina, in 1938, it was excavated, removed and rebuilt in its present location to celebrate the 2,000th anniversary of Augustus' birth. It was decreed by the Roman Senate on 4 July 13 BCE to celebrate the return of Augustus to Rome after three years away pacifying the recalcitrant provinces of Hispania and Gaul, although it would not be dedicated until four years later, on 30 January 9 BCE. On its north-facing and south-facing walls, it bears reliefs probably depicting the ceremonial processions that were made in 13 BCE by Augustus, his immediate family, and other significant Romans such as the members of the four priestly colleges, lictors and attendants. When visiting you can wander around the entire altar, and even inside it. If Cleopatra Selene is depicted on the processional frieze of the northern wall of the Ara Pacis along with Augustus' family members, among whom are also thought to be her half-brother Iullus Antonius and half-sisters Antonia Major and Antonia Minor, the child with her could be a son born soon after her marriage but who died before he reached maturity. The fact that Cleopatra Selene seems to appear first on coins in conjunction with Juba during his sixth regnal year, around 20–19 BCE, when she would have been around twenty-one years old, could be seen as an indicator that this is when she bore their first child and this joint coin is how she and Juba chose to mark the occasion. The fact that the woman and child on the frieze are both wearing fringed mantles marks them out as a pair.

A section from the processional relief on the northern side of the Ara Pacis Augustae in Rome. Cleopatra Selene may be one of those depicted here, the second figure from the right.

This type of article of clothing, usually dyed purple with a fringe of gold, has Hellenistic royal origins and was particularly associated with the flamboyant inhabitants of the regions in the eastern Mediterranean. This would have made it an inappropriate costume for an ordinary Roman citizen to don (bear in mind the criticism that Antony received for his purple and gold clothing choices), but perfectly acceptable for an allied monarch or a member of their immediate family. On one occasion, Juba's father King Juba of Numidia reportedly rebuked a Roman general for wearing such a cloak in his presence, as a mere general should not be dressed the same as a king, so it is clear that African monarchs favoured these trappings in addition to eastern ones.[4] This purple mantle would have been an excellent way for Cleopatra Selene and her son to display not only themselves but also the Kingdom of Mauretania, as presumably the purple dye was sourced from the dyeworks located on the Purple Islands of the Mauretanian coast.

Assuming that these figures are Cleopatra Selene and her older son, their inclusion on this monument makes it clear just how important she and her family were during the Augustan Principate, as human manifestations of Augustus' policies, representing the Roman presence in North Africa. If Cleopatra Selene did travel to Rome with her son for the dedication of the Ara Pacis in 9 BCE, it is possible that he succumbed to the city's climate and disease environment just as her younger brother Ptolemy Philadelphos seems to have done in 29 BCE, at around the same vulnerable age. Unfortunately, the woman's face is so damaged that she is impossible to identify definitively, and though the child's face shows a resemblance to the surviving portraits of Juba and Ptolemy, since he is otherwise unknown in the historical record, we cannot say for certain any more than this.

Like his parents, Ptolemy may have spent some of his childhood in Rome. There he would have been part of first Augustus' and then his successor Tiberius' households, educated and trained in a manner befitting his status as a future allied monarch much as both of his parents had been, before eventually returning to Mauretania as a mature man in 21 CE to rule in tandem with his father for two years until Juba's death in 23 CE.[5] Perhaps Juba was used to having a co-ruler, or ruling Mauretania was too much for one person to manage alone when dealing with the recalcitrant tribes that required time away from the capital?

After that, Ptolemy ruled alone until his own death seventeen years later in 40 CE. He was summoned to Rome by his cousin, the emperor Gaius, better known as Caligula, and executed for reasons that, beyond the workings of Caligula's notoriously cruel and unstable temperament, remain obscure.[6] Owing to Caligula's famous paranoia and resultant penchant for having his once beloved family members and friends either exiled or murdered, none of the ancient sources dwell for too long on this episode or Caligula's reasoning, although it is recorded elsewhere that he tested Ptolemy by sending him a messenger bearing the words 'Do neither good nor ill to the man whom I have sent you'.[7] According to Caligula's biographer Suetonius, Ptolemy had been a faithful ally to his cousin, but the emperor was jealous about how fine he looked, entering an amphitheatre to watch the gladiatorial games dressed in a splendid purple cloak.[8] This is perhaps another instance upon which the fabulous fruits of Mauretania's Purple Islands were put on public display – it would make sense for Ptolemy to follow his mother's example in presenting himself at the imperial court dressed in such finery, displaying not just himself and his kingdom, but also honouring the Roman Empire as worthy of such an effort. The historian Cassius Dio records that Caligula was jealous of Ptolemy's wealth, and Ptolemy was not the only well-known individual that he treated in this way. Caligula made a point of stripping anyone he considered a potential rival of indicators of rank such as triumphal regalia that had been passed down to them through their families from generation to generation.[9] Subsequent attempts to rationalise Caligula's actions have included suggestions that he was concerned about a conspiracy against him, and the possibility that Ptolemy might have had links with the conspirator Cornelius Lentulus Gaetulicus, since they had met when young men.[10] Like his father, Ptolemy was an extremely capable general. In recognition of his military prowess, Tiberius – Caligula's predecessor as emperor, Augustus' adopted son and Cleopatra Selene and Juba's childhood friend – had rewarded him with triumphal honours in 24 CE. These included the right to wear the highly distinctive triumphal regalia of a laurel wreath worked in gold, a tunic embroidered with palm leaves, a toga dyed purple and with an embroidered gold border, and to carry an ivory baton in 24 CE. Augustus had rewarded Juba for his own military prowess with triumphal regalia in 6 CE.[11] It may even have been a version of this outfit that Ptolemy had worn in Caligula's presence, and the reason why the emperor was driven into a murderous frenzy.

Caligula himself was a complete failure as a general, and unable to live up to the glorious reputations of his father Germanicus Julius Caesar (Cleopatra Selene's nephew), or his grandfather Nero Claudius Drusus (another of Cleopatra Selene's childhood friends who married her half-sister Antonia the Younger), who had been awarded the name Germanicus in 9 BCE because of his victories over the Germanic peoples on the Roman Empire's Rhine frontier.[12] In line with this focus on personal appearance, it has also been suggested that the prematurely balding Caligula was jealous of Ptolemy's glorious mane of hair.[13] In any case, it would appear that whether because of Ptolemy's physical appearance, his fashion sense, his illustrious lineage, or his military prowess, Caligula believed that Ptolemy cut a finer figure and looked more like an emperor than he, and was moved to do something about it. It is notable that Ptolemy's loyal subject Aedemon did not take his king's execution lying down and attempted to lead a revolt against Caligula's successor Claudius (his uncle, brother to his father Germanicus, and so another of Cleopatra Selene's nephews).[14]

It appears that Cleopatra Selene and Juba also had at least one and potentially several daughters, whose names are not known for certain, and they seem to have gone on to marry into other Near Eastern royal families.[15] Two inscriptions from Athens refer to Libyan princesses, one specifically mentioning a 'daughter of King Juba', and may have been set up during one of the family's numerous visits to the famous Greek city, as Juba was known on occasion as 'the Libyan'.[16] In neither case is the name of the princess preserved but, based on Cleopatra Selene and Juba's choice of Ptolemy as a name for their son, it is possible that they also used Ptolemaic names for their daughters, and these would have been one or more of the following: Cleopatra, Arsinoe and Berenike.

However, the historian Tacitus records that one Antonius Felix, an imperial freedman who subsequently served as the governor of the Roman province of Judea, married a woman named Drusilla, a granddaughter of Antony and Cleopatra.[17] Felix seems to have been a thoroughly unpleasant individual, and was of significantly lower status than a princess of an ancient and illustrious lineage (his name indicates that he was a formerly enslaved person, probably originating in the household of one of Cleopatra Selene's sisters). This suggests that after Ptolemy's death and the annexation of his kingdom in 40 CE, his remaining immediate family members were not accorded the level of sympathetic patronage by their imperial kin that Cleopatra Selene had enjoyed. Felix was the brother of the emperor Claudius' favourite, Antonius Pallas, so presumably his brother had a word in the emperor's ear about the possibility of making a match. So, if Tacitus was correct and this Drusilla was a granddaughter rather than a great-granddaughter of Antony and Cleopatra, Cleopatra Selene and Juba would seem to have had a daughter called Drusilla. This was an odd choice of name but one we can assume was made to honour either Livia Drusilla, the wife of Augustus, or Nero Claudius Drusus Germanicus, more commonly known as Drusus the Elder, her son and a peer of both Cleopatra Selene and Juba, and the former's brother-in-law thanks to his marriage to her half-sister Antonia Minor.[18] If this Drusilla was Cleopatra Selene and Juba's daughter, her name may have resulted from the fact that she was born around 9 BCE, shortly after the death of her uncle Drusus the Elder, who fell from his horse while on a military campaign in Germany. But this would make her too old to marry Felix over half a century later. However, if she was Cleopatra Selene and Juba's granddaughter, in all likelihood the daughter of their son Ptolemy, she could have been named either after Livia Drusilla, who died in 29 CE, or Caligula's sister Drusilla, who died in 38 CE, both of whom Ptolemy would have known well, and still have been of an appropriate age to marry Felix. It would make sense that, as an infant at the time of her father's execution, Drusilla was taken to Rome and raised in the imperial household until such a time as she could be used as a tool in imperial political and dynastic machinations, just as both of her grandparents had been, and this appears to be exactly what happened during the reign of the emperor Claudius.

Ptolemy's murderer did not long survive him: Caligula fell victim to a conspiracy between members of his Praetorian Guard, the Senate and the imperial court and was assassinated at the beginning of 41 CE. After a short period of political and military upheaval, he was succeeded by his paternal uncle Claudius, and it was during his reign that the Kingdom of Mauretania was finally dissolved in 44 CE. The territory was subsequently annexed and converted into two Roman provinces, Mauretania Tingitana in the west, named after its capital city Tingis (modern Tangier), and Mauretania Caesariensis in the east, named after its capital city Caesarea. The ancient kingdom and its fledgling dynasty were soon forgotten, both by their contemporaries and by later generations.

Writers and scholars tend to pay little attention to the Ptolemaic dynasty after Cleopatra VII's death, since it was no longer in possession of Egypt and thus no longer thought to be of any historical significance. In so doing, they are neglecting Cleopatra Selene and her descendants. On those rare occasions when they do give her some consideration, this usually extends no further than her son Ptolemy. This reluctance, displayed by both ancient and modern commentators, to consider matrilineality means that the possibility that Cleopatra Selene's descendants continued to play a significant role in ancient Mediterranean politics for centuries after her death is often overlooked. An inscription recovered from Cherchell, an epitaph to a woman named Julia Bodina, states that she was the freedwoman of a queen named Urania, whose full name, going by the name of her freedwoman, was probably Julia Urania.[19] Her name indicates that she could have been a member of the royal family of the eastern client kingdom of Emesa (modern Homs in Syria), one of several that arose from the ruins of the Hellenistic kingdom of the Seleucid dynasty in the Arabian peninsula after its annexation by the Roman Empire, and protected the empire's eastern frontier from incursions by the Parthian Empire.[20] Since ancient historians recorded much of Juba's activity during his long reign, including the names of his first and second wives, it seems likely that, if the Queen Urania mentioned in the Cherchell inscription was his third wife, they would have said as much. But they do not. However, Ptolemy's reign is much less well recorded, and the name of his wife not at all, so it seems more likely that Urania was his wife, and the mother of his daughter Drusilla. Like many eastern communities, the Emesenes had supported Antony in the civil war before eventually being reconciled with Augustus in around 20 BCE, and thereafter had a close relationship with the Julio-Claudian dynasty, until the dissolution of the client kingdom in the early 70s CE.[21] The genealogies of the Emesene royal family and the Emesene priesthoods can be partially reconstructed using inscriptions. It seems that the mysterious Drusilla would go on to further cement the links between the Mauretanian and Emesan royal families by marrying Gaius Julius Sohaemus, King of Emesa. Their great-, great-, great-grandson was Gaius Julius Bassianus, High Priest of Elagabalus, a solar deity worshipped in the form of a conical black baetyl stone at the Temple of the Sun at Emesa, from 187 CE until his death in 217 CE. Although he bore a Roman name, his *cognomen* Bassianus is thought to derive from *basus*, an eastern title for a priest.[22] A marble portrait bust that has been tentatively identified as depicting him in his role as high priest has survived and is currently on display at the Galleria Borghese in the Villa Borghese in Rome.[23] A distinguishing feature is his top-knot hairstyle, known as the *ushnisha*, that appears in Buddhist iconography as a symbol of the supernormal knowledge and consciousness of the Buddha, attesting that Indian influences were present in Syria during this period.[24]

Gaius Julius Bassianus, High Priest of Elagabalus at the Temple of the
Sun at Emesa, Syria, in the second and third centuries CE, and a possible
descendant of Cleopatra Selene.

His daughter Julia Domna married Lucius Septimius Severus,
who had been informed by an astrologer that he would find his
future wife in Syria, and he would go on to become the emperor
Septimius Severus.[25] He was born in Lepcis Magna in the Roman
province of Africa (modern Leptis Magna in Libya), and like
Cleopatra Selene and Juba added a multicultural dimension to
the Roman Empire's imperial family. Julia Domna was the mother
of his sons Lucius Septimius Bassianus, later renamed as Marcus

Aurelius Antoninus in 195 CE after his father's accession (and known to posterity as Caracalla), and Publius Septimius Geta. Caracalla would murder his brother in the arms of their mother in 211 CE and subject him to *damnatio memoriae* in his pursuit of absolute power after their father's death. A tondo decorated with a portrait of Septimius Severus' family, created around 200 CE, originally from Djemila in Algeria but now housed in the Altes Museum in Berlin, shows how all reference to Geta was systematically removed from monuments and inscriptions across the Roman Empire.[26]

After Caracalla was murdered in 217 CE, although the throne was initially usurped he was eventually succeeded by his fourteen-year-old cousin Varius Avitus Bassianus (better known to posterity as Elagabalus, after the god he worshipped), the son of Julia Domna's sister, Julia Maesa. Elagabalus was likewise murdered in 222 CE, and again, although the throne was initially usurped, it was eventually restored to the family and his fourteen-year-old cousin, Alexander Severus, acceded to it, ruling until his death in 235 CE, when he was assassinated by his generals. Since Alexander Severus did not father any children, this marked the end of the Severan dynasty's tenure as the Roman Empire's imperial family.

This notional eastern line of descent from Ptolemy of Mauretania could also account for the fact that a few years later the rebel Queen Zenobia of Palmyra (modern Tadmor in Syria) would claim to be descended from Cleopatra, Queen of Egypt, and from Dido, Queen of Carthage. Assuming that these were genuine rather than purely fantastical claims intended to bolster her status and legitimise her claims to Rome's African territories, these lineages could only have come via Cleopatra Selene and Juba.[27] Their veracity is not completely beyond the realms of plausibility. Bearing in mind how unusual Zenobia's name was, it is possible that she could have been related to Julius Aurelius Zenobius, the governor of Palmyra in 229 CE, whose paternal ancestry is known and contains names that are reminiscent of those that are known from the Emesene royal and priestly families. Additionally, Juba did claim to be descended from the sister of Hannibal Barca, and the Barcids – Hannibal's family – in turn claimed to be descended from the younger brother of Dido.[28] Perhaps as an attempt to validate these claims, Zenobia said that she was in possession of some of Cleopatra's belongings: her famous gold and bejewelled tableware.[29] The idea that Cleopatra's possessions were still in circulation three centuries after her death and were imbued with an aura of power and prestige that could be assumed by their possessor is found elsewhere. One of Zenobia's contemporaries, a woman named Calpurnia married to a man named Titus Quartinus who attempted to seize power by proclaiming himself emperor, was apparently in possession of Cleopatra's famous pearls and a silver platter weighing one hundred pounds.[30] Thus we can imagine how powerful and prestigious her former possessions, never mind her blood relatives, would have been considered in the years immediately after her death, and how Cleopatra Selene and her family would have sought to capitalise on this.

While admittedly we cannot trace Cleopatra Selene's descendants around the ancient Mediterranean over the ensuing decades and centuries with any degree of certainty, what we can do with the information we have is appreciate the extent to which her complex combination of Greek, Roman, Egyptian and North African heritages and identities was not anomalous during this period in history. Apart from Josephus' accounts of events at the royal court in the allied kingdom of Judea, we may not have much detailed information about the politicking going on outside of the imperial court based on the Palatine Hill in the centre of Rome, but we do know that it *was* going on. The allied kingdoms were not just in close contact with Rome but also with each other, and their royal families frequently made their own alliances independent of Rome that did not necessarily have Rome's interests first and foremost (as exemplified by Juba's brief marriage to Glaphyra). In this vein, Cleopatra Selene's son Ptolemy seems to have married an Emesene princess, and if we assume that Julia Domna was their descendant, she married an African member of the Roman equestrian order whose father was of Punic and whose mother was of Italian descent, and whose family members included men who had held the consulship. Therefore, in our final chapter, we will shall explore further Cleopatra Selene's complex range of heritages and identities.

12

An African Princess?

BORN AND RAISED IN Egypt, queen first of Cyrenaica and later of Mauretania, Cleopatra Selene was certainly African, just as I, born and raised in the United Kingdom, am certainly European. Not only did she clearly self-identify as African, and, more specifically Egyptian, she was so African in the eyes of her contemporaries, in fact, that at times it is difficult to differentiate between portraits of her in her guise as an African queen, and personifications of Africa itself, whether on the silver dish from Boscoreale or one of her husband's coin issues.[1] But what was her race? Was she, in addition to being African, of African descent?

It has long been argued, sometimes using more credible evidence, sometimes using less, that Cleopatra VII was Black. 'Black', however, is a modern and contemporary classification and identity that is not entirely appropriate to use about an ancient person, as neither an ancient Greek, Roman, Egyptian, nor even African would have considered themselves, or referred to themselves, in that way. Rather, they would have considered themselves, and referred to themselves, as Greek, more specifically a citizen of a city-state such as Athens or Sparta, a Roman, an Egyptian, or a member of an indigenous group that the Greeks and Romans referred to as a tribe, such as the Garamantes, for

A coin with Juba II and the Latin legend REX IUBA on the obverse,
and a woman who may be Cleopatra Selene, wearing the elephant scalp
favoured by ancient African rulers, on the reverse.

example. A Roman citizen born in North Africa, in the province of
Africa Proconsularis, for example, established in 146 BCE following
the Roman defeat of Carthage, would have considered themselves
Roman first and foremost, although their place of origin would
have been an important part of their identity, and their race and
ethnicity may well have been what we would consider Black
African. Cleopatra was certainly considered to be Egyptian by
her Greek and Roman contemporaries, who often referred to her
as such: Strabo and Florus, for example, called her 'the Egyptian
woman' in their works.[2] More importantly, she appears to have
self-identified as an Egyptian, and self-presented as an Egyptian,
at least when at home in Egypt, judging by the archaeological
evidence which has survived from Egypt in the form of statues,
and stelae depicting her in the Egyptian style.[3]

When modern commentators claim that Cleopatra was 'Black',
do they mean to say that she was a person of colour? Are they
making a judgement about the colour of her skin, and other aspects
of her physical appearance? Since no literary physical description
of Cleopatra has survived from antiquity, we know nothing

A silver drachm depicting Cleopatra VII on the
obverse face, and the Ptolemaic eagle on the reverse.

about the colour of her skin, or any other aspect of her physical
appearance. If we take her coin portraits to be a relatively realistic
and naturalistic representation of her, all that can be said on this
matter is that she had a rather prominent nose, potentially hooked,
inherited from her father and seemingly a distinguishing feature of
the Ptolemaic dynasty (assuming that it was not simply a stylistic
quirk of the people responsible for cutting the dies used to create
the dynasty's coin issues). For an example, see a silver drachm
minted in Alexandria around 47–46 BCE, depicting a portrait of
Cleopatra on the obverse and the Ptolemaic eagle, a bird that was
sacred to Zeus, the king of the Greek gods, on the reverse.[4]

Observations about an individual's skin colour, or the skin
colour of entire peoples, were certainly made in antiquity, and the
Greeks and Romans certainly endeavoured to understand the cause
of these variations in the human condition, a favourite explanation
being environmental determinism, but there were many competing
theories. The mythical Aethiopians, referred to as early in classical
literature as Homer's *Iliad* and *Odyssey*, and Hesiod's *Theogony*,
written in the middle of the eighth century BCE, and discussed

extensively in the third book of Herodotus' *Histories*, written in the fifth century BCE, were believed to have their counterparts in the inhabitants of the Upper Nile and Africa. The designation 'Aethiops' was a reference to their skin colour. A portmanteau derived from the combination of the Greek words *aithō* and *ōps*, it can be translated literally as 'burned face' and it is from this that we derive the modern terms Ethiopia and Ethiopians. The ancient Greeks and Romans were certainly familiar with people of colour, and often depicted them in beautifully detailed works of art. If Cleopatra was a person of colour, there is no reason why she would not have been portrayed as one. Although ancient works of art often appear today to have been coloured entirely white due to the use of white substances such as marble to create them, leading to the contemporary misapprehension that not only ancient art but also ancient people were, for the most part, white, they would actually have subsequently been coloured with paint, a practice known as the art of polychromy. It is simply that most of the paint has worn away, either through the ravages of time or because of overly enthusiastic cleaning and restoration by well-meaning yet misguided museum and gallery staff in centuries and decades gone by.[5] To get a sense of how distinctions were made between different skin colours in classical antiquity, you only need to look at one of the beautiful janiform (i.e. depicting two faces) vases that have survived from this period, such as an Attic red-figure *aryballos*, which would have been used to store perfume or scented oil, dating to around 520–510 BCE and currently housed in the Louvre in Paris, that juxtaposes a Black male with a white female.[6] The neck of the *aryballos* is painted with the Greek word *kalos*, which means 'beautiful, fair, good'.

No intrinsic value judgement was automatically placed on an ancient person simply because of the colour of their skin: people who would today be referred to as white were not automatically considered superior to those who would today be considered

Black.[7] In fact, in some ways, very dark skin and very light skin were viewed in much the same way, as extreme departures from the somewhat olive skin of the Greeks and Romans.[8] Consequently, the ancient Greeks and Romans did not actually think of themselves as white.[9] There was no singular overriding concept of ethnicity at all.[10] The ancient Mediterranean was an extremely diverse place, and the extent to which racism existed in classical antiquity is fiercely debated.[11] While ancient Africans are often mentioned in ancient literary sources in the context of slavery, this is because enslaved individuals of African origin were considered to be particularly exotic and fashionable to own, and were the showpieces of elite households, not because that was the only place for them in ancient society.[12] In fact, Cicero notes that the tall, pale-skinned, fair- or red-haired enslaved individuals who originated from northern Europe were considered likewise, and Ovid makes it clear that their presence in Rome set a new fashion for bottle-blonde hair and blonde hairpieces and wigs, for which we have not only a considerable amount of literary but also archaeological evidence, as many of them have survived interred in the sarcophagi of their owners.[13]

In the absence of definitive new proof, such as would be provided by the discovery of Cleopatra VII's tomb and the forensic analysis of her physical remains, we cannot be certain one way or the other on the issue of her ancestry, race or ethnicity beyond the fact that she was a direct descendant of Ptolemy I Soter. However, in recent years a theory has been advanced concerning Cleopatra VII's younger sister Arsinoe IV that may have some bearing on the question of Cleopatra VII's, and by implication Cleopatra Selene's, ethnicity. According to Strabo, Cleopatra VII, Arsinoe IV, Ptolemy XIII and Ptolemy XIV were Ptolemy XII's children by either a second wife or a mistress, whose identity is not known.[14] As discussed earlier, during Cleopatra VII's civil war with her brother and co-ruler Ptolemy XIII (or perhaps, since Ptolemy XIII was only ten years old at the time, we should say that the war was between Cleopatra VII and his advisers, Pothinus, Achillas and Theodotus), Arsinoe IV sided with her brother rather than her sister.[15] She and Ptolemy XIII proclaimed themselves the rightful co-rulers of Egypt, although their joint reign was brief, lasting only a matter of months from late 48 to early 47 BCE. The young couple went so far as to declare war on their sister, Caesar and his Roman legions. In his account of the civil war, Caesar makes it very clear that Arsinoe IV was instrumental in the military action, not only participating in but actually directing the Siege of Alexandria in 47 BCE, during which he and his forces were trapped on Pharos island, where the famed octagonal lighthouse was located. Caesar only escaped by diving off the causeway and into the sea, swimming away with his papers held over his head to keep them dry.[16] She also had Ptolemy XIII's general Achillas executed, replacing him with her own adviser, the eunuch Ganymede. Caesar did not forget that Arsinoe IV had brought about this humiliating retreat. After he had regained control of the situation and defeated the Egyptian forces, and Ptolemy XIII had drowned in the Nile, weighed down by his golden armour while retreating, he captured Arsinoe IV and transported her to Rome where he exhibited her in his unprecedented quadruple triumph in 46 BCE. She was paraded alongside a burning effigy of the Pharos.[17] Much to Caesar's chagrin, the spectators were not entirely pleased about this.[18] She was apparently the first woman to be so exhibited in a Roman military triumph, and the sight of her aroused pity and sympathy rather than scorn. After the triumph Arsinoe IV was banished to the Temple of Artemis in Ephesus where she remained until she was assassinated on the orders of Antony at the behest of Cleopatra VII in 41 BCE. There was clearly no love lost between the sisters, at least not where Cleopatra's safety, and the safety of Caesarion, was concerned.

In 1926, archaeological excavations in Ephesus uncovered an unusual octagonal tomb containing the skeleton of a young woman, and it has been proposed that the young woman is Arsinoe IV, with the octagonal tomb a reference to the Pharos serving to commemorate her great victory over Caesar and his legions.[19] Unfortunately, the skull of the skeleton was lost, like so many other precious archaeological finds, during the Second World War, and all that remains of it are sketches and measurements. The technique of establishing someone's ethnicity based on a visual examination of their cranium and the identification and measurement of specific craniomorphometric traits has a long history of being put to use in racially motivated and often overtly and explicitly racist ways. Today it is considered incredibly problematic and has been discredited (indeed, it is commonly referred to as scientific racism), with forensic ancestry assessment methods such as isotopic and DNA analysis much preferred. In any case, even the most comprehensive and detailed assessment of an individual's cranial and facial features can tell us nothing about their skin colour or other aspects of their physical appearance such as eye colour, hair colour and texture etc., or how they self-identified. However, based on these old-fashioned techniques, and calculations undertaken using the measurements of the skull that were recorded when the tomb was first excavated in the 1920s, it has since been suggested that the young woman was of African descent and that, if the young woman is in fact Arsinoe IV, then not only she but also, by implication, her three siblings were of African descent.[20] The tomb has been dated to between 50 and 20 BCE on stylistic grounds, while the remaining bones of the skeleton have been radiocarbon dated to between 200 and 20 BCE, so it is not entirely beyond the realm of possibility that the woman is Arsinoe IV. However, it is important to note that there is no definitive proof, only circumstantial evidence, and this evidence is incredibly weak, both flawed and problematic by contemporary historical and archaeological standards. Archaeological excavations are currently going on in Alexandria and Taposiris Magna, just outside Alexandria, in pursuit of Cleopatra VII's mausoleum. Until that is found, assuming it ever is, and any human remains interred inside revealed, and found to be well preserved enough to withstand forensic analysis, we shall have to look elsewhere in our attempts to add leaves to the Ptolemaic family tree.

Although both Cleopatra VII and Cleopatra Selene were direct descendants of Ptolemy I Soter, there are significant gaps in the Ptolemaic family tree. We do not know who Cleopatra VII's mother, maternal grandparents, or paternal grandmother were. Ptolemy XII Auletes, Cleopatra VII's father, was himself an illegitimate son of Ptolemy IX, born to a royal mistress who could, perhaps, have been Egyptian or even Nubian.[21] There is certainly a precedent for a Ptolemaic king taking an Egyptian woman as his mistress: Ptolemy II Philadelphos' mistress Didyme was described by his son Ptolemy III Euergetes as 'a native woman, and extremely good-looking'.[22] Intriguingly, a woman named Didyme is mentioned in a rather lovely poem written around that same time by the erotic epigrammatist Asclepiades of Samos, in which he rhapsodised about her beauty: 'Didyme captured me with her eye. Oh! I melt like wax by a fire when I see her beauty. If she is black – so what? Coals are too, but when we heat them, they glow like rosebuds.'[23] This description of her as dark-skinned supports the identification of the Didyme in question as Ptolemy II Philadelphos' mistress.[24] Additionally, the name Didyme means 'Twin' in ancient Greek, so if Didyme was an Egyptian, she may originally have been named Hatre, which means 'Twin' in Egyptian, but took on a Greek name upon her arrival at the royal court in Alexandria.[25]

It has recently been suggested that Ptolemy XII Auletes' mother was in fact a member of an indigenous Egyptian elite family, perhaps one dedicated to the god Ptah, the creator god of craftsmen and architects.[26] Certainly, a connection seems to have been made between the Ptolemaic dynasty and the indigenous Egyptian population in the late second century BCE in the form of the marriage of a woman named Berenike (probably, based on her name which, along with Cleopatra and Arsinoe, was a favoured moniker for royal women, a daughter of Ptolemy VIII) and the High Priest of Ptah Psenptais II. Perhaps this couple had a daughter who went on to form an attachment to Ptolemy XII Auletes, as there does appear to have been an enduring close personal relationship between his family and that of the High Priest of Ptah, not only during his reign but also the reign of Cleopatra VII, and the reign of Cleopatra Selene in Mauretania. Strabo did, after all, differentiate between Ptolemy XII Auletes' marriage to his sister Cleopatra VI which resulted in their daughter Berenike IV, and his relationship with another unnamed woman, which resulted in his other four children.[27] He stated that only Berenike was legitimate, but he is the only ancient writer who casts aspersions on Cleopatra and her siblings' legitimacy, something that would surely have been included in the invective directed at Cleopatra by any number of Roman authors in later years had it been true. Perhaps what Strabo meant was simply that Ptolemy XII Auletes' younger children's mother was not a member of the primary line of descent of the Ptolemaic dynasty, and perhaps the reason that other Roman authors did not weaponise Cleopatra's parentage was that her mother was a woman of considerable status rather than an enslaved person. The funerary stele of Psenptais II's son, Petubastes III, records that Ptolemy XII had several wives, each of sufficient status to produce royal children.[28] This is in sharp contrast to Ptolemy XII Auletes himself, who was frequently referred to as a bastard in Roman sources, presumably because his mother was not a woman of sufficiently high status.

The closeness of Ptolemy XII Auletes and his family to the High Priest of Ptah and his family is noted on a limestone stele set up in Memphis upon the death of the High Priest Pasherenptah ('Son of Ptah') III on 14 July 41 BCE, which includes a detailed biography of Pasherenptah, composed by his brother-in-law

Horimhotep and carved by his nephew Khahap. This biography recorded how he was appointed High Priest at the age of fourteen on 76 BCE and then soon afterwards was called on to perform the coronation of Ptolemy XII Auletes in accordance with ancient Egyptian pharaonic rituals.[29] When on a subsequent occasion Pasherenptah was visiting Alexandria, Ptolemy XII Auletes showed him a singular level of favour by stopping his chariot on his way to the Temple of Isis to meet him, appoint him priest of the royal cult of Arsinoe and gift him with a golden chaplet. Although Pasherenptah and his wife Tayimhotep had three daughters, and Pasherenptah had an additional daughter from a previous relationship, they had no son to hold the priesthood after him. The pair prayed to the god Imhotep and, when Pasherenptah was forty-three and Tayimhotep twenty-nine, they were blessed with a son they named Imhotep, who would later serve as the High Priest of Ptah Imhotep-Pedubast/Petubastes IV. Pasherenptah's wife Tayimhotep's limestone stele, set up upon her death on 15 February 42 BCE, has also survived, confirming many of these details.[30] This closeness between the royal family and the priestly family could indicate blood ties between the two.

It must also be remembered that Cleopatra VII was the first member of the Ptolemaic dynasty to bother to learn Egyptian.[31] Considering the pride that Cleopatra Selene took in her Egyptian heritage later in life, it is entirely plausible that she learned Egyptian, too, perhaps at her mother's insistence, or perhaps on her own initiative. She would certainly take care to commemorate her Egyptian heritage in her adopted kingdom, displaying many Egyptian sculptures, both ancient and contemporary, in the capital city of Iol Caesarea, including an inscribed basalt statue of the aforementioned High Priest of Ptah Imhotep-Pedubast/Petubastes IV.[32] The inscription, carved in hieroglyphs, records that he died on 31 July 30 BCE, on the very eve of the Roman invasion of Egypt (the point at which the gods were thought to have abandoned the city, and Dionysos was thought to have abandoned Antony). He was the distressingly young age of sixteen, almost the same age that Cleopatra Selene's elder brother Ptolemy XV Caesar (Caesarion) was when he died, later that summer. Whether they were or were not related, it is highly probable that the three youngsters were well acquainted. If events had transpired differently, Petubastes may well have been the one tasked with crowning Caesarion and Cleopatra Selene as King and Queen of Egypt at Memphis, in accordance with the ancient Egyptian ritual upon the death of Cleopatra VII, just as Pasherenptah had crowned their grandfather there in 76 BCE.

It is fascinating to me (and this is a point that I belabour to my students) that there is such firm insistence that Cleopatra VII was Black, and such equally firm insistence that she was not, and yet this insistence does not tend to extend any further than her. The race, ethnicity and identity of her four children are not considered at all, despite the fact that, if Cleopatra's race, ethnicity and identity are relevant to the ways in which she has been treated from antiquity to the present, then surely Caesarion's, Cleopatra Selene's, Alexander Helios' and Ptolemy Philadelphos' are too? While Cleopatra Selene's precise ethnicity, like Cleopatra's, cannot be definitively established with any degree of certainty, it is important to note that she was certainly considered to be of mixed heritage by her ancient peers: she was half-Egyptian and half-Roman. More conclusively, however, her husband Juba, the son of King Juba of Numidia, was a person whom we would today describe as a Black African, meaning that their children were indeed of mixed race and ethnicity in addition to being of mixed heritage (Greek, Roman, Egyptian, African). This heritage is clearly displayed in the couple's official communications with their subjects, notably their coin issues. While Juba's contributions to the coins are fairly pedestrian, a portrait of himself wearing a diadem, the symbol of his kingship, in profile accompanied by the

A Mauretanian coin depicting Juba II and the Latin legend
REX IUBA on the obverse face, and a crocodile and the Greek
legend BASILISSA KLEOPATRA on the reverse face.

Latin legend REX IUBA, 'King Juba', Cleopatra Selene's are much
more varied and thoughtful, with many of her contributions
Egyptian-themed, and accompanied by the Greek legend
BASILISSA KLEOPATRA, 'Queen Cleopatra'. On one issue,
we see a crocodile, an animal particularly associated with Egypt
in this period that had previously appeared on the coinage issued
in her name on Crete in the 30s BCE.[33]

On another, we see an ibis attacking a snake, perhaps a veiled
reference to her mother's death and the mythology that had started
to grow up around it during the Augustan Principate.[34] On a
third, we see the accoutrements of the goddess Isis, her crown
featuring the sun disk and cow horns and her *sistrum* atop the
Greek legend KLEOPATRA, and on another we see Isis' crown
atop a crescent moon, the symbol of the Greek goddess Selene,
after whom Cleopatra Selene had been named, and the Greek
legend KLEOPATRA BASILISSA. And on a fourth, intriguingly,
we see Isis' crown surmounted by a crescent moon containing a
globe, the symbol of the *oikoumene*, the 'known world' or the

'inhabited world' in Greek and Roman eyes, accompanied by the Greek legend BASILISSA KLEOPATRA. Evidently Cleopatra Selene continued her mother's patronage of her favourite goddess. On occasion, Juba joined in and honoured his wife's heritage by replacing his portrait with one of the ram's-horned god Amun accompanied by the Latin legend REX IUBA, while Cleopatra Selene followed in her mother's footsteps by depicting herself in the guise of the goddess Isis accompanied by the Greek legend BASILISSA KLEOPATRA.[35]

Since a statue of Amun has been found in Iol Caesarea, it is possible that Juba went further than simply depicting Amun on his coinage and actually presented himself as a living manifestation of him, with Cleopatra Selene presenting herself as Isis, just as her parents had presented themselves as Hercules or Dionysos and Isis on numerous ceremonial occasions. Perhaps Cleopatra Selene was responsible for this suggestion. Amun was a highly suitable choice for Juba as he was king of the Egyptian pantheon, and often equated with Zeus, the king of the Greek pantheon, elsewhere in the ancient Mediterranean. Indeed, her renowned relative Alexander the Great had claimed to be the son of Amun, and consequently he was often depicted with the god's ram's horns by his general Lysimachus who became the King of Thrace after Alexander's death.

Cleopatra Selene also had the authority to issue coins herself, one issue depicting a portrait of her wearing a diadem and the Greek legend KLEOPATRA BASILISSA on the obverse face, and a crocodile and the Greek legend KLEOPATRA BASILISSA on the reverse.[36]

In addition to Cleopatra Selene demonstrating consistent use of Egyptian-themed iconography throughout her reign, she also went to considerable lengths to import Egyptian influences into Mauretania, with the capital city Iol Caesarea being modelled after Alexandria and decorated with Egyptian sculptures, and

Cleopatra Selene had the authority to issue her own coinage: this coin shows her with the Greek legend BASILISSA KLEOPATRA on its obverse, and a crocodile – accompanied by the same legend – on the reverse.

Egyptian religious and cultural institutions being established. Clearly, despite spending her adolescence in Rome being encouraged to assimilate into Roman ways of doing things, and presumably presenting a reasonable façade of having been sufficiently Romanised to her Roman family, Cleopatra Selene remained very much an Egyptian at heart.

Afterword

ROMAN ALLIED QUEENS SUCH as Cleopatra VII, Boudicca of the Iceni, Cartimandua of the Brigantes and Zenobia of Palmyra, have been featured in countless works of art, poems, plays, novels, TV programmes and even films over the last two thousand years. Unlike them, until relatively recently Cleopatra Selene – like many ancient women of comparable importance and influence – has been almost completely overlooked by high, popular and mass culture. This is not necessarily because we know less about her and her life than we do about the others: while we certainly know far more about Cleopatra and Zenobia than we do about Cleopatra Selene, we know far more about Cleopatra Selene than we do about either Boudicca or Cartimandua. It is perhaps because, unlike the aforementioned women, she did not have what we might call an 'epic' moment, such as Cleopatra's meeting with Antony at Tarsus, or her dramatic suicide, or Boudicca's confrontation with Roman legions, or Cartimandua's handover of Caratacus, or Zenobia's military conquests or her declaration of herself as empress, or at least not one that we are aware of today. Instead, because she succeeded quietly rather than failed loudly, she did not catch the imagination of later writers and artists in quite the same way. Much the same can be said of her contemporaneous allied queens such as Dynamis of Bosphorus and Pythodoris of Pontus.[1]

Remarkably, considering that he had used Plutarch's *Antony* as his main literary source, and lived and worked during the successful reign of a female monarch, William Shakespeare excluded her entirely from his play *Antony and Cleopatra*. Although she appears in several other works produced in the seventeenth and eighteenth centuries, including Gauthier de Costes' novel *Cléopâtre* and Johann Matheson's opera *Die unglückselige Cleopatra*, Shakespeare's exclusion seems to have influenced generations of historians who systematically ignored her, preferring instead to focus on her elder brother Caesarion and her twin brother Alexander Helios, despite the fact that it appears that neither did anything of note and both died young.[2] It also seems to have influenced the makers of television series and films, who, while frequently turning to the Late Republic, its fall and the subsequent foundation of the Julio-Claudian dynasty as subjects, often excise Cleopatra's three children by Antony entirely. HBO's *Rome* (2005–7) is a notable exception here, as it does include the twins in the second season episodes set at the royal court in Alexandria, and during the series' final moments it is made clear that they were raised by Octavia after their parents' deaths, clearly differentiating them from the other children featured while marking them as a pair with their clothing and styling (Ptolemy Philadelphos is the only one excised from this particular retelling). Yet Sky's *Domina* (2021), despite having been heavily influenced by *Rome*, returns to the common practice of excluding them, and Juba, entirely.

Thus, perhaps it is not a coincidence that in recent years Cleopatra Selene has become something of a favourite for writers of historical fiction and has featured in a variety of novels aimed at both adults, young adults and children, though the extent to which these portrayals deal with the historical reality of her life is debatable. I first became aware of Cleopatra Selene while I was investigating crocodiles in ancient Rome as part of my PhD research in 2008 and stumbled across her coinage (my thesis was on healing strategies in Egypt during the Roman period, and crocodiles both caused injuries and were thought to cure them, with their hide, fat, teeth and excrement all appearing in various remedies prescribed in this period). It was not lost on me what a fantastic protagonist for an historical novel she would make, blessed not only with a story arc but also a character arc, with the historical and archaeological record providing a broad outline of both, while simultaneously leaving enough space and scope for an author to create something of their own.

While several authors writing during the twentieth century recognised this, with Beatrice Chanler's *Cleopatra's Daughter, Queen of Mauretania* (1934), Alice Curtis Desmond's *Cleopatra's Children* (1971), and Andrea Ashton's *Cleopatra's Daughter* (1979), none of these works seems to have received any significant attention or achieved any sort of longevity, and none of them remain in print today. More recently, Michelle Moran's *Cleopatra's Daughter* (2009), Stephanie Dray's trilogy *Lily of the Nile* (2011), *Song of the Nile* (2011) and *Daughters of the Nile* (2013), Vicky Alvear Shecter's *Cleopatra's Moon* (2011), and Phyllis T. Smith's *The Daughters of Palatine Hill* (2016), have all focused on her, while Michael Livingston's historical fantasy novel *The Shards of Heaven* (2015) features her as a key supporting character. She seems to be a particular favourite of female authors looking for female historical figures, either ancient or more recent, to serve as the protagonist of a standalone for the North American market.

Perhaps unsurprisingly, where Cleopatra Selene is the heroine, Octavian is the villain, and while the choices these authors have made regarding Cleopatra Selene's characterisation have varied considerably, to a greater or lesser extent they all emphasise her dedication to Egypt and her hopes of returning to the kingdom and regaining her lost throne. Considering Cleopatra Selene's parentage, another consistently popular element in retellings of her story is an emphasis on love and romance. This is certainly something that I have found catches the imagination of people who have attended talks I have given on Cleopatra Selene, particularly young women: on one memorable occasion, I gave a talk on Cleopatra Selene to a group of students considering reading Classics at university, and their questions all revolved around her relationship with Juba, and the extent to which it was possible to know if it was a love match. The couple and their relationship have a notable presence on social media platforms such as Tumblr.

Personally, I think reducing Cleopatra Selene's story to a binary tale of good versus evil, or even a straightforward trajectory of riches to rags to riches again, does her (not to mention Octavian, and everyone else) something of a disservice. It diminishes a person who was clearly incredibly complex – an intelligent and shrewd politician, an imaginative and creative innovator, and probably an incredibly charismatic and effective manipulator of those around her – and turns her into a simplistic and rather colourless stereotype. But however questionable (even anachronistic) some of these choices are, at least this sudden surge of popularity means that Cleopatra Selene has belatedly started receiving the attention that she has long deserved, and awareness of the fact that she existed in the first place has been raised. And, hopefully, this, combined with the fast-developing interest in non-classical history and historical figures, means that it will not be long before her female contemporaries, such as her fellow African queen Amanirenas of Kush, start to receive the same treatment.

ACKNOWLEDGEMENTS

Since this book owes its existence to Doug Young at PEW Literary, it's only right that he should be the first person mentioned in these acknowledgements. If he hadn't read an article that I originally wrote for *History Today* back in 2013, believed that I had potential as a writer of popular history, and offered to be my agent, I probably wouldn't have stepped outside of my academic comfort zone and attempted this. He's been my and Cleopatra Selene's champion for the last three years, and shepherded this book from an idea to a proposal to a manuscript. Simultaneously, his colleagues at PEW Literary have worked their magic spreading word of *Cleopatra's Daughter* around the world.

I would also like to thank Richard Milbank and Georgina Blackwell, my editors at Head of Zeus. They've made the transition from academic to trade publishing seamless and actually rather fun, and this book is undoubtedly better for their input than it would otherwise have been. Gina in particular has spent many hours tracking down suitable images and seeking permission for us to use them, and is in large part responsible for this book turning out as beautiful an object as it is. Also Matilda Singer has dealt patiently with my queries and administrative matters, not to mention provided me with books whenever I requested them.

And special thanks are due to Dan Jones for being a source of encouragement, support, and advice, as well as a human blueprint of how to be a public historian, prolific writer of high quality works of popular history, and now historical fiction.

*

I started thinking about Cleopatra Selene in earnest while I was a doctoral student at the University of Nottingham from 2008 to 2011. My supervisors Mark Bradley and Doug Lee and my academic reviewer John Rich patiently read through drafts of my earliest academic articles and offered constructive criticism that would prove crucial not just to my work on Cleopatra Selene but also to my entire academic career. I completed my first significant academic article on Cleopatra Selene while I was a postdoctoral fellow at the British School at Rome in 2011-2012, and the people that I met, the resources that I was able to access, and the experiences that I had there were formative and foundational to my academic career. I worked at the University of Sheffield in 2013 and the University of Wales Trinity Saint David in 2013-2016, and whenever I discussed Cleopatra Selene with staff, students, or even prospective students I came away with much food for thought. My former colleague Kyle Erickson was particularly informative and insightful with regard to all things related to the Hellenistic period, Alexander the Great, the Seleucids, and the Ptolemies.

I've been able to think about Cleopatra Selene in a more sustained way while working at the University of Glasgow from 2016 to the present as part of my 'Cleopatra: Life and Legend' module. The undergraduate and postgraduate students who've taken this course over the last six years, in particular Ellen Wilson who devoted her undergraduate dissertation to Cleopatra Selene in 2021, have given me much to think about in lectures, seminars, and assessments. My colleagues Catherine Steel and Angela McDonald have both provided ample opportunities for stimulating conversations about women in the Roman Republic and Graeco-Roman Egypt respectively.

A further removed but no less valued type of colleague is the one that can found online as part of the 'Classics Twitter' community. People that I know personally, such as Sarah Bond and Hannah

Čulík-Baird, and people that I don't, such as Adrienne Mayor, Andrew Kenrick, and Liv Mariah Yarrow, and a wide range of others who have simply replied to my random tweeted questions and comments, have provided me with invaluable information for no other reason than our shared enthusiasm for the ancient world.

And of course this book has benefitted from the scholarship of various forerunners who have worked on different aspects of the lives and reigns of Juba II and Cleopatra Selene, such as Duane W. Roller, and a range of other relevant topics such as Republican Rome, Hellenistic Egypt, the Augustan Principate, Egyptomania, client rulers, Cleopatra VII etc. No historian works in a total vacuum, but rather stands on the shoulders of those who have gone before them, and I am no exception in this.

*

I'm very lucky that some of my closest friends are also classicists, ancient historians, and archaeologists, and they have been indispensable in reading numerous drafts of this manuscript, making suggestions for inclusions and exclusions, and, most importantly, catching any literary and historical errors I inadvertently made. Amy Russell, Virginia Campbell, Claire Millington, and Robert Cromarty have enriched my life and my work in Roman history and archaeology for many years now, and I'm greatly appreciative.

Finally, my partner Olly has believed in and supported my academic ambitions for the last sixteen years, and I wouldn't have been able to start or finish my doctorate or pursue my academic career without him. The first draft of this book was written during the first period of lockdown in 2020, subsequent drafts in the second and third periods of lockdown, before finally being completed in early 2022, and he was my constant companion throughout while both of us worked from home. An honourable mention goes to our Norwegian Forest Cat Magnus, who joined me and my cup of coffee for many an early morning writing session and on occasion even attempted to contribute to the manuscript himself by walking across my keyboard.

Ancient Literary Sources
for Cleopatra Selene

LIKE MANY ANCIENT WOMEN who were, during their lifetimes, of extremely high status, considerable political importance, and famous to the point of being household names, Cleopatra Selene has left little explicit trace in the historical record. Herein, I have included all the ancient literary references that are concerned with her, whether they mention her explicitly by name (it is worth noting that she is often referred to simply by her first name, Cleopatra), or implicitly (such as when discussing Cleopatra's children collectively).

CRINAGORAS OF MYTILENE (70 BCE–18 CE)

Greek Anthology 9.235 (*c.*25 BCE, to celebrate the wedding of Cleopatra Selene and Juba)

Great bordering regions of the world which the full stream of Nile separates from the black Aethiopians, you have by marriage made your sovereigns common to both, turning Egypt and Libya into one country. May the children of these princes ever again rule with unshaken dominion over both lands.

Greek Anthology 7.633 (*c*.5 BCE, to eulogise Cleopatra Selene upon her death)
The moon herself, rising at early eve, dimmed her light, veiling her mourning in night, because she saw her namesake, pretty Selene, going down dead to murky Hades. On her she had bestowed the beauty of her light, and with her death she mingled her own darkness.

STRABO OF AMASYA (64/63 BCE–23 CE)

Geography 17.3.7
Now a little before my time the kings of the house of Bogus and of Bocchus, who were friends of the Romans, possessed the country, but when these died Juba succeeded to the throne, Augustus Caesar having given him this in addition to his father's empire. He was the son of the Juba who with Scipio waged war against the deified Caesar. Now Juba died lately, but his son Ptolemy, whose mother was the daughter of Antony and Cleopatra, has succeeded to the throne.

PLUTARCH (46–after 119 CE)

Antony 36.3–4
[Antony] heightened the scandal by acknowledging his two children by [Cleopatra VII], and called one Alexander and the other Cleopatra, with the surname for the first of Sun [Helios], and for the other of Moon [Selene]. However, since he was an adept at putting a good face upon shameful deeds, he used to say that the greatness of the Roman empire was made manifest, not by what the Romans received, but by what they bestowed; and that noble families were extended by the successive begettings of many kings. In this way, at any rate, he said, his own progenitor was begotten by Heracles, who did not confine his succession to a single womb, nor stand in awe of laws like Solon's for the regulation of conception, but gave free course to nature, and left behind him the beginnings and foundations of many families.

Antony 54.3

[Antony] was hated, too, for the distribution which he made to his children in Alexandria; it was seen to be theatrical and arrogant, and to evince hatred of Rome. For after filling the gymnasium with a throng and placing on a tribunal of silver two thrones of gold, one for himself and the other for Cleopatra, and other lower thrones for his sons, in the first place he declared Cleopatra Queen of Egypt, Cyprus, Libya, and Coele Syria, and she was to share her throne with Caesarion. Caesarion was believed to be a son of the former Caesar, by whom Cleopatra was left pregnant. In the second place, he proclaimed his own sons by Cleopatra Kings of Kings, and to Alexander he allotted Armenia, Media and Parthia (when he should have subdued it), to Ptolemy Phoenicia, Syria, and Cilicia. At the same time he also produced his sons, Alexander arrayed in Median garb, which included a tiara and upright head-dress, Ptolemy in boots, short cloak, and broad-brimmed hat surmounted by a diadem. For the latter was the dress of the kings who followed Alexander, the former that of Medes and Armenians. And when the boys had embraced their parents, one was given a bodyguard of Armenians, the other of Macedonians. Cleopatra, indeed, both then and at other times when she appeared in public, assumed a robe sacred to Isis, and was addressed as the New Isis.

Antony 81.2

Cleopatra's children, together with their attendants, were kept under guard and had generous treatment.

Antony 87.1

Antony left seven children by his three wives, of whom Antyllus, the eldest, was the only one who was put to death by Caesar; the rest were taken up by Octavia and reared with her own children. Cleopatra [Selene], the daughter of Cleopatra [VII], Octavia gave in marriage to Juba, the most accomplished of kings.

SUETONIUS (69–after 122 CE)

Augustus 17.1

[Octavian] had the will which Antony had left in Rome, naming his children by Cleopatra among his heirs, opened and read before the people.

Augustus 17.5

[Octavian] spared the rest of the offspring of Antony and Cleopatra, and afterwards maintained and reared them according to their several positions, as carefully as if they were his own kin.

Augustus 48

Except in a few instances [Octavian] restored the kingdoms of which he gained possession by the right of conquest to those from whom he had taken them or joined them with other foreign nations. He also united the kings with whom he was in alliance by mutual ties, and was very ready to propose or favour intermarriages or friendships among them. He never failed to treat them all with consideration as integral parts of the empire, regularly appointing a guardian for such as were too young to rule or whose minds were affected, until they grew up or recovered; and he brought up the children of many of them and educated them with his own.

Caligula 26.1

It would be trivial and pointless to add to this an account of his treatment of his relatives and friends, Ptolemy, son of king Juba, his cousin (for he was the grandson of Mark Antony by Antony's daughter Selene), and in particular Macro himself and even Ennia, who helped him to the throne; all these were rewarded for their kinship and their faithful services by a bloody death.

CASSIUS DIO (*c.*155–*c.*235 CE)

Roman History 49.32.4

Antony was not so severely criticised by the citizens for these matters, – I mean his arrogance in dealing with the property of others; but in the matter of Cleopatra he was greatly censured because he had acknowledged as his own some of her children – the elder ones being Alexander [Helios] and Cleopatra [Selene], twins at a birth, and the younger one Ptolemy, called also Philadelphus, – and because he had presented them with extensive portions of Arabia, in the districts both of Malchus and of the Ituraeans (for he executed Lysanias, whom he himself had made king over them, on the charge that he had favoured Pacorus), and also extensive portions of Phoenicia and Palestine, parts of Crete, and Cyrene and Cyprus as well.

Roman History 49.41.1–2

After this Antony feasted the Alexandrians, and in the assembly made Cleopatra and her children sit by his side; also in the course of his address to the people he commanded that she should be called Queen of Kings, and Ptolemy, whom they named Caesarion, King of Kings. And he then made a new distribution of provinces, giving them Egypt and Cyprus in addition; for he declared that in very truth one was the wife and the other the son of the former Caesar, and he professed to be taking these measures for Caesar's sake, though his purpose was to cast reproach upon Caesar Octavianus because he was only an adopted and not a real son of his. Besides making this assignment to them, he promised to give to his own children by Cleopatra the following districts: to Ptolemy, Syria and all the region west of the Euphrates as far as the Hellespont; to Cleopatra, the Cyrenaica in Libya; and to their brother Alexander, Armenia and the rest of the countries east of the Euphrates as far as India; for he even bestowed the last-named regions as if they were already in his possession.

Roman History 50.1.5

[Octavian] reproached [Antony] with Cleopatra and the children of hers which Antony had acknowledged as his own, the gifts bestowed upon them, and particularly because he was calling the boy Caesarion and was bringing him into the family of Caesar.

Roman History 51.15.6

Cleopatra [Selene] was married to Juba, the son of Juba; for to this man who had been brought up in Italy and had been with him on campaigns, Caesar gave both the maid and the kingdom of his fathers, and as a favour to them spared the lives of Alexander and Ptolemy.

Roman History 51.21.7–9

On the second day the naval victory at Actium was commemorated, and on the third the subjugation of Egypt. Now all the processions proved notable, thanks to the spoils from Egypt, – in such quantities, indeed, had spoils been gathered there that they sufficed for all the processions,

– but the Egyptian celebration surpassed them all in costliness and magnificence. Among other features, an effigy of the dead Cleopatra upon a couch was carried by, so that in a way she, too, together with the other captives and with her children, Alexander, called also Helios, and Cleopatra, called also Selene, was a part of the spectacle and a trophy in the procession. After this came Caesar, riding into the city behind them all.

Other Relevant
Ancient Literary Sources

Augustus (63 bce–14 ce)

Res Gestae 4
In my triumphs there were led before my chariot nine kings or children of kings.

Res Gestae 27
Egypt I added to the empire of the Roman people... I recovered all the provinces extending eastward beyond the Adriatic Sea, and Cyrenae, which were then for the most part in possession of kings.

Strabo of Amasya (64/63 bce–23 ce)

Geography 17.3.12
On this coast was a city named Iol, which Juba, the father of Ptolemy, rebuilt, changing its name to Caesareia; it has a harbour, and also, in front of the harbour, a small island.

Plutarch (46–after 119 ce)

Caesar 55.2–3
Next, [Caesar] celebrated triumphs, an Egyptian, a Pontic, and an African, the last not for his victory over Scipio, but ostensibly over Juba

the king. On this occasion, too, Juba, a son of the king, a mere infant, was carried along in the triumphal procession, the most fortunate captive ever taken, since from being a Barbarian and a Numidian, he came to be enrolled among the most learned historians of Hellas.

Antony 26–28.1

Though she received many letters of summons both from Antony himself and from his friends, she so despised and laughed the man to scorn as to sail up the river Cydnus in a barge with gilded poop, its sails spread purple, its rowers urging it on with silver oars to the sound of the flute blended with pipes and lutes. She herself reclined beneath a canopy spangled with gold, adorned like Venus in a painting, while boys like Loves in paintings stood on either side and fanned her. Likewise also the fairest of her serving-maidens, attired like Nereïds and Graces, were stationed, some at the rudder-sweeps, and others at the reefing-ropes. Wondrous odours from countless incense-offerings diffused themselves along the river-banks. Of the inhabitants, some accompanied her on either bank of the river from its very mouth, while others went down from the city to behold the sight. The throng in the market-place gradually streamed away, until at last Antony himself, seated on his tribunal, was left alone. And a rumour spread on every hand that Venus was come to revel with Bacchus for the good of Asia.

Antony sent, therefore, and invited her to supper; but she thought it meet that he should rather come to her. At once, then, wishing to display his complacency and friendly feelings, Antony obeyed and went. He found there a preparation that beggared description, but was most amazed at the multitude of lights. For, as we are told, so many of these were let down and displayed on all sides at once, and they were arranged and ordered with so many inclinations and adjustments to each other in the form of rectangles and circles, that few sights were so beautiful or so worthy to be seen as this.

On the following day Antony feasted her in his turn, and was ambitious to surpass her splendour and elegance, but in both regards he was left behind, and vanquished in these very points, and was first to rail at the meagreness and rusticity of his own arrangements. Cleopatra observed in the jests of Antony much of the soldier and the common man, and adopted this manner also towards him, without restraint now, and boldly.

For her beauty, as we are told, was in itself not altogether incomparable, nor such as to strike those who saw her; but converse with her had an irresistible charm, and her presence, combined with the persuasiveness of her discourse and the character which was somehow diffused about her behaviour towards others, had something stimulating about it. There was sweetness also in the tones of her voice; and her tongue, like an instrument of many strings, she could readily turn to whatever language she pleased, so that in her interviews with Barbarians she very seldom had need of an interpreter, but made her replies to most of them herself and unassisted, whether they were Ethiopians, Troglodytes, Hebrews, Arabians, Syrians, Medes or Parthians. Nay, it is said that she knew the speech of many other peoples also, although the kings of Egypt before her had not even made an effort to learn the native language, and some actually gave up their Macedonian dialect.

Accordingly, she made such booty of Antony that, while Fulvia his wife was carrying on war at Rome with Caesar in defence of her husband's interests, and while a Parthian army was hovering about Mesopotamia (over this country the generals of the king had appointed Labienus Parthian commander-in-chief, and were about to invade Syria), he suffered her to hurry him off to Alexandria.

VIRGIL (70–19 BCE)

Aeneid 1.697–756

As [Aeneas, here based on Antony] enters, the queen [Dido, here based on Cleopatra] has already, amid royal hangings, laid herself on a golden couch, and taken her place in their midst. Now father Aeneas, now the Trojan youth gather, and the guests recline on coverlets of purple. Servants pour water on their hands, serve bread from baskets, and bring smooth-shorn napkins. There are fifty serving-maids within, whose task it is to arrange the long feast in order and keep the hearth aglow with fire. A hundred more there are, with as many pages of like age, to load the board with viands and set out the cups. The Tyrians, too, are gathered in throngs throughout the festal halls; summoned to recline on the embroidered couches, they marvel at the gifts of Aeneas, marvel at Iulus, at the god's glowing looks and well-feigned words, at the robe and veil, embroidered with saffron acanthus. Above all, the unhappy Phoenician, doomed to impending ruin, cannot satiate her soul, but takes fire as she gazes, thrilled alike by the boy and by the gifts. He, when he has hung in embrace on Aeneas' neck and satisfied the deluded father's deep love, goes to the queen. With her eyes, with all her heart she clings to him and repeatedly fondles him in her lap, knowing not, poor Dido, how great a god settles there to her sorrow. But he, mindful of his Acidalian mother, little by little begins to efface Sychaeus, and essays with a living passion to surprise her long-slumbering soul and her heart unused to love.

When first there came a lull in the feasting, and the boards were cleared, they set down great bowls and crown the wine. A din arises in the palace and voices roll through the spacious halls; lighted lamps hang down from the fretted roof of gold, and flaming torches drive out the night. Then the queen called for a cup, heavy with jewels and gold, and filled it with wine – one that Belus and all of Belus' line had been wont to use. Then through the hall fell silence: 'Jupiter – for they say that you appoint laws for host and guest – grant that this be a day of joy for Tyrians and the voyagers from Troy, and that our children may remember it! May Bacchus, giver of joy, be near, and bounteous Juno; and do you, Tyrians, grace the gathering with friendly spirit!' She spoke, and on the board offered a libation of wine, and, after the libation, was first to touch the goblet with her lips; then with a challenge gave it to Bitias. He briskly drained the foaming cup, and drank deep in the brimming gold; then other lords drank. Long-haired Iopas, once taught by mighty Atlas, makes the hall ring with his golden lyre. He sings of the wandering moon and the sun's toils; whence sprang man and beast, whence rain and fire; of Arcturus, the rainy Hyades and the twin Bears; why wintry suns make such haste to dip themselves in Ocean, or what delay stays the slowly passing nights. With shout on shout the Tyrians applaud, and the Trojans follow. No less did unhappy Dido prolong the night with varied talk and drank deep draughts of love, asking much of Priam, of Hector much; now of the armour in which came the son of Dawn; now of the wondrous steeds of Diomedes; now of the greatness of Achilles. 'Nay, more,' she cries, 'tell us, my guest, from the first beginning the treachery of the Greeks, the sad fate of your people, and your own wanderings; for already a seventh summer bears you a wanderer over every land and sea.'

Aeneid 8.685–700

On the other side comes Antony with barbaric might and motley arms, victorious over the nations of the dawn and the ruddy sea, bringing in his train Egypt and the strength of the East and farthest Bactra; and there follows him (oh the shame of it!) his Egyptian wife. All rush on at once, and the whole sea foams, torn up by the sweeping oars and triple-pointed beaks. To the deep they race; you would think that the Cyclades, uprooted, were floating on the main, or that high mountains were clashing with mountains: in such huge ships the seamen attack the towered sterns. Flaming tow and shafts of winged steel are showered from their hands; Neptune's fields redden with strange slaughter. In the midst the queen calls upon her hosts with their native sistrum; not yet does she cast back a glance at the twin snakes behind. Monstrous gods of every form and barking Anubis wield weapons against Neptune and Venus and against Minerva.

HORACE (65–8 BCE)

Odes 1.37

Now let the drinking begin! Now let us thump the ground with unfettered feet! Now is the time, my friends, to load the couches of the gods with a feast fit for the Salii!

Before this it was sacrilege to bring the Caecuban out from our fathers' cellars, at a time when the queen, along with her troop of disgustingly perverted men, was devising mad ruin for the Capitol and death for the empire – a woman so out of control that she could hope for anything at all, drunk, as she was, with the sweet wine of success.

But her frenzy was sobered by the survival of scarcely one ship from the flames; and her mind, crazed with Mareotic wine, was brought down to face real terror when Caesar pursued her as she flew away from Italy with oars, like a hawk after a gentle dove or a speedy hunter after a hare on the snowy plains of Thessaly, to put that monster of doom safely in chains.

Determined to die more nobly, she showed no womanly fear of the sword, nor did she use her swift fleet to gainsome hidden shore. She had the strength of mind to gaze on her ruined palace with a calm countenance, and the courage to handle the sharp-toothed serpents, letting her body drink in their black venom. Once she had resolved to die she was all the more defiant – determined, no doubt, to cheat the cruel Liburnians: she would not be stripped of her royalty and conveyed to face a jeering triumph: no humble woman she.

TACITUS (c.56–120 CE)

Histories 5.9

The princes now being dead or reduced to insignificance, Claudius made Judea a province and entrusted it to Roman knights or to freedmen; one of the latter, Antonius Felix, practised every kind of cruelty and lust, wielding the power of king with all the instincts of a slave; he had married Drusilla, the grand-daughter of Cleopatra and Antony, and so was Antony's grandson-in-law, while Claudius was Antony's grandson.

BIBLIOGRAPHY

Primary Sources

Acro, *Commentary on Horace's Satires.*
Acts.
Aelian, *On the Nature of Animals.*
Aeschylus, *Fragments.*
Aeschylus, *Suppliants.*
Agatharchides, *On the Erythraean Sea.*
Ammianus Marcellinus, *Roman History.*
Appian, *Civil War.*
Appian, *Sicilian Wars.*
Aristotle, *Generation of Animals.*
Aristotle, *History of Animals.*
Aristotle, *Problems.*
Arnobius, *Against the Pagans*
Athenaeus, *Learned Banqueters.*
Augustus, *Res Gestae.*
Aulus Gellius, *Attic Nights.*
BT Niddah.
Caesar, *Alexandrian War.*
Caesar, *Civil War.*
Callimachus, *Hymn to Delos.*
Cassius Dio, *Roman History.*
Catullus.
Celsus, *On Medicine.*
Cicero, *Against Verres.*
Cicero, *In Defence of Caelius.*
Cicero, *In Defence of Rabirius Postumus.*
Cicero, *Letters to Atticus.*
Cicero, *Letters to Friends.*
Cicero, *On the Agrarian Laws.*
Cicero, *On the Manilian Law.*
Cicero, *On the Nature of the Gods.*
Cicero, *Philippics.*
Cicero, *Tusculan Disputations.*
Claudian, *On the Fourth Consulship of the Emperor Honorius.*
Dio Chrysostom, *Twelfth Discourse.*
Dio Chrysostom, *Thirty-Second Discourse.*
Diodorus Siculus, *Historical Library.*
Eusebius, *Chronicle.*
Eutropius, *Brief History of Rome.*
Festus, *Epitome.*
Florus, *Epitome.*
Galen, *Commentary on the Epidemics.*
Galen, *Compound Remedies According to Place.*
Greek Anthology.
Gregorius Magister, *The Marvels of Rome.*
Herodotus, *Histories.*
Hesiod, *Theogony.*
Hippocrates, *Airs, Waters, Places.*
Homer, *Iliad.*
Homer, *Odyssey.*
Horace, *Epodes.*
Horace, *Odes.*
Horace, *Satires.*
Hyginus, *Fables.*
Jerome, *Epistles.*
Josephus, *Jewish Antiquities.*
Josephus, *Jewish Wars.*
Juba, *Fragments.*
Justin, *Epitome.*
Juvenal, *Satires.*
Livy, *History of Rome.*

Livy, *Summaries.*
Lucan, *Civil Wars.*
Lucian, *Apology for the Salaried Posts in Great Houses.*
Lucian, *How to Write History.*
Macrobius, *Saturnalia.*
Marcus Minucius Felix, *Octavius.*
Martial, *Epigrams.*
Nonius Marcellus, *Doctrina.*
Ovid, *Art of Love.*
Ovid, *Fasti.*
Palatine Anthology.
Papyrus Cairo Zenon 1.59.
Papyrus London.
Papyrus Lugduno-Batava.
Papyrus Rainer 19.813.
Papyrus Tebtunis 33.
Parmenides, *Fragments.*
Pausanias, *Description of Greece.*
Persius, *Satires.*
Philo, *On the Embassy to Gaius.*
Philodemus, *On Signs.*
Plautus, *Epidicus.*
Plautus, *The Rope.*
Pliny the Elder, *Natural History.*
Pliny the Younger, *Letters.*
Plutarch, *Alexander.*
Plutarch, *Antony.*
Plutarch, *Caesar.*
Plutarch, *Cato the Younger.*
Plutarch, *Cicero.*
Plutarch, *Comparison between Demetrius and Antony.*
Plutarch, *Crassus.*
Plutarch, *The Malice of Herodotus.*
Plutarch, *Pompey.*
Plutarch, *Tiberius Gracchus.*
Polybius, *Histories.*
Pomponius Mela, *Description of the World.*
Pomponius Porphyrion, *Scholiast on Horace, Satires.*
Propertius, *Elegies.*
Pseudo-Asconius.
Publilius Syrus, *Sententiae.*

Quintilian, *The Orator's Education.*
Sallust, *History.*
Sallust, *Jugurtha.*
Scholiast to Aristophanes, *Nubes.*
Scribonius Largus, *Medical Compositions.*
Seneca the Elder, *Controversiae.*
Seneca the Elder, *Suasoriae.*
Seneca the Younger, *Consolation to Helvia.*
Seneca the Younger, *Epistles.*
Seneca the Younger, *On Clemency.*
Seneca the Younger, *On Providence.*
Seneca the Younger, *On Tranquillity of Mind.*
Servius, *Commentary on the Aeneid.*
Silius Italicus, *Punica.*
Solinus, *The Wonders of the World.*
Sophocles, *Oedipus at Colonus.*
Strabo, *Geography.*
Suetonius, *Augustus.*
Suetonius, *Caligula.*
Suetonius, *Claudius.*
Suetonius, *Grammarians.*
Suetonius, *Julius Caesar.*
Suetonius, *On Grammarians and Rhetors.*
Suetonius, *Tiberius.*
Synesius of Cyrene, *Phalakas encomium.*
Synkellos, *Extract of Chronography.*
Tacitus, *Annals.*
Tacitus, *Histories.*
Terence, *The Eunuch.*
Tertullian, *Against the Pagans.*
Tertullian, *Apology.*
Theocritus, *Idylls.*
Tibullus, *Elegies.*
Tosefta Niddah.
Trebellius Pollio, *Historia Augusta: Thirty Tyrants.*
Trebellius Pollio, *Historia Augusta: Aurelian.*
Trebellius Pollio, *Historia Augusta: Claudius.*

Trebellius Pollio, *Historia Augusta: Probus.*

Valerius Maximus, *Memorable Deeds and Sayings.*

Varro, *Sesqueulixus.*

Velleius Paterculus, *Roman History.*

Virgil, *Aeneid.*

Virgil, *Georgics.*

Vitruvius, *On Architecture.*

Secondary Sources

Ackert, Nick (2016) 'Animus after Actium? Antony, Augustus, and Damnatio Memoriae', *Discentes* 4.2, 32–40.

Ager, Sheila L. (2005) 'Familiarity Breeds: Incest and the Ptolemaic Dynasty', *Journal of Hellenic Studies* 125, 1–34.

Ager, Sheila L. (2006) 'The Power of Excess: Royal Incest and the Ptolemaic Dynasty', *Anthropologica* 48.2, 165–86.

Ager, Sheila L. (2013) 'Marriage or Mirage? The Phantom Wedding of Antony and Cleopatra', *Classical Philology* 108.2, 139–55.

Allen, Joel (2006) *Hostages and Hostage-taking in the Roman Empire.* Cambridge.

Ashton, Sally-Ann (2004) *Roman Egyptomania.* London.

Ashton, Sally-Ann (2008) *Cleopatra and Egypt.* Malden.

Bagnall, Roger S. (2002) 'Alexandria: Library of Dreams', *Proceedings of the American Philosophical Society* 146.4, 348–62.

Baldwin, B. (1964) 'The Death of Cleopatra VII', *Journal of Egyptian Archaeology* 50, 181–2.

Ball, Warwick (2000) *Rome in the East: The Transformation of an Empire.* London.

Barbara, Sébastien (2014) '"Memorial" Strategies of Court Physicians from the Imperial Period', in Maire, Brigitte (ed.) *'Greek' and 'Roman' in Latin Medical Texts: Studies in Cultural Change and Exchange in Ancient Medicine.* Leiden, 25–42.

Bennett, Chris (2003) 'Drusilla Regina', *Classical Quarterly* 53.1, 315–19.

Bicknell, Peter J. (1977) 'Caesar, Antony, Cleopatra and Cyprus', *Latomus* 36.2, 325–42.

Bingen, Jean (2007) *Hellenistic Egypt: Monarchy, Society, Economy, Culture.* Berkeley.

Birley, Antony (1999) *Septimius Severus: The African Emperor.* London.

Bond, Sarah (2017a) 'The Argument Made by the Absence: On Whiteness, Polychromy, and Diversity in Classics', *History From Below* (30 April 2017): https://sarahemilybond. com/2017/04/30/the-argument-made-by-the-absence-on-whiteness-polychromy-and-diversity-in-classics/

Bond, Sarah (2017b) 'Why We Need to Start Seeing the Classical World in Colour', *Hyperallergic* (7 June 2017): https://hyperallergic.com/383776/ why-we-need-to-start-seeing-the-classical-world-in-color/

Bowman, Alan K. (1996) 'Egypt', in Bowman, Alan K. (ed.) The Cambridge Ancient History Volume X: *The Augustan Empire, 43 BC–AD 69* (2nd edn). Cambridge, 676–702.

Braund, David (1984, reissued 2014) *Rome and the Friendly King: The Character of Client Kingship*. London.

Braund, David (1984) 'Anth. Pal. 9.235: Juba II, Cleopatra Selene and the Course of the Nile', *Classical Quarterly* 34.1, 175–8.

Braund, David (1984c) 'Berenice in Rome', *Historia* 33.1, 120–23.

Broughton, T. Robert S. (1942) 'Cleopatra and "The Treasure of the Ptolemies"', *American Journal of Philology* 63.3, 328–32.

Bueno, André (2016) 'Budistas no Mediterrâneo', *Revista Hélade* 2.2, 66–73.

Cairns, Francis (2012) 'Horace *Odes* 1.22 (and *Odes* 1.2.39): Juba II and the *Mauri*', in Cairns, Francis (ed.) *Roman Lyric: Collected Papers on Catullus and Horace*. Berlin, 244–61.

Caldwell, Lauren (2015) *Roman Girlhood and the Fashioning of Femininity*. Cambridge.

Cameron, Alan (1990) 'Two Mistresses of Ptolemy Philadelphus', *Greek, Roman, and Byzantine Studies* 31.3, 287–311.

Cherf, William J. (2008) 'Earth, Wind, and Fire: The Alexandrian Fire-storm of 48 B.C.', in El-Abbadi, Mostafa et al. (eds) *What Happened to the Ancient Library of Alexandria?*. Leiden, 55–72.

Coltelloni-Trannoy, Michele (1997) *Le royaume de Maurétanie sous Juba II et Ptolémée*. Paris.

Cravinho, Graça (2018) 'Roman Gems in the National Soares dos Reis Museum in Oporto', *Studies in Ancient Art and Civilization* 22, 141–89.

Crook, John (1957) 'A Legal Point about Mark Antony's Will', *Journal of Roman Studies* 47.1/2, 36–8.

Crook, John (1989) 'A Negative Point about Mark Antony's Will', *L'antiquité classique* 58, 221–3.

Dalby, Andrew (2000) *Empire of Pleasures: Luxury and Indulgence in the Roman World*. London.

Dasen, Veronique (1997) 'Multiple Births in Graeco-Roman Antiquity', *Oxford Journal of Archaeology* 16.1, 49–63.

Dasen, Veronique (2005) 'Blessing or Portent? Multiple Births in Ancient Rome', in Mustakallio, Katariina, Hanska, Jussi, Sainio, Hanna-Lee and Vuolanto, Ville (eds) *Hoping for Continuity: Childhood, Education and Death in Antiquity and the Middle Ages*. Rome, 61–73.

Dee, James H. (2003–2004) 'Black Odysseus, White Caesar: When did "Wite People" become "White"?', *Classical Journal* 99.2, 157–67.

Delia, Diana (1991) *Alexandrian Citizenship during the Roman Principate*. Atlanta.

Delia, Diana (1992) 'From Romance to Rhetoric: The Alexandrian Library in Classical and Islamic Traditions', *American Historical Review* 97.5, 1449–67.

Della Corte, Matteo (1951) *Cleopatra, M. Antonio e Ottaviano nelle allegorie storico-umoristiche delle argenterie del tesoro di Boscoreale*. Pompeii.

Dimitru, Adrian (2016) 'Kleopatra Selene – A Look at the Moon and her Bright Side', in Coşkun, Altay and McAuley, A. (eds)

Seleukid Royal Women: Creation, Representation and Distortion of Hellenistic Queenship in the Seleukid Empire. Stuttgart, 253–72.

Draycott, Jane (2010) 'The Sacred Crocodiles of Juba II of Mauretania', *Acta Classica* 53, 211–17.

Draycott, Jane (2012a) 'The Symbol of Cleopatra Selene: Reading Crocodiles on Coins in the Late Republic and Early Principate', *Acta Classica* 55, 43–56.

Draycott, Jane (2012b) 'Dynastic Politics, Defeat, Decadence and Dining: Cleopatra Selene on the So-called 'Africa' Dish from the Villa della Pisanella at Boscoreale', *Papers of the British School at Rome* 80, 45–64.

Empereur, Jean-Yves (2008) 'The Destruction of the Library of Alexandria: An Archaeological Viewpoint', in El-Abbadi, Mostafa et al. (eds) *What Happened to the Ancient Library of Alexandria?*. Leiden, 73–88.

Erskine, Andrew (1995) 'Culture and Power in Ptolemaic Egypt: The Museum and Library of Alexandria', *Greece & Rome* 42.1, 38–48.

Erskine, Andrew (2002) 'Life after Death: Alexandria and the Body of Alexander', *Greece & Rome* 49.2, 163–79.

Ejsmond, Wojciech, Ozarek-Szilke, Marzena, Jaworski, Marcin and Szilke, Stanislaw (2021) 'A Pregnant Ancient Egyptian Mummy from the 1st Century BC', *Journal of Archaeological Science* https://doi.org/10.1016/j.jas.2021.105371.

Etienne, Marc (2003) 'Queen, Harlot or Lecherous Goddess? An Egyptological Approach to a Roman Image of Propaganda', in Walker, Susan and Ashton, Sally-Ann (eds) *Cleopatra Reassessed.* London, 95–100.

Ferroukhi, Mafoud (2003) 'Les Deux Portraits de Cherchell Présumés de Cleopâtre VII', in Walker, Susan and Ashton, Sally-Ann (eds) *Cleopatra Reassessed.* London, 103–6.

Fishwick, Duncan (1971) 'The Annexation of Mauretania', *Historia* 20, 467–73.

Fishwick, Duncan (1972) 'The Institution of the Provincial Cult in Roman Mauretania', *Historia* 21.4, 698–711.

Fishwick, Duncan and Shaw, Brent D. (1976) 'Ptolemy of Mauretania and the Conspiracy of Gaetulicus', *Historia* 25.4, 491–4.

Flemming, Rebecca (2007) 'Women, Writing and Medicine in the Classical World', *Classical Quarterly* 57.1, 257–79.

Flory, M. B. (1993) 'Pearls for Venus', *Historia* 37.4, 498–504.

Fraser, Peter M. (1957) 'Mark Antony in Alexandria – A Note', *Journal of Roman Studies* 47.1/2, 71–3.

Fraser, Peter M. (1972) *Ptolemaic Alexandria.* Oxford.

Gardner, Andrew et al. (2013) *Creating Ethnicities and Identities in the Roman World.* London.

George, Michele (2002) 'Slave Disguise in Ancient Rome', *Slavery and Abolition* 23.2, 41–54.

Goddio, Franck and Masson-Berghoff, Aurélia (eds) *Sunken*

Cities: Egypt's Lost Worlds.
London.

Goldenberg, David (2003) *The Curse of Ham: Race and Slavery in Early Judaism, Christianity, and Islam.* Princeton.

Grant, Michael (1972) *Cleopatra.* London.

Gray-Fow, Michael (2014) 'What to do with Caesarion?', *Greece and Rome* 61.1, 38–67.

Griffiths, J. Gwyn (1961) 'The Death of Cleopatra VII', *Journal of Egyptian Archaeology* 47, 113–18.

Griffiths, J. Gwyn (1965) 'The Death of Cleopatra VII: A Rejoinder and a Postscript', *Journal of Egyptian Archaeology* 51, 209–11.

Grimm, Günter (2003) 'Alexandria in the Time of Cleopatra', in Walker, Susan and Ashton, Sally-Ann (eds) (2003) *Cleopatra Reassessed.* London, 45–9.

Gruen, Erich (2003) 'Cleopatra in Rome: Facts and Fantasies', in Braund, David and Gill, Christopher (eds) *Myth, History and Culture in Republican Rome: Studies in Honour of T. P. Wiseman.* Exeter, 257–74.

Gruen, Erich (2011) *Rethinking the Other in Antiquity.* Princeton.

Gruen, Erich (2013) 'Did Ancient Identity Depend on Ethnicity? A Preliminary Probe', *Phoenix* 67.1/2, 1–22.

Gurval, Robert A. (1995) *Actium and Augustus: The Politics and Emotions of Civil War.* Ann Arbor.

Gutzwiller, Kathryn J. (1995) 'Cleopatra's Ring', *Greek, Roman and Byzantine Studies* 36.4, 383–98.

Haley, Shelley P. (1993) 'Black Feminist Thought and Classics: Re-membering, Re-claiming, Re-empowering', in Rabinowitz, Nancy S. and Richlin, Amy (eds) *Feminist Theory and the Classics.* London, 23–43.

Hamer, Mary (2008) *Signs of Cleopatra: Reading an Icon Historically.* Liverpool.

Handis, Michael W. (2013) 'Myth and History: Galen and the Alexandrian Library', in König, Jason, Oikonomopoulou, Katerina and Woolf, Greg (eds) *Ancient Libraries.* Cambridge, 364–76.

Harders, Ann-Cathrin (2009) 'An Imperial Family Man: Augustus as Surrogate Father to Marcus Antonius' Children', in Hübner, Sabine R. and Ratzan, David M. (eds) *Growing Up Fatherless in Antiquity.* Cambridge, 217–40.

Hatzimichali, Myrto (2013) 'Ashes to Ashes? The Library of Alexandria after 48 BC', in König, Jason, Oikonomopoulou, Katerina, and Woolf, Greg (eds) *Ancient Libraries.* Cambridge, 167–82.

Hekster, Olivier (2010) 'Trophy Kings and Roman Power: A Roman Perspective on Client Kingdoms', in Kaizer, Ted and Facella, Margheritta (eds) *Client Kingdoms in the Roman Near East.* Stuttgart, 45–55.

Hemelrijk, Emily Ann (1999) *Matrona Docta: Educated Women in the Roman Elite from Cornelia to Julia Domna.* London.

Héron de Villefosse, Antoine (1899) *Le Trésor de Boscoreale (Monuments et Mémoires Eugene Piot 5).* Paris.

Hillard, T. W. (2002) 'The Nile Cruise of Cleopatra and Caesar', *Classical Quarterly* 52.2, 549–54.

Huss, Werner (1990) 'Die Herkunft der Kleopatra Philopator', *Aegyptus* 70.1/2, 191–203.

Huzar, Eleanor G. (1985–1986) 'Mark Antony: Marriages vs. Careers', *Classical Journal* 81.2, 97–111.

Isaac, Benjamin H. (2004) *The Invention of Racism in Classical Antiquity*. Princeton.

Jacobson, David M. (2001) 'Three Roman Client Kings: Herod of Judaea, Archelaus of Cappadocia and Juba of Mauretania', *Palestine Exploration Quarterly* 133.1, 22–38.

Jentel, M-O. (1981) 'Aigyptos', *LIMC* 1.1, 379–81.

Johansen, Flemming (2003) 'Portraits of Cleopatra – Do they Exist?', in Walker, Susan and Ashton, Sally-Ann (eds) *Cleopatra Reassessed*. London, 75–7.

Johnson, John Robert (1978) 'The Authenticity and Validity of Antony's Will', *L'antiquité Classique* 47.2, 494–503.

Jones, Prudence J. (2010) 'Cleopatra's Cocktail', *Classical World* 103.2, 207–20.

Joshel, Sandra R. (1986) 'Nurturing the Master's Child: Slavery and the Roman Child-Nurse', *Signs* 12.1, 3–22.

Kennedy, Rebecca F., Roy, C. S. and Goldman, Max L. (eds) (2013) *Race and Ethnicity in the Classical World: An Anthology of Primary Sources in Translation*. Indianapolis/Cambridge.

King, Helen (2016) *The One Sex Body on Trial: The Classical and Early Modern Evidence*. London.

Kleiner, Diana E. E. and Buxton, Bridget (2008) 'Pledges of Empire: the Ara Pacis and the Donations of Rome', *American Journal of Archaeology* 112.1, 57–89.

Konrad, Michaela (2017) 'The Client Kings of Emesa: A Study of Local Identities in the Roman East', Dossier: *Archéologie des rituels dans le monde nabatéen*, 261–95.

Kostuch, Lucyna (2009) 'Cleopatra's Snake or Octavian's? The Role of the Cobra in the Triumph over the Egyptian Queen', *Klio* 91.1, 115–25.

Kudryavtseva Tatyana V. (2019) 'Reconsidering the *imperium infinitum* of Marcus Antonius Creticus', *Vestnik of Saint Petersburg University. History* 64.3, 937–50.

Lange, Carsten Hjort (2009) Res Publica Constituta: *Actium, Apollo and the Accomplishment of the Triumviral Assignment*. Leiden.

Leach, Stephany et al. (2009) 'Migration and Diversity in Roman Britain: A Multidisciplinary Approach to the Identification of Immigrants in Roman York, England', *American Journal of Physical Anthropology* 140.3, 546–61.

Leach, Stephany et al. (2010) 'A Lady of York: Migration, Ethnicity and Identity in Roman Britain', *Antiquity* 84, 131–45.

Lefkovitz, Mary (1983) 'Wives and Husbands', *Greece & Rome* 30.1, 31–47.

Leveau, Philippe (1984) *Caesarea de Maurétanie: une ville romaine et ses campagnes*. Rome.

Linderski, J. (1990) 'The Surname of M. Antonius Creticus and the *cognomina ex victis gentibus*', *Zeitschrift für Papyrologie und Epigraphik* 80, 157–64.

Linfert, Andreas (1983) 'Die Tochter – nicht die Mutter. Nochmals zur "Africa" Schale von Boscoreale', in Nicola Bonacasa and Antonino di Vita (eds) *Alessandria e il mondo ellenistico-romano: studi in onore di Achille Adriani (Rome: Studi e Materiali 4–5)*, Palermo, 351–8.

Luce, J. V. (1963) 'Cleopatra as Fatale Monstrum (Horace, *Carm.* 1.37.21)', *Classical Quarterly* 13, 251–7.

MacLeod, Roy. (ed.) (2004) *The Library of Alexandria: Centre of Learning in the Ancient World*. London.

Macurdy, Grace H. (1936) 'Iotape', *Journal of Roman Studies* 26.1, 40–42.

Macurdy, Grace H. (1937) *Vassal-Queens and Some Contemporary Women in the Roman Empire*. Baltimore.

Makemson, Maud W. (1937) 'Note on Eclipses', in Macurdy, Grace H. (1937) *Vassal-Queens and Some Contemporary Women in the Roman Empire*. Baltimore, 60–62.

Malloch, Simon J. V. (2004) 'The Death of Ptolemy of Mauretania', *Historia* 53.1, 38–45.

Maras, Daniele F. (2020) 'Traces of Orality in Writing', in Whitehouse, Ruth D. (ed.) *Etruscan Literacy in its Social Context*. London, 125–34.

Maritz, J. A. (2001) 'The Image of Africa: The Evidence of the Coinage', *Acta Classica* 44, 105–25.

Marković, Nenad (2015) 'Death in the Temple of Ptah: the Roman Conquest of Egypt and Conflict at Memphis', *Journal of Egyptian History* 8, 37–48.

Marković, Nenad (2016) 'A Look through his window: The Sanctuary of the Divine Apis Bull at Memphis', *Journal of Ancient Egyptian Architecture* 1, 57–70.

Marshman, Ian J. (2017) 'All that Glitters: Roman Signet Rings, the Senses, and Self', in Betts, Eleanor (ed.) *Senses of the Empire: Multisensory Approaches to Roman Culture*. London, 137–46.

Martín, Alfredo Mederos (2019) 'North Africa: From the Atlantic to Algeria', in Doak, Brian R. and López-Ruiz, Carolina (eds) *The Oxford Handbook of the Phoenician and Punic Mediterranean*. Oxford, 627–43.

Matthews, Victor J. (1972) 'The *Libri Punici* of King Hiempsal', *American Journal of Philology* 93.2, 330–35.

Mazard, Jean (1955) *Corpus Nummorum Numidiae Mauretaniaeque*. Paris.

Mazard, Jean (1981) 'Un denier inedit de Juba II et Cléopâtre-Séléne', *Schweizer Münzblätter* 31, 1–2.

McDonough, Christopher Michael (2002–2003) 'The Swallows on Cleopatra's Ship', *Classical World* 96.3, 251–8.

McWilliams, Janette (2013) 'The Socialization of Roman Children', in Evans Grubbs, Judith and Parkin, Tim (eds) *The Oxford Handbook of Childhood and Education in the Roman World*. Oxford, 264–85.

Meiklejohn, K. W. (1934) 'Alexander Helios and Caesarion', *Journal of Roman Studies* 24.2, 191–5.

Miles, Margaret M. (2011) *Cleopatra: A Sphinx Revisited*. Berkeley & Los Angeles.

Morgan, Llewellyn (2000) 'The Autopsy of C. Asinius Pollio', *Journal of Roman Studies* 90, 51–69.

Moussa, Farès (2013) 'Berber, Phoenicio-Punic, and Greek North Africa', in Mitchell, Peter and Lane, Paul J. (eds) *The Oxford Handbook of African Archaeology*. Oxford, 765–76.

Oldfather, W. A. (1924) 'A Friend of Plutarch's Grandfather?', *Classical Philology* 19, 177.

Oliver, James H. (1965) 'Attic Text Reflecting the Influence of Cleopatra', *Greek, Roman and Byzantine Studies* 6.4, 291–4.

Olson, Kelly (2008) *Dress and the Roman Woman: Self-Presentation and Society*. London.

Olusoga, David (2016) *Black and British: A Forgotten History*. London.

Orlin, Eric M. (2008) 'Octavian and Egyptian Cults: Redrawing the Boundaries of Romanness', *American Journal of Philology* 129.2, 231–53.

Osgood, Josiah (2019) 'African Alternatives', in Morrell, Kit, Osgood, Josiah and Welch, Kathryn (eds) *The Alternative Augustan Age*. Oxford, 147–62.

Östenberg, Ida (2009) *Staging the World: Spoils, Captives, and Representations in the Roman Triumphal Procession*. Oxford.

Otele, Olivette (2020) *African Europeans: An Untold History*. London.

Parca, Maryline (2013) 'Children in Ptolemaic Egypt: What the Papyri Say', in Evans Grubbs, Judith and Parkin, Tim (eds) *The Oxford Handbook of Childhood and Education in the Roman World*. Oxford, 465–83.

Parca, Maryline (2017) 'The Wet Nurses of Ptolemaic and Roman Egypt', *Illinois Classical Studies* 42.1, 203–26.

Patterson, Lee E. (1974) 'Antony and Armenia', *Transactions of the American Philological Association* 145.1, 77–105.

Pearce, Sarah (2017) 'The Cleopatras and the Jews', *Transactions of the RHS* 27, 29–64.

Peek, Cecilia M. (2011) 'The Queen Surveys her Realm: The Nile Cruise of Cleopatra VII', *Classical Quarterly* 61.2, 595–607.

Pelling, Christopher (1996) 'The Triumviral Period', in Bowman, A. et al. (eds) *The Cambridge Ancient History: Volume X, The Augustan Empire, 43 BC–AD 69*. Cambridge, 1–69.

Perdrizet, Paul (1911) *Bronzes Grècques d'Égypte de la Collection Fouquet (Bibliothèque d'art et d'archéologie)*. Paris.

Pietrobelli, Antoine (2014) 'The Pharmacological Treatise Περὶ εὐφορβίου of Juba II, King of Mauretania', in Maire, Brigitte (ed.) *'Greek' and 'Roman' in Latin Medical Texts: Studies in Cultural Change and Exchange in Ancient Medicine*. Leiden, 157–82.

Plant, Ian (2004) *Women Writers of Ancient Greece and Rome: An Anthology*. London.

Pomeroy, Sarah (1984) *Women in Hellenistic Egypt: From Alexander to Cleopatra*. New York.

Posener, Georges (1936) *La première domination perse en Egypte: Recueil d'inscriptions hiéroglyphiques*. Cairo 11, 30–55.

Prioux, Évelyne (2014) 'Poetic Depictions of Ancient *Dactyliothecae*', in Wellington Gahtan, Maia and Pegazzano, Donatella (eds) *Museum Archetypes and Collecting in the Ancient World*. Leiden 54–71.

Puech, Pierre-François, Puech, Bernard and Puech, Fernand (2014) 'The "As de Nîmes", a Roman Coin and the Myth of Antony and Cleopatra: Octavian and Agrippa Victorious over Antony', *Revue Numismatique Omni Revista Numismática* 8, 58–66.

Raven, Susan (1993) *Rome in Africa*. London.

Rehak, Paul (1990) 'Livia's Dedication in the Temple of *Divus* Augustus', *Latomus* 49.1, 117–25.

Retief, Francois. and Cilliers, Louise (2005) 'The Last Days of Cleopatra', *Acta Theologica Supplementum* 7, 79–88.

Ricci, Cecilia (2011) '"In Custodiam Urbes": Notes on the "Cohortes Urbanae" (1968–2010)', *Historia* 60.4, 484–508.

Roller, Duane W. (2003) *The World of Juba II and Kleopatra Selene: Royal Scholarship on Rome's African Frontier*. London.

Roller, Duane W. (2014) *Cleopatra: A Biography*. Oxford.

Roller, Duane W. (2018) *Cleopatra's Daughter and Other Royal Women of the Augustan Era*. Oxford.

Rostovtzeff, M. (1919) 'Queen Dynamis of Bosporus', *Journal of Hellenic Studies* 39, 88–109.

Roullet, Anne (1972) *The Egyptian and Egyptianizing Monuments of Imperial Rome*. Leiden.

Royster, Francesca T. (2003) *Becoming Cleopatra: The Shifting Image of an Icon*. New York.

Ryholt, Kim (2013) 'Libraries in Ancient Egypt', in König, Jason, Oikonomopoulou, Katerina and Woolf, Greg (eds) *Ancient Libraries*. Cambridge, 23–37.

Salway, Benet (1994) 'What's in a Name: A Survey of Roman Onomastic Practice from c. 700 B.C. to A.D. 700', *Journal of Roman Studies* 84, 124–45.

Sanchez, Anne Bielman (2019) 'Power Couples in Antiquity: An Initial Survey', in *Power Couples in Antiquity: Transversal Perspectives*. London, 179–208.

Sarolta, Anna Takács (2011) 'Cleopatra, Isis, and the Formation of Augustan Rome', in Miles, Margaret (ed.) *Cleopatra: A Sphinx Revisited*. Berkeley, 78–95.

Scheidel, Walter (2003) 'Germs for Rome', in Edwards, Catherine and Woolf, Greg (eds) *Rome the Cosmopolis*. Cambridge, 158–76.

Scott, Kenneth (1933) 'The Political Propaganda of 44–30 BC', *Memoirs of the American Academy in Rome* 11, 7–49.

Settipani, Christian (2000) *Continuité gentilice et continuité familiale dans les familles sénatoriales romaines à l'époque impériale: mythe et realité.* Oxford.

Shatzman, Israel (1971) 'The Egyptian Question in Egyptian Politics (59–54 BC), *Latomus* 30.2, 363–9.

Siani-Davies, M. (1997) 'Ptolemy XII Auletes and the Romans', *Historia* 46.3, 306–40.

Sloan, Michael C. (2016) 'Mauri versus Marsi in Horace's Odes 1.2.39', *Illinois Classical Studies* 41.1, 41–58.

Snowden, Frank Jr (1983) *Before Color Prejudice: The Ancient View of Blacks.* Cambridge.

Snowden, Frank Jr (1991) 'Asclepiades' Didyme', *Greek, Roman, and Byzantine Studies* 32.3, 239–53.

Sorek, Susan (2014) *The Emperors' Needles: Egyptian Obelisks and Rome.* Liverpool.

Southern, Pat (1998) *Mark Antony.* Stroud.

Southern, Pat (2008) *Empress Zenobia: Palmyra's Rebel Queen.* London.

Speidel, Michael P. (1979) 'An Urban Cohort of the Mauretanian Kings', *Antiquités africaines* 14, 121–2.

Speidel, Michael P. (1993) 'The Fustis as a Soldier's Weapon', *Antiquités africaines* 29, 137–49.

Stoner, Lillian Bartlett (2015) 'A Bronze Hellenistic Dwarf in the Metropolitan Museum', *Metropolitan Museum Journal* 50.1, 92–101.

Sullivan, Richard D. (1990) *Near Eastern Royalty and Rome, 100–30 BCE.* Toronto.

Tarn, W. W. (1932) 'Alexander Helios and the Golden Age', *Journal of Roman Studies* 22.2, 135–60.

Thompson, Dorothy J. (1994) 'Egypt, 146–31 BC', in Crook, J. A. et al. (eds) The Cambridge Ancient History: Volume IX, *The Last Age of the Roman Republic, 146–43 BC.* Cambridge, 310–26.

Thompson, Dorothy J. (2009) 'The Multilingual Environment of Persian and Ptolemaic Egypt: Egyptian, Aramaic, and Greek Documentation', in Bagnall, Roger S. (ed.) *The Oxford Handbook of Papyrology.* Oxford, 395–417.

Thompson, Dorothy J. (2013) 'Hellenistic Royal Barges', in Buraselis, Kostas, Stefanou, Mary and Thompson, Dorothy J. (eds) *The Ptolemies, the Sea and the Nile: Studies in Waterborne Power.* Cambridge, 185–96.

Thompson, Lloyd (1989) *Romans and Blacks.* London.

Thür, H. (1990) 'Arsinoe IV, eine Schwester Kleopatras VII, Grabinhaberin des Oktogons in Ephesos? Ein Vorschlag', *Jahresh d Österr Archäol Inst* 60, 43–56.

Totelin, Laurence (2012) 'Botanizing Rulers and their Herbal Subjects: Plants and Political Power in Greek and Roman Literature', *Phoenix* 66.1/2, 122–44.

Totelin, Laurence (2017) 'The Third Way: Galen, Pseudo-Galen, Metrodora, Cleopatra and the Gynaecological Pharmacology of Byzantium', in Lehmhaus, Lennart and Martelli, Matteo (eds) *Collecting Recipes: Byzantine and Jewish Pharmacology in Dialogue.* Berlin, 103–22.

Tracy, Jonathan (2010) 'The Text and Significance of Lucan 10.107', *Classical Quarterly* 60, 281–6.

Tran, Nicolas (2013) 'Le cuisinier G. Iulius Niceros et la domesticité royale de Maurétanie', *Zeitschrift für Papyrologie und Epigraphik* 187, 310–16.

Tronson, Adrian (1998) 'Vergil, the Augustans, and the Invention of Cleopatra's Suicide – One Asp or Two?', *Vergilius* 44, 31–50.

van Minnen, Peter (2000) 'An Official Act of Cleopatra (with a Subscription in her Own Hand)', *Ancient Society* 30, 29–34.

van Minnen, Peter (2003) 'A Royal Ordinance of Cleopatra and Related Documents', in Walker, Susan and Ashton, Sally-Ann (eds) (2003) *Cleopatra Reassessed*. London, 35–44.

Versluys, Miguel J. (2002) *Aegyptiaca Romana: Nilotic Scenes and the Roman Views of Egypt*. Leiden.

Walker, Susan (2008) 'Cleopatra in Pompeii?', *Papers of the British School at Rome* 76, 35–46 and 345–8.

Walker, Susan and Ashton, Sally-Ann (eds) (2003) *Cleopatra Reassessed*. London.

Walker, Susan and Higgs, Peter (eds) (2001) *Cleopatra of Egypt: From History to Myth*. London.

Wardle, David (2006) 'The Bald and the Beautiful: Imperial Hair-envy and the End of Ptolemy of Mauretania?', *Arctos* 40, 175–88.

Watkins, Thomas H. (2019) *L. Munatius Plancus: Serving and Surviving in the Roman Revolution*. London.

White, Peter (1992) '"Pompeius Macer" and Ovid', *Classical Quarterly* 42.1, 210–18.

Whitehorne, John E. G. (1994) *Cleopatras*. London.

Whittaker, Dick (2009) 'Ethnic Discourses on the Frontiers of Roman Africa', in Derks, Ton and Roymans, Nico (eds) *Ethnic Constructs in Antiquity: The Role of Power and Tradition*. Amsterdam, 189–205.

Winsbury, Rex (2010) *Zenobia of Palmyra: History, Myth and the Neo-Classical Imagination*. London.

Wiseman, T. Peter (1974) 'Legendary Genealogies in Late-Republican Rome', *Greece and Rome* 21.2, 153–64.

Wiseman, T. Peter (2019) *The House of Augustus: A Historical Detective Story*. Princeton.

Woods, David (2005) 'Caligula, Ptolemy of Mauretania, and the Danger of Long Hair', *Arctos* 39, 207–14.

Wright, Andrew (2001) 'The Death of Cicero. Forming a Tradition: The Contamination of History', *Historia: Zeitschrift für Alte Geschichte* 50.4, 436–52.

Zachos, Konstantinos L. (2003) 'The *Tropaeum* of the Sea-battle of Actium at Nikopolis: Interim Report', *Journal of Roman Archaeology* 16, 65–92.

Zanker, Paul (1990) *The Power of Images in the Age of Augustus*. Ann Arbor.

ABBREVIATIONS

AE = L'Année épigraphique
ANS = American Numismatic Society
CIL = Corpus Inscriptionum Latinarum
FGrHist = Greek Fragmentary Historians
ILS = Inscriptiones Latinae Selectae
Kaibel = Epigrammata graeca
LIMC = Lexicon Iconographicum Mythologiae Classicae
Mazard = Corpus Nummorum Numidiae Mauretaniaeque
NTDAR = New Topographical Dictionary of Ancient Rome
OGIS = Orientis Graeci Inscriptiones Selectae
PIR = Prosopographia Imperii Romani Saeculi
RIC = Roman Imperial Coinage
RPC = Roman Provincial Coinage
RRC = Roman Republican Coinage
RSC = Roman Silver Coins
SNG = Sylloge Nummorum Graecorum

ENDNOTES

Foreword

1 Lefkowitz (1983) grapples with the issue of how much it is reasonable to expect from ancient women, given their circumstances.
2 Plant (2004) See Hemelrijk (1999) for discussion of the literature produced by women during the Roman period specifically.
3 Maras (2020) 129–30.
4 National Archaeological Museum of Naples inv. 9084.
5 National Archaeological Museum of Naples inv. 9018.
6 Pliny the Elder, *Natural History* 35.40.147.
7 In 2018, Dr Julie Hruby of Dartmouth University was awarded a Mellon New Directions grant from the Andrew W. Mellon Foundation to apply modern forensics to ancient pottery and investigate these prints: https://news.dartmouth.edu/news/2018/04/julie-hruby-wins-fellowship-study-ancient-fingerprints (accessed July 2020).

8 Roller (2003) and Roller (2018) are both excellent books and I highly recommend them to anyone interested in learning more about Cleopatra Selene, but they are not solely focused on her.
9 See, for example, the so-called 'Ivory Bangle Lady', a high-status woman who died in Eboracum (modern York) during the second half of the fourth century CE, but who was born in North Africa, and whose skeleton and grave goods can be viewed as part of the Yorkshire Museum's 'Roman York – Meet the People of the Empire' exhibition, Leach et al. (2010); for other Roman Africans in York, see Leach et al. (2009). There is also literary, documentary and archaeological evidence for the presence of many other people of colour in Roman Britain.
10 See Haley (1993), where she discusses her experience as a Black female classicist looking for role models.

Introduction

1 According to the Roman letter writer Pliny the Younger (61–*c*.113 CE), who witnessed the eruption and whose uncle, Pliny the Elder, died during it, it occurred 'nine days prior

to the Kalends of September',
i.e. 24 August 79 CE. He
was, however, describing it in
response to a question asked
by a friend twenty-five years
later, see his letters 6.16 and
6.20. But archaeological and
archaeobotanical evidence
has cast doubt on this, since
the clothing that many of the
deceased were wearing, and the
presence of wine made from
grapes that would not have been
harvested until September, and
pomegranates and walnuts that
would not have been harvested
until October, points to a date
later in the autumn rather
than the summer. Then, just
last year, a graffito was found
written in charcoal on the wall
of a house that has only recently
been excavated referring to 'the
sixteenth day before the Kalends
of November', i.e. 17 October,
and it is possible that it could be
referring to 17 October 79 CE.
The debate is ongoing.

2 Fragment of a fresco from the
Villa della Pisanella, featuring a
woman on a black background
presenting fruits, dating to
around 40–20 BCE, currently
housed in the Antiquarium di
Boscoreale. Image courtesy of
Wikimedia Commons.

3 A gilded silver dish from
the Villa della Pisanella at
Boscoreale, which may depict
Cleopatra Selene. Musée du
Louvre inv. Bj 1969.

4 For a sense of what this would
have looked like, you can see a
fresco of a similar set of silverware on display in the tomb of

the twenty-two-year-old aedile
Gaius Vestorius Priscus, located
near the Vesuvian Gate at
Pompeii.

5 Draycott (2012b).

6 The debate over the woman's
identity is ongoing and lively.
Héron de Villefosse, who originally published the silverware,
thought she was Africa, see
(1899) 177; Perdrizet suggested
she might be the city of Alexandria, see (1911) 39; Jentel
suggested she might be the province of Egypt, see (1981) 380;
Della Corte proposed she might
be Cleopatra VII (1951) 35–48.

7 Linfert (1983) 351–8.

8 Gray-Fow (2014).

9 See Suetonius, *Augustus* 17.5 for
the claim that Octavian 'raised
them as carefully as his own kin'.

10 Alexander: *ANS* 1980.109.90.
Ptolemy: *ANS* 1957.172.2020.

11 Maritz (2001) 109.

12 See, for example, Scribonius
Largus (*c*.1–50 CE), the imperial physician to the emperor
Claudius (10 BCE–54 CE,
reigned 41–54 CE), whose work
Medical Compositions, a collection of recipes for 271 remedies,
contains a number which he
claims were used and endorsed
by members of the imperial
family.

13 From the earliest history and
mythology of Rome, women
were associated with spinning
and weaving. While the production of cloth was certainly an
important part of the household
economy, and spindles and loom
weights are ubiquitous in the
Roman archaeological record,

this stereotype was so powerful that if someone wanted to praise a woman for her virtuous qualities, they would include reference to her weaving in preference to anything else that she may have done; for example, this compliment frequently finds its way into epitaphs.

14 *Palatine Anthology* 9.235.

15 Top: a coin depicting Juba and the Latin legend REX IUBA on the obverse face and the sun and the moon and the Greek legend BASILISSA KLEOPATRA on the reverse face, Mazard 299. Bottom: a coin depicting Juba and the Latin legend REX IUBA on the obverse face and the crown and sistrum of the goddess Isis and the Greek legend BASILISSA KLEOPATRA on the reverse face, Mazard 222.

16 Tacitus, *Annals* 12.36, 40; Tacitus, *Histories* 3.45.

17 Tacitus, *Annals* 14.31–37; Cassius Dio, *Roman History* 52.1–12.

1. Alexandria: Cleopatra Selene's Birthplace

1 Shatzman (1971); Siani-Davies (1997).

2 Thus, with the benefit of hindsight, it can be said that Cleopatra VII's choice of name for her only daughter seems to have been particularly apt, as, just as her namesake had done, the second Cleopatra Selene would technically rule Egypt alongside two of her brothers and then leave Egypt to reign alongside her husband in another kingdom before producing a son. On the first Cleopatra Selene, see Dimitru (2016).

3 Graeco-Roman Museum inv. 21739.

4 Yale University Art Gallery inv. 1932.1735. Dating to around 540 CE, it was donated to the church by a bishop named Anastasios but is now housed in the Yale University Art Gallery in New Haven in Connecticut.

5 Plutarch, *Alexander* 26.4–7.

6 *Papyrus Rainer* 19.813.

7 Fraser (1972) 38–60.

8 This would not be the case under Roman rule, as detailed in Philo, *On the Embassy to Gaius*, and the Emperor Claudius' letter to the Alexandrians, *Papyrus London* 1912.

9 Strabo, *Geography* 17.1.13.

10 It is not known for certain exactly how long an ancient stadion was, as this unit of measurement was equal to 600 Greek feet, and the length of the foot varied around the Greek world, but estimates have been made and it has been suggested that the Ptolemaic stadion was 185 metres. If so, this would mean that Alexandria was 5,550 x 1,480 metres.

11 Diodorus Siculus, *Historical Library* 15.52.6.

12 Delia (1991).

13 Strabo, *Geography* 17.6–10. For information on the underwater archaeological surveys of Alexandria and their findings, see the work of Franck Goddio: https://

www.franckgoddio.org/projects/
sunken-civilizations/alexandria.
html (accessed 2 November
2020).

14 Pliny the Elder, *Natural History*
36.18.83. See Lucian, *How
to Write History* 62 for the
lighthouse's dedicatory inscription: 'Sostratus of Cnidus,
son of Dexiphanes, on behalf
of mariners, to the Divine
Savours' – the 'Divine Saviours'
were probably the Dioscuri, the
brothers Castor and Pollux, who
were believed to be especially
protective of sailors. If the Ptolemaic stadion was 185 metres,
this would mean that the
Heptastadion was 1,295 metres
long.

15 Josephus, *Jewish Wars* 4.10.5.
If the Ptolemaic stadion was
185 metres, this would mean
that the Pharos was visible from
approximately 55.5 kilometres
away.

16 American Numismatic Society
inv. 1974.26.3475.

17 Suetonius, *Claudius* 20.3. For
an illustration, see the reverse
face of *RIC* 178, or the Torlonia
Portus Relief.

18 See also Diodorus Siculus,
17.52.5.

19 Empereur (2008) 80.

20 Aulus Hirtius accompanied
Caesar to Alexandria in 48 BCE,
added an eighth book to Caesar's
Gallic Wars, edited Caesar's
African Wars and Spanish Wars
and is probably the author of
the *Alexandrian War*. For the
observation, see Caesar, *Alexandrian War* 1. However, virtually
fireproof is not the same as

totally fireproof, as would be
discovered when this section of
the city burned in 48 BCE during
Caesar's Alexandrian campaign
against Ptolemy XIII and
Arsinoe IV, see Cherf (2008).

21 Polybius, *Histories* 15.25. See
Grimm (2003) for discussion.

22 Caesar, *Civil War* 3.112.

23 Delia (1992) 1449–1450.

24 Synesius of Cyrene, *Phalakas
encomium* 6; Ammianus Marcellinus, *Roman History* 22.16.12.
One statue base, upon which
stood a statue of the rhetor
Aelius Demetrios, dedicated
by Flavius Hierax on behalf of
his colleagues at the Museum,
has been recovered from Sherif
Pasha Street in Alexandria, and
it may have graced the halls of
the complex.

25 Agatharchides, *On the
Erythraean Sea* fragment 1. See
also aviary: Athenaeus, *Learned
Banqueters* 14.654; Aelian, *On
the Nature of Animals* 17.3;
Athenaeus, *Learned Banqueters*
5.196, 14.654b, c; giant snake:
Diodorus Siculus, *Historical
Library* 3.36–37. For Ptolemy II
Philadelphos receiving a gift of
exotic animals from an Ammo-
nite chief from the territory east
of the Jordan river, see *Papyrus
Cairo Zenon* 1.59.075 – it is
likely that other foreign rulers
made similar gifts once they
were aware of the existence
of the royal menagerie, just
as rulers exchange gifts today.
And it is likely that the royal
menagerie was the source of
many of the animals exhibited
in Rome in 29 BCE in the wake

of Octavian's Triple Triumph, see Cassius Dio, *Roman History* 51.22.5 for mention of a hippopotamus and a rhinoceros. The animals of the royal menagerie were used in royal processions, and an account of one of these has survived at Athenaeus, *Learned Banqueters* 5.198d.

26 Athenaeus, *Learned Banqueters* 1.22d.

27 Athenaeus, *Learned Banqueters* 6.240b–c.

28 Ryholt (2013).

29 A granite block inscribed with the words 'Dioskourides 3 volumes' that was discovered in the garden of the Prussian consulate general has been identified as a storage been for papyrus scrolls, and if this identification is correct, it provides some idea of the Library's storage arrangements. On the Library, see Erskine (1995); Bagnall (2002); MacLeod (2004). On the mythologisation of the Library in antiquity, see Delia (1992); from antiquity up to the modern day, see Handis (2013).

30 Athenaeus, *Learned Banqueters* 1.3b.

31 Galen, *Second Commentary on Hippocrates' Epidemics* 3.239–240.

32 Athenaeus, *Learned Banqueters* 5.206d–209b.

33 Galen, *Commentary on the Epidemics* 3.17.1.606.

34 Caesar, *Alexandrian War* 3.111.

35 Cherf (2008); Empereur (2008); Hatzimichali (2013). On the extent of the damage, see, for example, the contradictions in Plutarch, *Caesar* 49.6–7 and Cassius Dio, *Roman History* 42.38. Many ancient accounts propose suspiciously precise figures for the number of books that were lost.

36 Plutarch, *Antony* 58.5. On the rivalry between Alexandria and Pergamum, see Erskine (1995).

37 Erskine (2002).

38 Pausanias, *Description of Greece* 1.6.3, 1.7.1.

39 Plutarch, *Antony* 80.

40 Philo, *On the Embassy to Gaius* 149–51; see also Strabo, *Geography* 17.1.9; Pliny the Elder, *Natural History* 36.69. It was at the Caesareum that the philosopher Hypatia would be murdered by a mob of Christians in 415 CE.

41 Marković (2016).

42 Herodotus, *Histories* 3.28; Strabo, *Geography* 17.3.31; Pliny the Elder, *Natural History* 8.71.

43 See Posener (1936) n. 3 and n. 4 for epitaph and sarcophagus inscriptions of Apis Bulls.

2. Antony and Cleopatra: West Meets East

1 See, for example, Lucian, *Civil War* 10.59–62, and this link has continued to be made over the centuries since, for a relatively recent example, see Carol Ann Duffy's poem 'Beautiful' (2002).

2 Tacitus, *Annals* 2.56; Josephus, *Jewish Antiquities* 18.46; Justin, *Epitome* 41.1.1.

3 Plutarch, *Crassus* 18–33; Cassius Dio, *Roman History* 40.16–27.

4 Plutarch, *Cicero* 46.3–5; Appian, *Civil War* 4.8.35; Seneca the Elder, *Controversiae* 7.2. See also Velleius Paterculus, *Roman History* 2.66.1 for Octavian's 'defence' of Cicero at that time. See also Wright (2001).

5 Cicero, *Letters to Friends* 10.28.

6 Scott (1933).

7 Cicero, *Philippic* 2; Plutarch, *Antony* 9.4.

8 Pliny the Elder, *Natural History* 14.28.22.

9 Seneca the Younger, *Epistles* 73.25.

10 See Cicero, *Philippic* 2 for the specifics. These details were subsequently included in Plutarch's *Antony* and Cassius Dio's *Roman History*.

11 Suetonius, *Augustus* 69.1.

12 Suetonius, *Augustus* 70.1–2. The secret was so poorly kept that it was lampooned in anonymous verse.

13 Southern (1998).

14 Vatican Museums inv. 2236.

15 Appian, *Civil War* 5.7.

16 Suetonius, *Augustus* 62.1; Cassius Dio, *Roman History* 48.5.3.

17 Martial, *Epigrams* 11.20.

18 Plutarch, *Antony* 24.2.

19 Strabo, *Geography* 14.1.41.

20 Gruen (2003).

21 Appian, *Civil War* 5.8.1.

22 Plutarch, *Antony* 25–29; Appian, *Civil War* 5.8–9.

23 Vatican Museums inv. 38511. For discussion, see Johansen (2003).

24 Caesarion's full name was Ptolemy XV Caesar, although he was known as Caesarion, 'Little Caesar': Suetonius, *Julius Caesar* 52.

25 Strabo, *Geography* 17.1.13; Dio Chrysostom, *Orations* 32.35.

26 Apparently Auletes' restoration had cost him (or rather Egypt) 17.5 million drachmas, see Plutarch, *Caesar* 48.

27 Plutarch, *Antony* 27.2.

28 Plutarch, *Antony* 27.2. He claims that she spoke the languages of the Ethiopians, Troglodytes, Hebrews, Arabians, Syrians, Medes and Parthians, and many others besides.

29 Thompson (2009).

30 Plutarch, *Antony* 27.1.

31 Plutarch, *Antony* 26.1. Dellius must also have been a first-rate diplomat, as Antony would send him on numerous embassies and highly sensitive missions around the eastern Mediterranean over the next few years, as detailed in Josephus, *Jewish Antiquities* 14.394; Josephus, *Jewish Wars* 1.290.

32 British Museum inv. GR 1865,1118.252.

33 Athenaeus, *Learned Banqueters* 5.204e–205d. See Thompson (2013) for discussion.

34 Museo Nazionale Romano, Palazzo Massimo alle Terme inv. 33785 and inv. 33786.

35 This scene is frequently recreated in television series and films, perhaps most famously in the 1963 film *Cleopatra* directed by Joseph L. Mankiewicz starring Elizabeth Taylor as Cleopatra and Rex Harrison as Caesar.

36 Plutarch, *Caesar* 49.1–3; Plutarch, *Cato the Younger* 35.3.

37 Seneca the Elder, *Suasoriae* 1.7.

38 Plutarch, *Antony* 26.1.
39 Athenaeus, *Learned Banqueters* 4.147f–148a.
40 Athenaeus, *Learned Banqueters* 4.148a–b.
41 Athenaeus, *Learned Banqueters* 4.148b.
42 A bronze sculpture of this momentous occasion can be found today on display next to the Secession Building in Vienna.
43 Pliny the Elder, *Natural History* 8.21.55.
44 Appian, *Civil War* 5.11.
45 Lucan, *Civil Wars* 10.111–174.
46 Athenaeus, *Learned Banqueters* 5.196c.
47 Athenaeus, *Learned Banqueters* 5.196e.
48 Cicero, *Philippic* 2.42, 44; Plutarch, *Antony* 2.3.
49 Pliny the Elder, *Natural History* 33.14.
50 Goddio and Masson-Berghoff (2016).
51 Athenaeus, *Learned Banqueters* 4.147f–148a.
52 Pliny the Elder, *Natural History* 21.12.
53 Plutarch, *Antony* 28.3–4.
54 *OGIS* 195, discussed in Fraser (1957).
55 Pliny the Elder, *Natural History* 9.119–121; Macrobius, *Saturnalia* 3.17.14–17.
56 This is apparently possible, see Jones (2010).
57 Watkins (2019) 123.
58 Horace, *Satires* 2.3.239–241; Pliny the Elder, *Natural History*

9.59, 10.52. Cleopatra's actions in turn seem to have influenced Antony's grandson, the emperor Gaius, better known as Caligula, see Suetonius, *Caligula* 37.
59 Macrobius, *Saturnalia* 3.17.18. Pearls were often dedicated to Aphrodite/Venus in antiquity, appropriate due to the belief that the goddess had been born from the sea off the coast of Cyprus, see Flory (1988).
60 Lucian, *Apology for the Salaried Posts in Great Houses* 5.
61 Lucan, *Civil Wars* 10.141. On the use of slave disguise in ancient Rome, see George (2002) – Antony had previously used it under much more serious circumstances, in an attempt to escape an angry mob after the assassination of Caesar in 44 BCE.
62 Plutarch, *Antony* 29.2.
63 Velleius Paterculus, *Roman History* 2.83.1–2, 83.1–2.
64 Plutarch, *Antony* 29.1–3.
65 Plutarch, *Antony* 29.4.
66 Hillard (2002); Peek (2011).
67 Sacred crocodiles of Sobek = *Papyrus Tebtunis* 33. Labyrinth = Herodotus, *Histories* 2.148.
68 Plutarch, *Comparison between Demetrios and Antony* 3.3; Cassius Dio, *Roman History* 50.27.2.
69 Appian, *Civil War* 5.9 claims she was at the Temple of Artemis Leucophryne at Miletus.
70 Appian, *Civil Wars* 5.9.

3. The Birth of a Queen

1 Cicero, *Letters to Atticus* 14.20.2.

2 Celsus, *On Medicine* proem 23–6.

3 Hyginus, *Fables* 274. For discussion of this story, see King (2016).

4 Ejsmond et al. (2021). Non-invasive examination of the mother and foetus that will hopefully tell us much more about pregnancy and child-birth in this period is currently ongoing.

5 Pliny the Elder, *Natural History* 7.37; Aristotle, *Generation of Animals* 4.6.775a; Aristotle, *Problems* 10.894a.

6 Parca (2013).

7 Callimachus, *Hymn to Delos* 209–11.

8 British Museum inv. 1992,0811.1.

9 Cleveland Museum of Art inv. 1940.613.

10 Parca (2017).

11 For discussion of this complex relationship, see Joshel (1986).

12 Suetonius, *Nero* 42.1, 50.1; Suetonius, *Domitian* 17.3.

13 Publilius Syrus, *Sententiae* 600.

14 Their elder brother Caesarion's date of birth is recorded as 23 June 47 BCE in *Papyrus Lugduno-Batava XV* 82.

15 Egyptian Museum inv. JE 46278.

16 On twins in antiquity, see Dasen (1997) and (2005).

17 Aristotle, *History of Animals* 7.4.585a; Pliny the Elder, *Natural History* 7.49 – we might also consider the famous example of Helen of Troy's twin brothers Castor and Pollux, also known as the Dioscuri, one of whom was fathered by King Tyndareus of Sparta, the other by the god Zeus: as a result, Castor was mortal and Pollux was divine.

18 *RPC* 1.3901.9. This was a particularly pointed combination of religious and philosophical theatre, as the goddess Aphrodite was believed to have been born in the sea just off the coast of Cyprus, after the castrated genitals of the god Uranus were thrown into it – see Hesiod, *Theogony* 188.

19 Plutarch, *Antony* 36.

20 Although we do not know who Cleopatra VII's mother was, if she was Cleopatra V, as has often been suggested, then Cleopatra's maternal grandfather would have been Ptolemy X Alexander I Philometor, so the name Alexander could have been chosen to honour his maternal grandfather.

21 *RRC* 496/2 (issued in 42 BCE) or *RRC* 533/2 (issued in 38 BCE).

22 Tarn (1932); Meiklejohn (1934).

23 Cassius Dio, *Roman History* 50.25.3.

24 Pliny the Elder, *Natural History* 7.10. See also Macrobius, *Saturnalia* 2.28 for Antony rewarding musicians from Toranius. In fact, Toranius seems to have been a particularly well-connected dealer of enslaved people, operating at the highest echelons of Roman society at this time, as Suetonius, *Augustus* 69.2, also refers to him in relation to Octavian's friends procuring him beautiful women to take as his lovers.

25 State Hermitage Museum inv. ГР-12706. The gold setting is of a later date.

26 An inscription bearing an epitaph for an attendant who died suddenly was set up in Athens by a king's daughter from Libya, and it has been suggested that the princess was Cleopatra VII visiting Athens with her father Ptolemy XII during his exile from Egypt, see Grant (1972) 15. This is not entirely certain, as while Libya was often used as a way of referring to the entirety of North Africa, we might expect such an inscription to be more specific and use Egypt instead.

27 Horace, *Satires* 1.3.46–47; Pomponius Porphyrion, Scholiast on Horace, *Satires* 1.3.46. See also Philodemus, *On Signs* 3, column 2.18 for Antony supplying dwarfs from Syria for gladiatorial games. Stoner (2015) 96.

28 Philostratus, *Lives of the Sophists* 1.5; Galen, *Compound Remedies according to Place* 1.1, 1.2, 1.7. For discussion, see Flemming (2007); Totelin (2017).

29 This idea survives in the Jewish tradition, Tosefta Niddah 4.17; BT Niddah 30b.

30 Huzar (1985–1986).

31 Cicero, *Philippic* 13.10.23; see also Cicero, *Philippics* fragment 19.

32 On Pythodoria, see Roller (2018) 99–120, although he is not entirely convinced that

Pythodoria's mother Antonia was Antony's daughter.

33 One of Cleopatra Selene's ancestors had proposed marriage to the widowed Cornelia, widely considered a paragon of Roman womanhood, but rather than becoming Queen of Egypt she had preferred to remain a *univira*, a woman who had only been married once, and concentrate on raising her children, see Plutarch, *Tiberius Gracchus* 14.

34 *RRC* 541/1–2.

35 Although ultimately this dynastic marriage did not take place, the name Iotape subsequently appears in the genealogies of the royal families of the kingdoms of Commagene and Emesa, so it is possible ended up marrying King Mithridates III of Commagene, see Macurdy (1936). This marriage may even have been arranged by Augustus, as he gave the kingdom of Commagene to Mithridates in 20 BCE, and marriage to the kingdom's princess would have served as a way of reinforcing Mithridates' position.

36 Plutarch, *Antony* 52.1–3, 53.12; Cassius Dio, *Roman History* 49.33.1–2, 49.40.2.

37 British Museum inv. EA 1325, the so-called 'Caesarion Stele', dated to 19 January 30 BCE. See also Gary-Fow (2014).

38 Ager (2005), (2006).

4. Death of a Dynasty?

1 Plutarch, *Antony* 30; Cassius Dio, *Roman History* 48. 28.3.

2 Cassius Dio, *Roman History* 48.30.1.

3 Velleius Paterculus, *Roman History* 2.78.1.
4 British Museum inv. G.2204.
5 Plutarch, *Antony* 33.4; Appian, *Civil War* 5.76.
6 Palazzo Massimo alle Terme inv. 121221.
7 Athenaeus, *Learned Banqueters* 4.148b–c.
8 Velleius Paterculus, *Roman History* 2.82.4; Athenaeus, *Learned Banqueters* 4.148c.
9 Seneca the Elder, *Suasoriae* 1.6; Cassius Dio, *Roman History* 48.39.2.
10 Seneca the Elder, *Suasoriae* 6–7.
11 There is some debate between scholars over whether Antony and Cleopatra ever actually married. No ancient source records a wedding, although a number do refer to Cleopatra as Antony's 'Egyptian wife'. It is worth noting that although Romans did have formal wedding ceremonies and recognise several different types of marriage (depending upon the type of marriage you had, your legal rights were different, something which primarily affected women in relation to their autonomy and their property), men and women who simply cohabited were also classed as spouses. See Ager (2013) for discussion; she is of the opinion that they never did actually marry.
12 Plutarch, *Antony* 35; Cassius Dio, *Roman History* 48.54.
13 Cassius Dio, *Roman History* 48.54.4.
14 Cassius Dio, *Roman History* 48.54.5.
15 Plutarch, *Crassus* 31.6 records Crassus being decapitated (but notes that the precise manner of his death is pure conjecture) while 33.2–3 mentions his severed head subsequently being used as a prop; Cassius Dio, *Roman History* 40.27 includes the gory detail of the molten gold.
16 Plutarch, *Antony* 37.4.
17 At this point in time, the Roman client kingdom of Armenia was ruled by the Artaxiad dynasty and comprised a much larger geographical area than the country we refer to by that name today, occupying parts of Asia Minor (modern Turkey) and the Caucasus.
18 Plutarch, *Antony* 53.3.
19 Livy, *Summaries* 131; Plutarch, *Antony* 50.3–4; Velleius Paterculus, *Roman History* 2.82.3; Cassius Dio, *Roman History* 49.39.3–49.40.1; Tacitus, *Annals* 2.3. Patterson (1974).
20 Hekster (2010).
21 Athenaeus, *Learned Banqueters* 197c.
22 Velleius Paterculus, *Roman History* 2.82.4.
23 Cassius Dio, *Roman History* 49.40.2–3.
24 Cassius Dio, *Roman History* 49.40.3–4; Velleius Paterculus, *Roman History* 2.82.4; Plutarch, *Antony* 50.6–7.
25 Cassius Dio, *Roman History* 49.41.2.
26 Diodorus Siculus, *Historical Library* 40.1. For discussion, see Kudryavtseva (2019).
27 Cicero, *Against Verres* 2.3.213; Livy, *Summaries* 97; Appian,

Sicilian Wars 6.2; Florus,
Epitome 1.42.2–3.

28 Plutarch, *Antony* 1; Appian,
Sicilian Wars 6.2. For discussion,
see Linderski (1990).

29 Cassius Dio, *Roman History*
49.41.4.

30 *Sibylline Oracle* 8; *Sibylline
Oracle* 3.46; *Sibylline Oracle*
9.290.

31 *Sibylline Oracle* 3.350 361,
367–80.

32 Grant (1972) 175.

33 Plutarch, *Antony* 56–68; Cassius
Dio, *Roman History* 50.2–51.5;
Livy, *Summaries* 132.

34 The woman's epitaph recounts
how her mother travelled to
Alexandria to be with her during
her last illness but unfortunately
arrived too late and all that was
left to do was return her daughter's remains to Athens, where
she set up her funerary monument, Kaibel 118.

35 Cassius Dio, *Roman History*
50.26.1.

36 Plutarch, *Antony* 58; Cassius
Dio, *Roman History* 50.3.3–4;
Suetonius, *Augustus* 17.1. For
discussion of this episode, see
Crook (1957), (1989); Johnson
(1978).

37 Suetonius, *Augustus* 17.

38 Suetonius, *Augustus* 69. The
sentence 'Is she my wife?' can
also be translated as 'She is my
wife', which has contributed
to the debate over the nature
of Antony and Cleopatra's
relationship.

39 Cassius Dio, *Roman History*
50.4.5; Augustus, *Res Gestae*
25. This was an accusation
that Cleopatra Selene and Juba

would be careful to avoid,
although their son Ptolemy
would prove less successful.

40 Plutarch, *Antony* 63.3.

41 Plutarch, *Antony* 68.4.

42 British Museum inv.
1872,1214.1.

43 See for example Velleius Paterculus, *Roman History* 2.85.

44 Horace, *Odes* 1.37; Virgil,
Aeneid 8.671.

45 His epitaph is *CIL* 5.2501.

46 Pliny the Elder, *Natural History*
19.22. Later it would be said
that their defeat had been fore-
told by omens, see McDonough
(2002–2003).

47 Plutarch, *Antony* 67.4.

48 Strabo, *Geography* 17.9.

49 Plutarch, *Antony* 69–71.

50 Plutarch, *Antony* 69.2–3.

51 British Museum inv. EA1325.

52 Suetonius, *Augustus* 17.3; Aelian,
On the Nature of Animals 9.11;
Galen 14.235–236.

53 Plutarch, *Antony* 81.

54 On Cleopatra's treasure, see
Broughton (1942).

55 Plutarch, *Antony* 84–6; Cassius
Dio, *Roman History* 51.13–14;
Florus, *Epitome* 2.21.10–11.

56 Griffiths (1961), (1965).

57 Pompeii VIII.2.39.

58 There is a longstanding theatrical convention that Cleopatra
is accompanied by one white
attendant and one black
attendant.

59 Archaeological excavations in
this area are ongoing, so we may
soon find out if that is in fact
the case.

60 Plutarch, *Antony* 81.1; Cassius
Dio, *Roman History* 51.15.5;
Suetonius, *Augustus* 17.5.

61 Areius was paraphrasing Homer, *Iliad* 2.204: 'No good thing is a multitude of lords'.

5. The Aftermath of Actium

1 Bowman (1996) 676.
2 Marković (2015).
3 This may be the reason why Cleopatra Selene eventually set up a statue to commemorate him in Iol Caesarea.
4 Erskine (2002).
5 Cassius Dio, *Roman History* 51.16.5.
6 Cassius Dio, *Roman History* 51.16.5.
7 Cassius Dio, *Roman History* 51.16.5; Suetonius, *Augustus* 93.
8 Cassius Dio, *Roman History* 51.17.4.
9 Plutarch, *Antony* 86.5. A talent of gold is estimated to have weighed around 50 kilograms, so 2,000 talents of gold would equate to 100,000 kilograms.
10 Cassius Dio, *Roman History* 51.16.3. For discussion, see Gray-Fow (2014).
11 Seneca the Younger, *On Clemency* 1.9.1, 1.11.1.
12 Suetonius, *Augustus* 18.1.
13 Cassius Dio, *Roman History* 51.17.4–5.
14 Suetonius, *Augustus* 17.5.
15 Scheidel (2003).
16 Livy, *Summaries* 133. Lange (2009) 147.
17 Lange (2009) 150.
18 Horace, *Odes* 1.37.
19 Plutarch, *Antony* 86.3; Cassius Dio, *Roman History* 51.21.8–9; Eusebius, *Chronicle* 2.190. For discussion, see Östenberg (2009) 141–8.
20 Propertius, *Elegies* 3.11.52–54.

21 Virgil, *Aeneid* 8.714–721; Cassius Dio, *Roman History* 51.22.51–53.
22 Cassius Dio, *Roman History* 51.22.5–6. Although Dio claims it was the first time that either of these creatures had been displayed in Rome, according to Pliny the Elder, *Natural History* 8.39, a rhinoceros was displayed in Rome for the first time by Pompey the Great in 55 BCE, and a hippopotamus (along with five crocodiles) by Marcus Aemilius Scaurus in 58 BCE.
23 Suetonius, *Augustus* 43.4.
24 Suetonius, *Augustus* 41.1; Cassius Dio, *Roman History* 51.21.5.
25 Cassius Dio, *Roman History* 51.19.
26 There is some debate over whether the arch that has been excavated was the Actian Arch or the Parthian Arch, dedicated in 19 BCE to commemorate Augustus' achievement of convincing the Parthians to return the standards they had captured from Marcus Licinius Crassus and his legions at the Battle of Carrhae in 53 BCE. A compromise is that it is the Actian Arch, and the recovered standards were later displayed there, pressing the Arch into service to commemorate both the Actian and Parthian victories. For discussion, see Lange (2009) 163–6.

27 Gregorius Magister, *The Marvels of Rome*.
28 Propertius, *Elegies* 4.6.47–50.
29 British Museum inv. 1926,0930.54. See also Virgil, *Aeneid* 10.195–197, which mentions a ship with a figure-head of a centaur throwing rocks, and 5.151–243.
30 Vatican Museums inv. 31680.
31 Strabo, *Geography* 7.7.6; Suetonius, *Augustus* 18.2; Cassius Dio, *Roman History* 51.1.2.

32 British Museum inv. 1897,0604.4. There is also a version of this coin that depicts a hippopotamus in place of a crocodile, but it is of questionable authenticity. For discussion of the use of crocodiles on coins at this time, see Draycott (2012a).
33 British Museum inv. 1994,0915.263. For discussion, see Peuch et al. (2014).
34 Augustus, *Res Gestae* 27.1, and also alluded to it at 3.

6. When in Rome…

1 Room 62, the House of Marcus Fabius Rufus in the Insula Occidentalis at Pompeii.
2 Appian, *Civil War* 2.102.424; see also Cassius Dio, *Roman History* 51.22.3 for a slightly different account of the statue's backstory.
3 For this identification, see Walker (2008).
4 The only ancient author that suggests otherwise is Cassius Dio, *Roman History* 51.15.6, who claims that Octavian spared Alexander Helios and Ptolemy Philadelphos as a wedding present to Cleopatra Selene and Juba, but contemporary historians find this hard to believe, both because the dates do not line up and because both boys would have grown up to be significant men whose actions would have merited including in the historical record.
5 Cassius Dio, *Roman History* 53.27–28, 30–32.

6 Virgil, *Aeneid* 6.882–886; Servius, *Commentary on the Aeneid* 6.861.
7 Suetonius, *Virgil* 32.
8 I envy the people who live in the luxury apartments that have been built into it – one was recently on the market and priced at 30,000,000 euros.
9 Tacitus, *Annals* 16.6.
10 Suetonius, *Augustus* 5, 72; Velleius Paterculus, *Roman History* 2.81–83.
11 Suetonius, *Augustus* 29.3; Cassius Dio, *Roman History* 49.15.5.
12 Cassius Dio, *Roman History* 53.1.3.
13 Cassius Dio, *Roman History* 49.15.5.
14 Cassius Dio, *Roman History* 53.16.4; Ovid, *Fasti* 1.509, 4.951.
15 Pliny the Elder, *Natural History* 16.5. This award was subsequently celebrated on his coinage, *RIC* Augustus 277 and *RIC* Augustus 419.
16 Suetonius, *Augustus* 72.3.

17 Suetonius, *Augustus* 71.1. Murrhine, *murrha* to the Romans, is a type of fluorite that was used to make expensive vessels with an unusual multi-coloured appearance.

18 Athenaeus, *Learned Banqueters* 6.229c.

19 Cassius Dio, *Roman History* 51.15.7.

20 Athenaeus, *Learned Banqueters* 5.196a.

21 British Museum inv. EA29586.

22 Fillets: Propertius, *Elegies* 4.11.33–34. *Toga praetexta*: Cicero, *Against Verres* 2.1.113; Propertius, *Elegies* 4.11.33–34; Festus 282–284L.

23 Plautus, *Epidicus* 639–40, *The Rope* 1171. Walters Art Museum inv. 57.525.

24 See for example British Museum inv. 1772,0314.32, which dates to between the first and third centuries CE.

25 Nonius 836L.

26 Olson (2008) 68–70. See also Aulus Gellius, *Attic Nights* 2.15.4.

27 Caldwell (2015) 91.

28 Persius, *Satires* 2.69–70; the commentary of Acro on Horace, *Satires* 1.5.65–66; Jerome, *Epistles* 128.1. British Museum inv. 1905,1021.13.

29 Antiquarium Comunale inv. 469.

30 Nonius 863L; Arnobius, *Against the Pagans* 2.67.

31 Suetonius, *Augustus* 89.1.

32 White (1992).

33 Suetonius, *On Grammarians and Rhetors* 20.

34 Appian, *Civil Wars* 4.32–34; Valerius Maximus, *Memorable Deeds and Saying* 8.3.3.

35 Plutarch, *Antony* 2; Suetonius, *Augustus* 86.

36 Strabo, *Geography* 14.5.14; Suetonius, *On Grammarians and Rhetors* 18.3.

37 Suetonius, *Augustus* 64.2.

38 Suetonius, *Augustus* 73.1.

39 Cicero, *In Defence of Caelius* 34; Ovid, *Fasti* 4.

40 Plutarch, *Antony* 2.1.

41 Cassius Dio, *Roman History* 47.15.4.

7. Egyptomania!

1 National Archaeological Museum of Palestrina. One panel is housed in the Altes Museum in Berlin.

2 Walker and Higgs (2001) 334.

3 This nickname was bestowed upon him by Cicero although other ancient authors were not necessarily in agreement – Plutarch published a treatise entitled *The Malice of Herodotus* – and today he is often referred to as 'the Father of Lies'.

4 Herodotus, *Histories* 2.35.

5 For Hecateus, see Parmenides, *Fragment* 8.57; Hippocrates, *Airs, Waters, Places* 19.

6 Juvenal, *Satires* 10.81.

7 Palazzo Massimo alle Terme 253.

8 Pliny the Elder, *Natural History* 6.26.6.

9 For an overview, see Isaac (2004) 352–70.

10 See, for example, Juvenal, *Satire* 3; Seneca, *Consolation to Helvia* 6.2–3.

11 Trickiness: Aeschylus, *Fragment* 373. Thievery: Scholiast

to Aristophanes, *Nubes* 1130;
Theocritus, *Idylls* 15.48; Seneca
the Younger, *Epistles* 51.13.
Wantonness: Aeschylus, *Suppliants* 817. Softness: Lucan, *Civil
Wars* 8.543; Florus, *Epitome*
2.13.60.

12 Cicero, *In Defence of Rabirius
Postumus* 35.

13 Caesar, *Alexandrian War* 24.

14 Herodotus, *Histories* 2.35;
see also Sophocles, *Oedipus at
Colonus* 337–41.

15 Florus, *Epitome* 2.21 = 4.11.3

16 Horace, *Epodes* 9.11–12; Cassius
Dio, *Roman History* 48.24.2,
49.34.1, 50.4.5; Plutarch,
Antony 58.10; Florus, *Epitome*
2.21 = 4.11.1; Josephus, *Jewish
Wars* 1.243.

17 Plutarch, *Antony* 58.6.

18 Cassius Dio, *Roman History*
50.27.2.

19 Cassius Dio, *Roman History*
50.27.3–7.

20 Virgil, *Aeneid* 8.688.

21 Propertius, *Elegies* 3.11.51.

22 Propertius, *Elegies* 3.11.30, 39.

23 Florus, *Epitome* 2.21 = 4.11.2.

24 Josephus, *Jewish Antiquities*
15.97–103.

25 Seneca the Elder, *Suasoriae* 1.7.

26 Horace, *Odes* 1.37.6–10;
Horace, *Epodes* 9.13–14.

27 Livy, *History of Rome* 38.17.

28 Strabo, *Geography* 17.1.11.

29 Propertius, *Elegies* 3.11.40.

30 Plutarch, *Antony* 60.1; Josephus,
Jewish Antiquities 15.93; Jose-
phus, *Jewish Wars* 1.358; Cassius
Dio, *Roman History* 49.34.1.

31 Cassius Dio, *Roman History*
51.12.5.

32 Cassius Dio, *Roman History*
51.12.6.

33 See for example Horace, *Satires*
1.8, *Epodes* 5.

34 British Museum inv.
1865,1118.249. For discussion,
see Etienne (2003).

35 Cicero, *Tusculan Disputations*
5.78, *On the Nature of the Gods*
1.16.43.

36 Virgil, *Aeneid* 8.698–700; Propertius, *Elegies* 3.11.41 also refers
to 'barking Anubis'.

37 Tertullian, *Against the Pagans*
1.10, *Apology* 6; Arnobius,
Against the Pagans 2.73.

38 Cassius Dio, *Roman History*
40.47.3.

39 Valerius Maximus, *Memorable
Deeds and Sayings* 1.3–4; Cassius
Dio, *Roman History* 42.26.

40 Cassius Dio, *Roman History*
47.15.4.

41 Tibullus, *Elegies* 1.3.27–30;
Ovid, *Art of Love* 1.77–78.

42 Catullus 10; Ovid, *Amores* 2.13.

43 Cassius Dio, *Roman History*
53.2.4.

44 Naples National Archaeological
Museum inv. 8924.

45 Museo Nazionale Romano
Palazzo Altemps inv. 77255.

46 National Archaeological
Museum of Naples inv. 8920.

47 Valerius Maximus, *Memorable
Deeds and Sayings* 7.3.8; Appian,
Civil War 4.47.

48 Josephus, *Jewish Antiquities*
18.4.66–80.

49 Pliny the Elder, *Natural History*
37.10. See also Woods (2013).

50 *RIC* Augustus 492.

51 Cassius Dio, *Roman History*
51.22.2.

52 Pliny the Elder, *Natural History*
36.14.70.

53 *CIL* 6.702. Pliny the Elder, *Natural History* 36.72–73. A

gnomon is used to observe the sun's meridian altitude.

54 *CIL* 6.1374, 1375.

8. A Queen in the Making

1 And do not forget that Antony also had another daughter named Antonia, Antonia Prima, the product of his second marriage to Antonia Hybrida Minor, who had been born in 50 BCE and was, by this time, married and living with her husband and infant daughter in Smyrna in Asia Minor (modern Izmir in Turkey). This daughter, Pythodoria, would become Queen of Pontus and Cappadocia, and Antony's descendants would rule this kingdom for the next four hundred years.

2 See Horace, *Odes* 2 for that poet's comment of Iullus Antonius' poetry.

3 Cassius Dio, *Roman History* 55.10.12–16.

4 Antonia Major: Musei Capitolini inv. MC922; Antonia Minor: Palazzo Massimo alle Terme inv. 620.

5 Octavia had three other children, a son Marcus Claudius Marcellus and two daughters Claudia Marcella Major and Claudia Marcella Minor, Livia Drusilla had two sons Tiberius Claudius Nero and Nero Claudius Drusus, and Augustus one daughter Julia Caesaris.

6 Catullus 53.5; Seneca the Elder, *Controversiae* 7.4.6.

7 Suetonius, *Augustus* 72; Suetonius, *On Grammarians and Rhetors* 17; Pliny the Elder, *Natural History* 17.2.

8 *NTDAR* 281.

9 Braund (1984, reissued 2014).

10 This was a fairly common practice during the Late Republic: remember, Caesar and through him Augustus famously claimed descent from the goddess Aphrodite/Venus via the Trojan hero Aeneas who had settled in Italy after the Trojan War, and other Roman families claimed descent from Trojan heroes such as the Geganii (Gyas), the Cloelii (Clnous), the Sergii (Sergestus) and the Nautii (Nautes). Indeed, the Antonii were not the only Roman family to associate themselves with Hercules, although they were the only ones to do so in such a direct way: the Fabii claimed descent from one of the hero's companions who accompanied him on his trip to Italy and assisted him in his labours there, and the Pinarii claimed descent from the individuals he made responsible for establishing his cult in Italy. For discussion, see Wiseman (1974).

11 Plutarch, *Antony* 4.1–2.

12 Plutarch, *Comparison between Demetrius and Antony* 3.3.

13 Naples National Archaeological Museum inv. 9004.

14 Palatine Museum.

15 Suetonius, *Augustus* 2.3, 4.2, 7.1.

16 Suetonius, *Julius Caesar* 83.2.

17 Amusingly, due to Augustus' strategic matchmaking, all the

emperors of the Julio-Claudian dynasty apart from Tiberius would actually descend from Antony as well as from Octavia and, in the case of Nero, Augustus himself.

18 Seneca the Elder, *Suasoriae* 7.14; Seneca the Younger, *On Providence* 2.10. This means of suicide would subsequently become a moral paradigm studied by generations of Roman students.

19 Plutarch, *Julius Caesar* 55.3.

20 Cassius Dio, *Roman History* 53.26; Suetonius, *Tiberius* 9. Considering his age, it is not beyond the realms of plausibility that Juba accompanied Octavian on his Egyptian campaign and was actually present not just at the Battle of Actium in 31 BCE but also the Fall of Alexandria in 30 BCE. This could account for Cassius Dio's odd and dubious

claim, made by no other ancient author, that Alexander Helios and Ptolemy Philadelphos had been spared as a favour to Juba, since if present when the children were captured, he may have intervened on their behalf and presented himself as a positive example of what could happen when the children of foreign rulers were embraced by Rome. But this is pure speculation.

21 *RSC* 1, Syd 1210, Cr543/1.

22 *Greek Anthology* 6.345.

23 *Greek Anthology* 9.235.

24 Strabo, *Geography* 17.1.

25 British Museum inv. 1911,0901.1.

26 Braund (1984, reissued 2014).

27 Massinissa was King of Numidia (roughly modern Algeria) from 202 to 148 BCE and became a firm ally of Rome after switching to the Roman side in the latter part of the Second Punic War.

9. A Fresh Start: The Kingdom of Mauretania

1 See for example an illustration of this myth in a lovely fresco from the triclinium in the House of the Priest Amandus at Pompeii, Region I, Insula 7.7. The fresco is still in situ on the north wall of the triclinium.

2 Brooklyn Museum inv. 70.59.

3 See, for example, Horace, *Odes* 1.22.15–16, who refers to it as 'the land of Juba, that dry wet-nurse of lions', and Vitruvius, *On Architecture* 8.3.24, who refers to it as 'the mother and nurse of wild creatures'.

4 Pliny the Elder, *Natural History* 8.24.

5 Lions: Livy, *History of Rome* 39.21.1.2, Pliny the Elder, *Natural History* 8.20; elephants: Livy, *History of Rome* 44.18.8, Pliny the Elder, *Natural History* 8.7; rhinoceroses: Pliny the Elder, *Natural History* 8.29; hippopotami: Pliny the Elder, *Natural History* 8.40; crocodile: Pliny the Elder, *Natural History* 8.40.

6 Moussa (2013).

7 Silius Italica, *Punica* 1.211–213.

8 Cicero, *On the Manilian Law* 34.

9 On Rome's inexhaustible taste for the exotic and luxurious goods produced by its provinces

and neighbours, see Dalby (2000).

10 Pliny, *Natural History* 6.199, 9.133–135.

11 Homer, *Odyssey* 5.59–61.

12 Dio Chrysostom, *Twelfth Discourse* 49; Martial, *Epigrams* 14.3.

13 Martial, *Epigrams* 14.3, 14.91, 9.59.7; 14.89; Pliny the Elder, *Natural History* 13.29.

14 Pliny the Elder, *Natural History* 13.29. As of 2019, 1,200,000 sesterces equate to approximately £1,651,160, and 1,100,000 sesterces equate to approximately £1,510,811.40. Cicero was actually the first ancient author to mention citronwood tables, at *Against Verres* 2.4, although he refers to one that was already an antique. Gaius Asinius Gallus Saloninus was the man who had the misfortune of marrying the wife whom Tiberius truly loved yet was forced by Augustus to divorce in order to marry his daughter (and Tiberius' stepsister/adopted sister) Julia, whom he did not.

15 Pliny the Elder, *Natural History* 13.29.

16 Pliny the Elder, *Natural History* 13.29.

17 Pliny the Elder, *Natural History* 13.31.

18 Virgil, *Georgics* 3.339–347.

19 Strabo, *Geography* 17.3.7.

20 Virgil, *Aeneid* 8.724.

21 Osgood (2019).

22 Pliny the Elder, *Natural History* 5.37.

23 Horace, *Odes* 1.22.1–3.

24 Suetonius, *Augustus* 45.1.

25 Suetonius, *Augustus* 45.1.

26 Morgan (2000).

27 Sallust, *Jugurtha* 17.7; Ammianus Marcellinus, *Roman History* 22.15.8; Solinus 32.3 = *FGrH* 764 F19b. For discussion, see Matthews (1972). It was common practice for Romans to seize the libraries of the territories they conquered, and the texts contained within them were either retained by the conquering generals for their own private libraries, or, particularly from the late first century BCE onwards, donated to Rome's public libraries.

28 This is according to the calculations of ORBIS, the Stanford Geospatial Network Model of the Roman World.

29 Strabo, *Geography* 17.3.12.

30 For detailed discussion of the city, see Leveau (1984).

31 Suetonius, *Augustus* 29; see also Cassius Dio, *Roman History* 56.30.3 for a variation on this.

32 Martín (2019) 636. Just as Antony had once gifted Cleopatra with notable works of art such as the statues of Zeus, Athena and Hercules crafted by the famous Greek sculptor Myron from the Heraeum on the island of Samos, so too did Cleopatra Selene and Juba have their pick from around the ancient Mediterranean.

33 Strabo, *Geography* 14.4.

34 *AE* 1992, 19027. There is also an inscription from the royal household that refers to an unnamed individual who may have been a stone carver or engraver, *CIL* 8.9346.

35 Athenaeus, *Learned Banqueters* 8.343e–f (Juba, *Fragment* 104).
36 Pliny the Elder, *Natural History* 5.51.
37 Draycott (2010).
38 *Papyrus Tebtunis* 33.
39 National Soares dos Reis Museum in Oporto inv. 4/34 CMP – OURIV.PEDRAS; Cravinho (2018) 153–54, n. 9.
40 Mazard 149, British Museum inv. 1930,1101.3; Mazard 154, 1938,0510.189.
41 Pomponius Mela, *Description of the World* 1.31.
42 Strabo, *Geography* 5.3.8.
43 Pliny the Elder, *Natural History* 5.16; Plutarch, *Julius Caesar* 55.2; Tertullian, *Apology* 19.6. One inscription from the royal household refers to an unnamed copier or transcriber of books who may have worked for Juba in the royal library, *CIL* 8.21097.
44 For more detail about Juba's scholarship, see Roller (2003).
45 Athenaeus, *Learned Banqueters* 6.229d–e.
46 *Greek Anthology* 7.633.
47 Prioux (2014).
48 Pliny the Elder, *Natural History* 37.5.11; 37.6.12–13.
49 Pliny the Elder, Natural History 37.5.11; 37.34; 37.10.27; 37.21.81–82
50 Suetonius, *Augustus* 50.
51 Metropolitan Museum of Art inv. 10.110.1.
52 Plutarch, *Alexander* 4.
53 British Museum inv. 1867,0507.318.
54 Pliny the Elder, *Natural History* 25.38.77.

55 While Pliny the Elder, *Natural History* 25.77–78 states that Juba discovered the plant himself, 5.16 states that Euphorbos discovered it. For discussion, see Totelin (2012); Barbara (2014) 31. Of course, it is highly probable that neither Juba nor Euphorbos were the first people to discover the plant, merely the first Romans, as the indigenous inhabitants of the region would have been entirely familiar with it and its medicinal uses, see Pietrobelli (2014) 176–7.
56 Galen, *On the Composition of Drugs According to Places* 9.4; for discussion, see Pietrobelli (2014).
57 *CIL* 8.9344; *AE* 1960, 00105.
58 Plutarch, *Antony* 10.2, 21.2, 32.3; Plutarch, *Pompey* 40.5.
59 *CIL* 6.10110.
60 *CIL* 6.9046; *CIL* 6.35602.
61 Suetonius, *Augustus* 83.
62 Hyacinthus: *AE* 1976, 750; Crestus: *CIL* 8.9435; Gaius Julius Dapnus: *CIL* 8.21038. If the way these soldiers are presented is compared with the way another member of the company, Balaterus, is presented (Balaterus: *AE* 1921, 31), it would appear that the first two individuals were operating prior to the annexation of Mauretania and its transformation into a Roman province, as Balaterus is depicted wearing a much more Roman manner of dress.
63 *AE* 1976, 741.
64 Speidel (1979) 122.
65 Speidel (1993) 144.
66 Ricci (2011) 494.

67 Pliny the Elder, *Natural History* 8.25; Suetonius, *Augustus* 43.3. There are the remains of a sculpture of a tiger on display in the Palatine Museum that are dated to the Augustan Principate, and the sculpture may have been commissioned to commemorate this event.

68 Pliny the Elder, *Natural History* 5.51.

69 Cleopatra Selene would have been in good company here; the empress Livia dedicated a huge lump of rock crystal to the Temple of Jupiter Optimus Maximus on the Capitoline Hill in Rome, and a sizeable cinnamon root to the Temple of the Deified Augustus on the Palatine Hill in Rome. For discussion and examples, see Rehak (1990).

70 For discussion, see Pomeroy (1984) 11.

71 Sanchez (2019) 182.

10. Wedded Bliss?

1 Mazard (1981) 1–2.

2 The reverse face of British Museum inv. 1931,0303.2, a silver coin issued in Mauretania around 25–24 BCE, Mazard 369.

3 For discussion, see Ferroukhi (2003).

4 Cherchell Museum inv. S66 (31).

5 Plutarch, *Antony* 86.5. This process would not be reversed until the reign of the emperor Claudius, Antony's grandson (his mother was Antonia the Younger), see Suetonius, *Claudius* 11.3 – this seems to have occurred because, coincidentally, Claudius' father Drusus, the son of Augustus' wife Livia, and his grandfather Antony shared a birthday. For discussion of the precise extent to which Antony's memory was damned, see Ackert (2016).

6 Plutarch, *Antony* 86.5.

7 Cherchell Museum inv. S66 (31).

8 Musée du Louvre inv. MA 1885. Cicero, *On the Agrarian Laws* 2.22.58; Suetonius, *Julius Caesar* 71.

9 Mazard 84, British Museum inv. RPK,p218A.2.Jubl.

10 According to Marcus Minucius Felix, *Octavius* 21.10, Juba was voted a god by the Mauretanians, but he does not specify whether he means Juba I of Numidia, or Juba II of Mauretania.

11 British Museum inv. 1859,0301.140.

12 For discussion of this network, see Roller (2018).

13 For Cleopatra and Olbe, see Strabo, *Geography* 14.5.10; and Roller (2028) 122 for discussion. For Livia, see Roller (2018) 69 (Salome), 90 (Dynamis), 108 (Pythadoris and Antonia Tryphaina).

14 One notable exception here is Macurdy (1937), although this is quite dated now. See also Roller (2018) for more recent coverage of the same subject.

15 Hekster (2010) 52–3; see also Braund (1984c).

16 Josephus, *Life* 343, 355; Quintilian, *The Orator's Education* 4.1.19; *Acts* 25–6.
17 Cassius Dio, *Roman History* 66.15.5.
18 *Greek Anthology* 6.244.
19 Suetonius, *Claudius* 1.6.
20 *Greek Anthology* 7.633.
21 Makemson (1937) 61.
22 Makemson (1937) 61.
23 There were also lunar eclipses visible in Mauretania in 9 BCE, 3 CE, 7 CE, 10 CE, 14 CE and 23 CE, but circumstantial evidence such as Juba's remarriage (as a Roman citizen, he would not legally have been permitted to be polygamous) indicates her death occurred in 5 BCE. In fact, in the second half of the second century BCE, an earlier member of the Ptolemaic dynasty had likewise died upon the occasion of an eclipse of the moon, and his death and the eclipse that followed had been commemorated in poetry by Antipater of Sidon, so if

Crinagoras knew that, it makes sense that he would follow suit, and so here we have yet another way in which Cleopatra Selene's ancestry and pedigree were invoked to lionise her, albeit, on this occasion, not by her or Juba. See Antipater of Sidon, *Greek Anthology* 7.241. See Ypsilanti (2018) for discussion.
24 Musée du Louvre Ma508.
25 Macurdy (1937) 51.
26 An inscription that seems to have been fixed to the base of an honorific statue of the pair found in Athens refers to the marriage, *IG* III 1.549.
27 Whitehorne (1994) 201.
28 See, for example, Plutarch's remarks on Antony's dealings with Octavia and Cleopatra, *Comparison of Demetrius and Antony* 4.1.
29 Rostovtzeff (1919) 104–5.
30 Cassius Dio, *Roman History* 51.15.6.
31 Harders (2009) 236.
32 Harders (2009) 237.

11. Family Matters: The Second Ptolemaic Dynasty

1 Musée du Louvre inv. MA 1887.
2 Pomeroy (1984) 6.
3 Kleiner and Buxton (2008).
4 Caesar, *Civil War* 57.5.
5 Jacobson (2001) 26.
6 Seneca the Younger, *On Tranquillity of Mind* 11.12; Suetonius, *Caligula* 26.1; Cassius Dio, *Roman History* 59.25.1.
7 Suetonius, *Caligula* 55.1.
8 Suetonius, *Caligula* 35.1.
9 Cassius Dio, *Roman History* 35.1.
10 Fishwick and Shaw (1976).
11 Tacitus, *Annals* 4.26.2.
12 Malloch (2004).
13 Suggested by Woods (2005); argued against by Wardle (2006).
14 Pliny the Elder, *Natural History* 5.11.
15 Macurdy (1937) 56 thinks there was only one child, Ptolemy.
16 *IG* II2 3439; IG I111 1309; Pausanias, *Description of Greece* 1.17.2. See also Josephus, *Jewish Antiquities* 17.349 and *Jewish Wars* 2.115.

17 Tacitus, *Histories* 5.9. For discussion, see Bennett (2003).

18 This was not entirely unprecedented: the Herodian dynasty of Judea named a number of its members after prominent members of Augustus' extended family such as Herod Agrippa I, named after Marcus Vipsanius Agrippa who had died the year prior to his birth, his son Drusus, named after the emperor Tiberius' son Drusus who had died just prior to his birth in 23 CE, and his daughter Drusilla, named after the emperor Caligula's sister Drusilla who had died around the time of her birth in 38 CE, so this may have been another instance of competition between the Mauretanian and Herodian dynasties.

19 *PIR*2 I 710. It has been suggested that this title of queen was an informal one, and that Julia Urania was a concubine rather than a queen consort, see Coltelloni-Trannoy (1997) 38.

20 Settipani (2000) 438 n. 11. For a brief overview of the Emesene dynasty, see Sullivan (1990) 326–7.

21 Konrad (2017).

22 Ball (2000) 405.

23 Galleria Borghese inv. LXVII.

24 Ball (2000) 401; Bueno (2016) 69–70.

25 Sullivan (1990) 327.

26 Altes Museum inv. 31.329.

27 Trebellius Pollio, *Historia Augusta: Thirty Tyrants* 27, 30; *Aurelian* 27; *Claudius* 1; *Probus* 9.5. For discussion, see Southern (2008) 93 for the suggestion that Zenobia saw Cleopatra as a role model, and 97 for refutation of the claim of descent, but the explanation that it was either Zenobia's attempt to enhance her rule and her claim to Egypt, thus endearing herself to the indigenous population, or by her enemies to discredit her. Winsbury (2010) 39 also sees this as invention.

28 Juba's descent from Hannibal: Scholia on Lucan, *Civil Wars* 8.287; Hannibal's descent from the younger brother of Dido: Silius Italica, *Punica* 1.71–77.

29 Trebellius Pollio, *Historia Augusta: Thirty Tyrants* 30.

30 Trebellius Pollio, *Historia Augusta: Thirty Tyrants* 32.

12. An African Princess?

1 Mazard 125, British Museum inv. 1930,0622.4. For discussion, see Maritz (2001).

2 Strabo, *Geography* 13.1.30; Florus, *Epitome* 2.21.1–3.

3 Ashton (2008).

4 British Museum inv. 1857,0822.46.

5 This is, incidentally, another topic that has recently been subjected to a storm of manufactured controversy by the far right and alt-right, see Bond (2017a), (2017b).

6 Musée du Louvre inv. CA 987.

7 See Snowden (1983) for the earliest influential discussion of Black people in classical antiquity.

8 Thompson (1989) 65–80 argues for a tripartite colour scheme based on the Latin and Greek terminology used to refer to each type, and the ways in which they are used together.

9 Dee (2003–2004) 163.

10 Gruen (2013); Gardener et al. (2013).

11 While Snowden (1983) says it did not exist, Goldenberg (2003) and Isaac (2004) argue that it did, although in a different way to how it exists today.

12 Dee (2003–2004). See, for example, Juvenal, *Satires* 5.52–55, 6.597–600, 8.30–33, 12.4 – while these are satirical poems that play on stereotypes rather than sincere ones, and present a negative view, Juvenal presents a negative view of just about everyone.

13 For enslaved Britons being considered exotic, see Cicero, *Letters to Atticus* 4.17.13. On blonde hair dye, referred to as 'German herbs', see Ovid, *Art of Love* 3.159–68. On blonde hairpieces and wigs, see Ovid, *Amores* 1.14.45–46, *Art of Love* 3.163–8, 3.242–50; Martial, *Epigrams* 5.37.8, 5.68, 14.26; Juvenal, *Satires* 13.164–5; Claudian, *On the Fourth Consulship of the Emperor Honorius* 4.446–7, Eutropius, *Brief History of Rome* 1.383.

14 Strabo, *Geography* 17.1.11.

15 Lucan, *Civil War* 10.107. For discussion of these gifts, see Tracy (2010).

16 Appian, *Civil Wars* 2.90.

17 Florus, *Epitome* 2.13.88.

18 Cassius Dio, *Roman History* 43.19.2–4. For discussion, see Östenberg (2009) 141–2.

19 Thür (1990).

20 The documentary *Cleopatra: Portrait of a Killer,* broadcast on BBC Four in 2009, detailed this theory, but was rather more positive about it than the evidence warrants.

21 Huss (1990) 191, 203.

22 Athenaeus, *Learned Banqueters* 576E–F = FGrHist 234F4.

23 *Greek Anthology* 5.210.

24 Cameron (1990); Snowden (1991).

25 Cameron (1990) 288.

26 Huss (1990).

27 Strabo, *Geography* 17.1.11; Pausanias, *Description of Greece* 1.9.3.

28 British Museum inv. EA886.

29 British Museum inv. EA886.

30 British Museum inv. EA147.

31 Plutarch, *Antony* 27.4.

32 Cherchell Museum inv. S75 (94).

33 Mazard 344, British Museum inv. 1938,0510.166.

34 Mazard 349, British Museum inv. 1909,0102.30.

35 Mazard 355, British Museum inv. 1938,0510.205.

36 Mazard 395, British Museum inv. G1874,0715.491.

Afterword

1 Roller (2018).

2 Duane W. Roller is a notable exception.

IMAGE CREDITS

Maps: Jeff Edwards
Family Trees: Ben Cracknell

Plate Section Credits

1. Woman with Wax Tablets and Stylus by Carole Raddato
2. Photo: akg-images
3. Villa della Pisanella by Jebulon
4. © Louvre / Rmn Grand Palais / Jane Draycott / Dist. Photo SCALA, Florence
5. Private Collection / Photo © Christie's Images / Bridgeman Images
6. Yale University Art Gallery
7. Photograph © The State Hermitage Museum
8. Edith Perry Chapman Fund, 1949 / The Metropolitan Museum of Art
9. Jose Lucas / Alamy Stock Photo
10. Lana Vdovina / Alamy Stock Photo
11. Stefano Ravera / Alamy Stock Photo
12. Pyramid of Cestius by Francesco Gasparetti
13. Affresco Romano by Stefano Bolognini
14. Heritage Image Partnership Ltd / Alamy Stock Photo
15. Royal Mausoleum of Mauretania by TCHOKETCH KEBIR Faiza (Rosy Picture)
16. Charles Edwin Wilbour Fund / Brooklyn Museum
17. Rogers Fund, 1910 / The Metropolitan Museum of Art
18. The Picture Art Collection / Alamy Stock Photo

Integrated Images Credits

p.29 © Bibliothèque nationale de France
p.39 American Numismatic Society
p.52 Bust of Antony by Sergey Sosnovskiy
p.54 Cleopatra VII by Sergey Sosnovskiy
p.59 © The Trustees of the British Museum
p.76 © The Trustees of the British Museum
p.77 Bequest of James Parmelee 1940.613 / The Cleveland Museum of Art
p.80 Chronicle / Alamy Stock Photo
p.82 American Numismatic Society
p.90 American Numismatic Society
p.97 American Numismatic Society
p.98 Historia / Alamy Stock Photo
p.111 © The Trustees of the British Museum
p.130 Schiffsrelief Palestrina by Rabax63
p.131 American Numismatic Society
p.132 American Numismatic Society
p.143 Acquired by Henry Walters / The Walters Art Museum
p.145 The History Collection / Alamy Stock Photo
p.154 Lanmas / Alamy Stock Photo
p.159 © The Trustees of the British Museum
p.161 Heritage Image Partnership Ltd / Alamy Stock Photo
p.167 (two images) Female Portrait by Marie-Lan Nguyen; Lanmas / Alamy Stock Photo

INDEX

Page numbers in **bold** indicate images in the text.